A SUSPICION OF SPIES

To dearest Mother
from her loving son
with lots of
love
J.

Kenneth V. Collins

TIM SPICER

A Suspicion of Spies

Risk, Secrets and Shadows –
the Biography of Wilfred 'Biffy' Dunderdale

With a foreword by General David H. Petraeus

BARBRECK

First published in 2024 by Barbreck Publishers
Copyright © Tim Spicer 2024
This edition © Barbreck Publishers, 2024

Foreword copyright © General David H. Petraeus, 2024

Quotations on pages 349, 350, 351, 352 and 353 of the Epilogue reproduced
with the permission of Ian Fleming Publications Ltd, London
FROM RUSSIA WITH LOVE Copyright © Ian Fleming Publications Ltd, 1957
www.ianfleming.com

Quotations on page 356 of the Epilogue reproduced
with the permission of Ian Fleming Publications Ltd, London
YOU ONLY LIVE TWICE Copyright © Ian Fleming Publications Ltd, 1964
www.ianfleming.com

ISBN 978-1-9995891-4-1

A CIP catalogue reference for this book is available from the British Library

All rights reserved. Published in the United Kingdom by
Barbreck Publishers, 50 Albemarle Street, London W1S 4BD
and distributed by Penguin Random House UK,
20 Vauxhall Bridge Road, London SW1V 2SA

Typography and typesetting by Clarendon Road Studio

Printed and bound by CPI, Moravia

All reasonable steps have been taken to locate the appropriate
copyright holders of photographic and other material.
The author and publisher apologise for any errors or omissions.

'In a whole army's affairs, there is no one closer to you than a spy, no one to reward more richly than a spy, and no business more secret than a spy's.
Unless you are sagacious and wise, you cannot deploy spies. Unless you are humane and just, you cannot send out spies. Unless you are wonderfully subtle, you cannot get the substance of what spies provide. Subtle, so subtle! – there is nothing spies cannot be used for.'

Sun Tzu, c.544 BC – 496 BC, *The Art of War*

With my complements.

Mr. W. A. Dunderdale.

1, Avenue Charles Floquet, VIIe
Paris.

'Nothing is more worthy of the attention of a good general than the endeavour to penetrate the designs of the enemy.'

Niccolò Machiavelli

'The first, last and most necessary essential of a secret service is secrecy.'

Mansfield Cumming

'Intelligence is an activity which consists, essentially, of three functions. Information has to be acquired; it has to be analysed and interpreted; and it has to be put into the hands of those who can use it.'

F. H. Hinsley

'A great part of the information obtained in war is contradictory, a still greater part is false, and by far the greatest part is of doubtful character.'

Carl von Clausewitz

'Capital sport.'

Mansfield Cumming describing intelligence work

CONTENTS

FOREWORD

It is a pleasure to provide the foreword to *A Suspicion of Spies*, Tim Spicer's wonderful tale of the extraordinary Wilfred 'Biffy' Dunderdale. Dunderdale was an intrepid, diabolically creative and exceedingly effective intelligence officer whose contribution to winning World War II has often been overlooked and underestimated. Tim's splendid biography will do much to get Dunderdale the recognition he deserves for what Dunderdale described as his '*40 years of licensed thuggery*'.

I have known and admired Tim since he and his team engaged in various endeavours in Iraq and Afghanistan when I was privileged to command the wars in those countries. In the past decade, I have watched with enormous respect his transition from soldier to author (while he has also watched my transition from soldier to spymaster to author). In his first book, *A Dangerous Enterprise*, Tim demonstrated an excellent grasp of the intricacies of the clandestine world. Now, with this superb biography of Biffy Dunderdale (amazingly, the first biography of Biffy Dunderdale), Tim's mastery of spies and espionage is on display once again. He takes us deep into the intrigues of intelligence operations in Tsarist Russia and later the Soviet Union and eastern Europe, when Britain and the western powers needed urgently to understand and influence the unfolding dramas there during a period that encompassed two world wars.

Dunderdale was engaged by British Naval Intelligence in 1917 at the age of 18 as an interpreter, given his mastery in key foreign languages. But his first exploit came in 1916 when he was 17 and working for his father, taking submarines from Vladivostok to St Petersburg for the Imperial Russian Navy. While taking a submarine out for sea trials with a dockyard crew, he spotted a group of German ships, engaged them and sank four of them. He was knighted for military valour by Tsar Nicholas II. Decades of distinguished service later, he smuggled the first ENIGMA machine from Poland to the code breakers at Bletchley, contributing to one of the most significant intelligence breakthroughs of World War II.

This is a story wonderfully told, superbly researched, as exciting as any James Bond novel (in fact, Dunderdale was a lifelong friend of Ian Fleming and may have been one of the models for James Bond) and full of new material unearthed from long forgotten archives and private sources.

It is, in sum, a truly cracking read! I congratulate Tim on it and commend it to those looking for the real-world story of a buccaneering member of Britain's Secret Intelligence Service. It is one that rivals fiction, except that it isn't fiction but a wonderfully readable account of the actual actions of an iconic British spy.

General David H. Petraeus,
Former Director, CIA,
General, US Army (retired),
March 2024,
Arlington, Virginia

ACKNOWLEDGEMENTS

This has been a difficult book to write. Trying to write the biography of an intelligence officer, who spent almost all of his life working for the Secret Intelligence Service, inevitably runs up against the wall of security surrounding the activities of SIS. Of course much has been written about SIS, in particular its *Official History 1909–1949* by Keith Jeffery and other works by Nigel West, Dermot Turing, Christopher Andrew, Mike Smith, Damien Lewis and Stephen Dorril, all of which have been very useful. However, I wanted to get at more. In this I have been helped by many, with facts, anecdotes, photographs, documents, artefacts, advice and encouragement.

In particular, I am totally indebted to a group of people that I call the 'Biffologists': family or close friends of Biffy or those who worked with him. Without their help this book could never have been written. Chris Perowne and Anthony Fraser, in the first instance, closely followed by Sebastian Allaby, Philip Heath, Anthony Johnson, Danielle Golden, James Grey, Georgina and Robert Woods, Jane Garton, Pascal Sandevoir, Eric le Roux, Giles and Michael Keun, Colin Cohen and Anne Alexandre, '*Volunteers of the First Hour*', all of whom provided me with a mass of material about Biffy which is not in the public domain, as well as boundless enthusiasm for the project.

Paul Biddle, a renowned military collector who owns an extensive archive of original material relating to Biffy, gave me full unrestricted access and allowed me to copy and publish many original documents.

Additionally, the following helped with research: Phil Tomaselli, the best researcher you could find. In France, Catherine Courtauld, Blodwyn Sherriff and David Sbrava at the French Military Archives Vincennes, Jean Jacques Bucher at the Yacht Moteur Club de France, Oliver du Plessis at the Travellers Club Paris, Alan Bryden and

Micheline Billard in Montigny and Jérôme Maubec at the Fondation de La France Libre.

Elsewhere, Anna Gorka at the Pilsudski Institute, Paul Reuvers at the Crypto Museum, Charles Hutcheon, the curator of the Tangmere Museum, Doreen Fraser-Smith, Lynn Amos and Tim Worthington at Blundell's School, Liam Shaw at Duxford, General Jonathon Riley and the Trustees of the Royal Welch Fusiliers Museum and Craig Encer of the Levant Heritage Society as well as Colin and Sally McColl, Alan Judd, Sara Keeling, Philip Boulton, Andrew Fulton, Paul Beaver and Geoffrey Pidgeon. In America, Dimitri Sevastopoulo, Sam Hoskins, Gene Smith and Charles Schaefer. From the OSS Society, Peter Sichel and Charles Pinck. In Germany, Sabina Stern at the Buchenwald Archive and in Austria, Florian Gushe at the Mauthausen Archive.

In addition, I have had considerable help from André Kervella, Diana Mara Henry, Tim Austin and Peter Larson. Part of my research was funded by a grant from Michael Martin and the Trustees of the Gerry Holdsworth Special Forces Charitable Trust. A special thanks to General David H. Petraeus for writing the foreword.

I was lucky to have had the strong support of my publisher, David Campbell, and the intrepid Nell Richmond-Tanner at Barbreck, Christina Usher at Penguin Random House, Christian Lewis PR, Tom Bromley for his editorial work and my outstanding PA Lauren Smith for many long hours of typing. Rachel Glenn for her maps and diagrams, Isabella Ballanti at Ultimate Languages for translation and Paul and Anna Potgieter of Focus Media Markets for photography.

As ever, I had great encouragement from friends who are well-established writers: Jon Swain, Charles Glass, Justin Marozzi and Mike Scott as well as motivational support from Jamie Lowther-Pinkerton, Don and Catherine McCullin, Sarah Smith, James Ellery and 'The Captain'.

Nigel West, Damien Lewis and Mike Smith were also particularly helpful as was Kate Grimond and Ian Fleming Publications.

Thanks also to Richard Perrett, Master Watchmaker, who repaired Biffy's desk clock on several occasions.

Of course all of this could not have been done without the support of my wife Pauline and my son Sam; Sam often by remote control when on overseas deployments and Pauline between her own work, painting, writing and most recently making her film *Branded: Born Criminal (ЗАТАВРОВАНА)*, a harrowing tale of the suppression of free speech and culture, with particular reference to Ukraine, where Biffy was born, and who, if still around, would have been at the forefront of the war against his old enemy.

Thank you all.
Tim Spicer, Devon 2024

INTRODUCTION

'I've got a story to tell you.
It's all about spies...'

Ricki Tarr to George Smiley, *Tinker Tailor Soldier Spy*

I first encountered Wilfred 'Biffy' Dunderdale while researching
A Dangerous Enterprise, my history of the 15th Motor Gun Boat
Flotilla.[1] The flotilla was a clandestine naval transport operation run
by SIS into occupied France during World War II and Biffy was one
of its sponsors and clients. Research tends to take you down many
side streets and back alleys and I kept finding fleeting references to
Commander Dunderdale, 'Biffy', 'DOLINOFF', 'Wilski' or 'Bill'. He
was rather like a ghost that one knew was there but the apparition
never stood still long enough for a clear view.

Whilst there were lots of fleeting references to Biffy (he appears
in over 60 books and websites) no one has ever got the whole story
and written his biography. This seemed rather unusual for someone
who made such an impact in an intelligence career that spanned over
40 years – or as Biffy put it himself, '*40 years of licensed thuggery*'.
Perhaps, though, it is not so unusual in one whose life story seems to
be an awkward mix of reliable facts and legend. Tracing the life of an
intelligence officer is never easy. Little, if anything, will be consigned
to paper. It is a difficult task to bring someone out of the shadows,
when they have spent their whole life living in them.

Biffy Dunderdale has an exotic profile and reputation. Born in
Odessa of British and Austrian parents, he spoke, in addition to
English, fluent Russian, German, Turkish, French and Polish. He
grew up against the background of World War I and the Russian
Revolution, in a hotbed of strategic jockeying across the Levant, the
Black Sea, Odessa, Constantinople and Smyrna. By the time he was
21, he had been involved on the fringes of the Bolshevik Revolution

---

1 *A Dangerous Enterprise*, Tim Spicer, Barbreck Publishing.

and the Russian Civil War of 1917–1920, the disintegration of the Ottoman Empire and the emergence of modern Turkey.

Between 1918 and 1920 he worked for British Naval Intelligence, winning two Mentions in Dispatches (MID) by the time he was 19 and a military MBE gazetted when he was 21. He also had two Russian Imperial decorations earnt when he was 17 and later, decorations from France, Poland and the United States as well as the CMG. He formally joined SIS in 1921 although he had probably been working indirectly for them since 1918. That was just the beginning!

Many accounts testify to the fact that Biffy was stylish, dashing, charming and always immaculately turned out. He had impeccable manners, was a wonderful host and, more often than not, could be found smoking a Balkan cigarette in a long black ivory holder. He was also independently wealthy, a *bon vivant* and a ladies' man. He had enormous vitality and a real gift for friendship, was good-looking with swept-back black hair, a dimple on his chin and mischievous piercing eyes with '*an element of the pirate about him*'. He was also known as a grand raconteur and, towards the end of his life, it is felt by those who knew him well that some of his stories had more than a touch of embellishment.

In *A Dangerous Enterprise* I described Biffy as '*more Bond than Smiley*'. This is undoubtedly true and indeed there has been much speculation that he was the role model for James Bond. This, however, is not the case. Biffy was a close friend of Ian Fleming and maintained that friendship from when they first met in 1940 in France until Fleming's death in 1964. Fleming would regularly meet Biffy for lunch or dinner, often with their mutual friend Fitzroy Maclean. One of their first lunches together was with Robert Bruce-Lockhart on Wednesday the 10th of July 1940, just after Biffy and Fleming had got back from France. Bruce-Lockhart described Biffy as '*attractive, a little sleek*'. Biffy undoubtedly discussed Bond with Fleming and Biffy provided anecdotes which made their way into Fleming's novels. There are certainly parts of Biffy that made up the character of Bond. Comparisons are often made between Ian Fleming's books and the real world of British Intelligence and how little they have in common. But when compared to some of the real-life plots of the Soviet

Intelligence agencies – particularly in books like *From Russia with Love* – they do not seem so fantastic.

As Winston Churchill put it:

> *In the higher ranges of Secret Service work, the actual facts in many cases were in every respect equal to the most fantastic inventions of romance and melodrama. Tangle within tangle, plot and counter-plot, ruse and treachery, cross and double-cross, true agent, false agent, double agent, gold and steel, the bomb, the dagger and the firing party were interwoven in many a texture so intricate as to be incredible and yet true. The Chief and the high officers of the Secret Service revelled in these subterranean labyrinths, and amid the crash of war pursued their task with cold and silent passion.*

Unlike Bond, Biffy was never asked to kill anyone,

> *although on one occasion when I was going back to Paris on the Golden Arrow boat train, it was suggested that I would render the country a great service if I nudged a certain individual into the English Channel. Unhappily the man concerned was not on board so there was no one to nudge.*

Admiral William Canaris[2] maintained that '*Intelligence is a gentleman's job*' and Biffy was certainly a gentleman. In the early days of SIS, the first 'C' Mansfield Cumming's recommendations for recruiting officers stated that he should be '*a gentleman and a capable one, tact, force of character combined with scrupulous honesty, for in the long run, it is only the honest man who can defeat the ruffian*'. Cumming also added, with his customary twinkle, given that intelligence is also about betrayal, deception and expediency, that his ideal officer should have '*a drop of cunning, and a drop of fun, enjoy a yarn and a good, very long lunch*'. Cumming was attracted to the unusual

---

2 Head of German Military Intelligence, the Abwehr. Eventually executed for plotting against Hitler and in all probability an SIS asset. The Abwehr's motto was '*Der nachrichtendienst ist ein Herrendienst*' – a service of gentlemen.

and the exotic. Biffy was just the sort of adventurous and resourceful maverick and 'scallywag' that appealed to him.

To quote Honoré de Balzac: '*The trade of a spy is a very fine one, when the spy is working on his own account. Is it not in fact enjoying the excitements of a thief, while still retaining the character of an honest citizen?*'

According to Paul Paillole,[3] the head of the Deuxième Bureau counterintelligence department and close friend of Biffy, honour was critical in such a seemingly amoral profession. '*We had to be all the more rigorous, for we were dealing with terribly ambiguous, frightening and sometimes sordid situations.*' Serving as an intelligence officer requires very different qualities from those of a regular soldier. It requires a byzantine mind. As Paillole had learned, you had to throw off the military straitjacket; flexibility and lateral thinking were key. You had to learn the rules, in order to break the rules, before rewriting the rules.

This suited Biffy down to the ground – it's no wonder he caught the selector's eye.

*

There are many amusing stories about Biffy – not least his nickname, which is reputed to stem from his fast right hook, demonstrated in boxing matches with the British Mediterranean Fleet. Given that Biffy spent most of his time with the Navy as a temporarily employed intelligence officer and ashore gathering intelligence in Southern Russia, the Crimea and Ukraine, it is unlikely that he had time for organised sports. He more likely developed these skills at school and in the back alleys and bars of Odessa.

One story reports him going ashore to gather intelligence in the docks in Odessa when he was just 18. He was ordered to find out if the Russian communists had succeeded in assembling several mini-submarines supplied in kit-form by Vickers during the war, which were still lying in Odessa. For some inexplicable reason he had the perfect disguise in his kit trunk, namely his old school uniform. This

---

3 Paul Paillole, 1905–2002. French intelligence officer. Worked closely with Biffy before and during World War II.

was not the 'cap and shorts' type of uniform, but a Naval Academy uniform. Biffy was put ashore with a rendezvous for exactly one week's time. He made for his friendly former schoolmaster's house where he knew he would find a 'safe house' and was let in by his very surprised wife. When her husband returned and found Biffy in his Naval Academy uniform, he could not believe his eyes.

'*What on earth are you doing here, Dunderdale?*'

Biffy explained his mission and fortuitously, the master had a relative in the docks who could find out the answer to Biffy's question. In the meantime, Biffy's presence was dangerous and had to remain undetected. He was hidden in the attic, where he was set to work.

'*Your Latin was always behind the class, Dunderdale, so you can work up there to improve it!*'

The schoolmaster had the answer from the docks for Biffy the next day. However, because of the timing of the pick-up rendezvous, Biffy now had the rest of the week in the attic to do his extra Latin and make up for his idleness in the classroom.

Biffy is also reputed to have stood in the corridor of the Trans-Siberian Express acting as an interpreter for a White Russian general and his English mistress, who were seducing each other in a closed compartment, until verbal direction ceased to be relevant. Biffy himself also told the story that one of his first jobs for SIS in Constantinople was paying off the British Nationals in the Sultan's harem with gold sovereigns and arranging passage out of the country on a Royal Naval cruiser. Another Biffy myth was that he drove around Paris in an armoured Rolls Royce. The true story of the Rolls Royce we will discover in a later chapter.

*

The purpose of this biography is to try and separate fact from fiction, to dispel some of the myths (probably encouraged and even perpetrated by Biffy himself), and in doing so tell the story of someone whose career with SIS was outstanding. There is no doubt Biffy was an exceptional intelligence officer from the outset. His early reports from the Crimea as a very young officer in Naval Intelligence were excellent. They were very well written and show a vast breadth of contacts, agents and networks. He clearly had highly placed sources and it is intriguing to know how these were developed. His subsequent work, particularly in France from 1926 and through World War II, certainly made a huge impact on and contribution to the ultimate Allied victory. He would remain with SIS until 1959 when, aged 60, he retired – or did he? Even in retirement, the myths about this remarkable figure continued.

TIMELINE

1899   24th December – Wilfred 'Biffy' Dunderdale born in Odessa.

1909   4th July – SIS created. Mansfield Cumming takes up post as first 'C', October.

1914   Outbreak of World War I.

1915   Biffy attends St Petersburg Military Engineering Technical University.

1916/17   Richard Dunderdale procures submarines for Russian Navy. Biffy joins delivery team as interpreter. Later, sinks four German ships on a sea trial of one of the submarines from St Petersburg.

1917   Russian Revolution.

1918   4th December – hired by Naval Intelligence as a 'civilian interpreter and agent'.

1919   4th March – Biffy civilian employment terminated. March – July – attends Sokolov investigation into murder of Tsar and family. 3rd July – Granted 'Temporary Commission' RNVR. Awarded 2 MIDs.

1920   Quells mutiny on submarine OUTKA. Awarded MBE. Moves to Constantinople.

1921   Joins SIS.

1923   Mansfield Cumming dies, replaced as 'C' by Hugh Sinclair.

1926   Biffy appointed Head of Station Paris. SIS moves headquarters to Broadway Buildings.

1928   19th December – Biffy marries June Woodbridge-Ament.

1929   Wall Street crash.

1933   30th January – Hitler appointed Chancellor.

1934   Philby recruited by Russians.

1935   Italy invades Abyssinia.

1936   March – Hitler invades Rhineland. 17th July – Spanish Civil War begins.

1937   5th November – Hitler outlines secret plans for invasion of Europe.

1938	Hugh Sinclair buys Bletchley Park.
	Section 'D' for Destruction set up.
1939	1st April – Spanish Civil War ends.
	16th August – Biffy delivers ENIGMA machine to London.
	1st September – Hitler invades Poland.
	3rd September – Britain at war with Germany and Italy.
	4th November – Hugh Sinclair dies. Replaced as 'C' by Stewart Menzies.
1940	10th May – Germany attacks Holland, Belgium and France.
	14th June – Germans enter Paris.
	20th June – SIS Station evacuated from France. Biffy flies back.
1940–1944	Biffy runs SIS sections: 'A4', 'P5', Special Liaison Controllerate.
1944	6th June – D-Day.
1945	Biffy Controller Special Liaison.
	8th May – war in Europe ends.
	6th August – atomic bomb. Japan surrenders 2nd September.
1947	Biffy marriage to June annulled.
1951	Burgess and Maclean defect.
	Philby under scrutiny and resigns from SIS.
1952	Biffy marries Dorothy Hyde.
1953	John Sinclair replaces Menzies as 'C'.
	Work begins on Berlin Tunnel.
1955	Philby 'cleared'. Berlin Tunnel operational.
1956	Dick White takes over as 'C'.
	Suez Crisis.
	Buster Crabb incident.
1959	Biffy retires.
1978	Dorothy dies.
1980	Biffy's third marriage to Deborah McCloud.
1990	First Gulf War.
1991	13th November – Biffy dies in New York.

CHAPTER 1 – A SUSPICION OF SPIES

'I have reports from agents everywhere – pedlars in South Russia, Afghan horse-dealers, Turcoman merchants, pilgrims on the road to Mecca, sheikhs in North Africa, sailors on the Black Sea coasters, sheep-skinned Mongols, Hindu fakirs, Greek traders in the Gulf, as well as respectable Consuls who use cyphers.'

Mansfield Cumming, First Head of SIS

Wilfred Albert Dunderdale was born on the 24th of December 1899 in Odessa. His parents were Richard Dunderdale and Sophie Urbanek. Richard and Sophie were married on May the 26th 1898, at the British Church in Odessa by Arthur Steven the Parish Priest and Chaplain for Odessa and Southern Russia: Richard was 28 and Sophie 19. Sophie, a language teacher, was an Austrian countess born in Lauband, East Prussia (now Poland). Richard was variously described at the time of Biffy's birth as 'Clerk' and later, 'Shipping Agent'. He came from a modest background, having been born at 94 Hudson Road East Plumstead in Kent on the 9th of November 1869, the son of Thomas and Annie Dunderdale. Thomas's profession is given as 'Blacksmith'. How Richard got to Odessa, married, produced a son and amassed a considerable fortune in 30 years remains a mystery. It is likely that his father Thomas was in reality an armaments engineer who worked for the Royal Arsenal at Woolwich. The Turkish Imperial Arsenal recruited many skilled Englishmen to work in Constantinople and it is likely Richard moved there with his parents and then struck out on his own. There is no doubt that he was a very entrepreneurial individual and it would appear that he made a lot of money very quickly. Along with his fellow trading families in the Levant and Black Sea – an area of growing strategic importance to Britain – Richard was an ideal candidate to have been of great assistance to the embryonic SIS. Biffy's fate was sealed almost at birth.

Although SIS was in its infancy at this time, the British have a long history of expertise in intelligence work. For centuries British monarchs and governments have recognised the essential need to gather foreign intelligence. Sir Francis Walsingham served as Queen Elizabeth I's spymaster from 1573 until his death in 1590, his favourite maxim was 'knowledge is never too dear'. Walsingham's most conspicuous success as a spymaster was against the Spanish Armada, despite the fact that his warnings were not acted upon. Oliver Cromwell also understood the value of intelligence. His Secretary of State, Thomas Thurloe, a worthy successor of Walsingham, had such an efficient secret service that, in the words of the diarist Samuel Pepys, 'Cromwell carried the secrets of all the princes of Europe at his girdle.'

The need to protect trade, particularly with India, subdue nationalist movements and secure frontiers against the threat from rival powers and expansionist neighbours all required accurate and timely intelligence. The Admiralty was the first to establish a global reporting system which monitored the strength, deployment and intentions of the French and Russian fleets. This network relied primarily on Naval attachés who gathered information from both open sources and paid agents. This was formalised by the creation of the Naval Intelligence Department in 1897 and would be how Biffy Dunderdale entered the world of intelligence.

Originally created as a joint venture between the Admiralty and the War Office, the Secret Intelligence Service was founded on the 4th of July 1909 when Biffy was 10 years old. It is the foreign intelligence service of the British Government and primarily a human intelligence agency, tasked with the clandestine collection and analysis of intelligence overseas, to find out what the departments of state cannot find out by overt means. It can also act as a 'back channel' link between governments and organisations whose overt relationships are non-existent, are in poor shape or need to be deniable. To quote from the SIS website, 'SIS works secretly around the world to make the UK a safer and more prosperous place. For over 100 years it has ensured the UK and our allies keep one step ahead of our adversaries.'

Mansfield Cumming, the first 'C'

In its early years, under the leadership of the first 'C', Captain Sir Mansfield Smith-Cumming, SIS intelligence collection priorities were the rising threat to Britain from Germany, the threat to India from the Russians and the threat to Egypt and the Suez Canal from the Ottoman Empire.

As such, the Eastern Mediterranean and Black Sea – the Levant – was an important area of intelligence interest. One of Cumming's continuing concerns was budget, or lack of it, and as a result he was keen to use loyal, entrepreneurial and adventurous British trading family businesses in Berlin, Moscow, St Petersburg, Odessa, Constantinople and Smyrna to gather intelligence for him. The group of trading families that had gravitated to the Levant and Odessa were a godsend to Cumming. The Gibsons, La Fontaines, Whittalls, Keuns and Dunderdales were to give long and valuable service to SIS.

Traditionally, SIS work was supplemented by reports and specific missions delivered by British subjects working overseas – bankers, industrialists, merchants, Merchant Navy captains and journalists. SIS bolstered its operational coverage by persuading British companies and individuals to use their 'natural cover' to carry out intelligence-gathering operations on its behalf. It fostered good relations with British firms such as Vickers, Shell, the British American Tobacco Company and the Hudson's Bay Company. Vickers in particular was very helpful and SIS came to rely on it more than any other company, to expand its reach. In its early days SIS used the cover name Rasen, Falcon Ltd Shippers and Exporters.[4]

Since the late 18th century, Britain's interests in the Mediterranean and Middle East had been secured by a powerful presence in India, Aden and Egypt. The overriding requirement was to prevent any other of the Great Powers from usurping Britain's dominant position and disrupting British trade routes and lines of communication with the Far East and India. The *Entente Cordiale* with France and friendly relations with Imperial Russia due to the interrelations of both Royal Families had eased the problem. From the early 1900s, increasing German involvement in the Ottoman (Turkish) Empire, which covered most of the Middle East, including Syria, Lebanon and Arabia, threatened Britain's regional security. The Foreign Office used secret funds to buy a substantial shareholding in the Constantinople Quays Company, a commercial trading company, to give Britain covert influence in Turkey.

Britain had effectively controlled Egypt since the 1880s and used a series of strategically important colonies, such as Gibraltar, Malta and Aden to secure the lines of communication to India. With the outbreak of World War I in 1914, everything would change. When Turkey entered the war on the side of Germany, Britain responded by taking direct control of Egypt, turning it into an important military base from which they could conduct military operations against Turkey in Arabia and Mesopotamia (Iraq).

The Levant had always been of strategic interest to Britain, ever since 1592 when Elizabeth I approved the original charter for the Levant Company. It traded continuously until 1825 and was run by the British Government from 1821–25. By the end of the 19th and early 20th century, the Levant had become one of the richest and most cosmopolitan regions in the world. It emerged from one of the most successful strategic alliances between France and the Ottoman

---

4 Like Ian Fleming's fictional 'Universal Export'.

Empire that lasted from the 16th to the early 20th century. It was the front line between East and West, with Russia to the northeast and Constantinople guarding the entrance/egress to the Black Sea and Mediterranean, and had always been of strategic importance. A 'Levantine' is defined as a person who originated from Europe but who settled in the major port cities of the Ottoman Empire such as Constantinople, Smyrna, Beirut and Aleppo. There existed a mix of language and culture with Muslims, Christians and Jews living and working alongside each another, a distinctive aspect of the later Ottoman Empire that belies its usual reputation for laziness and corruption, and which compares favourably with cultural and ethnic tensions in the region now. The Levant was also a 'state of mind', where trading and deal-making were more important than race, religion or politics. It was a melting pot attractive to, and ideal for, intelligence-gathering.

The Odessa into which Biffy was born at the end of the 19th century was a special place: European, cosmopolitan and modern, the gateway to Southern Russia. The large modern port was frenetically busy exporting grain from Ukraine and importing everything needed in Russia. Thousands of expatriate foreigners – businessmen, merchants, sailors, soldiers and tourists filled its cafés, bars and shops. Pushkin wrote, '*In Odessa you can smell Europe*', like in Constantinople and Smyrna, it was a frontier and a maritime crossroads of Europe and Asia, mixing high culture and a seamier wild side – a criminal underbelly '*packed with the poor, smugglers, pickpockets and thieves, lowlifes of every type*'. By the time Biffy was born, the population of 400,000 was a mix of Russians, Ukrainians, Tatars, Cossacks, British, Greeks, Italians, Armenians and Georgians.

Young Biffy, growing up in Odessa, soon learnt to operate at all levels of Odessan society, quickly becoming a typical Odessan – '*experienced, shrewd, a manoeuvrer and a man of ingenuity*'. While Richard Dunderdale was establishing himself in Odessa, Charlton Whittall arrived in Smyrna from Liverpool in 1889. He soon acquired a fortune and an exotic wife, Madeleine Giraud, the daughter of the Austrian Consul in Smyrna. The Whittalls were not only traders who became spies, they made discoveries of antiquities, new species of flora and fauna such as *Fritillaria Whittallii* and five Whittalls represented Turkey in the 1906 Olympics in Athens. The Whittalls' first involvement with SIS came in 1914. Cumming began developing intelligence operations against Turkey at the end of 1914. In December, his deputy, Captain Laycock, began to recruit potential agents amongst the English residents in Constantinople, Smyrna and Odessa. In January 1915, Cumming was instructed by Admiral Reginald 'Blinker' Hall at the Admiralty to provide support for a plan to bribe Turkey out of the war and Hall authorised a £4 million bribe. Edwin Whittall and George Griffin Eady were recruited to negotiate with the Turks. Cumming provided funds, administrative support and arranged secure communications. Whittall told Cumming that the project was a waste of time. Whatever chance there had been evaporated the moment the Allies launched their operation against Gallipoli in February 1915 to take control of the Dardanelles. Whittall reported to Cumming that '*the day he opened negotiations we bombarded the Dardanelles. The day his man landed at Smyrna we bombarded it! Money no use.*' Whittall had thought that he might be able to get an agreement if Constantinople was '*internationalised and left in nominal Turkish possession under international control*' but the landings in Gallipoli and the nine months of fighting that followed put an end to any deal that would take Turkey out of the war. This attempt at a covert strategic manoeuvre was exactly the sort of operation that a secret service was for. If it had succeeded it would have been cheap at the price and saved many Allied soldiers fighting in Gallipoli, Mesopotamia and Arabia.

Smyrna became the centre of the Levant trading hub and became a thriving mix of the Orient and the West. European hotels such as the Hotel de la Ville Sur les Quais flourished as did nightclubs, casinos and music venues – L'Alcazar d'Amerique, Trocadero, Cristal Palace, Petit Alhambra and Concert Monaco being the most famous. The major trading families developed their business trading in barley, cereals, opium, cannabis, wool, nuts, saffron, carpets and linen. Charlton Whittall's company C. Whittall and Co. had become the leading powerhouse in Smyrna. From trading in commodities, they branched out into shipping, insurance and finance. As Gertrude

Bell described in one of her letters from Smyrna dated April the 4th 1907:

> ... *Then to call on all my Whittall friends. They have the bulk of the English trade in their hands, branch offices all down the southern coast, mines and shooting boxes and properties scattered up and down the S.W. coast of Asia Minor and yachts on the seas. They all have immense quantities of children. The sons, young men now in the various Whittall businesses, the daughters very charming, very gay. The big gardens touch one another and they walk in and out of one another's houses all day long gossiping and laughing. I should think life presents itself nowhere under such easy and pleasant conditions.*

The Whittalls soon cemented their alliance with two other prominent trading families, the Keuns and La Fontaines. Charlton Whittall's son Jacques married Elmina Keun. Jacques and Elmina had a son, Arthur, born on the 7th of November 1893 in Constantinople. Arthur went on to serve in the Intelligence Corps in World War I and subsequently was recruited by SIS, serving in the Istanbul station. He became a hero in Israel because, in his career as Passport Control Officer, he processed many Jews fleeing the Holocaust. He was awarded an OBE in 1946. Arthur's sister Daisy married into the La Fontaine family. All of Arthur's brothers and cousins served in World War I. Arthur married Biffy's sister Lily Sophie on the 25th of August 1928. It is likely that Arthur was recruited to SIS after World War I, around the same time as Biffy.

The La Fontaines intermarried with the Whittalls. Many of them served with the military and intelligence services, adopting a double-barrelled name of 'La Fontaine Whittall'. Roland La Fontaine Whittall was killed in Gallipoli in 1915. Kenneth La Fontaine Whittall received an OBE for his military intelligence work. Hubert La Fontaine Whittall received the MC, Croix de Guerre and the Grand Order of Military Merit. Wilfred La Fontaine worked for SIS with Compton McKenzie in Greece and Turkey. Sidney La Fontaine was awarded the DSO and MC. His daughter Hillary joined SIS in 1967 and retired in 1994 having worked with Daphne Park in Africa and Hanoi, being personal assistant to 'C' and working on anti-Soviet operations.

Harold Gibson and his younger brother Archie both had long careers with SIS. They were not from the Levant but had been living in Moscow where their father managed a chemical works. The Gibson family had a long history of trading with Russia, stretching back to the 19th century. Harold, always known in SIS as 'Gibbie', was fluent in Russian, German and Czech. He worked in Southern Russia at the same time as Biffy was in Odessa and Sevastopol. In October 1919 he was posted to the SIS station in Constantinople where he remained until 1922, overlapping with Biffy who was posted there in 1921. Gibson was subsequently posted to Sofia, Bucharest, Riga, Prague and was Head of Station in Istanbul during World War II where Arthur Whittall worked with him. 'Gibbie', like Biffy and all Russian-born officers in SIS, came under some suspicion and scrutiny during the Philby era. All were exonerated. Sadly, Harold Gibson shot himself in Rome in 1960. Archie Gibson worked closely with his older brothers in Bucharest, taking over as Head of Station and working with a cover as a journalist for *The Times*. He then moved to Belgrade as Head of Station.

The Keuns were originally from the Netherlands. Benjamin Keun moved to Smyrna and set up a trading business, primarily trading in Turkish opium for the international pharmaceutical market. The business was taken over by his son Alfred, who married Virginia Amira from an Italian aristocratic family. They had two children, George and Valeria, who married Prince Paolo Borghese. George married Germaine Feydeau[5] in Paris in 1910. After the fire in Smyrna in 1922, the Keuns moved their business to Istanbul, Paris and London. George Keun became friendly with the Dunderdales in both Istanbul and France. Later in the 1920s and 1930s, Biffy would be a frequent guest at Tana Merah, the villa that George built in Antibes. Here he would have met George and Germaine's son Philip, born in Paris in 1911, who was to become one of Biffy's key agents and network organiser of the JADE AMICOL network during World War II.

---

5 Eldest daughter of Georges Feydeau, the French playwright.

Sacking of Smyrna

The success and prosperity of Smyrna was to come to a tragic end in two weeks of September 1922. The shocking events were the consequence of the chaos that ensued at the end of World War I and the dismemberment of the Ottoman Empire, including the Greco-Turkish War of 1919–22. The Turks, having chased the Greek Army into Smyrna, initially appeared to be highly disciplined. However very quickly discipline broke down and looting, murder and rape became commonplace. Eventually the Turks set fire to the city. By the evening, the quayside was packed with an estimated 500,000 people, driven to the waterfront by the wall of fire. *'The screams of the frantic mob on the quay could easily be heard a mile distant,'* one observer noted. *'There was a choice of three kinds of death: the fire behind, the Turks waiting at the side streets and the ocean in front.'* So ended the great run that Smyrna had as an important and cosmopolitan outpost.

By this time, the grand trading families, including the Whittalls and Keuns, had seen the writing on the wall and moved their operations to Constantinople,[6] and in the background their association with SIS, as had Richard Dunderdale, in the wake of the Russian Revolution and subsequent Civil War. Richard's son, Biffy, meanwhile, was setting out on the start of his long and distinguished career as a professional intelligence officer. It was a career that began, a few years earlier, in Odessa.

---

6 After the Great Fire of Smyrna in 1922.

CHAPTER 2 – ODESSA, 'A FABLED LAND OF GOLD, ABUNDANCE AND SIN.'

Jarod Tanny

'Never say "no" to adventure. Always say "yes", otherwise you will lead a very dull life.'

Ian Fleming

Richard Dunderdale is often described as having worked full-time for Vickers, the British Armaments Company, but there is no trace of him in the Vickers history or archives. It is more likely that, as an entrepreneur, he became an agent (in the commercial sense) for Vickers, amongst his other business interests. At various times he was involved in military equipment procurement, in particular, submarines, oil trading, ship broking and ship ownership. He was closely connected with Peter Regir and his very profitable shipping fleet of 10 ships, transporting coal and other cargos both to Black Sea ports and further afield.[7]

His career is tricky to follow and may well be deliberately opaque. There is more than a suggestion that he was one of Cumming's commercial contacts, and if not 'on the books' of SIS, he was certainly of great use to them, not only as a supplier of information, but of much wider use as an asset. Closely linked to the other Levantine families both by trade and intermarriage, there is no doubt he would have come into SIS's orbit. It was as an agent for Vickers that Richard became involved in the supply of submarines to the Russian Imperial Navy, a role which in turn would lead to Biffy's career as an intelligence officer.

The trail of supplying submarines to Russia can be traced back to Isaac Rice, an American entrepreneur, who had used his business acumen to corner the storage battery business in the US. He founded the Electric Boat Company and used his extended influence in Washington to get the US Navy to buy his submarines. Rice

---

7 Peter Regir supported the White Russians in the Russian Civil War. He was captured in Mariupol, tortured for a week, then shot. His son transferred the business to London.

Basil Zaharoff

also had his eye on the international market, with Britain as his first target. Rice was a millionaire; he had close business and social contacts among the leading New York bankers and brokers, and, through August Belmont & Company, he obtained an introduction to the Rothschilds in England. He arrived in London in July 1900, and, as he himself wrote, *'almost immediately, through the courtesy of Lord Rothschild, began negotiations with the Admiralty'*. With the Admiralty's approval, Rice got in touch with Vickers, with the result that the two companies signed an agreement which granted Vickers a licence to manufacture Holland submarines in accordance with Electric Boat's patents. The agreement was dated October the 27th 1900, and the licence was for 25 years. It covered not only Britain but the whole of Europe, including Russia, and gave Vickers the right to *'grant licences to any other firm, government, or state upon terms to be agreed with the Electric Boat Company'*.

Enter Basil Zaharoff. Born in Muğla in Turkey, his family later moved to Odessa. He became an astonishing linguist, reportedly mastering 10 languages. His early life was an extraordinary tale of adventure and criminality.

He became an agent for the Maxim-Nordenfelt Company which manufactured machine guns. Maxim-Nordenfelt was absorbed into Vickers in 1897. Vickers took on Zaharoff as their *'general representative for business abroad'*, paying him commissions on his sales. There are, not surprisingly, difficulties in ascertaining what exactly Zaharoff did, but the documentary evidence that survives suggests that his chief value to his employers was an instinctive understanding of when and to whom he should offer bribes – he wrote memos that told of '*doing the needful*' and '*administering doses of Vickers*'. Foreign Office records show that, in 1912, Zaharoff was instrumental in passing 100,000 rubles to officers in Russia's Ministry of Marine in order to divert government contracts to a local shipbuilding group in which Vickers had an interest. At much the same time, for reasons that remain obscure but can easily be guessed at, Vickers also won a contract to supply light machine guns to the Russian army, despite the fact that its bid was almost 50 per cent higher than the competition. Zaharoff's charm and powers of seduction were as helpful as his money; he made particularly effective use of his association with the ballerina Mathilde Kschessinska, the mistress of Grand Duke Sergei Mikhailovich, Inspector General of Russian Artillery.

Outside of Britain, bribery was not accidental or occasional, but considered both essential and quite normal practice in the armaments industry. It is clear that Zaharoff paid bribes to secure contracts in Latin America, Serbia, Turkey and Russia. He was the 'éminence grise' of Vickers' overseas sales. The French Government also believed that not only was he the chief '*actionaire*' of Vickers, but an agent of '*La puissante organisation occulte qui domine la politique anglaise depuis des siècles... L'intelligence service*' – SIS. There is more than a hint that he was involved with the Whittalls' attempt to bribe Turkey out of World War I and a second attempt in 1917, for which supposedly Lloyd George awarded him a knighthood. Vickers negotiated the sale of the Electric Boat Company submarines to Russia. Eighteen Holland class submarines were ordered early in the war. Generally known as the 'H' class, the submarines received the Russian designation 'AG' for 'Amerikanski Golland'. AG-11 to AG-15 arrived with the Baltic Fleet via a circuitous route. Hull sections, machinery and other equipment were manufactured in the US by the Bethlehem Steel Corporation with the Electric Boat Company acting as subcontractor. Because of America's neutrality laws, the submarines were sent by rail (along with an American workforce) to Montreal in Canada for final assembly at the Canadian Vickers yard. After the submarines were completed at Canadian Vickers, they were again disassembled for rail transport across Canada to Vancouver. Next, they were sent by ship to Vladivostok, whence they would again be placed on rail cars to arrive at their destination for reassembly.

It is at this point that Richard Dunderdale, acting as an agent for Vickers, stepped in to organise the shipment of the submarines, in kit-form, by rail via the Trans-Siberian Railway.[8] He used Biffy to act as interpreter, fixer and to accompany the party.

*

While Richard had been building his business, Biffy was educated first at the Richelieu Lyceum in Odessa, then the Alexandrovskaya Gimnazia in Nikolaev and, at age 16, the Saint Petersburg Military Engineering Technical University, a higher military education institute. Clearly highly intelligent with a gift for languages, by 16 he was studying Naval Architecture and Naval Engineering. He was also broadening his education in the waterfront bars and dodgy subculture of both Odessa and St Petersburg. In 1916, the submarine kits from Canada arrived in Vladivostok so that they could be transported to St Petersburg and Nikolaev by rail.

Richard sent Biffy to Vladivostok to meet a group of technicians from both Vickers and the Electric Boat Company including Captain Frank Cable, Edward Viler, Robert Gilmore, Herman Knoblett, Worth Foster, George Gill, Andrew Anderson and Edward Mayers. Biffy completed the team. The gun sights and control gear had been sent to Archangel in January 1916 and were picked up by a British engineer, Allan Monkhouse. Monkhouse is also believed to have worked for SIS.

In total, the Electric Boat Company provided 25 submarines for the Russian Imperial Navy. The first five kits were delivered in March 1916, shipped from Vladivostok to Petrograd (St Petersburg) for assembly at the Baltic shipyard (Baltiysky Zavod). Acceptance trials were then carried out from Kronstadt. These are the ones escorted by Biffy. Six more were delivered in 1917 and assembled at Nikolaev

---

8 The Electric Boat Company had a subsidiary – the Electric Launch Company – which specialised in luxury launches. Tsar Nicholas ordered a custom-made launch. It is believed that this was brokered by Richard Dunderdale.

Captain Frank Cable and his team

under the direction of Richard Dunderdale. This last shipment included an AG-22 named OUTKA which entered service with the Imperial Navy on June the 20th 1917. Biffy would meet the OUTKA again under different circumstances in 1920.

Biffy took his escort duties a stage further. Having assembled several of the submarines in Kronstadt Naval Dockyard, they needed to be tested at sea. Ever up for a challenge, Biffy manned one of the boats, A-16, with a Naval Dockyard crew and took it out for sea trials. Whilst out in the Baltic they spotted a group of German ships. Biffy gave the order to attack and sank four of them. Returning to Kronstadt to report the success of the sea trial, the submarine became entangled in an anti-submarine net at the entrance to the dockyard placed there by the Russians to catch German submarines.

Biffy's submarine was stuck and lay on the bottom for 18 hours. Oxygen was getting low and things were looking grim. Suddenly with a change in the tide and current, the submarine broke free and rose to the surface. Biffy immediately opened the hatch in the conning tower to get air into the boat, only to find every gun in the port trained on them. Thinking quickly, Biffy shouted to them in Russian and the situation was defused. For this action the Tsar personally

Submarine assembly in St Petersburg

Electric Boat Company submarines transferred to the Imperial Navy

recommended the award of Order of St Anne – the equivalent of a knighthood – for military valour and *'bravery in battle'*.[9] In order for the Tsar to award the Order of St Anne, the rules of Russian Orders and Decorations stated that the Order of St Anne could be awarded only if the recipient already had the Order of St Stanislav – so the Tsar gave him both.

9 In his 1926 wedding photo Biffy is clearly wearing the Order of St Anne, but also the Order of St Stanislav.

CHAPTER 3 – THE CRIMEA 1918–1920

'Secret operations are essential in war; upon them the army relies to make its every move. An army without secret agents is exactly like a man without eyes or ears.'

Sun Tzu, *The Art of War*

Biffy's intelligence career began on the 4th of December 1918 when he was hired as a *'civilian interpreter and agent'* by the Naval Intelligence Division of the British Mediterranean Fleet which was operating in the Black Sea in support of Russian counter-revolutionary forces. There is no doubt that Biffy's intellect, connections and linguistic ability would be well known within the considerable British expatriate community in Odessa and Nikolaev. Richard Dunderdale had entrusted him with a lot of responsibility in the Electric Boat Company submarine business and Biffy had shown himself to be both resourceful and adventurous. He was also getting a reputation amongst his friends for being quite handy with his fists in a tight corner.

The linkage between Naval Intelligence and SIS, particularly during the end of World War I and the mid-1920s, was very close. Naval Intelligence was very well established but SIS was still in its infancy. Between 1909 and 1918, SIS was shunted between the War Office, the Admiralty and the Foreign Office. However, it performed effectively during the war and was very alive to the newly emerging threat from Bolshevik Russia. Mansfield Cumming wrote in his diary in 1918, *'Russia will be the most important country for us in future and we should sow seed and strike roots there now.'*

British intervention in what became the Russian Civil War began in January 1918 and lasted until May 1923. The aim was to help White Russian forces defeat the Bolsheviks. Britain was not alone in this venture – 13 other nations also sent troops to assist. However, the Bolsheviks were not defeated by the White Russians and, by April

Pyotr Wrangel

1919, Allied troops were withdrawn from Odessa after further threats from Nikifor Grigoriev's army, before the defeat of the White Army's march against Moscow. General Pyotr Wrangel and his soldiers fled Russia aboard Allied ships on the 14th of November 1920. Subsequent British involvement in the Crimea was entirely naval. The Allied intervention is considered to have poisoned East–West relations forever and to have contributed to the origins of World War II and, subsequently, the Cold War.

The British support for the White Russians and Biffy's work in the Crimea were to set the tone for his subsequent 39 years with SIS. He joined an SIS which already had a presence in Odessa. Lieutenant Commander Malcolm Maclaren, a Russian and Polish expert, had arrived in Odessa in March 1919, just after Biffy was recruited as a civilian interpreter. Maclaren was accompanied by another Russian expert, Harold Gibson. These two joined Sidney Reilly, who had been born in Odessa and was already working for SIS. Maclaren reported to Cumming that Reilly had developed an effective network and was getting results. Maclaren and Gibson remained in the Crimea until August 1920, and Gibson moved to the SIS station in Constantinople at the end of 1919, where he would remain until 1922. Biffy would join him in 1921 on his first 'official' posting for SIS.

Biffy's employment as Civilian Interpreter/Agent was concluded on the 4th of March 1919. However, his success as an agent led to him being granted a *'Temporary Honorary'* Commission as a Sub-Lieutenant in the Royal Naval Volunteer Reserve on the 3rd of July 1919. It is believed that Biffy was working with SIS under the shadow of Reilly, Maclaren and Gibson from the days of his earliest engagement, developing and operating his own networks based on his and Richard Dunderdale's extensive contacts at all levels in the Crimea. As he proved his worth, he was taken on more formally, regularly signing his reports *'The Naval Intelligence Officer Crimea'*.

Biffy's initial recruitment coincided with the arrival in Nikolaev of Captain George Chetwode on the 5th of December 1918 in the destroyer HMS TRIBUNE, together with another Royal Naval ship, HMS SHARK and the French destroyer DEHORTER. Lieutenant Godfrey (later Admiral Godfrey, the Director of Naval Intelligence) was Chetwode's principal Staff Officer. To quote from Volume I of Godfrey's memoir:

> As soon as our little flotilla was secured alongside the jetty at Nicolaieff on 5th December 1918, the White Russian General Augustoff in command of the local Volunteer Army, Admiral Rimsky-Korsakoff, Captain of the port, the Governor of the City, the Mayor and several other leading officials came onboard. These included Mr Dunderdale of the firm of Peter Regir trading in the Black Sea and his son Bill, with whom I had much to do as DNI during the Hitler War.
>
> A large crowd on the pier greeted us with the greatest enthusiasm. A conference was held in the ward room, Mr Dunderdale translating, and the officials explained the political situation.

Biffy clearly made an impression from the start. Two weeks later, in a letter dated the 18th of December 1918:

H.M.S. CANTERBURY
18th December 1918

Mr. Dunderdale Junior has been appointed to assist on Staff of Senior Naval Officer of the Allies' Forces at Nikoliaeff.

*He is used as interpreter and temporary agent and installed
at British Headquarters in the town situated at PUSHKINSKAYA
No.1 under British Flag and guard, and where protection is given
to any Allies' subject or women and children.*

Signed: SENIOR ALLIED NAVAL OFFICER SEVASTAPOL

Biffy was based initially in Nikolaev and, using his many contacts, including his school-friends, he set up an extensive network of agents in the Crimea, Caucasus and Southern Russia. They reported mainly on naval targets, including the Black Sea Fleet and coastal defences, but also made highly detailed reports on the Bolshevik attitude to Britain, France and Germany, as well as economic conditions inside Russia. This was strategic and operational intelligence of the highest order. He also used his networks to intercept and expel German agents. As well as his friends, Biffy's agents also included fishermen who could pass close to the Russian fleet and move through coastal waters without arousing suspicion. Biffy's natural flair as an agent runner, his language skills and his highly detailed reports quickly came to the attention of Hugh Sinclair, then Director of Naval Intelligence, who ordered that his activities should be highly classified and that his name should be deleted from all but the most tightly controlled reports to protect both him and his agents.

His reports were very highly thought of. On the 10th of September 1920, one of his reports was annotated:

*It is requested that you will inform Lieutenant Wilfred A.
Dunderdale RNVR that the Commander-in-Chief has read with
much interest and appreciation his very lucid report on the situation in Odessa dated 21st August.*

J. M. de Robeck, Admiral Commander in Chief HMS Iron Duke

Sinclair also commended him. Biffy's extraordinary network enabled him to collect, collate and disseminate 52 very significant intelligence reports, covering all aspects of strategic, operational and tactical intelligence. They were valued greatly and often forwarded to the highest levels in the Admiralty, War Office, Foreign Office and even the Prime Minister and, of course, to SIS. Biffy's value as an intelligence officer is illustrated by the concern of the Commander in Chief when Biffy 'disappeared' for a few days in Odessa.

I should be glad if the question of Mr. Dunderdale could be examined. I have lost him. He told me he wanted to go to Odessa to make arrangements for intelligence in case of the evacuation of that place. He went up in 'Sportive' just before Odessa fell and since then I have heard nothing of him.

A sampling of Biffy's reporting shows great depth and breadth of information including the attitude of the Bolshevik Government to Britain, France and Germany. In a report dated the 2nd of August 1920, he outlined Bolshevik foreign policy, economic conditions, attitude of the civil population and intentions in Turkey, Persia, Afghanistan and the Holy Union of Mohammedans. Britain is described as follows:

BRITAIN. The strongest enemy of the Soviet Government is Britain, whose position in the world, her obstinate policy, her recent popularity in Russian circles, still make them feel anxious. This is why the Bolsheviks carry on a movement against the British on a great scale, not grudging expense, making use of well tested means, such as bribery and propaganda.

The state of the Soviet Navy:

13 December 1920

Herewith is forwarded information compiled by Lieutenant Dunderdale RNVR, from various sources concerning all classes of vessels known or credibly reported to be at various Russian Black Sea Ports.

Richard Webb
Rear Admiral
Senior Naval Officer

The report runs to four pages detailing 80 ships of all types, their armaments, crew and state of repair.

The operational effectiveness and intentions of White Russian troops:

> *I saw General WRANGEL this morning when he discussed the Polish advance with me and he told me that if the Polish right flank was advanced he would swing his left flank forward to join them. He had just got a telegram from the UKRAINIANS stating that they were ready to work under him, but they had very few troops.*

Other reports cover coastal and port defences, with detailed sketch maps and minute detail, such as which gun positions were connected by telephone to their headquarters and fire control centres.

Biffy was also involved in direct action operations:

> *18/19 March: 16 Bolshevik agents were rounded up last night. When a certain house was surrounded it was defended with a machine gun and there was some bloodshed.*

And a month later:

> *20th April: Last night the Bolshevik organisation which has been under observation here for some time was successfully rounded up, 26 men being captured, a large quantity of high explosives, arms, grenades, and bombs were seized, also much documentary evidence disclosing plans for blowing up General Wrangel in his train, destroying bridges in several places including the one over the Alma, and other trains and tanks under repair here.*
> *2. German agents are again in evidence here. After another meeting last night, two of sub-lieutenant Dunderdale's men followed one of these men from the meeting, held him up and went through his documents, amongst which was a copy of a document in the possession of another German agent who left for Varna in the 'Boris', ordering all German organisations here to assist him in every way.*

3. I am going to see General Mangin to see if any steps can be taken about this man. Sub-lieutenant Dunderdale's other two agents from Odessa and Nicolaef have just gone back to Eupatoria and should arrive here tomorrow evening.

I have the honour to be, Sir,
Your obedient servant,
(signed) W. S. Leveson-Gower.
Captain. B.S.N.O. Sevastopol.

Biffy also pioneered the use of wireless intercept. One of the intercepted messages is set out in full below:

I have the honour to submit the following Soviet wireless message addressed to Sevastopol, Constantinople, Theodosia, Kerich, Skadovsk, Khorli:-

(Begins). 'To the seamen of the White Fleet. Comrades, Seamen, we apply to you from the name of the Red Sailors of the Black Sea and the Sea of Azov, also from all the crews of the batteries and coast defences. I again propose that you should stop the tyranny over you by the Czar's servants, the shoulder-strappers and gold-braiders, who have been hiding under the name of the Volunteer Army, calling it the people's army and at the same time were leading you against your brothers, the workmen and the peasants, who have been heroically protecting the Soviet Authorities. Comrades, Seamen, how is it that you cannot understand that the Generals and officers of the Czar are your betrayers, making you work for them and are sacrificing your lives for their interests, making you serve the enemies of the working class? You are shedding blood for those who have squeezed all your juice out. Sailors, only here in Soviet Russia you will be protected by the working classes against the tyranny of the capitalists. It is not too late for you to return to your Proletarian family to unite in our combat against the Imperialists. You, the sons of the peasant and the workmen, must immediately pull down the horrible and hated St Andrew's flag under which the Czar's Generals executed and

drowned, hundreds of thousands of your best comrades who have been fighting for freedom and who were attempting to overthrow the remnants of the democratic army have converted you into gun fodder. The seamen of my fleet want you immediately to part with your executors, Generals and landowners. That is the only way you can free yourselves from slavery. You must boldly proceed to the red shores of Ukraine where the workmen, sailors and peasants will welcome you as their brothers. To the Commanding Officers who will honestly join the Red Army and Fleet, the Soviet Government forgets all the past and guarantees personal safety. This proclamation is to be read on board all the white ships. Time of departure is to be reported to me.

COMMANDER OF THE SEA AND RIVER FLOTILLA, IZMAILOV'

I have the honour to be,
Sir,
Your Obedient Servant,
W. Dunderdale
Sub Lieutenant, R.N.V.R.

Even at this early stage in his career, Biffy was very attuned to the use of technology in intelligence-gathering. This use of intercept and code-breaking would stay with him in Constantinople, Paris, World War II and into the Cold War.

Biffy was beginning to make a name for himself, being awarded two Mentions in Dispatches for his reporting, but he was not without his detractors. A report sent to the Commander-in-Chief in July 1920 stated:

I have been informed by both British Naval and Military Officers that this Officer (Sub-Lieutenant) Dunderdale is much disliked by General Wrangel's staff. I can only report that I find him very keen, and that that Captain of BENBOW gave me a very good report concerning him.

This type of report is often generated by professional jealousy and in Biffy's case, probably due to the fact that he operated outside the normal chain of command with his own networks and reporting lines. He fell out with Commander Hugh Woodward, the then Senior Naval Officer Odessa, but was supported by the C in C Fleet, who wrote: 'He will carry out special intelligence duties. He will not come under Woodward in any way, and the less Woodward has to do with him the better.' He wielded quite a lot of power. When he discovered that the British Consul in Sevastopol was conducting 'amateur intelligence work', he complained that this was getting in the way of his work and had it stopped.

*

One very significant incident that would further enhance Biffy's reputation and status concerns the OUTKA submarine AG-22, one of the original Electric Boat Company submarines that Biffy and his father had helped transport in 1916. Biffy's agents warned him that nine members of the crew were about to mutiny, take over the submarine, kill the officers and anyone else who resisted and then sail the submarine to join the Bolshevik Navy.

Biffy's report of the incident is set out in full below:

SEVASTOPOL
20th May, 1920

Sir,
I have the honour to submit the following report on an occurrence in the Russian Submarine 'OUTKA', a result of the Bolshevik Wireless Message offering amnesty forces handing their ships over to the Bolsheviks at the port of ODESSA (vide my report on this subject dated the 22nd April, 1920):-

It has been noticed for about six days previously that there was a certain unrest in the Russian Submarine 'OUTKA', but owing to the fact that she was undergoing a refit no undue cause for anxiety was felt. Towards the end of the refit it was reported to *me by my agent that the Quartermaster THEODORE KUZMICH GRUDICHEFF, who now appears to be a very dangerous and active Bolshevik agitator, had been spreading propaganda amongst the crew and terrorising the younger element by telling them that he was leaving SEVASTOPOL very soon and would come back with the Bolshevik forces especially to inform the Soviet authorities as to who had been working against them. He was supported in his agitation by a seaman, MAXIMOV, and an Engine Room Artificer named OLAINIKOV (who was one of the leading members of the KIEV Chresvichaika).*

It is now known definitely that GRUDICHEFF's plan was to arm nine of the pro-Bolshevik members of the crew, as evidently he could not rely on more than that number, and when the submarine went out for her trials, all officers and men were to be secretly disarmed, officers who resisted thrown overboard, and the red flag hoisted. As he said – 'No one would dare to resist the nine brave armed lads'. The submarine was then to be taken in triumph to ODESSA.

As soon as this propaganda and plan of campaign was reported to me, I secretly informed the Russian Naval Intelligence Department, who after verifying this information from knowledge obtained by their agents, arrested the three leaders of the proposed movement.

I consider the Bolshevik movement in the submarine can be attributed to the fact that officers did not take enough interest in their men, and were not careful enough in the selection of their crew. The Russian authorities are insisting on this matter being properly dealt with: at present the submarine is quite quiet, all disturbing elements in the submarines 'BOUREVESTNIE', 'TULHNE' and 'A.G.22' having been checked satisfactorily.

I have the honour to be, Sir,
Your Obedient Servant,
W. Dunderdale
Sub Lieutenant R.N.V.R.

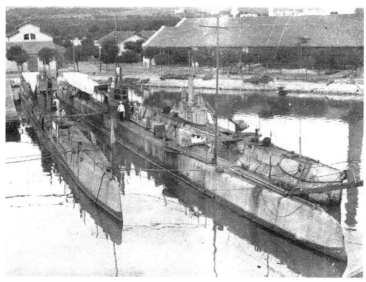
Submarine OUTKA AG-22

Having obtained information that this mutiny was about to happen, Biffy took a hand in proceedings himself and this may account for the concern when he dropped off the radar for a while. Biffy went onboard the OUTKA, warned the Captain and directly assisted in the prevention of the mutiny. For this particular action, he was awarded an MBE in 1920. His citation reads:

I wish to recommend him most strongly for promotion to Lieutenant R.N.V.R., and for the award of the Order of the British Empire. He has conducted himself most ably and successfully, his information was excellent and reliable, and he has been of the utmost value, not only to me, but to others. It was thanks to him that a Bolshevik plot to seize a submarine was baffled, and I cannot overstate the assistance he has given me in every way. He has an intimate knowledge of the Russians and their character, which he has used to the best of his advantage of H.M.Service, and his services are thoroughly worthy of reward.

The OUTKA was sailed to Bizerte, impounded and eventually sunk.

Nikolai Sokolov

Biffy also provided intelligence about another Bolshevik uprising in June 1920. The British war diary for the Black Sea Fleet reads:

Sunday, 6th June. At 2200 hours Sub-Lieutenant Dunderdale, R.N.V.R. came off to say he had reliable information that a Bolshevik rising was expected during the night and that the warships' crews had been recalled to their ships.

As a precautionary measure, cleared for action and prepared Marines for landing.

Message intercepted from Concord saying that Wrangel's AZOV expedition entered the AZOV on 4th June.

Monday, 7th June. The prompt measures taken during the night prevented the local insurgents from rising.

Biffy and his family were very well connected to pre-Revolution Russian society, including the Russian Royal Family, and these connections enabled him to subsequently work to great advantage with the White Russian émigré community in Constantinople and Paris. Between March and July 1919, Biffy was sent as an observer to the Sokolov investigation into the murder of the Tsar.[10] He was sent at the behest of Admiral Kolchak and the British Government, as the Tsar was the King's cousin. This was facilitated by Richard Dunderdale, a close friend of the Russian Royal Family and the Tsar in particular.

10 Recorded in Biffy's entry in the *Dictionary of National Biography* written by John Bruce Lockhart, a fellow SIS officer.

The investigation was funded by the Tsar's mother, the Empress Dowager Maria. Despite the overthrow of the monarchy in 1917, the former Empress Dowager Maria at first refused to leave Russia. Only in 1919, at the urging of her sister, Queen Dowager Alexandra, did she begrudgingly depart, fleeing Crimea over the Black Sea to London. King George V sent the battleship HMS MARLBOROUGH to retrieve his aunt. The party of 17 Romanovs included her daughter the Grand Duchess Xenia and five of Xenia's sons, six dogs and a canary. After a brief stay in the British base in Malta, they travelled to England on the British battleship HMS LORD NELSON and she stayed with her sister, Alexandra.

Biffy was sent as intelligence officer and interpreter to join the Royal party on their evacuation from Yalta on HMS MARLBOROUGH, already being well known and respected by the Russian Imperial family. The surviving members of Biffy's family and his godson who knew him later in life also attest to his significant collection of Fabergé, including an ebony cane with a Fabergé top. In his later years, he was adamant that the emergence of the person claiming to be Anastasia, the Tsar's daughter who supposedly survived the massacre, was a fraud.

*

After being taken on more formally by Naval Intelligence, Biffy worked with Sidney Reilly and George Hill. They were on a specific mission for Mansfield Cumming in November 1919, reporting on 'certain important information' about the Black Sea coast and Southern Russia, which was needed for the forthcoming Paris Peace Conference. Hill and Reilly were impressed by Biffy's excellent reports and, on returning to London, they recommended Biffy for full-time employment by SIS.

By the end of 1920, the British Naval support operations in the Crimea and the Black Sea were closing down and the SIS intelligence centre of gravity had moved to Constantinople. Biffy and his networks had shown their value, with Biffy proving to be an effective and wily intelligence operator. It was no surprise, therefore, that he was formally taken on by SIS in 1921 and posted to Constantinople.

CHAPTER 4
CONSTANTINOPLE 1920–1926
'A BALLET OF LUNATICS'

'For anyone who is tired of life, the thrilling life
of a spy should be the very finest recuperator.'

Sir Robert Baden-Powell

At the end of World War I, following the defeat of the Ottoman Empire and the signing of the Armistice of Mudros on the 30th of October 1918, British, French and Italian troops occupied Constantinople. Like Odessa, the population was a melting pot of Muslims, Greeks, Armenians and Jews, as well as a substantial Western population. They had been joined by a large community of White Russians who had fled the Revolution as well as Muslims from the Balkans, Crimea and Caucasus. It was described as '*une place marchande et militaire*' – a marketplace and military hub. The Bosphorus was dominated by Allied warships and the streets were filled with the uniforms of the occupying armies, British, Italians and French.

The Allies set up a military administration, largely dominated by the British. The city was divided into three zones, a precursor to the partition of Berlin and Vienna in 1945. Stambul, the old city, was assigned to the French, Pera-Gelata to the British and Kadıköy and Scutari to the Italians. Admiral Somerset Gough-Calthorpe was appointed Military Commander of Constantinople and British High Commissioner. His headquarters were HMS IRON DUKE, to which Biffy was assigned. Some welcomed the military occupation; others resented it, particularly the emerging Turkish nationalist movement.

After the turmoil of the Russian Revolution and the destruction of Smyrna, Constantinople became the home and trading hub for the group of families closely linked to SIS. Richard Dunderdale, the Whittalls, Keuns and La Fontaines all set up there, as well as in

Constantinople, 1920

London and Paris in the case of the Keuns. They all lived in Moda, a village on the Asian side of the Bosphorus, and worked out of the same group of buildings in Galeta. This is where the Whittalls partnered with Calouste Gulbenkian to set up the Turkey Petroleum Company, which later became the Iraq Petroleum Company, beginning production in Mesopotamia in 1926. This cosmopolitan melting pot, *'The Ballet of Lunatics'*,[11] soon became a significant centre of operations for both Naval Intelligence and for SIS, with the establishment of the British Military Intelligence Headquarters at Hagodian Han in Galeta that became the hub for covert activity of *'very secret agents'*. Biffy and his ability to penetrate and run agents in Southern Russia was a significant part of this operation.

The SIS station in Constantinople had been set up in 1919 at the beginning of the Occupation. Its first Head of Station was 'Gibbie' Gibson. Other members of staff included Alfred Cumming, who had been born in Constantinople in 1895 and served in the Intelligence Corps in World War I, Arthur Whittall, recruited in 1920, and secretary Lucy Lunn.[12] Lucy, one of three sisters, had been born in Russia.

---

11 A description coined by George Theotokas, the Greek writer and artist.
12 Her sister Helen worked for the Government Code and Cypher School. Her other sister Edith had worked for SIS in Finland but was sacked for her communist leanings. She later married Andrew Rothstein, one of Britain's most virulent communists.

Kemal Atatürk

She continued to work for SIS in London during World War II and her sister Helen was a Section Head at Bletchley.

By 1921, SIS had been in existence for 12 years. It had 200 staff worldwide, 60 in the UK and 140 overseas. The Constantinople Station was to become a very important part of this global network. In the aftermath of World War I, two new factors, nationalism and communism, emerged to challenge British interests. British government officials rather naively assumed them to be the same thing. In Turkey, the nationalist movement under Kemal Atatürk sought to depose the Sultan who had been kept in power by the victorious Allies, establish an independent Turkish republic and defeat the British-backed Greeks. There was a concern that Atatürk was leaning strongly towards the Russians, who were very keen to take control of his nationalist movement, and a real possibility of British forces in the region having to resume military operations.

Intelligence-gathering was vital. SIS was well aware of this and Cumming regarded the Constantinople operation as '*one of the most important, if not the most important, of all my agencies. A better service of information has never been organised regarding events in the Near East.*' Much of this intelligence came from a very effective signals intercept team, Number 3 Wireless Observation Group, working under army cover. In early 1922, in a cost-cutting move, it was proposed to close down the SIS station, but keep the signals intercept unit. Gibson responded robustly pointing out that 'SIGINT' (signals intelligence) on its own without corroboration from human intelligence sources was not ideal. He pointed out that SIGINT does *'get most valuable information regarding existing foreign relations, but it cannot pick up all the nuances of the subversion and intrigue which go on behind the scenes, for the latter are seldom if ever mentioned even in cypher cables'*. Furthermore, the SIGINT operation would only work effectively for as long as the Allies remained in Constantinople. Thereafter interception could only be conducted remotely and, if that failed, there would be an intelligence vacuum. Therefore, a HUMINT operation run by the SIS station needed to be maintained on the ground.

Initially Biffy's work in Constantinople was in continuation of his work in the Crimea for the NID. He was submitting reports throughout 1920 on key aspects of the strategic collection plan, including Franco-Russian relations, Russian naval operations in the Black Sea and Mediterranean and the current situation in the Caucasus. One report, dated February 1921, caught the attention of the DNI and SIS. It covered in detail relations between Georgia and Turkish nationalists and Soviet support operations to the Georgian Communist Party. It also covered the general situation in Baku and Armenia, relations between Armenia and Turkish nationalists, details of the Russo-Turkish Azerbaijan Conference at Moscow and the Russian involvement with, and funding of, Kemal's army.

Biffy's Turkish identity card

In 1921, Biffy went home to England on leave and to attend an investiture for his MBE. It is during this visit that he was invited to a meeting with Mansfield Cumming at the SIS headquarters at 1 Melbury Road in Kensington. At this meeting he was formerly invited to join SIS and his first posting was to return to the Constantinople station.

*

Biffy's remit was to continue to run his existing networks but also to recruit new agents from the Russian émigré community and other anti-Bolsheviks amongst the Turkish, Persian and Afghan communities. He was also to target members of the Ottoman government, the Turkish National movement, the Greek Orthodox Church, the Levant Consular Service, French and Italian intelligence officers and the local and foreign media. It was through his agents in the Turkish National movement that he helped prevent attempted coups against Allied forces. However, one of Biffy's first tasks was to arrange for the covert departure of the Sultan Mehmed VI. The Sultan did not want to leave Constantinople. He was protected by a battalion of the Grenadier Guards stationed in a barracks opposite the Palace. But as his power declined, he asked the British for help, first to arrange the transfer of his money to an overseas bank account and then to give him safe passage out of Turkey. He wrote to General Charles Harrington:

Sir,
Considering my life in danger in Constantinople, I take refuge with the British Government, and request my transfer as soon as possible from Constantinople to another place.

The SIS station was given the task of coordinating this with the military and the Sultan. Biffy was given the responsibility of planning and conducting the operation, with the Brigade Commander Julian Steele and the Commanding Officer of the Grenadiers, Colonel Colston.

At 08:00 on the 17th of November, with Biffy watching from the shadows, Mehmed VI left by the Orhaniye gate to the Palace, opposite the Grenadiers' barracks. The weather was conveniently miserable, it had rained continuously for eight days and most people remained indoors. The Grenadiers put out a protective cordon. The Sultan was accompanied by his son Ertuğrul, his first chamberlain, his bandmaster and six servants. Officers from the Grenadiers drove him away in an ambulance with the cross painted out (so that the British could not be accused of sheltering under the Red Cross) and were followed by another ambulance for the rest of the entourage and the luggage. The Sultan left Turkey on HMS MALAYA, which took him to Malta. From Malta he went to San Remo near Genoa, where he died in 1926.

Another delicate task that fell to Biffy after the departure of the Sultan was the repatriation of the European ladies of his harem, making sure that the Sultan's favourite was paid off generously. When Biffy asked how he would know which one she was, he was told '*oh you'll know alright*'. This task was hardly the stuff of agent running and other derring-do but, due to the Monogamy Diction of the new republic, it was an important job. Moreover, the fate of the ladies of the harem had caught the attention of the international press.

Biffy ensured a quiet departure smoothed with gold sovereigns. Biffy personally oversaw the departure of the British ladies on the Orient Express, including Anne Nevill who wrote a series of articles for *Thomson's Weekly News* in late 1923, 'My ten years in a Turkish Harem' and Grace Ellison, who later wrote *An English Woman in a Turkish Harem.*

Two years later Biffy was to oversee another departure, this time that of the Caliph, the heir to the Sultan's throne who had been kept in place by Kemal Atatürk as a sop to public opinion, until he was ready to fully proclaim a Republic and move the capital from Constantinople to Ankara.

On the 3rd of March 1924, the Caliphate was abolished and the Caliph ordered to leave. He took with him his immediate family of six, three staff and two servants. At 05:30, with Biffy shadowing the operation discreetly, they were taken in three cars followed by a lorry of luggage along the Bosphorus, over Galata bridge and out of the city through the Edirne gate, heading for the station at Çatalca and the Orient Express. As the train sped through the Balkans, past the tomb of Suleyman the Magnificent in Hungary, the Caliph lamented: *'My ancestors came with horses and flags. Now I come as an exile.'*

*

Constantinople, or Istanbul as it had now become known, was a very fertile ground for SIS. The station would also be an excellent training ground for officers who would go on to have long and successful careers in SIS, including Valentine Vivian, Harold Gibson, Arthur Whittall and, of course, Biffy. Harold Gibson and Biffy, as well as continuing to run their agents and networks into Russia, also began to develop relations with the Jewish community who had extensive reach into the Caucasus.[13]

British rivalry with Russia in the 19th century, epitomised by Rudyard Kipling as *'The Great Game which never ceases day and night'*, coupled with the British experience during the Russian Civil War, created a tendency to overestimate the threat of Russian Bolshevism to British interests in the region. However, the threat was real. The Bolsheviks were keenly aware of the benefits of spreading their brand of revolution among the disenchanted people of Iraq, Afghanistan and India. For SIS, the intelligence priorities were the protection of India, penetration of the Turkish Nationalist Government and prevention of Russian subversion or expansion in Persia, Iraq and Afghanistan. This led to the development of three lines of operations: penetration of the Atatürk Government, support to offensive action against the Bolsheviks in Baku, Grozny and the Trans-Caucasus and the continuation and extension of existing intelligence-gathering against the Russians. Biffy was to have had a hand in all three.

Agent running was always Biffy's forte. He continued with his very successful work in Southern Russia and the Caucasus, as well as recruiting new agents in Istanbul. The station ran an eclectic mix of some excellent agents. One of the most successful was Mehmet

---

13 This assistance was repaid by Arthur Whittall during World War II where he helped many Jews to escape from Europe by securing visas and exit permits to Palestine under the SIS cover of Passport Control Officer. His work was later recognised by the State of Israel.

the Tailor, codenamed 'RV/5', who collected information in his shop in Üsküdar which was popular with nationalist officers. His contacts within the Turkish military were excellent. His tailoring skills gave him access to Atatürk's palace where he ran a network of sub-agents who worked there.

Another agent, a former Russian cavalry officer codenamed 'JQ/6', whom Biffy knew from the Crimea, was a *'Turkman of European appearance'*. He had set up a coffee shop in Beyoğlu, which soon became a centre of nationalist political meetings and intrigue. He reported what he overheard but, by January 1923, *'he was under suspicion having become known to many Azerbaijanis now working for the Turks'*. He was blown and the station had to get him out quickly, moving him to Romania. He was described by Biffy as *'one of the very best agents we have got'*. He continued to work for SIS in Berlin and later in Baghdad.

Biffy also recruited Bapsy Cursetji Pavry, codename PARSIFAL, who was originally from one of the wealthiest families in Bombay. She was the daughter of Parsi Zoroastrian Cursetji Pavry, the Head Priest of the Zoroastrians. Highly intelligent, speaking 12 languages, she was an excellent agent, penetrating Atatürk's inner circle and providing very good intelligence until blown in 1922.

Another of Biffy's recruits was a Georgian in exile, Noé Jordania, who conducted covert operations in the Caucasus, later becoming part of the Georgian Government in exile. He would stay in touch with SIS until the 1950s, having followed Biffy to Paris, then London.

In January 1923, the Station reported that Atatürk was reluctant to fall in with Russian plans to form a bloc consisting of *'Russia, Turkey, Persia, Afghanistan and other Moslem States'*. SIS's analysis suggested that the Turks were wise to Russian games and were more than happy to plot behind the backs of the Soviets in order to create a *'Moslem Federation'* which would exclude Moscow. Although SIS's principal preoccupation in Turkey was Soviet diplomatic and intelligence activity, SIS's assessment of the independence and integrity of Turkish nationalism showed that it could provide impartial and clear-sighted reports contrary to the popular view which, in the 1920s, saw every threat to be caused by the Russians.

Odette Keun

Biffy felt entirely at home with the émigré Russians and used his contacts in the large expatriate Russian community with great success. He had many contacts and part-time agents reporting everything from gossip to detailed conversations overheard in bars, cafés and restaurants opened by the Russians as they adapted to their new lives. Tsarist officers drove taxis and waited tables and Russian 'princesses' worked as nightclub hostesses, dancers and, on occasion, upmarket ladies of the night. In 1924, three Russian 'princesses' opened a restaurant called Ellie's. It was renowned for its volcanic dry martinis and its interesting clientele – Atatürk, Agatha Christie and Greta Garbo, to name but a few. It was a classic listening post. The three princesses were in fact middle-aged Russian ladies from one of the classier brothels of Odessa – quite possibly having a 'bit of a history' with Biffy. Biffy would regularly frequent the smarter restaurants such as L'Ermitage and Maxime, in the Pera as well as Victoire – '*un boui – boui Russe*' – a Russian 'greasy spoon' which became a centre for trading information.

It was through one of Biffy's agents that he discovered that a plot had been hatched to kill the C in C General Harrington. The General was due to attend a ball at the Summer Palace of Therapia when an urgent message was passed from the SIS station to military headquarters who relayed the intelligence to the General, urging him not to go. He remained at home without incident.

It was also during his time in Istanbul that Biffy made two important contacts. George Keun, a friend of Richard Dunderdale and the head of one of the largest trading families in the Levant, and, through him, his son Philip, who would go on to play an important role in Biffy's JADE network in occupied France. Another member of the Keun clan, Philip Keun's cousin Odette, was to prove a complication for Biffy during his time in Constantinople. Odette was the daughter of Gustave Keun, George Keun's brother, and was extremely rebellious and outspoken. She hated dogma, repressive religion, loved travelling and had a selection of interesting lovers: Bernard Laverge took her to the deserts of Algeria, a Georgian prince, Dodi Chavchavadze, to Georgia. Soon she transitioned from Dodi to another prince, Grisha Tsereteli.

In 1921, Georgian politics were complicated. France and Britain were conducting clandestine operations there against the Bolsheviks, which Biffy had a hand in, and the entire area was considered very sensitive. Most foreigners left before the Bolsheviks arrived in February 1921, but Odette decided to stay. In June 1921, she needed to go to Istanbul to sort out her affairs but on arrival she was arrested by the French, acting on behalf of the tripartite Allied Forces. Eventually she was released, but on the eve of her departure back to Georgia, she was arrested by the British Military Police, who took all her notebooks and her Bolshevik Laissez-Passer from Tbilisi. She was suspected of working for the Bolsheviks and accused of having some involvement in the plan to assassinate General Harrington. In the end, she was deported to the Crimea along with 36 other people with Bolshevik sympathies. She was most indignant and bombarded everyone she could think of with complaints about her treatment. Odette was now stuck and, on arrival in Sevastopol, was accused of being a British spy. Eventually she was allowed to come back to Constantinople and from there moved to the south of France where she lived with her lover H. G. Wells.

Biffy arrived in Istanbul in the autumn of 1921 and was not immediately involved. He was advised to keep out of this affair but maintain good relations with George and that side of the Keun clan. When Odette was finally allowed to return to Istanbul, it is very likely that Biffy would have debriefed her on her stay in Sevastopol and also on her contacts in Georgia, as one of his operational tasks was the delivery of weapons to Georgian anti-Bolshevik forces.

Not everything was plain sailing for Biffy in this period. During 1920, while still working for NID, Biffy was attending a parade which involved the 11th (Service) Battalion of the Royal Welch Fusiliers which was due to be disbanded after the end of World War I. The Fusiliers traditionally have a goat as a regimental mascot – either given to them by the Monarch or procured locally in overseas stations. The goat parades with the Battalion on formal occasions. For this parade Biffy was in his Naval dress uniform. At the end of the parade, Biffy jumped into his car, put it in gear and promptly reversed over the goat, killing it. The Commanding Officer, Lieutenant Colonel Yatman DSO, was unamused.

This was not only terribly embarrassing but upset him so much that he swore never to drive again, deciding to hire a chauffeur. A friend of his in the Russian émigré community recommended Paul Kilesso. Kilesso was born in the Ukraine, went to France in 1916 as part of the Russian Expeditionary Force and had fought at Verdun. After the war he did not want to return to a communist Russia and moved to Constantinople. Biffy had known Kilesso from Odessa and immediately hired him. This would be a fortuitous meeting. Kilesso would return to Paris with Biffy in 1926 and in 1940 become the linchpin for the JADE FITZROY and JADE AMICOL networks.

As well as conducting operations into Russia, Biffy and the SIS team targeted the Russian trade mission and Consul General for

Royal Welch Fusiliers parade where Biffy ran over the regimental goat

penetration and the recruitment of agents, as it was the cover organisation for their extensive disinformation and espionage activities.

By 1924 the SIS station in Istanbul was able to identify the Russian intelligence structure, which was sent to London in a report dated the 23rd of September 1924. The report begins:

The largest foreign Intelligence Organisation in Turkey is the Russian one, the others all being on a much smaller scale and primarily concerned with Military Intelligence.

It goes on to identify the local Head of Station as Comrade Goltz, working under diplomatic cover of the Repatriation Committee of the S.S.S.R., controlling all political and military intelligence-gathering in Turkey, Syria and Egypt and counterintelligence operations against the Russian émigré community. Goltz was supported by two deputies, Troitsky and Theophilsky. A subsidiary station operated in Smyrna working undercover of the Soviet Consulate, who 'ran' the Italian Consul General, an important Soviet agent who provided the Bolsheviks with genuine Italian passports.

Biffy had also identified Vladimir Vilenski, the Russian Consul General in Istanbul, as an intelligence officer. His operations officer, Kolomtytsev, worked out of the Trade Delegation, running a network of 16 agents including some 'doubles' in the White Russian community, such as Countess Savantzo and Prince Georgi Andronikoshvilli (who betrayed the operations of Georgian anti-Bolshevik operations in the Caucasus). The penetration of Russian émigré communities by the Soviet Intelligence Services was an ongoing problem for Biffy and for SIS. Comrade Vilenski was successful in penetrating not only the émigré communities, but also the Turkish army, police and media. The OGPU office in the trade mission was run by Konstantizovski who also reported to Vilenski. Vilenski was to move to Paris in 1929 working under the cover name of Janovitch, where he would cross paths with Biffy again.

*

SIS targeting of the Turks was very effective, successfully penetrating and recruiting agents in Parliament, the Council of Ministers and the General Staff. So successful was the penetration of the army that the detailed orders for military operations were usually in British hands well before the event. Reports regularly came from highly placed sources:

The following information has been obtained very confidentially from a close friend of Mustafa Kemel and a senior official of the Ankara administration.

In addition, Biffy helped set up a communications intercept operation against the Turks and the Russians, named 'Black Jumbo'. Its transcripts were sent to London as part of the overall Constantinople intelligence product. A young French officer Gustave Bertrand was attached to the Radio Intercept Cell of the Allied General Staff. Biffy met him and they became friends. Gustave Bertrand would later become a key player in Biffy's story when he moved to Paris and, later, in the run-up to, and throughout, World War II.[14]

Whilst the Turks had proved themselves not to be receptive to Bolshevik moves to form an anti-British Islamist nationalist bloc within the British Empire, others were more than happy to go along with Russian plans. Biffy debriefed an agent who had attended a conference held at the Schloss Café Salzburg on the 14th of August 1923. Sari Efe Edib Bey, a prominent Turkish nationalist, had played a significant role in organising the conference which was attended by Islamic nationalists from Egypt, Persia, Gaza and India, as well as Henry Stickman from Britain and a 'Russian Bolshevik' only known as Findrin. One of the key aspects of Biffy's debrief report relates to armed action against British troops including the possibility of biological warfare.

---

14 Another young French intelligence officer whom Biffy became friendly with was Roger Lafont, whom Biffy would meet again in Paris. He would go on to be the head of French counterintelligence after the war.

Stress was laid on the fact that wherever opportunity offered, enemies were to be got rid of. This was also to happen in the case of individual officers of the troops of occupation in the Orient. Sabotage was to be carried on wherever possible, on railways and other means of transport, in the mines and oilfields, and on animals such as horses, etc. The old question was raised regarding fighting with bacilli against men and animals, should actual hostilities break out.

The report also covered the possible assassination of Lord Curzon, the British Foreign Secretary, and the French Prime Minister, Raymond Poincaré. There is some speculation that Biffy's agent was Sari Efe Edib Bey. Bey was later executed in 1926 for his part in the assassination attempt against the first president of Turkey, Mustafa Kemal Atatürk, in Izmir.

The third and final line of operation was the support for offensive action. The British Government, infuriated by the Treaty of Rapallo, ordered the Istanbul station to organise offensive action in Transcaucasia. They got in touch with anti-Bolshevik forces and set up sabotage teams to attack bridges, oil installations and the Chiatura manganese mines. Weapons and explosives were provided by British forces in Constantinople and automatic pistols were provided by Arthur Launder, the local Vickers representative who was no doubt a friend of Richard Dunderdale. The equipment was delivered to the Trabzon area by British Motor Gunboats where they were transferred to Turkish feluccas for final delivery. Biffy and one of the local SIS staff, Khasan Karansaflei, travelled to Trabzon to organise reception of equipment and the hire of feluccas and the onward delivery of the weapons and equipment into Georgia. These operations were not particularly effective and were suspended in November 1922.

By 1925 things were quietening down in the region and Biffy, having continued to impress, was about to move on to what was to be his most effective posting. His promotion was helped by the appointment of Admiral Hugh 'Quex'[15] Sinclair as Head of the Secret Intelligence

15 He got his nickname from Sir Arthur Pinero's play 'The Gay Lord Quex, the most dangerous man in London'.

Service and Director of the Government Code and Cypher School. Sinclair succeeded Mansfield Cumming, who had developed heart problems at the beginning of 1923 and died on the 14th of June that year. Sinclair had an excellent professional reputation and also that of a *bon vivant*; a large crocodile-skin 'magazine' containing 100 cigars was usually close at hand. He was intolerant of any form of idleness or inefficiency, which he would immediately chastise with *'an astonishing flow of forcible language, such as was traditional in an earlier generation of sea officers delivered without hurry or any change of expression'*. He was also a *'delightful companion, possessed of a fund of caustic humour and entertaining anecdote'*.

Quex Sinclair had been the Director of Naval Intelligence and was well aware of Biffy's activities, networks and reports in the Crimea, as well as his ongoing work in Istanbul. It would be Sinclair who would select Biffy to go to Paris as Head of Station in 1926 – a remarkably senior and responsible post for such a young officer.

CHAPTER 5 – PARIS 1926

'Oh what a tangled web we weave,
when first we practise to deceive
But when you've practised quite a bit
You really get quite good at it.'

Nicholas Elliott, SIS Officer 1939–69

The British Ambassador in Paris, Sir George Clark, established a tradition that on New Year's Day he would throw a lunch party for everyone who worked in the embassy. *That meant everybody, typists, the man who took the bag to Calais, everyone.*' The lunch took place in the state dining room in the residence. So, on New Year's Day 1935, the young, newly joined diplomat Fitzroy Maclean[16] found himself sitting next to a stunning, stylishly dressed American blonde. Fitzroy was struck by her beauty and curious as to who she was. So far, he had only met his fellow diplomats and had never seen her before, so asked her where she fitted into the embassy. She replied that her husband worked in the Passport Control Office. This didn't mean much to Fitzroy, but after lunch she introduced him to her husband and they invited him to dinner the following week. She was June Dunderdale, Biffy's first wife, whom he had married in Paris in 1928.

Fitzroy duly went to dinner at what he thought was their flat, but in fact was Biffy's office at 1 Avenue Charles Floquet, just underneath the Eiffel Tower. Dinner was a bit of an eye-opener for the young Fitzroy. The building was very impressive, with a vast marble entrance hall and upstairs a magnificent dining room looking out over the Champ de Mars and the illuminated Eiffel Tower. Two dozen people sat down to an excellent dinner and an endless supply of vintage champagne. After dinner Biffy and June took their guests to the Sheherazade nightclub on the Rue de Liège.[17] It was run by

16 Brigadier Sir Fitzroy Maclean, KT, CBE. British Embassy, Paris 1934–37. Moscow 1937–39. In World War II served with the SAS chosen by Churchill to lead the military mission to Tito's Partisans in Yugoslavia. Post-WWII a politician, retiring in 1974.
17 Opened on the 3rd of December 1927. It was extremely popular. Regulars included the Prince of Wales, Maurice Chevalier and Charlie Chaplin, as well as Biffy and June.

June Dunderdale in
French *Vogue*

Fitzroy Maclean

an émigré Tsarist General whom Biffy knew from Odessa and full of exotic atmosphere – tall Russian waiters, mostly ex-Imperial Guard officers, rose velvet curtains and dim lighting. The General greeted Biffy effusively. Biffy introduced Fitzroy – '*This is my friend Maclean, he must have free champagne whenever he comes here.*' The party watched the cabaret, which happened to be Josephine Baker, whom Biffy was to work with later during the war.

They stayed in the club till dawn then Biffy suggested a boat trip down the Seine. Fitzroy envisaged a 'Bâteau Mouche', but when they arrived at the river, they were piped aboard Biffy's motor yacht *My June*.

The champagne continued to flow as they watched the sun come up. Later Fitzroy staggered into his office, bleary-eyed and somewhat worse for wear and bumped into the military attaché Lt Col Tom Hayward OBE. He relayed his adventures and asked who exactly this fellow Biffy from the Passport Control Office was, speculating as to how he could afford such a lifestyle. Tom laughed: '*Don't you know what the Passport Control Office is? It's standard cover for SIS and Biffy Dunderdale is Head of Station.*'

*

The Paris to which Biffy was posted from Istanbul in 1926 was equally if not more exotic. The 'City of Light' was experiencing a cultural, intellectual and financial boom, as a counter to the miserable years of World War I and the social and economic unrest that followed. Paris

Cabaret at the Sheherazade nightclub

My June

had become a shadow of the glory days of the 1890s and early 1900s. Now Paris resumed its place as capital of the arts, and of the exotic, in what became known as 'Les Années Folles' – the crazy years. The city was buzzing with creative energy and the sound of jazz, attracting a host of international artists, writers and performers who came to create and share in the excitement.[18]

The bohemian atmosphere of Montparnasse, with its cafés, bars and studios, was a hub of creative energy. Montparnasse was to become a favourite haunt of Biffy's. Revolutionary art movements such as Cubism, Surrealism and Dada turned Paris into the home of the artistic avant-garde. Picasso and Matisse were just two of the leading lights in an art scene that included Chagall, Giacometti, Léger, Miró and Calder. Intellectual life thrived. In literary circles, Gide, Valéry and Malraux were at the forefront of French thought, while world writers who found inspiration there included Ernest Hemingway, F. Scott Fitzgerald and James Joyce. It was a golden age for haute couture too, with the houses of Chanel, Dior and Schiaparelli dressing the beautiful, rich and emancipated women who populated Paris's glittering social scene, while the exotic pleasures of the city's nightlife were embodied in the sensational glamour of Josephine Baker. The haute couture world soon homed in on June Dunderdale, inviting her to wear their latest creations when attending high-profile society events.

18 There were others who were not part of the glamour but would make their mark on history including a young pastry chef from French Indochina called Ho Chi Minh.

Many Russians had fled to the city in the wake of the Revolution and many of them were already well known to Biffy. When Biffy arrived in Paris, the émigré population numbered 60,000. Many of its Tsarist aristocrats were eking out a living driving taxis, setting up nightclubs and restaurants, including the Sheherazade, the Troika, L'Aigle Russe and the Bistrot Russe. The Kazbek at 12 Avenue de Clichy and L'Esturgeon, run by the former chef to the Tsar, were firm favourites of Biffy's. There were about 5,000 Russian taxi drivers in Paris. Their main gathering place was Le Petit Bistro Petrograd and again, Biffy was a frequent visitor. The Russians were joined by thousands of Armenians, Czechs and Slovaks, soon to be followed by Germans fleeing the rise of the Nazis. It was a heady cultural mix and after the horrors of a world war and a bloody Revolution, it made for a society keen to live only for today because, tomorrow, who knew what might happen? Politically, Paris reflected the extremes of much of the rest of Europe: fascism on the rise in Germany, Spain and Italy, and the communists in full control of Russia, which was by then the Soviet Union.

It was also the era of the Grand Brothels of Paris. Le Chabanais[19] was described as the 'Académie Française' of brothels and 122 and Le Sphinx catered to upmarket clients. 122 soon became the darling of everyone who was anyone in Paris. People went there for sex, or merely to have a good dinner at its famous restaurant called Le Bœuf à la ficelle (The Bull on a String). The champagne flowed freely – there were never fewer than 120 bottles consumed each day. The pianist tinkled out foxtrots, tangos and slow waltzes. It was where many of the glamorous stars of the era met: Humphrey Bogart, Cary Grant, Marlene Dietrich, Sacha Guitry, Mistinguett and Suzy Solidor with her lesbian lover, the antique dealer Yvonne de Brémond d'Ars. Biffy's new friends in the Deuxième Bureau took advantage of these 'maisons closes', either as listening posts for gathering intelligence, or on occasion for blackmailing a potential agent. It was also the era of great cafés and restaurants such as La Coupole, which opened in 1927, with 1,200 bottles of champagne drunk on its

19 Le Chabanais opened its doors in 1897 at Rue Chabanais, founded by Alexandre Jouannet who had started 'work' in Constantinople. Le Chabanais was a favourite of Edward VII.

opening night, Ciro's[20] and Maxim's, both of which were to become great favourites of Biffy's. Often at lunchtime his Rolls Royce would be parked outside.

Maxim's at 3 Rue Royale was opened in 1893 by Irma de Montigny, a very attractive courtesan, and Maxime Gaillard. It rapidly gained a reputation for delicious food and delicious ladies, '*les grandes cocottes*'. '*It was a restaurant to take ladies but never your wife.*' Whilst not a brothel per se, these ladies were on the lookout for rich men who could keep them in grand style, in return for horizontal companionship. They were witty as well as attractive. Their manners were good, they knew everything about the art of entertaining, and they knew even more about the art of spending money. Jean Cocteau said of the female clientele: '*It was an accommodation of velvet, lace, ribbons and diamonds. To undress one of those women is like an outing that calls for three weeks advanced notice. It is like moving house.*' The most famous of these 'demi-mondaines', as they were called, were queens in their own right and exerted absolute power over a court of admirers. They were naturally the fiercest of rivals. Magnificent jewels and famous lovers were their status symbols and Maxim's was the chosen place where they appeared nearly every night, to make sure that their stock market quotations did not drop.

Maxim's flourished until the crash of 1929 when it was put up for sale. In 1931 it was bought by Octave Vaudable who, in a stroke of genius, hired Albert Blazer as the Maître d'Hôtel. Albert had few friends, but Biffy, long established as a valued client, was one of them. Albert had excellent connections from the Aga Khan to the Duke of Windsor, not to mention the innumerable duchesses, film stars and millionaires in his address book. Albert's success in his career and in the comeback of Maxim's was based on his art of out-snobbing the snobs. He was far more than a Maître d'Hôtel; he was a court official of infallible judgement, instinctively assigning everyone to his proper place. All Paris society begged for his acknowledgement.

---

20 Ciro's: The eccentric James Gordon Bennett, owner of the *New York Herald*, patronised a small restaurant in Monte Carlo. He always had a table on the terrace and one day he arrived to find them all occupied. He bought the restaurant and then promptly gave it to a waiter as a tip. The waiter's name was Ciro and he was thus launched on a career of some distinction.

A very prominent Parisian lawyer remarked that '*I knew that I had succeeded in life the day that Albert called me by my name.*' Maxim's became like a private mansion where an introduction or invitation was necessary before entering. All this was to be a fertile ground for Biffy's intelligence-gathering activities.

*

Biffy had arrived in Paris in November 1926, accompanied by his trusty friend, chauffeur and bodyguard, Paul Kilesso, to set up a parallel SIS station to the one working under Passport Control Office cover, run by Maurice Jeffes[21] at 16 Avenue Hoche. Neither of the stations was to be based in the embassy. This suited Biffy – he was always very wary of working in 'Head Office' or under the watchful eye of the ambassador and his diplomatic staff.

After World War I, SIS was thinly spread across the world with 19 stations in Europe, one in New York and Vancouver, three in China, and one in Japan, Singapore, Hong Kong and Vladivostok. Cash was very tight, but Sinclair, with a degree of foresight, had realised the main threat was still Russia with stirrings elsewhere in Europe, notably in Germany, Italy and Spain. Following the crash of 1929, the world economy was in tatters with nationalism or fascism emerging. Even in France, in spite of the glitter of Paris, there was considerable social, economic and political unrest. It seemed to Sinclair that SIS should capitalise on close liaison with the French intelligence services who had a much greater budget and had made significant inroads against the threat from Russia and the emerging threat from Germany. So, Biffy was sent to set up his second station with the designation 5550, whereas Jeffes's station was designated 27000. Biffy transformed the Paris station and by 1935 he would have the biggest budget of any SIS station in the sum of £4,005.[22]

The central weapon in Biffy's armoury was his personality. He spoke English, Russian, German and Polish. His wife June spoke

---

21 Maurice Jeffes HOS 1922–37, Biffy Dunderdale 1926–40.
22 Worth £350,000 today. In spite of the rise of Hitler, SIS was starved of money. That same year further cuts were imposed on the SIS budget. Hugh Sinclair pointed out that SIS's entire annual budget amounted to the cost of maintaining one destroyer in home waters.

English, French and German. His substantial private income enabled him to live in sumptuous style and to entertain lavishly. His links with the leaders of French social and political life were close, and he developed excellent relations with the French intelligence services. His flat at 15 Avenue Elisée Reclus became a meeting place for international visitors and a venue for political gossip – part home, part 'salon'. His manners and demeanour were more continental than British, enabling him to blend in well with Paris society.

Biffy served with four ambassadors during his 14 years in Paris: the Marquis of Crewe from 1926–28, Sir William Tyrell 1928–34, Sir George Clerk 1934–37, Sir Eric Phipps[23] 1937–39 and Sir Ronald Campbell 1939–40. Biffy ensured he had as little to do with the embassy as possible and, due to his capability, character and very good relations with his French friends in the Deuxième Bureau, was able to operate more or less independently. Of all the ambassadors, he got on best with William Tyrell, whose own lifestyle echoed Biffy's. He was not impressed with Eric Phipps who, having been ambassador in Berlin from 1933–37 and witnessed the rise of Hitler and the Nazis first hand, followed the appeasement line, much to the irritation of Biffy and his French counterparts. Biffy was distinctly unimpressed with him and the functioning of the embassy. He felt they produced nothing of value to London except gossip and tittle tattle.

Biffy initially took a flat in the Rue Joubert, but soon moved to a much smarter part of Paris, taking a first-floor flat at 15 Avenue Elisée Recluse, overlooking the Champ de Mars and the Eiffel Tower. It was a very convenient 10-minute walk or a short drive in his Rolls Royce to his nearby office at 1 Avenue Charles Floquet and close to the Deuxième Bureau Office at 2 bis Avenue de Tourville.

On posting to Paris, Biffy did what all 'declared' intelligence officers did. Rather than getting involved in a complicated cover, he relied on a fairly transparent cover as an attaché at the British embassy and acted accordingly. 'Cover' is described in intelligence manuals as *'the life which you outwardly lead in order to conceal the real purpose of*

23 Sir Eric Phipps, father to Alan Phipps, killed on Leros 1943. Alan married Veronica Fraser, Lord Lovat's daughter. They had a son, Jeremy. After Alan was killed, Veronica remarried Fitzroy Maclean in 1945. Jeremy went on to be General Jeremy Phipps CBE, Director UK Special Forces.

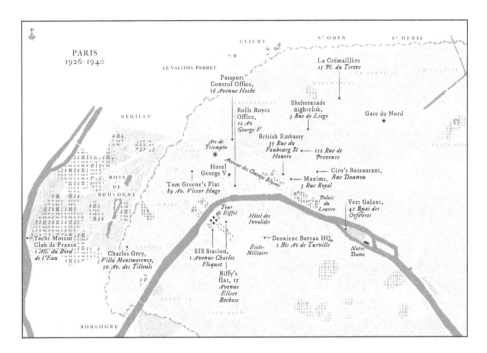

PARIS
1926-1940

CLICHY ST OUEN ST DENIS

LE VALLOIS PERRET

La Crémaillère
15 Pl. du Tertre

Passport
Control Office,
16 Avenue Hoche

NEUILLY

Rolls Royce
Office,
12 Av
George V

Sheherazade
nightclub,
3 Rue de Liege

Gare du Nord

British Embassy
35 Rue du
Faubourg St •——— 122 Rue de
Honore Provence

Arc de
Triomphe

Hotel
George V •

Tom Greene's Flat
89 Av. Victor Hugo

Ciro's Restaurant,
Rue Daunou
•— Maxims,
3 Rue Royal

Palais
du
Louvre

Vert Galant,
42 Quai des
Orfèvres

BOIS
DE
BOULOGNE

Tour
de Eiffel

Hôtel des
Invalides

Yacht Moteur
Club de France
1 All. du Bord
de l'Eau

Charles Grey,
Villa Montmorency,
50 Av. des Tilleuls

SIS Station,
1 Avenue Charles
Floquet

École-
Militaire

•— Deuxieme Bureau HQ,
2 Bis Av de Turville

Notre
Dame

Biffy's
flat, 15
Avenue
Elisee
Rechose

BOULOGNE

your presence and the explanation which you give of your past and present'. Biffy had to protect his true mission from public scrutiny, but why bother with the constraints and complexities of being under a full cover alias that had to be maintained 24 hours a day, seven days a week without any slip? In addition, the chosen cover, commercial, journalistic or military, might not get the access necessary for developing a full spectrum of intelligence. As he was also a man of considerable private means, he was able to develop and lead an extravagant lifestyle which gave him access to all levels of French as well as émigré society, including the White Russian, Americans, British and – increasingly – Germans escaping from the rise of Hitler and the Nazis. This was very fertile ground for making and developing a vast network of contacts and therefore agent recruitment and intelligence-gathering, in addition to his increasingly close relations with the key officers in the Deuxième Bureau.

Intelligence officers in any service can roughly be divided into two categories: those who sit in their offices analysing and evaluating the information as it comes in and those that go out into the world to get it. Biffy was certainly the latter. To quote Nicholas Elliott,[24] one of Biffy's protégés:

> *Field officers have three important characteristics: personalities*
> *in their own right, a humanity and a capacity for friendship and*
> *they will have a sense of humour which will enable them to avoid*
> *ridiculous mumbo-jumbo of over secrecy. This is because a large*
> *part of intelligence work in the field is all about the establishment*
> *of personal relationships; of gaining other people's confidence*
> *and on some occasions persuading people to do something that is*
> *against their better judgement.*

Biffy ticked all the boxes.

Underneath his extravagant exterior lurked a mind like quick-silver, fully attuned to his mission. He was not universally popular with his colleagues – Kenneth Cohen would later say that they did not get on particularly well, calling him a '*Quex Sinclair incubus*' – but others believed he was one of the best officers SIS had.

*

As well as the extensive social scene centred on the British embassy and the White Russian community, there was a large American expatriate community in Paris. One of these was June Woodbridge Ament, an exceedingly glamorous blonde. Her family were very wealthy and had come to live in Paris from Washington DC. June's mother Geraldine was the granddaughter of Samuel Morse, the inventor of the morse code. Biffy met June one evening at an embassy cocktail party in the summer of 1927 and was totally smitten. They were married on the 19th of December 1928; Biffy was 29 and June 17.[25]

The civil ceremony was held in the town hall of the 7th arrondissement of Paris, in the Rue de Grenelle, officiated by Paul Gaté, the

---

24 Nicholas Elliott, SIS 1939–68. Friend and protégé of Biffy's. Responsible for the Buster Crabb operation and for extracting a confession from Kim Philby in Beirut, although he failed to prevent Philby from escaping to Russia.
25 June was technically underage and the marriage was later annulled on the 30th of April 1947.

Biffy and June on their wedding day

deputy mayor. The best man was a close friend of Biffy's, George Cury. George Cury was born in Odessa in 1895 and was at school with Biffy. He later joined the 20th Regiment of Dragoons of the French Army. He was a chevalier of the Légion d'honneur and won a Croix de Guerre in World War I. At the time of the marriage, he was serving in the Headquarters of the French Army in Paris. June was attended by Charlotte Lawrence, another wealthy American 'sans profession' who lived with June and her mother at 52 Avenue Bosquet. After a honeymoon on the Riviera, they took up residence at Biffy's flat on the first floor, 15 Avenue Elisée Recluse, where they lived in considerable style, looked after by a famous Russian chef who had fled to Paris and Lucy,[26] whom Biffy hired as a maid for June. Their social circle included many of Biffy's friends and contacts in the Russian émigré community, including George and Diana Snopko. George had been a member of Tsar Nicholas's bodyguard, later serving with General Wrangel and then moving to Paris where he married

26 Both the chef and Lucy worked for Biffy and June until 1940. They remained in their flat, which was taken over by the Abwehr during the war. After the war, Biffy did not return to live in Paris, but arranged for funds to be transferred to them as they were destitute.

Princess Diana Eugina Kotchoubey de Beauharnais, a direct descendant of Nicholas I.[27] June and Biffy were regularly seen at the most prominent social events, like the Art and Tourism Ball, with the likes of Clarissa Churchill, Lord and Lady Acheson and Count Victor de Lesseps. They also could be found at the Sheherazade nightclub in the company of Baron de Freygary, Grand Duke Alexandre of Russia and Prince Krassinsky; at the Ritz with Prince and Princess Djurdjazé, Lady Orr Lewis and Princess Eristavi, who had been very close to the Tsar as her father was in the Imperial Duma and her sister a lady in waiting to Alexandra, and at Ciro's with Baron Édouard de Rothschild and Major Dudley 'Fruity' Metcalf.[28] They were also friends with Grand Duke Kirill Vladimirovich of Russia who had proclaimed himself head of the Imperial family of Russia. They were often mentioned in the social columns of the *New York Herald* (published in Paris), *Mode*, *Excelsior*, *Femina* and *Vogue*, which wrote about June:

L'élégance et le charme de Mrs W. A. Dunderdale lui ont acquis les plus vives sympathies tant dans les circles diplomatique que dans la société Parisienne – The elegance and charm of Mrs W. A. Dunderdale won her the warmest sympathy both in diplomatic circles and in Parisian society.

Outside Paris they travelled regularly to Deauville, Biarritz, Saint Jean-de-luz and Antibes, where they stayed with George and Germaine Keun at their villa Tana Merah[29] at 64 Avenue des Pins du Cap, George Keun being a close friend of Richard Dunderdale. The Keuns had left Smyrna, briefly spent time in Constantinople then settled in Paris and Antibes.

---

27 Diana's grandmother was Countess Daria Dmitrievna Beauharnais von Leuchtenburg, great granddaughter of Emperor Nicholas I, usually known as 'Dolly'. She had a sad life. Banished from Russia for insulting the Tsar, she worked as a nurse during the Revolution and was eventually shot in 1930 by the KGB after a long trial for plotting to assassinate Russian politicians.
28 Dudley 'Fruity' Metcalf, MVO MC, equerry to Edward VIII later the Duke of Windsor, who was living in Paris.
29 Designed by Barry Dierks, an American architect who also designed villas for the Aga Khan and Somerset Maughan amongst many others.

From left to right: Coosie Hottinguer, Biffy, Richard Dunderdale and June

Back in Paris, their inner circle included another wealthy American friend of June's, Allardyce Barclay Boyesen, who, after being educated at North Foreland Lodge in England, gravitated to Paris and became great friends with the Countess Tolstoi. She then married a Swiss banker, Philippe Hottinguer. Always known as 'Coosie', she became very close to Biffy and June. During the war she stayed in Paris working for one of Biffy's networks and was eventually arrested and imprisoned in Fresnes. She survived, divorced Philippe, and eventually lived with Ingram Fraser who was a fellow SIS officer and close friend of Biffy's.[30]

Biffy bought *My June,* his yacht, in 1930. It was a J. Taylor Bates Gentleman's Motor Yacht. Biffy saw a similar model at the Paris boat show at the Grand Palais in 1928 and ordered one. Once delivered, Biffy joined the Yacht Moteur Club de France where Biffy would keep *My June* at an exclusive berth.

Biffy would take part in races, often winning, or would cruise down the Seine in the company of close friends, mostly linked to his SIS station.

30 Ingram Fraser. Former advertising executive. Recruited to Section D of SIS. Head of Scandinavian operations. Lifelong friend of Biffy's.

Biffy and friends on his yacht, My June

'Uncle' Tom Greene at
Château le Chêsne

Membership to the YMCF also got Biffy alongside additional interesting contacts such as Doctor Eugenie Etchegoin, the Commodore of YMCF, an Argentinian lung bacteriologist who was working at the Pasteur Institute in Paris. Etchegoin raced powerboats and held the water speed record in 1927 and 1929 and regularly raced his speedboat in Venice and Lake Garda and was reputed to be close to the Italian Government. As such he would have been useful to Biffy during Mussolini's rise to power and the Abyssinian invasion of 1935.

In 1934, an Ulsterman, Tom Greene and his wife Lilly (who was always known as Sylvia) took up residence in Paris, renting a luxurious apartment at 69 Avenue Victor Hugo, accompanied by his two daughters Sheelagh and Lois and his niece Doreen. Upon meeting Biffy, they began a partnership in the secret world that would last until Tom retired from SIS in 1948.

Tom Greene was born on the 30th of October 1890 in Warrenpoint, Northern Ireland. He was part of the Mathew d'Arcy whiskey distilling family and, from their distillery, he derived considerable private income.[31] He was a massive man, 6' 6" tall, described by the French as '*built like Hercules*', a truly delightful character with a huge international network of friends and contacts. Tom's father John Greene was the owner of Mathew d'Arcy whiskey, a very successful business with many clients in Ireland and overseas, selling its unique brand

---

31 When Tom Greene died in Portugal in 1963, he left the equivalent of £2.3 million.

using laid-down whiskey from distilleries such as Jameson. Following John's death, the whiskey business was split between Tom and his brother Hulton. During World War I, whiskey was to be diluted in strength, its tax doubled and a compulsory three years in bond before sale imposed. In addition, in 1917, the government reduced by 50 per cent the amount that could be taken out of bond. Tom immediately put the company into liquidation, sold the stock, the premises in Newry and other assets for a considerable sum. As he was extremely wealthy, Tom offered to assist Biffy in his work for no renumeration. Biffy quickly took him up on the offer. In those days, the recruitment process for SIS was particularly informal. He became his Chief of Staff, working with Biffy up until they had to leave Paris in 1940. As he was the oldest in the Paris station, he quickly earned the nickname of 'Uncle' Tom. He continued to work for SIS and directly for Biffy throughout the war and returned to Paris in 1944, serving his last four years there, retiring to Portugal in 1948. Tom also had long dinners in his apartment with Biffy and June and Paul Paillole and his wife. Tom and Paul became close friends. Doreen, his niece, also worked in the SIS office in Paris.

The Dunderdales and Greenes became very close. As well as working together they socialised a great deal on Biffy's boat, often going on trips to the Château le Chêsne near Salbris in the Loire Valley, and on holidays to Le Touquet, Deauville and Zoute in Belgium.

The Château le Chêsne is sometimes referred to as Biffy's country

Château le Chêsne

Biffy and Sheelagh Greene relaxing at the
Château le Chêsne c. 1930

residence but was in reality an SIS 'off-site', used for operational
purposes as well as an escape from Paris life. The château dated from
the 14th century but was rebuilt and modernised in the 19th century.
It was set in a 60-acre park on the bank of a river near Salbris, south
of Orléans in the Loire Valley – very quiet and very discreet. Biffy had
leased it from the Comtesse de Gontaut-Biron in 1930. Another character who came into the Dunderdale orbit was the French playwright
Sacha Guitry, who lived opposite them on the Avenue Elisée Recluse
at number 18. Guitry was born in St Petersburg in 1895, where his
father Lucien ran the French Theatre Company, the Théâtre Michel.
He gradually rose to prominence in French theatre and cinema and,
by 1930, he was famous, well off and had started a collection of
wives. Whilst living opposite Biffy and June, he was married to his
most famous wife, Yvonne Printemps. Their marriage was stormy
to say the least and marked by many affairs on both sides. The
Dunderdales and their occasional guests from SIS head office such as
Fred Winterbotham were regularly amused by ferocious rows taking
place on the Guitry doorstep as Yvonne stormed off on some pretext,
probably to spend a few days with her latest lover. Guitry and his
next wife Jacqueline Delubac, whom he married in 1935, will make a

'guest appearance' assisting SIS in 1939. Later, he was to be arrested for collaboration with the Germans but was cleared of all charges.

*

In the period after the Russian Revolution and civil war many White Russians settled in Paris and, by 1926, there was a thriving community, the leaders of which were well known to Biffy. Inevitably this community, like its counterpart in Istanbul, continued to plot against the Bolsheviks and maintained many lines of communication to their friends and contacts in Russia. Biffy, with his background, capabilities and connections in the émigré world was, although still only 26, an obvious choice to establish a new station in Paris, primarily to liaise with the French Deuxième Bureau, but also to continue intelligence operations against the Soviets, later switching targets to Germany. He also did peripheral work such as being the nominal Head of Station in Norway, gathering intelligence on the Spanish Civil War and the ambitions of Mussolini. As part of his anti-Soviet work, he was also to handle relations with Grand Duke Nicholas,[32] the de facto leader of the White Russian community in Paris.

Whilst Biffy's primary task was intelligence development and agent recruitment, he was also tasked with setting up a close liaison with the French intelligence services, which in 1926 consisted of the Service de Renseignement (SR) – Intelligence Service – based at 2 bis Avenue de Tourville right alongside Napoleon's Tomb at Les Invalides in central Paris and the Renseignement Généraux de la Préfecture de Paris (RGPP). These two services often failed to talk to each other, let alone share information. The SR was attached to the Deuxième Bureau of the Army Staff[33] and had three responsibilities: Human Intelligence (agent-running), military counterintelligence

---

32 Grand Duke Nicholas Nikolaevich of Russia (1856–1929). Grandson of Tsar Nicholas I. Commander of the Russian army until 1915. He was replaced and appointed Commander-in-Chief of the Caucasus. He was evacuated from the Crimea in 1919 aboard HMS MARLBOROUGH. In exile, he lived at Choigny, 20 miles from Paris, protected by the Deuxième Bureau and a group of Cossack bodyguards. He was the head of all anti-Soviet Russian forces. He died of natural causes in Antibes in 1929.
33 Military Staffs are divided into branches: G1 – Personnel, G2 – Intelligence, G3 – Operations, G4 – Logistics, hence 'Deuxième' or 'Second' Bureau.

Walter Sleator

and the interception and analysis of foreign communications. Biffy was to work closely with the Deuxième Bureau in all three areas and was a frequent visitor in their offices.

In addition, SIS activity in France also cultivated British commercial connections, such as Rolls Royce. Biffy had got to know Walter Sleator, the 29-year-old head of Franco-Britannic Automobiles, Rolls Royce's front company in Paris whose offices were at 12 Avenue George V, just across the river from Biffy's office. By 1934, Sleator was head of all Rolls Royce operations in France. At some point in the 1930s, Sleator was recruited by Biffy to assist SIS operations both then and in the future. Sleator loaned Biffy a Rolls Royce. The Rolls, a 20/25, was not armoured – to dispel another Biffy myth.

SIS found it exceptionally useful being able to run an organisation in Paris which 'underpinned close secret services relations with the French who not only had six times the staff of SIS, but had clearly

Rolls Royce 20/25, similar to the one Biffy was loaned by Walter Sleator

worked out that while Russia was still the primary target, Germany was catching up fast'. To this end, the French developed close working relations with the Polish intelligence services. Maurice Jeffes had been sent to Paris as Head of Station in October 1922. His station, coded 27000, worked under Passport Control cover. While Jeffes continued to target Russia, he began, together with Stewart Menzies – then Deputy Head of SIS in London – to develop close relations with the Deuxième Bureau which Biffy would take over and run from his second station, specifically to deal with the Deuxième Bureau on Soviet and German order of battle, military capability and intelligence.[34]

In time, there was to be a third station working under commercial cover as part of Claude Dansey's 'Z' organisation. It would be run by Kenneth Cohen, a former naval officer who had known Biffy in the Crimea. Cohen stayed with Biffy and June but felt like *'an unwanted lodger'*. Cohen and Biffy were wary of each other and during the war were to be on different sides of the Free French/Vichy dilemma. However, they were to remain friends and continued to socialise after the war.

Biffy immediately established a good working relationship with the Deuxième Bureau. He got on well with his French counterparts. Paul Paillole, the Head of Counterintelligence, described him as a *'congenial and refined officer – un camarade séduisant d'une élégance raffinée. We liked his easy going manner, the fact that he spoke fluent French, and the efforts he made to foster friendly relations with us.'*

Biffy also arranged for his French counterparts to visit London. Paillole described his visit: *'We were given a friendly welcome as comrades in arms and shown round the British capital, spending two evenings at a music hall and a concert at the Albert Hall.'* These visits further cemented personal relationships and interservice cooperation. Paillole again: *'The British Services were really brotherly services. We acted hand in hand.'*

---

34 Major General Sir Kenneth Strong, who was Eisenhower's Chief of Intelligence for the D-Day landings and went on to be Director of Joint Intelligence at the Ministry of Defence from 1948–64, considered that in the 1930s the Deuxième Bureau was *'the most competent intelligence organisation in the world'*.

Biffy became a regular visitor to the Deuxième Bureau offices. According to Paul Paillole, '*He would come at least two or three times a week and we often had lunch or dinner together.*' The Deuxième Bureau offices were entered by a large green gate in the high wall close to the École Militare. An ancient concierge, Hervé Dourain, would open the door and send you to a little wooden hut just inside the gate to sign the visitor's register. There was a bare table and a pen with a broken nib which one dipped into a bottle of very diluted ink. Its run-down appearance gave the impression that the French Government did not spend much money on its intelligence service. Inside the courtyard, the headquarters consisted of a collection of wooden huts, freezing in winter and roasting in summer. The offices were sparsely furnished with bare trestle tables and hard wooden chairs, a few filing cabinets and maps on the wall. In spite of the spartan nature of the headquarters it had a certain reputation in France, where it was generally known as 'Le Temple Mystérieux'.

By comparison, the SIS offices in Broadway Building were positively luxurious. As Biffy entered, he would always check to see if he was being followed. On one occasion his counter-surveillance procedure was interrupted by the arrival of an ancient, rickety old van whose driver got out of his cab, opened the rear doors, took two mail bags from the back, threw them on the pavement and shouted: '*Voilà, pour les espions.*'

So much for secrecy.

Street number of the Deuxième Bureau headquarters

CHAPTER 6
ÉMIGRÉS AND DEFECTORS

'Can we dream of reforming Russia?
I don't think so. Therefore, we must be
courageous and in spite of all, try to live.'

Vera Evdokimova

'Defectors are like grapes; the first
pressings are always the best.'

Maurice Oldfield, 'C', 1973–78

The end of World War I did not bring an end to conflict in Europe or elsewhere. Wars of independence, nationalist resistance to European colonialism, frontier readjustments of the new Eastern European states created in the aftermath of the peace treaties, brutal civil wars in Russia and Spain and territorial aggression by Japan and Italy in Asia and Africa, all ensured that the intelligence services of France and Britain were busy. For more than half of the interwar period, British and French intelligence services focused on the emerging Soviet Union, which, despite its efforts to foster communist revolutions either by invading a neighbour (Poland, 1920) or by fomenting internal uprisings of communist workers, sailors and soldiers (Germany, Hungary and Austria), remained the only communist country. After the Russian Civil War ended in 1921 with the Bolshevik victory, a secret war was beginning which pitted the British and French secret services against the expanding intelligence services of the Soviet Union. Biffy was to be at the forefront of this.

Soviet intelligence services sought to discover the military capabilities and intentions of potential enemies such as Britain, France, Germany and the United States, as well as Japan to which it had lost the 1904 Russo-Japanese War and continued to have territorial disputes in the Far East. In addition, Soviet spies sought to obtain Western industrial and economic secrets in order to improve industrial capacity and enable Russia to compete with the West.

The Soviets employed different types of spies: 'legals', who used diplomatic cover at Soviet consulates and embassies, and 'illegals', who used all sorts of cover, including Soviet press and trade associations established in foreign capitals, as well as a variety of ideologically sympathetic agents who infiltrated trade unions, defence industries and government departments. The targeting of workers and merchant seamen in major ports in Germany, Holland, Belgium and Scandinavia had the dual purpose of encouraging the overthrow of capitalism and creating a 'fifth column' to cause disruption by strike action and sabotage in the event of war with the Soviet Union.

Stalin, like Mr Putin, used the long arm of Soviet intelligence to murder exiled White Russians and other enemies of the USSR wherever they were living abroad. These tactics became well known in Paris when the press reported that opponents or defectors were being kidnapped or murdered in France. These operations were carried out by the Special Division (Chastny Otdyel) of the Second Directorate of the Cheka.[35]

During 1924, there were serious discussions between the British and French governments about Bolshevik subversion in both countries and Europe as a whole. The French wanted to put anti-Bolshevik counterintelligence on a more formal and aggressive footing. The Foreign Office, in an internal note dated December the 18th 1924, suggested that this might be misconstrued as a direct threat to Russia and too aggressive. It was suggested that liaison between the Police Special Branch and the French counterintelligence department should continue but not be formalised. This loose arrangement did not work well. Later, in 1925, a decision was taken that the second SIS station should be set up in Paris to affect this as well as other intelligence activities.

Biffy, with his fluent French and obvious style and flair, must have been an easy choice. The other reason for choosing Biffy was his experience with the Russians and he was to continue to use his extensive contacts in the large White Russian émigré community which had settled in Paris between 1917 and 1922. Biffy was able to develop

---

35 The Bolshevik/Soviet Intelligence Services changed names throughout the timespan of Biffy's career: Cheka 1917–22; GPU 1922–23; OGPU 1923–34; NKVD 1934–46; MVD 1946–54; KGB 1954.

good intelligence and recruit agents such as his White Russian aviation expert Nikolai Baranov. Another of Biffy's agents within the émigré community, Leonard Narbevich, was able to obtain official manuals from the Russian Military Publishing Office, via '*a friend to whom he frequently sent presents*'. The same agent supplied '*reports on the Russian Navy as well as obtaining newspapers prohibited for exportation*'. Another of Biffy's contacts from Istanbul worked in a Soviet army office in the Georgian capital Tbilisi and regularly sent information about military deployments as well as technical specifications of weapon systems and other military equipment to Paris, hidden in local newspapers. There was also a network of railway officials in Southern Russia whose reports on railway traffic and troop movements in the '*central Asian Military District*', were described as '*very valuable*'. Baranov and Narbevich left France in 1940 with Biffy and continued to work for SIS into the 1950s.

Whilst Biffy developed excellent sources and continued to use contacts from his time in the Crimea and Istanbul, the émigré community in Paris had to be treated with a great deal of circumspection. This community and others elsewhere had two weaknesses: it made a huge business out of peddling forged documents, 'fake news' in modern parlance, and it was also heavily penetrated by the Soviet intelligence services, the Cheka and its successor, the OGPU.

Ever since the controversy over the Zinoviev letter in 1924, SIS had been quite rightly concerned about the veracity of intelligence coming out of Russian exile communities. This was made more difficult to detect because of their determination to destroy Bolshevism and that some of the Anglo-Russian SIS Officers, including Biffy, were inclined to trust them. In May 1925, SIS sent out a sharp reminder to all stations that they must '*use every precaution in accepting as genuine any alleged communist document that may be offered to you*' and to check their sources thoroughly.

As the Russian émigré communities settled in Paris, Berlin, Warsaw and the Baltic States they formed mutually supporting centres for anti-Soviet plotting, propaganda and intelligence-gathering. Their operational security was lax and they became obvious and easy targets for penetration and exploitation. A central figure in this business was Vladimir Orlov, described by Desmond Morton[36] as '*a born intriguer and ambitious*'. Orlov had '*an elaborate machinery for forging documents*' and, '*with information supplied by the OGPU*', his organisation prepared bogus intelligence reports which they sold or leaked to European intelligence services as part of a disinformation programme.

The largest and most important White Russian group was the All-Military Union (ROVS-Russky Obshche-Voinsky Soiuz), which had emerged from the remnants of General Wrangel's White Army. When the ceasefire with the Bolsheviks had been signed in October 1920, the French had assisted in the evacuation of Wrangel's army to Turkey. After much messing about by the French, three countries, Bulgaria, Yugoslavia and Hungary, agreed to take the troops and they were dispersed between them while still retaining some semblance of an army. With his troops scattered and many beginning to migrate westwards to work in France, where there was a large shortage of labour, Wrangel formed ROVS as a means of keeping in touch and maintaining links with his troops. Organised on a country level, each man paid a small subscription which offered a degree of social security and kept them in touch with fellow exiles. General Kutepov, whose strict military discipline had kept the army together in Constantinople, was appointed head of ROVS own intelligence/counterintelligence section dubbed the 'Inner Line' and became a high-priority target for the Bolsheviks.

General Kutepov's organisation was initially targeted by an OGPU 'sting' operation called 'The Trust' which was designed to disorganise, destabilise and discredit the Whites. An individual named Aleksander Aleksandrovich Yakushev, who had been a senior civil servant in the Tsarist Ministry of Communications, contacted émigré organisations in the early 1920s and through him they were introduced to an Edward Opperput, who claimed to represent an organisation in Russia which was planning a counter-revolution against the Bolsheviks. They were seeking financial support and details

36 Major Sir Desmond Morton KCB, CMG, MC, head of SIS section V dealing with counter-Soviet operations in the 1920s. Later became Winston Churchill's PA handling all ENIGMA/ULTRA intelligence.

General Alexander Kutepov

of existing White networks so they could work with them. Various groups fell for it, sending large amounts of money and details of their networks, which were then infiltrated and rolled up.

Kutepov sent several agents into Russia, including his own niece Maria Zakharchenko-Radkevich and her husband who believed they were working with The Trust. They tried to get Sidney Reilly back to Russia. During his preparations to return to Russia, Reilly was certainly in touch with Kutepov, who was planning to meet two allegedly senior Trust members in Paris at about the same time. Kutepov's people in Finland, including Maria Zakharchenko-Radkevich, helped him get Reilly into Russia on the 25th of September 1925. On arrival he was arrested, interrogated and eventually executed. His death effectively blew The Trust, though it took some people a while to realise it.

One lingering legacy of The Trust was to sow seeds of distrust about the White organisations. Generally, SIS seem to have taken a pretty poor view of the Whites, though they did use them from time to time when it suited; several key SIS agents were Whites, but they were kept well away from their compatriots and operated directly under SIS control because SIS was keenly aware of the OGPU penetration operation. In spite of his close contacts with the émigré community, Biffy was rightly sceptical. He reported that:

Like most White Russian information, it is very voluminous and a good deal of it is untrue and merely a compilation or rehash of old information. In all probability a good deal of what does not come into these categories is the result of denunciation of one White Russian by another, a habit which, as you know, this community are prone to.

Wrangel died in April 1928 of tuberculosis but there were inevitably suspicions that the infectious bacteria had been administered incrementally, over a long period, by an OGPU agent on his staff. Kutepov now found himself as the unchallenged though not entirely popular head of White anti-Soviet operations. Kutepov was certainly still a power to be reckoned with, ably demonstrated when a team of his agents were able to detonate a bomb inside OGPU Headquarters in Moscow.

*

Following the end of the Russian Civil War and the Russo-Polish War (where France had given Poland extensive support) there was a general move among the western European countries to establish diplomatic relations with the Bolsheviks. The motivation for this was a hope that trade with Russia would help boost their flagging economies. They were encouraged in this by Lenin's New Economic Policy. By 1925, the Bolsheviks had established an embassy in Paris and there was a rapid growth of cultural and commercial contacts. Under cover of these new contacts, the Bolsheviks deployed agents into France, working from the embassy, the Consulate and the Trade Delegation. Others maintained cover as journalists, businessmen and artists.

Operations at the Trade Delegation were run by Soloman Kharin, under cover of the Economic and Statistical Section, where he collated all agent reports on military matters. In the embassy, Second Secretary Lev Borisovich Helfand was Head of OGPU operations, assisted by Vladimir Borisov Janovitch (real name Vladimir Volensky) who had previously served in Constantinople where he had worked chiefly against Russian émigré targets and was well known to Biffy.

General Evgheni Karlovich Miller

Biffy reported to London in a CX cable dated the 22nd of November 1930, that Volensky was *'below medium height; dark; about 30; nimble and lively with shifty eyes; looks like a shop assistant; curly hair, sly and clever. Likes money.'* His wife, Aleksandra, a former ballet dancer and singer, was also an OGPU agent, responsible for acting as a cut out between the OGPU clandestine agents and the embassy. Volensky and his wife were closely monitored by one of Biffy's agents.

On Sunday the 26th of January 1930, General Kutepov set out from his flat in the Rue Rousselet for the Russian Orthodox Church and never returned, having been snatched off the street by OGPU agents. He was stopped by a police patrol – in reality a snatch squad led by Yakov Serebryansky. In Moscow it was felt that a show trial would cause international complications and it is believed that he was quietly executed. In fact, as confirmed by General Alexander Orlov of the NKVD (successors to OGPU) who defected to the USA in 1938, Kutepov had been given an accidental overdose of anaesthetic during the kidnap and had a heart attack and died as a result.

Kutepov's disappearance was a hard blow to ROVS, from which it never really recovered. His successor, General Evgheni Karlovich Miller, who had been in charge of ROVS administration and finances, was more of a diplomat and administrator than a fighting soldier.

He quickly appreciated the effects of the depression caused by the Wall Street Crash and began to turn the organisation towards

Nikolai Skoblin and Nadezhda Plevitskaya

providing financial support for its poorer members to enable them to survive. This change wasn't popular with some of the younger and more aggressive officers who still wanted to overthrow the Bolsheviks. Though Miller continued to work towards this end it was very much secondary and the 'Young Turks' turned to General Nikolai Vladimirovich Skoblin for leadership. He was a proper fighting soldier, who was both ruthless and a tactical genius. He had married a beautiful young Russian folk singer, Nadezhda Plevitskaya,[37] and helped her to develop a successful singing career which included international concert tours and made the couple very well off.

Rumours began to circulate about Skoblin and his wife. She had spent a lot of time with Kutepov in the weeks before he disappeared. Her singing career also seemed to be slowing, yet the couple had recently bought a new house in Paris and a new car, spending as freely as ever. Then Captain Fedessenko, one of the 'Young Turks', revealed in a Parisian Russian-language newspaper that he had allowed himself to be recruited by the OGPU. He had been told after his recruitment that Skoblin was also an OGPU agent. Fedessenko was not to get close to him in case he revealed him as a fellow agent. Fedessenko took this information to General Miller but was not believed. Miller promised not to reveal this accusation, but word soon reached Skoblin. Skoblin questioned Fedessenko about his knowledge of other Soviet agents within ROVS. Fedessenko was then

---

37 Plevitskaya was known as the Kursk Nightingale and said to be a favourite of Stalin.

expelled from ROVS and also quickly dropped by the OGPU. Having also leaked the whole story to the press, he was lucky not to be quietly executed.

A further report from Finland informed Miller that the Finns refused to work with ROVS because *'someone in Paris, especially in Ozoir-la-Ferrière, would surely betray them'*. Ozoir-la-Ferrière was where Skoblin lived.

On Sunday the 22nd of September 1937 at 12:10, General Miller left his office at ROVS Headquarters. Before he left, he handed a sealed envelope to General Kossonsky, his Chief of Staff, with the words: *'Please do not think I have gone out of my mind, but if I don't happen to return, open this and read it.'* He left but had not said where he was going. He was scheduled to attend a meeting at 17:00 of veterans who had served under him at Archangel in 1919 but by 20:00 he'd still not returned home. His wife became very alarmed and she began phoning round to try and find him. No one had seen or heard from him. Eventually someone got through to General Kossonsky to ask him to call the police. He took a taxi back to his office, found the letter in a drawer and opened it. It read:

> *Today at 13:30pm I have an appointment with General Skoblin at the corner of Rue Jasmin and Rue Raffet. He is supposed to take me to a meeting with a German officer by the name of Strohman – reputedly a German military attaché in one of the Balkan countries – and one Werner, of the German embassy here. They both speak good Russian. The meeting was arranged at Skoblin's initiative. This is perhaps a trap, which is why I am in any event leaving this note.*

Skoblin was tracked down and taken to ROVS Headquarters where he was confronted and accused of treachery, which he denied and agreed to accompany his accusers to the police. He was first out of the door and, when he saw that the other officers were not immediately behind him, he promptly disappeared. His wife denied all knowledge of his whereabouts or about the events leading up to Miller's disappearance. The police, by good old-fashioned detective work, traced

Skoblin's escape route to the point when he turned up at the house of an ROVS veteran and borrowed 200 francs and then disappeared again. Mrs Skoblin gradually broke down under interrogation. Both her and her husband's alibis for the timeframe of Miller's disappearance didn't stand up. It became clear that she was closely involved in the operation and was able to warn others to get clear.

Later in the investigation it was discovered that a Soviet freighter, the *Marya Ulyanova* in Le Havre, had been loaded with a large packing case that had arrived from Paris in a van with diplomatic plates. The van was registered to the embassy and the driver and another man were embassy officials. A witness emerged, a Russian veteran, who had seen Skoblin and Miller together entering a Russian villa owned by the embassy in the early afternoon of the disappearance. Skoblin had completely disappeared. His wife was tried for her part in the planning of the operation at a trial that gripped Paris and on the 9th of December 1938 was sentenced to 20 years, hard labour. She died in prison in 1940.

Miller arrived in Russia alive. He was kept in solitary confinement for 19 months, regularly interrogated and was shot on May the 11th 1939. Skoblin reached the Russian embassy and was smuggled out to Russia. He later fell foul of Stalin's purges and show trials; his fate is unknown, but probably, like Miller, he died from a bullet in the back of the head in the basement of the Lubyanka.

*

Against this background of intrigue and internecine strife within the émigré community, Biffy was able to keep a finger on the pulse, discern what was going on and still run his reliable agents, keeping them compartmentalised from the rest of the chaos and confusion, and from those working for the Bolsheviks.

One of Biffy's first jobs in Paris was to debrief the first high-level Soviet Party official to defect to the West after the Revolution, Boris Georgievich Bazhanov, a Politburo secretary and Stalin's Personal Assistant.

Boris Bazhanov

He had been working as an agent for SIS since 1919 and worked his way up through the party hierarchy. He was recruited in Ukraine and it may be that Biffy recruited him in the first place, although it's more likely to have been Harold Gibson.

In early 1928, together with a Russian cavalry officer, Arkady Maximov, he arrived in India. He claimed to have detailed intelligence on the structure of the Central Committee of the Communist Party, on Soviet finances and on the order of battle and operational detail of the OGPU both in the Soviet Union and overseas. Word of their arrival was sent to SIS in London. Sinclair thought that their desire to get to London was simply '*a transparent ruse to effect their desire to make their way to Europe*'. This was to prove short-sighted, but it was arranged with the Deuxième Bureau to bring the two men to France, where Biffy helped run their interrogation and debrief.

Bazhanov had escaped to British India via Persia. Maximov who accompanied him was in fact Captain Birgar of the OGPU, his assignment to stop Bazhanov leaving Russia, but Bazhanov knew all about him. As they approached the Persian boarder Bazhanov turned to him, pointing a hunting rifle at his chest, and said:

Now listen, I know your real name. I know what your real job is, and I know what order you were given about me in Moscow. There will be little difficulty crossing today because the guards will still be drunk from last night. The other side is Persia and beyond that British India. That's where I am going. Don't try and stop me.

Leo Steveni

If you do, I will kill you. You can join me although they will hound us wherever we are. If you turn back without me you're dead anyway. Make up your mind.

Maximov/Birgar clearly got the message and nodded his agreement. Having crossed into Persia, it was not long before the OGPU went into action trying to kill both of them, first with poison, then using a hitman who was stopped in his tracks by a local police chief who was on the SIS payroll. Bazhanov and Maximov found their way to Duzdap where they got in contact with Leo Steveni[38] the 'Military Attaché', who was in fact an SIS officer.

One of his informers reported that the Soviet Consul, Comrade Platte, had been joined by a known OGPU officer Osipov and a team of six trained Turkoman killers. Steveni realised that they were there to kill or capture Bazhanov and Maximov to prevent them falling into British hands. The threat was real and imminent and they needed to be got out to British territory without delay. No trains were to leave for three days and, in any event, Steveni considered trains unsafe as they could easily be stopped and intercepted. Steveni takes up the story:

I accordingly arranged with Mr Jamaluddin Mullick, a prominent Muhammadan merchant of Duzdap and a gentlemen whom

38 Colonel Leo Steveni OBE MC, later full-time SIS officer and Head of SIS Operations Far East 1942–44. He, like Biffy, was born in Russia in 1893.

I knew I could trust, that he should drive Bazhanov and Maximov in his private car that night to Kacha levy post, some 36 miles east of Duzdap. I had myself motored most of the way to Kacha not long before, and knew that the frontier was unguarded; the 17 miles between Kacha Road railway siding and the levy post lie among rugged and uninhabited mountains, and the track is very seldom used. Although Mr Mullick had never been to Kacha and was doubtful whether even with my driver as guide, he would be able to get there in the dark, and although he was naturally anxious not to compromise himself with the Persians, he agreed at once, refusing to accept even the cost of the petrol he would consume, and it was arranged that he should leave with the two refugees at 11 p.m. Their last few hours in Duzdap were spent by Bazhanov and Maximov writing against time to complete the intelligence reports they had promised to Major Steveni, and it was nearly midnight before we were able to put them in Mr Mullick's car, together with the food, blankets etc. which had been procured for them.

Mr Mullick had considerable difficulty owing to the bright moonlight in making his way through the station precincts and out of Duzdap without attracting the attention of the Customs police, but he succeeded in doing so and in reaching Kacha before dawn. In the gorge through which the track leads at mile 22–3, scarcely eight feet wide in some places, he scraped the sides of his car (an almost new 8-cylinder Hupmobile) but suffered no other mishap. Leaving the refugees with a letter from me in the hands of the levy jemadar, he managed to return to Duzdap and enter the town by a devious route without his absence having been remarked.

The next day (8th April), according to intelligence reports, the Soviet Consul and his associates hunted high and low for Bazhanov and Maximov in the bazaar and at the station. On the 9th May they enlisted the aid of the police, who spent most of that day searching for the refugees. The Superintendent of Police evidently suspected the Trade Assistant, M. Mahmud Gul (wrongly) of knowing their whereabouts, for he sent a subordinate to try and 'pump' him, but without success. On 10th April

Comrade Platte visited the Governor of Duzdap and asked him to surrender Bazhanov and Maximov on the pretext that they had committed a murder in Russia. The Governor wrote an order to the Police to produce the refugees before him; this order was taken to the Superintendent of Police by the Soviet Consul himself. The Superintendent, who must have suspected by this time that Bazhanov and Maximov were out of reach, denied equally knowledge of their whereabouts and responsibility for their disappearance. The same evening the Soviet Consul sent urgent cypher telegrams to Meshed, Sistan and Kerman. He spent another three days in Duzdap making enquiries and then returned to Sistan. Except for some unofficial attempts on the part of the Governor to find out from Mahmud Gul whether Captain Macann or I had had anything to do with the disappearance of the refugees, the Persian authorities have made no further move in the matter. I have reason to believe that they are, if anything, relieved to be rid of two embarrassing visitors.

Bazhanov eventually got to Simla where he was rather indifferently debriefed by the British authorities. They gradually understood what a big fish they had caught but were hamstrung by the seeming lack of interest in London. Both British India and London seemed very sluggish about this high-value catch. Communications were batted back and forth between London and India for seven months. The main barrier to sending them immediately to London for debriefing seemed to be Vernon Kell, Head of MI5, in spite of the British authorities in India being *'convinced of their bona fides and the great importance of revelations they are able and willing to make'* which included *'the organisation of the central Soviet committee, location of secret funds, the Comintern budget and how foreign communist parties [were] funded, the workings of OGPU inside and outside Russia and details of planned Coups in Persia and Afghanistan. We recommend they are sent under police protection to Karachi and from there to London with a conducting officer from SIS.'*

Still, London prevaricated. In June 1928, frustrated with this absurdity, Biffy took a hand in the negotiations by speaking to his friends in the Deuxième Bureau, who agreed to them coming immediately to France: '*Negotiations to that end have been successfully conducted by a member of SIS. We have now succeeded in preparing the way for the grant of permission by the French for these two people to journey to France, they're to be interviewed by the French authorities.*'

Eventually on August the 19th 1928, they sailed from Bombay on the SS MALOJA, arriving in Marseilles on the 30th.

The French had jumped at the chance of having the opportunity to pick the brains of Stalin's former secretary. Bazhanov arrived in Paris on the 1st of September 1928. Biffy was immediately involved in the debriefing. He reported that Maximov was of '*absolutely no interest to us as he is a typical low-class post-revolutionary officer*', but Bazhanov was '*an exceptionally intelligent man*', from whom he had extracted 140 pages of information. '*We are producing a whole book mainly on the Polit Bureau [sic] and the OGPU*', which he hoped would '*be a very important guide*'. This included a '*description of the Government mechanism*' and profiles of the Bolshevik leadership. While the former was described as '*very accurate*', Biffy felt the latter less reliable, being '*the somewhat prejudiced views of an unsuccessful Communist who now has leanings towards Fascism*'. Biffy thought that Bazhanov '*considerably exaggerates the strength of the anti-Bolsheviks and the results attained by them in their secret anti-Soviet work abroad*'.

By the end of 1928, the OGPU, having realised the vast amount of intelligence that Bazhanov had taken with him, put out an urgent order to all their agents in Paris and London '*to render him innocuous*' at the earliest opportunity. However, Bazhanov was reported to be ill. Valentine Vivian[39] thought the Russians had missed their chance and '*that Tuberculosis [was] likely to save the GPU agents the expense of a cartridge*'. In fact, Bazhanov survived until the 1970s.

The French were quicker on the uptake than their British counterparts in Simla. They wasted no time in summoning Bazhanov to the Deuxième Bureau Headquarters in the Avenue de Tourville, where they began a very detailed debrief in complete contrast to

---

39 Valentine Vivian joined SIS in 1925 running their counterintelligence department. He became Vice Chief of SIS in 1941 and retired in 1951. His latter career was marked by a long-running power struggle with Claude Dansey.

the nugatory efforts of the British in Simla. Biffy was immediately invited to join the debrief team and Bazhanov was interrogated intensively every day for the next two weeks. The French focused almost entirely on politics with little attention to military matters. Colonel Josse, the Deuxième Bureau team leader, wanted exact details as to how Moscow financed the French Communist Party and those in other Western countries. Bazhanov was invited to explain the machinations of the Kremlin power game and who was likely to come out permanently on top. The result was a document, over 200 pages long, which provided the first detailed and authentic picture, given from the inside, of the Soviet leadership and the divisions and factions within it.

Biffy sent the report to London where the SIS and MI5 hierarchy now had, rather belatedly, realised their initial mistake in not bringing Bazhanov to London. It was clear from the Paris report that Boris Bazhanov was a unique and irreplaceable expert on the complicated puzzle of Soviet leadership and politics.

In early 1929, Biffy again went to see Bazhanov and asked for his advice. SIS had a particularly interesting problem that they needed Bazhanov to comment on.

It concerned the activities of Comrade Gaidouk, OGPU Head of Station in Riga, the capital of Latvia, which was still an independent Baltic state. He had made contact with the local SIS station, offering to sell the British Government copies of the minutes of the Soviet Politburo. The price was astronomical, but so was the potential intelligence and Gaidouk's samples looked genuine. So, a deal was done and London started rubbing their hands in anticipation of what they thought would be a very significant espionage coup. As with all intelligence, it needed validation and corroboration. Gaidouk's information seemed to be enhanced when the Politburo's decisions reported by him became official policy. There was always the possibility that this was an elaborate disinformation operation on the OGPU's part. Bazhanov was the only person who could provide this validation, so Biffy asked Bazhanov to look at some of the documents Gaidouk had produced.

Bazhanov immediately pronounced the documents to be fakes

and Gaidouk to be a fraud. Bazhanov was emphatic: for a start, he knew that the OGPU 'Resident' in Riga would never have access to this level of material and it was extremely unlikely that the Politburo minutes could have reached him unofficially. The most detailed and elaborate precautions were always taken to ensure that what went on inside the Politburo was only communicated in a very abbreviated form to a very closed group of senior figures outside it.

Bazhanov emphasised that although Stalin never sat as chairman of the Politburo, he always edited the minutes of each meeting himself. Only when he had approved the final text were copies made for limited distribution to the members of the Central Committee. Those in Moscow received them that same evening by hand – delivered in pink envelopes, by the Kremlin couriers mounted on bicycles. Those away from the capital had their copies delivered to them by special messengers belonging to the Kremlin specialist Courier Service. Every document was copy numbered as specified on a distribution list for individual recipients and each copy had Stalin's personal stamp and signature. They also had to be returned after reading, so that they could be burnt by the Politburo's Secretariat.

It was possible there might have been a Western agent in place in the top echelons of the party who could copy the document, but that was unlikely as Western intelligence agencies would know about him. Couriers could be overpowered and the document stolen but that would soon be known about and compromised.

Bazhanov was also able to point out that there were some glaring errors in the documents – errors of fact, or mistakes in style and layout. However, the real reason why he knew that they were forgeries was that Gaidouk had actually come to Paris and offered him a business proposal. Freely admitting that he was doing a very lucrative trade in 'Politburo minutes' with the British, but that he was now running rather low on inspiration, he proposed that Bazhanov should join him in the deception in return for a share of the profits. Bazhanov threw him out.

Perhaps understandably, both Biffy and SIS in London were reluctant to accept Bazhanov's verdict. It was not pleasant, when you thought you had hit the jackpot, to be told that it was all completely worthless. Bazhanov's verdict had to be accepted and Biffy reluctantly reported this to London. Comrade Gaidouk found that his services were no longer required by London, which in hindsight may have been short-sighted as he could have been persuaded, by a bit of judicious blackmail, into working for SIS.

For Bazhanov, this was the beginning of a long-term relationship with Biffy, who consulted him at intervals over the next 10 years on a variety of Soviet issues. The relationship was a happy one and it was only a change in British policy which brought it to an abrupt end. In 1939, the British Government sent a mission to Moscow to establish better relations with Russia. Biffy went to see Bazhanov to seek his advice. Bazhanov felt let down by the British and said that he was no longer prepared to help a country that was seeking to ally itself with his sworn enemy.

Biffy concluded their last meeting by warning him: '*Remember, we have long arms*'; Bazhanov replied: '*Stalin's are longer and so far I have kept out of them.*'[40]

*

In October 1929, Biffy became involved with a second Russian defector, Grigory Bessadovsky, the Chargé d'Affaires at the Soviet Embassy in Paris.

Bessadovsky was under suspicion of either embezzlement or espionage, or both. He had been under surveillance for some time and received a summons to return to Moscow for 'official consultations', which at best usually meant an extended stay in the Gulag, at worst a bullet in the back of the head in the cellars of the Lubyanka. Bessadovsky ignored two of these summonses, so inevitably the Kremlin dispatched Comrade Roizenman, one of their most effective executioners, to bring him back to Moscow or eliminate him in situ. As soon as he arrived at the embassy, Roizenman armed two of the embassy security guards and told them to prevent anyone leaving, most especially Comrade Bessadovsky. As soon as Bessadovsky heard

---

40 There was an ironic twist to Bazhanov's story. The third Russian defector to arrive in France in June 1930 was Georges Agabekov who had led the operation to kill Bazhanov in Persia in 1928. Eventually they met in Paris, a somewhat tense encounter.

Grigory Bessadovsky

that Roizenman was in the embassy and had summoned him to the OGPU office, he knew he was in real trouble. He stalled and warned his wife and son to pack and leave. He was then confronted by his executioner, who told him that he was taking him back to Moscow *'dead or alive'*. Bessadovsky ran for it, avoided the two guards, got into the embassy courtyard and, seeing his escape route blocked, dodged sideways and clambered over the embassy wall, making his escape through some neighbouring gardens to a local police station. He eventually found his way to the Prefecture of Police, was immediately granted asylum and his wife and son were rescued from the embassy by the police.

Bessadovsky and his family were installed in the Hotel Marigny on the Rue des Arcades under police protection. However, the Russians soon let him know that they knew exactly where he was. Very quickly, Biffy's friends in the Deuxième Bureau arranged for him to see Bessadovsky, so, on Saturday the 5th of October, two days after his defection, Biffy had a two-hour meeting with him, followed by a second session four days later. Biffy was unimpressed, describing him as *'smart and intelligent, but neither frank nor principled and quite possibly not honest. Extremely talkative, shifty, indiscreet and a poor judge of people.'* However, Bessadovsky did divulge a lot of detail about how the OGPU operated in France and Britain, both under diplomatic and commercial cover. He also gave Biffy the name of an Englishman who had tried to sell the British diplomatic code to the Head of the OGPU Station, Vladimir Yanovich, who not only got the code, but tricked the Englishman out of the US $2,000 he had asked for it.

He also explained to Biffy how Russian 'black' funds were channelled to agents and sympathisers in the West. All proceeds of foreign trade were being sent to a current account at the Equitable Trust Company in New York. From there it was distributed via the international banking system, to individuals' accounts in the target country. The only exception was funds for France, which were sent to Germany, then Belgium and, only then, to France. Biffy was able to pass this routing detail to his friends in the Deuxième Bureau.

Bessadovsky's defection, whilst not as significant as Bazhanov's, nevertheless gave both SIS and the Deuxième Bureau a very good insight into the intelligence-gathering methodology of Soviet overseas missions and the funding of agents and subversive groups. It is another example of the close cooperation with the French that was to set the tone for Biffy's tenure in Paris from 1926 to 1940 and was to pay great dividends during the war.

CHAPTER 7 – GERMANY, ITALY
AND THE SPANISH CIVIL WAR

'I smell the rain, and with it, pain,
and it's headed my way.'

Led Zeppelin, *Ramble On*

By the early 1930s, Germany was beginning to emerge as a greater threat than the Soviet Union. This was recognised from 1930 onwards by the French, Polish and British intelligence services, even if their respective governments were not so perceptive. While Biffy was still working on the Russian threat, it was from this point that he began his close involvement with the Deuxième Bureau and through them the Poles. This close cooperation was to last until the end of World War II.

When the Deuxième Bureau uncovered Hitler's plan to annex Western Poland and invade Western Europe, they began to develop, with the Poles, a significant intelligence-gathering operation against Germany. France had an agent in place close to the German High Command. He had provided them with intelligence in January 1936 about Hitler's plan to invade the Rhineland, which he did in March. On the 5th of November 1937, Hitler called a meeting in his private apartment at the Chancelry for the chiefs of the three armed forces, his closest ministers and the heads of the Abwehr, Gestapo and SS. He outlined his grand design for reviving the economy, rearmament and, most importantly, for expansion and the creation of 'buffer' states around Germany, i.e. the invasion of Poland and Western Europe over the period 1938–48. The meeting ended at 16:20 and it was followed by a cocktail party and ball. General Rudolf Schmidt, who had not been at the conference, dined with his friend Colonel Friedrich Hossbach, who had attended. Hossbach briefed Schmidt on the plan. Schmidt was horrified and rushed home to confide in his brother Hans-Thilo Schmidt. By 11:00 the next morning the plan was in the hands of the Deuxième Bureau: Hans-Thilo Schmidt was their highly placed agent in Berlin, codenamed ASCHÉ.

Ever since arriving in 1926, Biffy had worked hard at his job of close liaison with the Deuxième Bureau. He became increasingly close to Colonel Louis Rivet, who ran the bureau from 1936, Gustave Bertrand, who ran the crypto analyst department and whom he had first met in Constantinople, and Paul Paillole, Head of Counterintelligence.

Interpersonal relations and a good rapport are very important elements in intelligence liaison, often facilitating both understanding and problem-solving to mutual benefit. Biffy was very good at this.

During the early 1930s, links between SIS in London and the Deuxième Bureau became even closer. Rivet was well known to Menzies, 'C''s deputy, who would regularly send experts and heads of departments in Broadway over to Paris to liaise with their opposite numbers. These visits were coordinated by Biffy who would usually have the visitors to stay with him. One of the first visitors was John Tiltman from the GC + CS, who came over with Stewart Menzies in May 1933 to meet Gustave Bertrand. Tiltman describes the meeting:

I flew over to Paris, and I spent one day with Bertrand and two other French officers. Bertrand, I had then met for the first time. I had very definite instructions that if I found the French were unaware of Russian additive ciphers, and particularly the one-time pad, which had been introduced by then, I wasn't to talk about them. This was my first experience of Bertrand's intuition.

Colonel Louis Rivet

Gustave Bertrand, 1934

Paul Paillole

Fred Winterbotham

He started off (he didn't speak English… all had to be through an interpreter, because my French wasn't good enough) … saying, 'I realise that you probably have been instructed not to tell us everything you know, so we put down on paper everything we knew about Russian ciphers, which made it easy for me.' This is typical of Bertrand.

Meetings usually took place in Biffy's office or flat.

A typical interview with Bertrand, who as I said didn't know English, would be in Biffy Dunderdale's office. I would be talking, Bertrand would be sitting on the edge of his chair opposite to me, and when he saw you about to ask a question that he couldn't answer, always he'd say, 'ne pas demander'. He always knew what was going on.

Another frequent visitor was Fred Winterbotham.[41] Winterbotham had been seconded from the RAF to run a new SIS air section. One of his first jobs was to establish a link with Colonel Ferrand, Head of the Deuxième Bureau Air Section. Biffy facilitated this by arranging

41 Frederick William Winterbotham. Born in 1897 in Stroud. In 1914 joined the Royal Gloucestershire Hussars. Transferred to the Royal Flying Corps in 1916 as a fighter pilot. He was shot down and captured. During captivity he learnt fluent German. In 1919 he took a law degree then farmed in Kenya and Rhodesia. In 1929 he rejoined the RAF.

Lieutenant (Paymaster)
P. S. Sykes

for Winterbotham to travel to France every three or four months for a liaison meeting.

> *In those early thirties I took the Golden Arrow train from Victoria Station to Dover, crossing by passenger boat, then taking the train on to Gard du Nord in Paris, where Biffy would meet me and drive me to their flat in his chauffeur-driven car. It was very grand.*

Biffy and June entertained the guests from Head Office in the lavish style they had developed, ensuring that they had, for a few days, a taste of the restaurants and nightlife of Paris. Another regular visitor was Lieutenant (Paymaster) P. S. Sykes who ran the complicated finances of SIS. Colloquially known as 'Pay', he was not averse to a good night out and Biffy and June would ensure that he was properly entertained, helping to ensure continued funding for the station. Sykes and Biffy became firm friends and maintained a regular correspondence. One letter, written in 1955, regaled Biffy with stories of Mansfield Cummings and harked back to their sorties in Paris referring to dinners fit for Biffy's *'elegant palate'*.

Biffy would regularly meet Deuxième Bureau officers, usually accompanied by Tom Greene and any visitors from London, for lunch at the Vert Galant Restaurant – Auberge Du Vert Galant at 42 Quai des Orfèvres on the Île de la Cité, close to the Prefecture of Police.

It was a very popular restaurant but lower key than Maxim's or

Auberge Du Vert Galant

Ciro's. Its advertisement in *La Revue Diplomatique* describes '*Une ambiance tres agréable, un endroit frais et reposant, une cuisine delectable.*' A very pleasant atmosphere, a cool and relaxing place, a delectable cuisine. It was famous for its lobster newburg and 'La Poule au Pot d'Henri IV' was always on the menu. Lunch, always in an upstairs private room, was presided over by Colonel Rivet and Biffy. Most of the officers of the Deuxième Bureau who worked with the SIS station or with their visiting opposite numbers from London would attend. The conversation would be kept convivial, usually centring around the delights of the latest dancers at the Bal Tabarin[42] and that they were all English or that the principal dancer at the Bar Nudiste, who had the most perfect figure in Paris, was married to a very wealthy industrialist who collected her in his Rolls Royce every night after the show. Professional matters would be discussed later. Lunch would go on for about two hours until nearly 15:00, when the younger members of the party would excuse themselves to the Colonel and depart just in time to get to the exclusive brothel not far away, reserved for serving officers. Once the 'young blades' had left, Biffy, the senior officers and the visitors from London would get down to real business and go through the key points on the agenda.

---

42 Bal Tabarin was the name of a cabaret at 36 Rue Victor-Massé. Its shows were spectacular – a mix of classical music or ballet and the erotic. One of its most famous dancers was a young South African Sadie Rigel, made even more famous by a series of photographs by Man Ray, the surrealist photographer.

By late afternoon the meeting was over and visitors from London were thankful to get away and back to Biffy's flat to have a cup of English tea.

One of the regulars at lunch was the Deuxième Bureau Air Section Chief, Colonel Ferrand, particularly if Fred Winterbotham was visiting. He had been a fighter pilot in World War I and was an expert on the Russian Air Force, at that time a preoccupation of Paris and London. He wore strange shirts with horizontal stripes rather than vertical and a hat with a brim turned up all the way round which he rarely took off. His sartorial elegance certainly left something to be desired, but he soon adopted a British-style suit and plain or vertically striped shirts. Also on the air intelligence side, Biffy had recruited Nikolai Baranov, a former White Russian Air Force General. Winterbotham usually met him with one of Biffy's team, Mr Parkinson (or 'Parky') in Parky's flat. Parky was another of Biffy's old friends who had also been brought up in Russia. He had married the daughter of a Russian Admiral whom Parky had helped to escape from Russia after the Revolution. Parky, Baranov and Winterbotham used to gather in the sitting room of their small flat and try to work out the real existence, strength and disposition of what the Russians called their air force. Parky of course did all the interpretation while the old General chain-smoked Russian cigarettes. Once it was explained to him what information was needed, he devised an ingenious way of getting information out of Russia.

He was still in touch with many of his old air force comrades who were scattered all over Russia. As letters were heavily censored, but newspapers were allowed to be sent between Russia and the outside world without censorship, he asked his friends to post him copies of their local newspapers, which always contained a lot of information about local goings-on. They would report social events connected with the local Russian Air Force base such as weddings, usually mentioning the pilot's unit. This enabled Baranov to compile a list of the location of Russian Air Force squadrons. It was not possible to describe the type of aircraft at a particular airfield but a small, pencilled figure in the corner of the outside page, which didn't arouse suspicion, would give the actual number of aircraft known to be stationed there. It was not a very accurate picture of the whole Russian Air Force, but it did confirm that the figures coming out of Moscow were all overinflated. Gradually, over the next few years, it was possible to get a fairly accurate idea of the size and strength of the whole force. Biffy never let on to his French friends how exactly the information was obtained, but they were impressed and very glad to have it.

Winterbotham became a frequent visitor and got to know Biffy and June very well.

June loved riding and my arrival was always the signal to hire a couple of horses so that we could ride in the Bois de Boulogne every morning. She also loved dancing, which was not one of Biffy's accomplishments. The couturiers had not wasted much time in spotting this lovely girl, and they provided her with lovely evening gowns which she was duly expected to show off. For myself white tie and tails were of course order of the day in better restaurants. It was always a thrill to lead this lovely girl onto the floor, and watch all the heads turning in her direction. When we sat down, there would inevitably follow little notes brought to us by the waiters from some women in the restaurant asking if June would mind giving the name of her couturier. It was obviously good business. I got to know Paris's smaller restaurants, where one could get the best food. As the franc was two hundred and fifty to the pound, it wasn't difficult to enjoy oneself. After the first year, Colonel Ferrand retired and a new man came to take his place. Georges Ronin was a very different person, tall and absolutely sincere, eventually becoming one of my best friends. We both knew what we were really after and there was absolute coopera-tion between us. He spoke no English, but by now my French was capable of coping with all the intricate details of aviation.

The Ethiopian Crisis of 1935–36 highlighted Mussolini's foreign policy of seeking to expand Italy's African colonies, which included Libya, Eritrea and Italian Somaliland. Italy invaded Ethiopia in October 1935 and in seven months had conquered the country.

Mussolini ignored international protest which was weak and ineffective – a lesson not lost on Hitler (or Vladimir Putin). As the situation escalated, Biffy was tasked with developing intelligence operations against Italy from Malta. Biffy, always meticulous about covering his tracks, would go into Malta unannounced. He would travel from Paris to Antibes, stay the night with George Keun and the next day pick up a private motorboat, crewed by sailors from the DNI, and head for Malta. On one occasion the crew was led by Pat Southby[43] who recalls the method of Biffy's arrival in Malta:

> When we reached Malta from Cannes he remained on board
> till after dark and was put ashore on Manoel Island in Sliema
> Harbour, just as the evening naval cinema was ending, to enable
> him to join some two hundred sailors plus wives or girlfriends as
> they left the cinema and went across the only bridge that con-
> nected the island with Malta.

Many years later, Southby had retired to Spain where one of his neighbours was Bertram Ede, who had been the MI5 Defence Security Officer for Malta from 1933–42. They were reminiscing about old times and Southby recounted this story. Ede roared with laughter – '*I always wondered how Dunderdale got into Malta unannounced.*'

Biffy's operations in Malta also included clandestine visits to Italy to meet agents and set up networks. He often went by submarine and was rowed ashore on the southern Italian coast. It was on one of his trips to Malta that he interviewed and recruited Anthony Heath.

Another plan involved a slightly ludicrous disinformation operation, whereby rumours were leaked to known Italian intelligence officers and their Maltese agents that a special technical operation, involving a '*shattering interference apparatus*' which could bring down aircraft, was being set up at RAF Kalafrana in the southeast of the island. However, Biffy's Malta operations had barely started before they were stopped, due to lack of funding.

43 Lieutenant Commander Patrick Southby (1913–2003). Son of Sir Archibald Southby and Phillis Garton. The Gartons were an SIS family. Southby was the cousin of Charles Garton who worked for Biffy during the war and married Sheelagh Greene.

The second crisis requiring SIS attention was the Spanish Civil War, which broke out in July 1936 between the left-wing Republican government and Nationalist forces led by General Francisco Franco. Despite the British and French brokered Non-Intervention Agreement, Germany and Italy provided both manpower and equipment to Franco in the shape of the CONDOR Legion. France and the Soviet Union intervened on the Republican side, which was also supported by many foreign volunteers who joined the International Brigades, within which SIS was able to develop many sources.

Biffy had a well-developed network of agents in Paris, Marseilles and Perpignan which had completely penetrated the Russian support network for the Spanish Republicans in France. His sources had identified Moscow's principal agent in Spain as a well-known German communist, Margarita Nelken. Timely and detailed reports were provided from Marseilles about the movement of weapons, ammunition, personnel and funds. Teams in Perpignan monitored cross-border movement. In Paris, Biffy's agents identified key Republican recruiting centres working under front organisations such as the 'Maison des Syndicats Unitaires' at 8 Avenue Mathurin Moreau. Altogether about 40,000 volunteers for the Republicans, French, Russian, Polish, Italian and German, passed through France to Spain as opposed to only 150 for Franco.

One area that Biffy investigated in detail across Europe was a clever Russian plan to facilitate the movement of volunteers who wished to fight on the Republican side. Recruiting offices were established in Sweden, Italy and France and other European countries where volunteers, including those from Britain, were required to surrender their national passports in exchange for Spanish passports. The genuine European passports were then passed to the OGPU who would use them as alias passports for their agents moving to western countries. Biffy also monitored the activities of Soviet intelligence officers operating in support of the Republicans. On the 14th of July 1938, he submitted a report to London:

The motor car used for the most important and secret trips of Soviet agents from France to Barcelona, bears No. E5490M

('E' stands for Espagne and 'M' means the car is registered in Madrid). Customs officials pass this car immediately and without examination.

Other reports contained detail of Russian pilots supporting the Republicans, Anarchist Party activities, the state of Franco-Russian relations and inventories of equipment supplied by the Russians.

SIS was less well positioned with sources on the Nationalist side and Sinclair ordered a special effort *'regarding General Franco's position, policy and prospects'*. Biffy was getting good intelligence from the French, who had a high-level agent in Franco's headquarters. Attempts were made to recruit an agent inside General Eoin O'Duffy's headquarters, who commanded a group of Irish volunteers, and also to recruit an agent in a civilian relief organisation working both sides of the conflict. Biffy also began developing some recruitment operations from Gibraltar. Also, in October 1937, London told Biffy that the War Office needed more on the technical details of new German and Russian weapons being used in Spain. Biffy responded quickly and within a short space of time he had recruited an agent who had contacts among the interrogators of Russian prisoners-of-war who provided photographs of new Soviet weaponry and intelligence on Soviet aircraft deployment. Biffy was also keeping track of Soviet pilots passing through Paris on their way in or out of Spain and had some of his Russians engage them in conversation over several vodkas, designed to loosen their tongues, in a bar in the Rue de Rennes, a well-known watering hole for Russian pilots.

Biffy was not above playing office politics with Broadway, probably to keep or enhance his budget. Occasionally he would drip feed information to London. He had obtained a copy of the German JU88 'Stuka' dive bomber manual from an agent in Spain. He sequenced the information to the Air Section in Broadway – first engines, then avionics and finally weapon systems. When challenged by the Head of the Air Section, he came clean, saying that all Heads of Station did it, as it was necessary to keep Broadway motivated and his station well-funded.

On the 10th of March, Sinclair put out a signal to all the SIS stations in Europe and North Africa to find suitable agents to target Italy. Soon Biffy believed he had discovered a good candidate, a French travelling salesman, but who was already working for the Deuxième Bureau. Biffy reported that his motivation to work for the British too was both patriotic and financial: *'he believes our two countries should stand together whilst he is also desirous of adding to his income'*. Having cleared this recruitment with the Deuxième Bureau, Biffy sent him to report on the strategically important island of Pantelleria, west of Malta between Sicily and Tunisia, which was a target specified by the War Office. When his report went to London, SIS Air Section questioned its accuracy. They thought it *'extremely doubtful'* that the agent had been to Pantelleria at all. Biffy began to have doubts about employing him as he thought he had been *'doing this kind of work far too long under too many masters'* and claimed that *'in normal circumstances I should never employ such an individual but in view of the present situation I thought I would give him a trial'*. Recruiting a source who was an existing French agent could have upset Biffy's excellent relations, even though he had cleared it and that, combined with the questionable intelligence provided, led Biffy to drop him quickly.

*

In his hunt for agents in the Mediterranean, Biffy came across Anthony Heath, who was to become a key member of Biffy's team in Paris. Anthony was educated at Emmanuel School in Wandsworth. He left school when he was 18 in 1930 and took up a job as Junior Administrator on the Duke of Bronte's[44] estate, Castello di Maniace in Sicily, where he worked for five years. During the course of his work on the estate and his inclination to explore the surrounding mountains, he eventually bumped into the Sicilian Mafia. Out riding one day he came across a mule train. The men were wearing dark clothes, capes and slouch hats. The first man looked him straight in the eye and said nothing. The last man stopped him and said to him *'caccia e pippa'*, effectively, *'push off and keep your mouth shut'*.

---

44 Given to Admiral Nelson in 1799 after the Battle of the Nile. 15,000 hectares in Catania Province.

Anthony Heath at the Duke of Bronte's
(Admiral Nelson) estate Castello di Maniace

Heath maintained his sang froid, nodded and kept moving. Three weeks later he was in one of the estate's orange groves when a boy of about 10 came up to him and said 'vossia,[45] le sue spalle son guardate' – 'your back is being watched, nothing to worry about'. In 1935, things began to change.

> *The day began with the arrival of a motorcar. Two Generals in full uniform got out. They were on an important mission and had come to ask for assistance. I was only too anxious to help. We exchanged names and over a glass of wine became quite friendly. One general was bringing over a military unit and wanted to go over a certain number of issues. The soldiers were to carry out manoeuvres.*

It wasn't difficult to work out that this was connected with the imminent war in Ethiopia. This unit was coming to Maniace for pre-deployment training before taking part in the Abyssinian campaign. Heath continued to be friendly towards the Generals and was happy to discuss their plans with them. Arrangements were made to receive

45 *Vossia* is short for vostra signoria – your lordship.

Anthony Heath on *My June*

the troops and to accommodate them on the estate. Heath described what followed:

Two or three days later, there were troops on one side of the hill and guns were placed, with targets three or four miles away. An aircraft flew over to see how accurate the shelling was. A dress rehearsal, you could say, of what was going to happen a month later. And I had made up my mind. I was leaving Sicily because I felt Italy was going to war. I did not want to be mixed up in something I did not believe in.

He had become party to military plans, troop deployments and tactics, which were part of the preparations for the Italian take-over of Abyssinia, information he passed to the British consulate in Catania which in turn made its way to SIS, and eventually to Biffy in Paris who also had responsibility for the Mediterranean, including Malta, Italy, Spain and Gibraltar.

Eventually Heath was given the hint by the local Police Chief, who came to visit every Friday, that he should probably leave in a hurry. Anthony took the hint and made a quick exit to Catania and then to Syracuse where he took passage to Malta on *The Knight of Malta*.

When the boat docked in Malta, he was met at customs and immigration by a naval officer who asked to accompany him to an office in the Military Headquarters. There, Biffy was waiting to meet him. Biffy knew all about his predicament and fast exit from Sicily and offered him a job. Biffy understood that Anthony's experiences in Sicily had formed a character which could be put to intelligence use and that he had valuable knowledge to impart, particularly the time spent with Mussolini's troops, having been privy to the plans and the discussions over terrain and manoeuvres in preparation for the war in Abyssinia. Also, during his time in Sicily, Heath had travelled extensively, not only in Sicily and other parts of Italy, but also in countries on the north coast of Africa, such as Libya, Tunisia, Morocco and Algeria. Anthony's experience with the wary, secretive, suspicious people of Sicily would be instrumental in helping form the mindset of an intelligence officer. The hours of solitude and having to make decisions on the spot would of course be valuable lessons for the future. For Anthony, disentangling and dis-embroidering versions of a story to arrive at the truth, whilst working with Sicilians, strengthened his interrogative powers and his patience and allowed him to be aware of acts of deceit and taught him how to deal with them. It also taught him how to use them himself.

Anthony stayed in Malta working for Biffy from September 1935 until August 1936. He worked for Biffy under two covers – as a technical advisor at 'Combined Services Mediterranean Headquarters' and as a journalist with 'Photo Features Incorporated'. He was posted to Palma de Mallorca between November 1936 and January 1937 where Alan Hillgarth of SIS had diplomatic cover as Vice Consul. In 1937 he joined Biffy's Paris station. Later, Heath was to say that working for Biffy gave him great 'comfort and pleasure as well as a clearly defined sense of purpose and morality in a world of intrigue and adventure'. He and his new French wife, Simone Damart, became very close to Biffy and June who welcomed them as part of the 'family' that Biffy encouraged in his station. Heath regularly wrote to his wife while she was away at her parents' house in Bordeaux.

Biffy is always as kind to me as ever he was; he is more like a brother in certain ways than my Chief. I am sure that he will always need me and that I can serve him faithfully and well. I do want to make as successful a job of it as I can – both for his sake and mine. As days go on I realise that I am indeed very lucky to

have such a kind and considerate Chief. It does make all the differ-
ence and I can assure you that I am certainly making progress in
every way.

When he joined the station in Paris, he worked closely with Colonel
Bertrand, but also joined the glittering high life that Biffy encouraged in his team. Cocktails, dinner parties, long lunches at Maxim's
or Le Vert Gallant – listening, observing, watching. After a particularly hard day in the office, Biffy would take him to the bar at the
George V for several martinis, followed by dinner at Maxim's or La
Crémaillère. Sometimes he would join Biffy and the Greenes at the
Château le Chêsne. On other occasions Anthony and his wife would
join Biffy and June on their yacht.

Anthony, like the others in the station, was frustrated by the events
leading up to war. In a letter dated the 23rd of August 1939, he wrote
to his wife, '*our warnings have gone unchecked and our reports thrown
into the waste paper basket*'. As war approached, June, who was an
inveterate traveller, usually with Coosie Hottinguer as her companion, came back to Paris on the 18th of August 1939. Heath wrote:

*June is coming home tonight and I shall be very glad when she
gets here because Biffy was very worried lest she should have
decided to go to Italy or any of the central European states with
Mme Hottinguer. At least that is one responsibility less for him,
and incidentally for me too.*

On her return she took a job with the American Hospital in Paris.
Anthony Heath again:

*June is working very hard; she is now in charge of one of the
wards at the American Hospital. She certainly is quite different
from the June of before the war. No lying in bed a-mornings. She is
up and dressed at 7:30 and usually at the hospital at 8:15.*

Anthony was evacuated in 1940 with the rest of the station and
their wives, mistresses and children on a British merchant ship, the

SS MADURA, anchored at Le Verdon at the mouth of the Gironde Estuary near Bordeaux, to Falmouth. He then joined Biffy in London and became a liaison officer with the Polish Intelligence Service.

The rapid rise of the Nazi party in the early 1930s with Hitler becoming Chancellor in 1933 gave stimulus to the activities of the German Military Intelligence Service – the Abwehr – against all their neighbouring countries, particularly France and Britain. The realisation that Germany was now the primary threat began a period of ever closer cooperation between Biffy and his station and the key players in the Deuxième Bureau – Ronin, Rivet, Bertrand and Paillole. Biffy not only tightened relations with the French, but through them got close to the Poles and his close relations with the French and the Poles were to continue from the 1930s, right through the war, until 1945.

Colonel Louis Rivet maintained close relations with Biffy, directly or via his department heads, but he also had close links with the SIS Deputy Chief, Stewart Menzies and, through him, the various departments of SIS and the Security Service MI5. Rivet's office diary shows that he travelled to London in February 1937 for three days and that Menzies travelled to Paris on three occasions, October 1936, October 1937 and January 1939. On one occasion in 1938, when Bertrand came on a visit to London for a lunch given by Menzies, he presented Bertrand with a gold cigarette case engraved with the Royal Cypher. There were 23 official high-level meetings between June 1936 and March 1939. Paul Paillole: *'The British Services were really brotherly services. We acted hand in hand.'*

There were also many other less formal meetings, usually over lunch at Le Vert Gallant, in Biffy's flat or in the Deuxième Bureau offices. Biffy was quick to understand that he had much to learn from the French about the German threat and would meet with them two or three times per week. At these meetings they would exchange what they knew but Biffy would leave with more information than he could deliver to his French friends.

Biffy was always keenly aware of this imbalance and was always on the lookout for a chance to pay them back. One such opportunity arose in June 1938. MI5 in London had uncovered an Abwehr mailing

Lieutenant Colonel William Hinchley-Cook

The traitor, Marc-Elot Aubert

address in Dublin and were intercepting the letters sent there. One of them had a Paris postmark and its contents indicated a spy in the French Navy who was passing Fleet dispositions and preparing to deliver French naval codes to the Germans. They dispatched 'Cookie', Lieutenant Colonel William Hinchley-Cook, to Paris where he briefed Biffy.

Biffy took him to see Paul Paillole. Based on the information provided, Paillole's counterintelligence department was able to track down the traitor, Marc-Elot Aubert, serving on a destroyer in Toulon. He was arrested, tried and executed by firing squad at dawn on the 8th of March 1939.

SIS was quite slow to look at the impending war in Europe as a major concern, even though German direct involvement in the Spanish Civil War from 1936 was a pretty clear indication that things might not go well in the rest of Europe. It was really only after the Anschluss[46] that they realised that the information and warnings from the French, Poles and Czechs[47] had a very serious basis. The Polish and Czech services were even more aware of the danger than the French because they felt directly threatened. They knew they were in a race against time and probably wouldn't win.

---

46 Anschluss: The German annexation of Austria. 12th of March 1938.
47 Biffy's old friend and colleague Harold 'Gibbie' Gibson was Head of Station in Prague.

CHAPTER 8 – ENIGMA

'You can't start a fire
You can't start a fire without a spark
This gun's for hire
Even if we're just dancin' in the dark.'

Bruce Springsteen

'The king hath note of all that they intend.
By interception which they dream not of.'

William Shakespeare – *Henry V*

The story of how Biffy was able to get an ENIGMA machine to London in August 1939 has its early beginnings in fashionable society in 1920s London. Like Paris, London was enjoying a backlash to the privations of the war years. Life was exciting, full of frivolous gaiety and almost as louche as Paris. In the midst of this, a scandal was developing involving an affair between Florence Robinson, wife of Charles Robinson, and Sir Hari Singh, heir to his uncle the Maharajah of Kashmir. The lovers were subject to a blackmail scam perpetrated by William Hobbs – the 'Mr Big' of the London criminal fraternity, and Rodolphe Lemoine, one of Hobbs's many partners in crime. Lemoine was a real 'operator', who loved the good life – *'money, good meals, risqué stories and especially cigars rolled on the naked thighs of dusky maidens'*. He had been talent spotted by the Deuxième Bureau and had been working for them as an agent recruiter since 1908, using the codename REX. Despite being a crook, he was very effective. Paul Paillole described him as a *'l'homme a tout faire'* – a Mr Fix-it. He was the stuff of the fictional spy, with 15 different aliases, able to compromise a target, pick locks, produce fake passports or seemingly do the impossible, get you a reservation at Maxim's even if you weren't known to Albert. One of Lemoine's most important recruits and subsequent agents was Hans-Thilo Schmidt.

Arthur Scherbius was a brilliant German engineer and inventor. Just after World War I he set up business in the Berlin suburb of Wilmersdorf where he began working on encryption and cipher machinery. By 1923, Scherbius was confident enough to gather together a group of investors to back his company Chiffriermaschinen Aktiengesellschaft (Coding Machines Incorporated) which was based at 2 Steglitzer Straße Berlin. Its purpose was to manufacture and sell an encryption machine called the 'Scherbius ENIGMA'. The launch of the company was accompanied by a huge publicity campaign across Europe.[48] In spite of this, the company was not a commercial success until 1926 when the German Navy cryptographic department took an interest. The Navy bought several machines and began to adapt them for military use. Their interest spread to the embryonic German Army, the Reichswehr and Air Force, the Luftwaffe.

Germany's military capability had been severely curtailed under the Treaty of Versailles in 1919, but there had been no mention of Secure Communications. After considerable success during World War I, the Admiralty 'Room 40'[49] cryptanalysts continued to monitor German communications. In 1926, they began to intercept messages which baffled them completely. ENIGMA had arrived and, as the number of ENIGMA machines increased, Room 40's ability to gather intelligence diminished rapidly. The Americans and the French also tried to tackle the ENIGMA cipher, but their attempts were equally dismal and they soon gave up hope of breaking it. Germany now had the most secure communications in the world. Totally secure communications are the aspiration of all governments, intelligence services and armed forces. The speed with which the Allied cryptanalysts abandoned hope of breaking ENIGMA was in sharp contrast to their perseverance just a decade earlier in World War I. Confronted with the prospect of defeat, the Allied cryptanalysts had worked night and day to penetrate German ciphers. However, after World War I, the Allies no longer feared anybody. Germany had been crippled by

---

48 This campaign resulted in early purchases by Edward Travis, future Director of Bletchley, who bought one in Berlin in 1921 and Dilly Knox, another future star of the Bletchley team, who bought one in Vienna in 1925.
49 Room 40. The forerunner of the GC + CS and subsequently GCHQ.

defeat, the Allies were in a dominant position and, as a result, they seemed to lose their cryptanalytic zeal. Allied cryptanalysts dwindled in number and deteriorated in quality.

One nation, however, could not afford to relax. After World War I, Poland re-established itself as an independent state, but it was concerned about threats to its new-found sovereignty. To the east lay Russia, a nation ambitious to spread its communism, and to the west lay Germany, desperate to regain territory ceded to Poland after the war. Sandwiched between these two enemies, the Poles were desperate for intelligence information and, in 1919, they formed a new cipher bureau, the Biuro Szyfrów. Its mission was signals intelligence (SIGINT), both cryptography and cryptanalysis. Its first test came during the Polish Russian War of 1919–21 when it had considerable success, enabling the Poles to read the majority of Russian military radio traffic. So successful were they that radio intercept formed the basis of all operational decisions which allowed the Polish Commander-in-Chief, Joseph Pilsudski, to outwit the Russians.

One Saturday in 1928, a parcel arrived in the Polish customs office in Warsaw from Germany marked '*Radio Equipment*'. Its shipper demanded its return even before it went through customs. This inevitably made the customs officers suspicious. They informed the Polish Intelligence Service, who in turn informed the Cipher Bureau. An operation was mounted to open the parcel covertly. They found it contained a commercial ENIGMA machine of no military significance, which even so alerted the Cipher Bureau to activity that might lead to the development of a military version. Before repacking the machine and returning it to its owner, they took detailed photographs and measurements and then purchased an identical commercial ENIGMA through a front company.

On the 15th of July 1928, the first encrypted messages were broadcast by German military radio stations. Polish monitoring stations picked them up and the Cipher Bureau started to try and decipher them, without success. The officer responsible for deciphering German messages was Captain Maksymilian Ciężki. Ciężki had access to the commercial version of the ENIGMA machine, but the commercial version was distinctly different from the military one in terms of the wirings inside each scrambler. Without knowing the wirings of the military machine, Ciężki had no chance of deciphering messages being sent by the German army. Almost at the point of despair, he started to look for a new approach to apply to the ENIGMA problem, including the application of pure mathematics. A course in cryptology was set up at Poznan University and 20 mathematicians who could speak German were invited to attend. By the end of the course, three had demonstrated an aptitude for this work. The most gifted of the three was Marian Rejewski.

The three mathematicians were immediately recruited by the Cipher Bureau and put to work on German naval hand cipher, which they were able to break. However, there was a problem with the 'unbreakable' German military traffic. Instead of putting all three of them to work on this together, Rejewski was separated from his colleagues, Zygalski and Rozycki, by Colonel Gwido Langer, and he was given a small room on his own in the Polish Army Headquarters to work specifically on ENIGMA. Langer felt that Rejewski, the most capable of the three, was most likely to have success with ENIGMA. The room that he was put into contained nothing but a table and a chair and on the table a stack of ENIGMA messages and a Scherbius commercial ENIGMA. *'There you are Rejewski. Do what you can.'* Langer walked out and left him to it. Rejewski felt a mounting degree of excitement. He began by dismantling and examining meticulously every single part of the ENIGMA machine. After he had done this, he turned his attention to the messages. Eventually he worked out that:

Rejewski, Rozycki and Zygalski,
the three mathematicians

The preface of any message of German Military ENIGMA was produced by the operator encoding a three-letter group of his choice twice at a certain scrambler setting. And the scrambler setting in question was the same for all messages of the day in question, but different from one day to another.

This was a eureka moment and would form the basis for all work on ENIGMAs from then on. Eventually, with considerable help from intelligence supplied by the French agent Hans-Thilo Schmidt (ASCHÉ), the Poles were able to build their own replicas of the military ENIGMA and decode German military traffic between 1932–36. In 1936 the Germans added additional technical security measures which the Poles in turn cracked. From 1934, the Polish effort was helped considerably by a Pole who had been working in the ENIGMA factory in Germany and was able to help build replicas. He became the subject of a completely embellished version of events put out by Fred Winterbotham and subsequently further embellished by Anthony Cave Brown.[50] The man in question was given the name 'Richard Lewinski'.

The story goes that Lewinski was a Polish Jew working in the ENIGMA factory in Germany. Having seen the writing on the wall (literally) in late 1934, he fled Germany back to Poland, where he was spotted by Polish intelligence and more precisely by the Cipher Bureau. He was put to work helping to build replica ENIGMA machines. So far, true. It is also possible that Biffy met him in Warsaw as he later described him as reminding him of '*a raven plucking an abacus*'.

What is not true is that Biffy arranged for Lewinski and his wife to go secretly to Paris via Stockholm with British diplomatic passports so as to avoid Germany, where, together with Bertrand, SIS and the Deuxième Bureau set him up with the task of building replica ENIGMAs. To avoid him being captured by the Germans, the story goes that Sidney Cotton[51] was summoned to collect him – hence the unfortunate incident which was the final straw for the RAF as far

50 Anthony Cave Brown, *Bodyguard of Lies*.
51 Sidney Cotton. Contract pilot for SIS, flying clandestine missions – see Chapter 11.

as Cotton was concerned. This incident did indeed take place, but the agent was not Lewinski. Quite why Fred Winterbotham put out this story is not known unless it was part of an overall cover story about ENIGMA – as the full story of ENIGMA did not emerge until the 1970s.

On the 15th of September 1938, ENIGMA procedures were again changed and further layers of security were added. This made the Poles' job much harder, but again they persevered, enabling them to read traffic up until July 1939 when even more security measures were put in place by the Germans which brought their ability to crack ENIGMA to an end.

*

Hans-Thilo Schmidt was born into a Prussian aristocratic family. He and his elder brother Rudolf had both fought in World War I and both were decorated with the Iron Cross for bravery. At the end of the war, Hans was a Lieutenant and demobbed. His brother had reached the rank of Captain and was retained in the small German Army, the Reichswehr, allowed under the Armistice of 1919. He was a highflyer and by 1936 would be a Lieutenant General.

Hans-Thilo struggled after the war as his expensive tastes had got him into debt. Paul Paillole described him as leading '*a life of debauchery and scabrous enterprises*'. After drifting through various jobs, by 1930 he had joined the six million unemployed. However, his brother Rudolf soon stepped in to help. In the German War Ministry, Rudolf was in command of the department of codes and ciphers – including ENIGMA. Rudolf was due to be promoted and move to another job. He heard that his successor was looking for an assistant, so immediately recommended Hans-Thilo. Rudolf was very influential and highly respected, so this 'recommendation' was effectively an order and Hans-Thilo got the job. The regular salary helped him, but he was still saddled with his mountain of debt. Inevitably he began to think how he might profit from his access to secrets, including ENIGMA. Gradually, he decided the only course of action was to sell the secrets of ENIGMA to a foreign government and that France was probably his best bet.

Rodolphe Lemoine (REX)   Hans-Thilo Schmidt

On the 8th of June 1931, he calmly walked into the French embassy in Berlin, approached a somewhat surprised official and told him that he wanted to sell highly valuable secrets to the French Government. He was initially given the brush-off but was persistent and was told eventually to write to an address in Paris.

> *I confirm what I said on the 8th June 1931 to your representative of the French embassy in the Parizer Platz who gave me your address. I am in a position to bargain over some documents of the greatest importance. In order to convince you of the genuineness of my offer I have given you some references below. Your specialists will appreciate their value. Please reply before the 1st October 1931 at the following address: Hans-Thilo Schmidt, 2 Kauthesgasse – Basle – Switzerland. If there is no reply by that date I shall look elsewhere. If you give me a rendezvous, arrange for it to be on a Sunday, and preferably in Belgium or Holland close to the German border.*

Schmidt also enclosed two documents about the ENIGMA keys and other operating details. The address, 75 Rue de l'Université, was a 'cut-out' address for the Deuxième Bureau. The letter eventually landed on the desk of Gustave Bertrand who commanded Section 'D', the cryptology section. Bertrand was fully aware of ENIGMA and jumped at the chance of recruiting a well-placed agent. He entrusted the detailed recruitment of Schmidt to Lemoine – agent REX whom we first met perpetrating a large fraud in London – who was considered to be one of the Deuxième Bureau's best agent recruiters and handlers. The Bureau always intervened on his behalf whenever he was in danger of having his collar felt for one of his many shady deals.

Having run some preliminary checks on Hans-Thilo, Lemoine invited him to a meeting at the Grand Hotel in Verviers in Belgium, close to the German border. The rendezvous was for 12:00 on Sunday the 1st of November 1931. After a slow start, the meeting went well. Schmidt, his tongue loosened by copious supplies of alcohol and cigars, answered all of REX's questions in considerable detail. Schmidt also showed REX some highly sensitive documents. REX was convinced he must quickly arrange a follow-up meeting with Schmidt, asking him to bring additional classified documents. These would be paid for in cash on the spot. A rendezvous was then arranged in the same hotel for the following week.

For the second rendezvous on Sunday the 8th of November 1931, Bertrand, Lemoine and a photographer were installed in interconnecting rooms. Bertrand and the photographer set up an improvised dark room in the bathroom of Bertrand's room and tested the Leica camera to be used for photographing Schmidt's documents. It was agreed that Bertrand would wait for a call from Lemoine. The call came at 10:00. Bertrand went to join them, very excited to see the contents of Schmidt's documents. Suite No. 31 was full of cigar smoke and there was a blaring radio turned on by Lemoine to prevent anyone eavesdropping. Lemoine introduced Schmidt, who was already well lubricated with whisky. In typical Prussian style, he bowed to Bertrand and clicked his heels. Lemoine: '*Monsieur Barsac*' (Bertrand's alias), '*you are going to be very well satisfied. Monsieur Schmidt will give us the documents to photograph. He needs them back by 1500 hours at the latest in time to catch the train to Berlin.*' Schmidt then handed Bertrand a very large envelope. Bertrand glanced at the contents, at least 100 documents, which he immediately could see were of great interest. It was clear to Bertrand that they needed to hook him immediately and he agreed a considerable cash payment on the spot with a promise of more to come. They set to work copying the documents which they finished just in time, returning to find REX and ASCHÉ in fine form and the recruitment sealed.

'*Alles ist in ordnung*,' Schmidt bowed and left with his package and his money. Bertrand, normally described as '*as silent as an oyster*', was ecstatic and could hardly contain himself as he now felt that he had the key to unlock ENIGMA.

Back in Paris, Bertrand hurried to see Colonel Gauché, the head of the Deuxième Bureau. Gauché was amazed at the haul and congratulated Bertrand. The next day, Bertrand went to see Colonel Bassières, the head of the cryptographic section at French Army Headquarters, and left him a sample of Schmidt's documents, emphasising their potential value for re-creating an ENIGMA machine. However, when he returned on the 21st of November, Bassières gave Bertrand a polite, but very firm negative response; they simply did not have the time or resources to use Schmidt's intelligence to re-create an ENIGMA. Bertrand was astonished.

With the full agreement of his superiors at the Deuxième Bureau, Bertrand then went to see Biffy, with some of Schmidt's documents. Biffy transmitted the documents to London. To both Biffy and Bertrand's intense irritation, the response from London was just as negative as from the French. Bertrand was now in despair, but on the advice of his chief, who was as convinced as Bertrand of the extreme importance of Schmidt's documents, approached the Polish Cipher Bureau with whom a meeting was fixed for the 8th of December 1931. At the meeting, Schmidt's documents were received '*like manna in the desert*', especially those relating to the technical details and method of usage of the ENIGMA machine; according to Bertrand these '*produced an explosion of stupefaction and joy*'. Altogether, Bertrand met Hans-Thilo, or ASCHÉ, 19 times. Four in Belgium, once in Denmark, 12 times in Switzerland, once in Czechoslovakia and once in France.

As well as face-to-face meetings, Bertrand also used another route to recover information from his agent. This route was made possible by Abbé Vorage, a native Dutchman from Limburg who was a long-term French intelligence asset. Limburg is a Dutch state that shares a border with Germany, where there were some houses in which one could walk from their back garden in Germany to their front door into Belgium, ideal for smuggling operations. Vorage volunteered his services to the Deuxième Bureau in 1914. His natural cover as a priest was invaluable. He worked on cross-border operations until 1917 by which time there was a substantial price on his head. He withdrew to France and was found a small parish near Versailles from where he continued to serve the Deuxième Bureau with '*boundless enthusiasm*'.

During the 1930s, Vorage acted as a cut-out between Bertrand, Rodolphe Lemoine (REX) and Hans-Thilo Schmidt (ASCHÉ),[52] bringing Bertrand documents relating to ENIGMA. He was an expert at clandestine border crossings. In September 1935, he escorted a funeral cortege from Cologne to Paris with an enormous volume of documents relating to German order of battle and mobilisation plans, as well as ENIGMA material hidden in the coffin. In 1940, after the invasion of France, he continued to provide Bertrand with intelligence on Wehrmacht and Luftwaffe order of battle and dispositions. Bertrand put him in direct contact with Biffy. He went on the run in October 1943 after being betrayed by a collaborator. Biffy arranged for him to be picked up by Lysander on the 15th of October, flown by Flight Lieutenant James 'Mac' McCairns DFC MM. On his return to London, he worked for Biffy at Caxton Street until returning to Paris after the liberation. In 1948 he would marry Sheelagh Greene and Charles Garton.

Although rebuffed by the British and welcomed by the Poles, Bertrand was still determined to get the British to wake up to the German threat and to forge strong links between the French, Polish and British code breakers. Biffy would be his conduit. This determination was to set Biffy on a course of action which was to be one of the greatest achievements of his career in SIS, in obtaining details of the Polish breakthrough on ENIGMA, and bringing an ENIGMA to London.

In August 1938, Bertrand made another attempt to get the British code breakers interested. He asked Biffy to put him directly in touch

---

52 Hans-Thilo Schmidt's codename ASCHÉ derived from pronunciation of the letters HE when being spelt out in French.

Left to right: Gustave Bertrand, Tom Greene, Biffy, Abbé Vorage

with Alastair Denniston at GC + CS, in order to give him some of the ASCHÉ intelligence on ENIGMA, in an attempt to establish full cooperation between the Poles, British and French. In fact, this was a waste of time and effort as the Poles had already cracked ENIGMA. In 1974, when the ENIGMA secret became public, Biffy revealed in a GCHQ enquiry that the Head of Polish Army Intelligence, Colonel Stefan Mayer, had told him that the ASCHÉ intelligence '*contributed nothing to the Polish success*'. This is very hard to believe. Cracking ENIGMA was a collective effort. The Poles undoubtedly made the breakthrough in technical code-breaking but were helped by the French with their good old-fashioned spy. This work was in turn supported by the application and brainpower of those at Bletchley.[53] Biffy and Bertrand between them made this work.

After the Munich Crisis in September 1938, Bertrand wrote to Langer suggesting a tripartite meeting in Paris. Biffy got in touch with Stewart Menzies, who knew both Bertrand and Rivet, who by then was the director of the Deuxième Bureau, to get him to send British representatives. The Paris meeting took place in January

---

53 This 'triumvirate' is covered in full detail in *X Y & Z* by Dermot Turing.

Polish ENIGMA

ENIGMA machine coding wheels

1939. It was of historic importance as the first face-to-face meeting between British and Polish cryptographers. Biffy acted as lead interpreter. The Poles clearly wanted to find out what the British knew about ENIGMA – which was very little. The meeting broke up without much being acknowledged except a heads of agreement for future meetings.

Three months later, the Germans broke the Munich Agreement and occupied the whole of Czechoslovakia. This changed the attitude of both British and French Governments and resulted in the Franco-British guarantee to Poland. War was looming and the rather lukewarm attitude of GC + CS changed rapidly. They became very eager to meet and repeatedly asked Biffy for news from Bertrand. Eventually on the 10th of July, Biffy passed word to Denniston that the Poles wanted them to come to Warsaw for a meeting to be held between the 24th and 26th of July.

The French delegation, Bertrand and one of his cryptographers, Captain Braquénie, arrived by air from Paris. Biffy joined them to act as interpreter and to observe proceedings and no doubt to report back to Menzies. The British delegation consisted of Denniston, Dilly Knox and a representative from Naval Intelligence. John Tiltman was supposed to have gone but was away in Hong Kong. Both delegations stayed at the Bristol Hotel and later, on the 24th, Colonel Mayer held a preliminary meeting and reception in a room on the first floor which had been swept for listening devices. The waiters were vetted by Polish Intelligence. The next day, the Poles collected

Pyry, Polish intelligence cryptology headquarters

the British and French delegations and drove them 20 kilometres from Warsaw to a heavily forested area near the village of Pyry. They arrived through numerous security checkpoints at '*a new strongly built and strongly fortified building*' in a clearing where they met the three young mathematicians who had worked on ENIGMA.

They were given a full and lengthy explanation of what the Poles had been working on and were shown the replica ENIGMA and the 'Bombas'[54] the Poles had produced, under the codename Operation WICHER. The British were astounded. The next day, the 26th, it was agreed that the Poles would send two of their replica ENIGMA machines through Germany by diplomatic bag to Paris, one for the French and one for the British. The Poles also promised to send copies of the transcripts of their decoded German ENIGMA traffic direct to London.

In return, the British would send the Poles everything they had achieved in their work on ENIGMA. Both French and British teams were delighted, much hand-shaking and back-slapping. Alcohol was forbidden in the centre, but Biffy and Bertrand were able to round up some beer with which to celebrate and drink to joint success.

The Poles were as good as their word. The two machines duly arrived in Paris on the 11th of August. Bertrand sent word to Denniston that he hoped to get the British one – by this time safely with Biffy at the SIS office – to London around the 16th.

---

54 A device invented by the Poles before the war. It consisted of a number of ENIGMA machines wired together.

Roy Archibald, 1936

Henry Archibald, 1931

At this point, a popular 'Biffy story' emerges which is completely untrue – that Biffy stored both machines in a large safe in an SIS purchased hotel, the Hotel du Havre, and that the safe had two doors, one at the front and a concealed one at the back with different locks and, while Bertrand and Biffy both had keys to the front lock, Biffy had a key to the back one, which he used to remove both machines and spirit them to London.

Colonel Langer also arrived in Paris on his way to a series of meetings in London. Bertrand and Biffy took him for a serious lunch in Drouant, a classic Parisian restaurant in the Rue Gaillon, where they consumed a good deal of champagne in celebration.

Among Biffy's useful 'honourable correspondents'[55] were the senior partners of the Paris-based law firm Archibald's,[56] Roy and Henry Archibald. They had agreed to help Biffy and SIS when needed. Having sealed the bulky items in the largest diplomatic bags that they could find, on the morning of the 16th of August 1939, Biffy assembled his team, Uncle Tom Greene and the Archibald brothers, to take the Polish ENIGMA to London. They all squeezed into Biffy's Rolls Royce driven by Paul Kilesso and headed for the Gare du Nord to catch the Golden Arrow boat train which left at 12:00. They were

55 'Honourable correspondent': Someone trusted by an intelligence service but not serving, who uses their contacts or position to assist in the development of intelligence work or operations.
56 Archibald's was originally set up in Paris by a Canadian, Roy Archibald. It became a conglomerate of Canadian, American, French and British lawyers and would eventually be absorbed into the accounting firm Arthur Anderson as their legal department.

joined on the train by Bertrand. Tom Greene did a walk-through of the train to check if there was anyone suspicious, or any known German agents on board. Both Biffy and Bertrand were concerned that they might be observed moving a very bulky diplomatic bag which could attract unwanted attention on the train at both Calais and Dover. Uncle Tom reported that there was no one he recognised as the enemy, but that Sacha Guitry, Biffy's neighbour, was on board. Guitry was travelling to London with his wife Jacqueline Delubac for the London opening of Guitry's latest play *Pearls in the Crown*. Needless to say, they had large amounts of luggage in numerous Louis Vuitton trunks and cases. Biffy, in a flash of genius, thought this would make excellent cover and concealment for the diplomatic bags to avoid the prying eyes of anyone watching the ports. He also rightly surmised that the Guitrys would have in their luggage large amounts of dutiable goods such as scent and cognac. He went to see his neighbour and struck a deal – conceal the diplomatic bags and the Guitry luggage would pass through Dover customs unchecked. At Dover, Tom Greene disembarked ahead of the Guitrys and Biffy's team, had a word with the Senior Customs Officer and they all moved quickly through customs onto the train for Victoria.

Sacha Guitry and Jacqueline Delubac

That evening, the Golden Arrow pulled into Victoria at 18:35. Having recovered their precious cargo from the Guitry luggage mountain, Biffy and his party stepped onto the platform to be met by Stewart Menzies and Alastair Denniston. Menzies was wearing Black Tie with the rosette of the Légion d'honneur in his lapel *'en smoking, avec rosette de la Légion d'Honneur à la boutonnière'* and greeted the party effusively. *'Accueil triomphal'* (triumphal welcome), declared Bertrand. Denniston and a team from SIS took the ENIGMA away for immediate delivery to Bletchley Park.[57]

*

Biffy always played down his role in the ENIGMA business. To quote the 1974 GCHQ report on the exposure of the ENIGMA story in Gustave Bertrand's book *ENIGMA*:

Dunderdale's role, even though a small one, in obtaining information about the successful Polish attack on the ENIGMA machine was one of the most significant SIS actions during the war. It was interesting therefore to hear Dunderdale describe the work he did on this as 'peanuts' compared with his other activities in Paris. Dunderdale told C that GC + CS were very slow to admit that the Poles might have anything to teach them and it is quite clear that Dunderdale did not at the time in the least appreciate the importance of what he was doing. Even now he is clearly bemused by the idea that this was the most important thing he ever did, and not really particularly pleased about it.

Biffy saw himself as merely a facilitator for the tie-up between the Poles, French and British cryptanalysts. But in fact, Biffy probably

---

57 Between 1928 and 1931 GC + CS had also been working on their own version of an ENIGMA machine – *'a copy of the ENIGMA with additions and alterations'*. Developed by GC + CS in conjunction with the RAF, slightly bigger than the ENIGMA machine, it was known as Typex or Type X. To quote Alan Judd *'It was ENIGMA which we'd also bought and adapted, the Germans couldn't penetrate their own system. Type X was used successfully throughout the war providing secure communications – to protect the fact that ENIGMA was cracked.'* Type X continued in service into the 1950s.

saved the reputation of SIS which was at an all-time low in Whitehall. The delivery of the machine to London was very much his style. Whether it was pre-empting the mutiny on the OUTKA, sneaking around the Crimea setting up networks and contacting agents, conducting intercept operations, debriefing defectors or the whole business of 'pinching'[58] – he was, by nature, a man of action who liked to be in the thick of the excitement, danger and intrigue of actual intelligence-gathering in the field. He was someone who got the raw intelligence, rather than analysing it.

In his mind some of his other preparations for war during the Paris years were much more significant. However, without the link with the Poles, the brilliant and unorthodox team at Bletchley might not have made the breakthrough that they did and the war might have gone very differently. As Winston Churchill described it: *'The intelligence that never fails.'*

The timing of Biffy's arrival in London could not have been more crucial: 16 days after the delivery of ENIGMA, on the 1st of September, the Germans invaded Poland. On the 3rd, Britain was at war.

---

58 'Pinch', as one former SIS officer described to the author, was the action of obtaining by covert or any acceptable method secret documents or equipment, especially those relating to cryptography.

CHAPTER 9 – 'A CORRIDOR OF DEEPENING AND DARKENING DANGER...'

Winston Churchill, 31st of May 1935

'Everyone has a plan until they get punched in the face.'

Mike Tyson

Clare Hollingworth, the renowned war correspondent, had been working as a *Daily Telegraph* journalist for less than a week when she was sent to Poland to report on worsening tensions in Europe. She persuaded the British Consul General in Katowice, John Anthony Thwaites, to lend her his chauffeured car for a fact-finding mission into Germany. Whilst driving along the German-Polish border on the 28th of August, Hollingworth observed a massive build-up of German troops, tanks and armoured cars facing Poland after the camouflage screens concealing them were disturbed by wind. Her report was the main story on the *Daily Telegraph*'s front page on the following day. Her report was headlined: '*1,000 Tanks Massed on Polish Frontier; 10 Divisions Reported Ready for Swift Stroke; From Our Own Correspondent.*'

On the 1st of September, Hollingworth called the British Embassy in Warsaw to report the German invasion of Poland. To convince doubtful embassy officials, she held a telephone out of the window of her room to capture the sounds of German armoured vehicles rolling past. Hollingworth's eyewitness account was the first report the British Foreign Office received about the invasion of Poland.

Fred Winterbotham happened to be the SIS duty officer that night. At 02:00, the duty secretary woke him up with a signal. The signal from the SIS station in Warsaw was short, containing only the pre-arranged codeword for the German invasion of Poland '77077'. Winterbotham calmly picked up the green scrambler telephone.

Vicky, get me the Cabinet Office on the scrambler, please. Hello, is that you, Cox? May we scramble, this is Zero C speaking? Just to let you know, the first bombs fell on Warsaw a few minutes ago. Yes, that's all, don't stay up too late.

As a matter of fact, he knew that Cox would be spending the rest of the night on the phone to all the cabinet ministers and military staff.

Life for Biffy was about to get very busy.

*

Two weeks earlier, having safely delivered his secret cargo, Biffy visited Broadway to give an overview of what was going on in France, his close liaison with the French, his other intelligence activities and, most importantly, his preparations as per part of his directive, 'to establish and enhance contacts in future occupied countries'.

Biffy may have taken time for a few days off to attend to personal matters such as house hunting, anticipating that events might force him to move out of Paris in a hurry. Richard Dunderdale had been in London in early August but had travelled back to Istanbul on the 9th, so they sadly missed each other. When Biffy got back to Paris, he received a letter from his father, dated the 28th of August 1940:

My dear Wilfred,
On August the 9th just before leaving London, I sent you a cheque on the Société Général for £200[59] to buy yourself a birthday present. I did this as we intended going right through from London to Marseilles without stopping at Paris which we did.

We had a very pleasant voyage on the 'Théophile Gautier'[60] and found all well on arrival. It was quite nice to get back to sunshine again after the continuous rainy weather we had in London. We have heard from our friends there since that the weather changed for the better as soon as we left.

The political situation seems to have gone from bad to worse in the last few days and it looks as if war cannot be avoided.

I see by the radio lots of people are leaving Paris for the country and presume you are amongst them. I don't know how long the

59 Worth about £1,500 today.
60 The '*Théophile Gautier*', named after a French poet, was a passenger liner which would carry 728 passengers. Built in Dunkirk in 1927 she was launched in Marseilles and her usual area of operations was between Marseilles, Naples, Beirut, Piraeus, Alexandria and Odessa. Used by the Vichy Government, she was torpedoed and sunk by the British submarine HMS TALISMAN on the 4th of December 1941.

Simplon Orient Express will be running out in their direction as I expect it will stop as soon as hostilities start.

Very few preparations are being made out here, people are not even buying gas masks. I expect this will be a rush when they get panicky. Arthur, Lily[61] and Lynette are all well as is mother and myself.

In going through different drawers of an old writing desk of mine, I came across the following documents which concern you:

Certificate of Baptism, issued by the British Chaplain at Odessa March 4 / 8th April 1900

Birth Certificate issued by the British Consul General at Odessa March 4 / 8th April 1900

Your agreement (Copy) with the senior Naval Officer in British Naval Forces, Royal Naval Volunteer Reserve as Sub Lieutenant.

Letter from St James Palace SW1 dated 27 June 1921 appointing you member of the order of the British Empire.

I am not sending you these now as the post depends on the movement of the trains which at present are not certain, so shall keep them here protem.

Love from us all to June and yourself.
Your very affectionate ...

It is likely that the letter's arrival coincided with the German invasion of Poland on the 1st of September 1939.

On the outbreak of war, all SIS officers were given military ranks as cover for their work, but also to give them appropriate status in a war machine now dominated by the military. Anthony Heath, who had been made an Army Captain, wrote to his wife: '*Biffy is now a Capitaine de Fregate (English equivalent Royal Naval Commander); we are all very glad that he has been given this rank as it is, of course, equal to the Army rank of Colonel. He is very busy and it will be quite a few days before we can settle down ...*'

Biffy's work in preparation for the coming war had started long before this date. Together with his friend Fred Winterbotham, he had

---

61 Arthur Whittall, SIS Istanbul ,was married to Lily, Biffy's sister.

helped SIS play an important part in their development of clandestine air photographs. On one of his visits to Paris in August 1938, Fred Winterbotham and Biffy went to see Georges Ronin at the Deuxième Bureau Headquarters. Ronin looked unhappy, sitting behind his bare wooden table, when Winterbotham and Biffy were shown in. The hut was unbearably hot, so they adjourned to a nearby café and continued their meeting there.

Ronin had a problem. The head of the French Air Force, General Joseph Vuillemin, had recently returned from a visit to Germany where he had been given a show of airfields, aircraft factories and assembly plants. He had also been treated to mass flypasts of very powerful fighters and bombers which added up to a massive offensive war fighting capability. The display had been designed to intimidate and it did. Vuillemin reckoned that the French Air Force would not last a week in the face of what he had seen. Winterbotham agreed with the assessment and explained that, in addition, it was getting harder to recruit agents and get information out of Germany, such was the reign of terror unleashed by the Gestapo and SS. An agent or suspected agent caught could expect a prolonged period of extreme torture of the medieval kind, followed by execution.

A new method was needed to observe the Luftwaffe and other military preparations that would give early warning of an impending attack. Georges Ronin explained that he had been experimenting with aerial photography – using an old aeroplane fitted with a large wooden camera. The plane was flown by a civilian pilot friend of Ronin's and the camera was operated by an elderly gentleman with a splendid flowing beard whose day job was portrait photography in Paris. They flew the aircraft up and down the Rhine photographing German military targets and, in spite of the Heath Robinson set-up, managed to get some good photographs. Ronin and Winterbotham agreed that, by developing the concept with the right technology, this could be a winner. Both Fred and Biffy liked the idea but immediately recognised that it must remain completely undetected.

Winterbotham returned to London and briefed the idea to Menzies who liked it but said that the Air Ministry would have to procure the aircraft. In fact, its Chief of the Air Staff Sir Cyril Newall, an

Sidney Cotton

Sidney Cotton's G-AFTL Lockheed 12 at Heston

experienced combat pilot, also liked the idea and gave authority to purchase two Lockheed 12A civilian aircraft, one for SIS and one for the French. He also agreed to loan SIS camera equipment from the RAF. To preserve their cover, Imperial Airways[62] would order them and have them delivered. Lockheed was able to deliver the first aircraft in three weeks but the one for the French would take three months.

Now SIS needed a pilot. Winterbotham was put in touch with a very unorthodox and adventurous pilot, Sidney Cotton, an Australian educated in England who flew with the Royal Naval Air Service in World War I. He was the inventor of the 'Sidcot' flying suit.[63]

Although unconventional and adverse to discipline, he was an excellent pilot, always heading for excitement wherever he could find it. Between the wars he flew all over the world, usually in dangerous places with little or no back-up. His abrasive self-confidence was not everyone's cup of tea, but Winterbotham liked him and gave him the job. SIS needed a cover story. Cotton was already involved in a colour photography firm in England and Germany and SIS built on this by providing him with travel documents identifying him as a film director seeking suitable film locations in Europe. The commercial cover was set up as 'The Aeronautical Research and Sales Corporation' of 3 St James's Square, London, W1. Biffy went to see Ronin and explained that SIS would share all the intelligence with them if the

---

62 Imperial Airways, the forerunner of BOAC and BA.
63 The Sidcot flying suit was designed to keep air crew warm at high altitude. It had three layers, fur, silk and a waterproof outer. It was used by aircrew until the 1960s.

French aircraft did not arrive in France by early October 1939. When it did, Biffy was asked to come and collect payment which was made in cash in high-denomination French bank notes.

Cotton and his team developed cutting-edge photographic techniques for air reconnaissance which provided better results than ever before. By the end of 1938, clandestine photographs were being taken of Italian bases and airfields. Cotton travelled all over Europe, flying at extremely high altitudes over Germany and Italy, photographing large numbers of airfields and other military intelligence targets, getting excellent results from 20,000 feet and, most importantly, remaining undetected. Indeed, he was so successful that, by mid-1939, there was a bottleneck in the production of his material due to a shortage of trained photographic interpreters. The Lockheed was in constant use throughout the summer of 1939 and Biffy kept Ronin up to date with all the available intelligence. Often, Cotton would take the Lockheed over to France with well-known people for 'holidays', so that he could keep up the cover of a wealthy tycoon with his own private aircraft. To build on Cotton's success, SIS persuaded the RAF to part with two highly valuable Spitfires. These were stripped of all non-essential equipment including guns, fitted with cameras and painted 'camotint' duck-egg blue.[64] They could operate undetected at 30,000 feet, producing excellent results. Cotton by this time was commissioned as a Wing Commander in the RAF and was destined to command the newly created Photo Reconnaissance Unit. Unfortunately, the success went to his head and this, combined with his unconventional nature and entrepreneurial skills, was to be his undoing. The RAF were beginning to worry about Cotton. Cotton's team were working hard with frequent, long and dangerous flights, with the ever present fear of being killed or captured. Cotton asked Winterbotham if SIS would rent a flat in Paris so they could relax properly when not on operations – a not unreasonable request. This was appreciated by the pilots. However, it was soon regarded by those in authority as another Cotton transgression. He was later accused of organising wild parties with naughty women and the flat became

---

64 Cotton was at Heston one day when the Maharajah of Jodhpur's private aircraft was painted a pale duck-egg blue, took off and within a few seconds was lost to sight.

known as his 'brothel'. Less well known was the fact that he was also running some of his many businesses and was still acting as agent for his gun-running friends who were organising the supply of weapons to the French.[65] Cotton preferred to use small French airfields such as Toussus-le-Noble, 40km south west of Paris, wherever possible, away from the scrutiny of the RAF. His general attitude is typified in his award of patches sewn onto his team's flying suits bearing the logo 'C.C.11', 'C.C.' standing for 'Cotton's Crooks' and '11' for the 11th Commandment *'Thou shalt not get caught.'* This did not go down well with crusty senior RAF officers.

SIS were also getting a little apprehensive about Cotton. Matters came to a head on the 18th of May 1940, when Cotton was ordered to fly to Orly Airport to extract some important passengers at Biffy's request. In April 1940, it had been agreed that eight French cryptologists would go to Bletchley to work on German, Italian and Russian codes. One of them, Marc Vey, was worried that his wife and daughter were stranded in France and asked if they could be got out. This was agreed and it was Vey's wife and daughter waiting with Biffy to catch this flight. Orly was crowded with wealthy Frenchmen trying to get themselves or their families out of France. Biffy was well known socially in Paris and was spotted by one of these Frenchmen, Marcel Boussac, the famous racehorse owner and textile magnate. Believing that a plane was coming to collect Biffy, he saw an opportunity to get out of France. He approached Biffy and offered him a small fortune to take the Frenchman and his family with him. Biffy refused. When the Frenchman saw Cotton arrive, he made a similar offer. Cotton was receptive, saying *'perhaps we can talk business'.* Biffy overheard this and ordered Cotton to get his passengers away without any further delay. When Cotton refused, Biffy made an urgent telephone call to London and Winterbotham threatened to have Cotton court-martialled and put in prison unless he took off immediately. Vey's family boarded the Lockheed while, for a tense few minutes, Biffy and French police held back panic-stricken Frenchmen from pushing

65 Cotton's business 'associates' were the Miranda brothers, Alfred and Ignacio, later convicted of arms smuggling in what became known as the 'Gran Chaco' case. The Mirandas had also been the brokers for the purchase of the two Lockheeds.

their way onto the aircraft. On return to England, Cotton was told that his services were no longer required by the RAF and SIS. There is an interesting sequel to this story.

In June 1940, the French at Bletchley Park, by now 10 in number, including Vey, were ordered back to France. There were eight naval officers and two from the Air Force. They were told a severe penalty would be imposed for not complying and a number went back. Vey and a colleague of his, Mirambel, bravely decided to stay but were deeply concerned as it meant losing their French nationality, their pay and the accusation of desertion. In fact, all of this happened. Denniston stepped in once again and immediately paid their salaries and expenses.

Biffy, back in England, had a brilliant idea to get round their loss of French nationality and the accusation of desertion. He let the Vichy Government know that Vey and Mirambel had refused to work for the British, been detained by force and interned in Oxford for the duration of the war. As proof of this, one of Biffy's team, Captain Blake-Budden, produced phoney alien registration papers and leaked them to Vichy. Some six months later their nationality was restored.[66]

Cotton was eccentric and unconventional and his side interests may have been a cause for concern, but his practical approach to operations was to be sorely missed later in the war. A report from January 1942 on SIS operations, written by Admiral John Godfrey, Director of Naval Intelligence, said:

> 'C' also showed foresight in making use of photographic reconnaissance before the war and obtained results of great value to the Admiralty in keeping movements of the German fleet under observation in the critical weeks before hostilities began. To this end, he employed a plane with civilian markings, piloted by Wing Commander Cotton, and hardly a month has passed since the outbreak of war when we have not regretted that this small illicit PRU organisation has been swallowed up in the larger and less enlightened machinery of the Air Ministry.

*

66 Related to the author by Geoffrey Pigeon, who had served at Bletchley and in SIS's Y Service. In 2021 he was giving a series of interviews to the author when he sadly died.

Charles Grey in Lafayette
Squadron uniform

Another adventurous pilot to come into Biffy's life was to become a longstanding friend, agent and fellow intelligence officer – Charles Gossage Grey. Biffy's charm and character made him a magnate for sophisticated, interesting, capable and adventurous people, many of whom he recruited, Tom Greene and Anthony Heath being two of them. Grey was to be a third.

Charles Gossage Grey was born in Chicago on the 20th of June 1894. He attended Columbia University School of Journalism and became a reporter for the *Chicago Evening Post*. He came from a wealthy family and was always marked with a taste for adventure. One of his first assignments for the *Chicago Evening Post* was reporting on the Mexican border war in 1916. In 1917, he volunteered for the American Ambulance Field Service in France, a volunteer ambulance service ferrying casualties from the battlefront to hospitals in Paris.[67] Grey served five months with them before joining the French Foreign Legion. He learnt to fly and eventually joined the Escadrille Spa.93 of the Lafayette Flying Corps. Between the 2nd of September and the 3rd of November 1918, he shot down five enemy aircraft and officially became an 'Ace'. Grey was awarded the Distinguished Service Cross for extraordinary heroism in action at Montmédy on November the 4th 1918. By the time the war ended, he was a Captain.

67 In July 1916 the Countess of la Villestreux and the Hottinguer banking family put the estate and five-acre private park at 12 Rue Raynouard at the disposal of the Field Ambulance Service for their HQ. Coosie Hottinguer became close friends with Biffy and June.

Charles Grey eating oursin

Charles Grey chose to stay in France after World War I and became a banker, becoming a Director of the Neidecker Travellers Bank, 20 Place Vendôme, and subsequently worked for the Banque de Paris. In 1935, he married an equally wealthy American divorcee, Cornelia O'Connor, née Wallace. They lived a very luxurious lifestyle, regularly commuting between the house in Paris at 50 Avenue des Tilleuls – Villa Montmorency – and their villa in Deauville, in Charles's private plane. They were regular guests of James Hazen Hyde.[68] Hyde was another very wealthy American who had come to live in France under a cloud, concerning what would today be called 'an expenses scandal'. The Greys were also close friends of Jacques Balsan who was married to Consuelo Vanderbilt.[69] They lived at 9 Avenue Charles Floquet, very close to Biffy's office. Balsan had helped set up the Lafayette Escadrille along with William Vanderbilt. The Balsans and Vanderbilts were also close friends of Biffy and June. During World War I, Balsan had been one of the patrons of the Ambulance Field Service where he met Charles Grey. Hyde had an enormous house in Versailles where he entertained lavishly with many well-connected

68 James Hazen Hyde: On his father's death, Hyde assumed the presidency of the Equitable Insurance Company. Other board members including JP Morgan and Henry Frick wanted to wrest control from Hyde. Unfortunately, Hyde played into their hands by organising a very extravagant ball using today's equivalent of $6 million to fund it. This resulted in charges of corporate malfeasance. Nothing was proved but Hyde resigned and moved to France where he lived on his considerable fortune.
69 Consuelo Vanderbilt. First married to the 9th Duke of Marlborough. This marriage was annulled and in 1921 she married Lt Col Jacques Balsan, a French aviator. They were neighbours of Biffy's in the Avenue Elisée Recluse.

Charles Grey's Beechcraft

and interesting guests, Ravel, Cole Porter, Josephine Baker – and Biffy and June Dunderdale. The Hyde salon was the ideal place for Biffy to expand his circle of important contacts and he and Charles Grey became close friends. Grey would also meet James Hyde's son Henry. Both would serve together as early recruits to the OSS. Biffy also became friendly with Hyde's wife, the Countess de Gontaut-Biron, from whom he was to lease the Château le Chêsne.

With the outbreak of war, the Greys remained in France. Charles and Cornelia were disappointed by the isolationist stance of the United States in the face of Nazi aggression, and both volunteered their services to fight the Germans. Cornelia joined the Infirmières Pilotes Secouristes de l'Air[70] as a nurse and air ambulance pilot and was awarded a Croix de Guerre for her work in 1940. Charles went to see his friend Biffy and volunteered to help SIS. Charles Grey continued his love of flying after World War I, purchasing first a small Curtis aircraft and then replacing it with a Beechcraft C17B, a state-of-the-art biplane which could take five passengers. He offered the use of it to Biffy for SIS work. Biffy took him up on it.[71] On the outbreak of war, Grey was 'commissioned' into the RAF. The Beechcraft was based at Le Bourget on permanent standby for SIS operations

70 IPSA: Formed in 1934 as the aviation section of the French Red Cross, they worked in France in 1940 and at the end of WWII recovering downed pilots and recovering prisoners from concentration camps. They were also involved in French military operations in Indochina and Algeria.
71 Charles Grey was a meticulous pilot and kept a very detailed flying log in which he noted everything about each flight he ever made. The log is completely blank after the 18th of October 1938 – the date at which he started working for SIS.

and Charles became known by the codename L'ANGE BLEU. Charles Grey would have an important role to play in the final days of the German invasion of France which would cement his relationship with SIS.

*

By 1939, Biffy had become incredibly well connected throughout 'Le Tout Paris' – Paris high society. This exotic lifestyle and enjoyment of Paris nightlife and his eye for a pretty girl inevitably led him to become friendly with Josephine Baker.

Certainly, he would have visited her own club 'Chez Josephine' in his early days in Paris. Later after the club closed in 1928, he would have seen her at his favourite nightclub Sheherazade and they would have got to know each other at James Hyde's Salon at Versailles.

Josephine Baker's ability to connect with her audiences had helped revive a depressed French society. Known as 'La Bakair', she came to epitomise the spirit of 'Les Années Folles'. Turning to France as an escape from racism in America, she came to both hate repression of any sort and represent a strong force against the emerging propaganda of Nazi Germany. Josef Goebbels, as part of his war on degenerate art, demonised her – she was black, female, exotic and

Josephine Baker

very sexy – worse still she was a tonic for French morale. Goebbels labelled her the 'Black Devil'. Her strong personality and her ability to forge connections did not go unnoticed by both Biffy and his friends in the Deuxième Bureau, who were well disposed to recruiting female agents – more so than other intelligence agencies of the period. It was only a matter of time before someone would recruit her. She came to the attention of the Deuxième Bureau via Daniel Marouani, the brother of Josephine's theatrical agent. Marouani, an impresario, who also owned a casino in Paris, was already an 'honourable correspondent' for the Deuxième Bureau. He suggested to his handler Captain Maurice Abtey, known to everyone as 'Jacques', that he recruit Josephine. Abtey initially didn't think it a good idea but took the idea to his boss Paul Paillole, who undoubtedly mentioned the idea to Biffy in one of their regular weekly meetings. They both agreed it was a good idea. She was recruited by Abtey and initially given a cover for her newfound military connection, enrolling in the Infirmières Pilotes Secouristes de l'Air (IPSA). Here she would have encountered Cornelia Grey and Coosie Hottinguer, both close friends of Biffy. Her first mission was to gather intelligence from the Italian and Japanese embassies. In the chaos of 1940, Baker fled to her Château, Château des Milandes, in the Dordogne. Abtey had rejoined his colleagues in the Deuxième Bureau but maintained close contact with her while Rivet and Paillole worked out how they would continue to fight the Germans and continue their work with SIS. How this played out is in Chapter 11.[72] Paul Paillole was to describe her as '*une résistante atypique, mais d'une résistante authentique*' – an atypical, but genuine resister.

Biffy was also friendly with Josephine's close friend and advisor Ada 'Bricktop' Smith who ran her own club, Bricktop's, which became very popular with the Duke and Duchess of Windsor, the Aga Khan, Cole Porter and Josephine Baker, as well as with Biffy.

Another of Biffy's social contacts was to develop into an important actor as the curtain rose on the events of 1940 and was also to become involved in one of Biffy's early networks in France after June 1940.

---

72 The story of Josephine Baker and her work for French intelligence and for SIS is excellently covered in *Flame of Resistance* by Damien Lewis.

In 1934, Walter Sleator had taken over all Rolls Royce operations in France. Rolls Royce had been beset by poor sales after the crash of 1929 and an impending massive tax bill from the French authorities. In a corporate manoeuvre that would be well recognised today, Rolls Royce in France became Franco-Britannic Motors. Sleator, although a British citizen, had been brought up in France and was completely bi-lingual. Sleator began his career in the luxury car world in 1924 when he went to work selling luxury cars for the Carrosserie Kellner Frères (Kellner custom bodyworks) at 127 Champs-Élysées, very close to the Rolls Royce showroom at 102. In 1934, Sleator moved to Rolls Royce and was soon in charge of Franco-Britannic Automobiles with a showroom at 12 Avenue George V, a repair services facility at 25 rue Gide in the suburb of Levallois-Perret and a storage depot at Biarritz on the Franco-Spanish border. Sleator certainly moved in the same circles as Biffy, was also a keen yachtsman and had an eye for the ladies. He was very close to a number of his female clients including Princess de Faucigny-Lucinge who bought a new Rolls Royce every year with a Kellner body, always in yellow and black.[73]

As Biffy and Walter Sleator's friendship developed, Biffy broached the subject of working for SIS in the event of war. Sleator confirmed this, writing to SIS in London:

> *I shall be taking an active part in Commander Dunderdale's organisation which, at the same time would enable me to attend to the company's interest.*

The much vaunted 'Biffy's armoured Rolls Royce' was in fact a car 'on loan' for official duties from Rolls via Sleator. Biffy also had another Rolls, a silver Ghost 45PK. Rolls Royce always maintained close contact with SIS and their Paris operation was no exception. Biffy also used their office safe to store some of the untraceable cash needed for SIS operations.

Biffy and Walter hatched a plan that, in the event of war and Biffy having to withdraw from France, Walter would leave Paris for the

---

73 Said to be the inspiration for the 1964 film *The Yellow Rolls Royce*.

Biffy's entry in the Gestapo Special Search List GB

Anglo depot at Biarritz and then across the Spanish border to Madrid where he would be the linchpin for SIS networks running across the Spanish border into France.

It was about this time that Biffy found out that he was included on the German SD Sonderfahndung Liste GB – the Special Search List GB – the immediate arrest and execution list for the planned invasion of Britain.[74] Biffy felt this was a mark of honour, rather like Rebecca West who sent a telegram to Noël Coward (they were both on the list) '*My Dear – the people we would have been seen dead with.*'

*

As the 'phoney war' of 1939/40 progressed, Biffy's office was officially designated the Allied Technical Liaison Office in all official documentation and correspondence. His team, now expanded to nine and including Tom Greene's eldest daughter Sheelagh and niece Doreen, who worked as secretaries, were issued with all sorts of permits enabling them to travel around France when most civilians were

74 Biffy was entry 124 on Page 45.

Biffy's SIS Paris station staff, 1939   Biffy's French ID card

being constrained in what they could do by wartime regulations. The SIS presence in France was enhanced in September 1939. At the same time as the Germans were moving into Poland, the 'Z' organisation was deploying to its battle stations in France and Switzerland. One section led by Kenneth Cohen and John Codrington made for Paris where they set themselves up in parallel with Biffy's station. Dansey and the main party drove to Switzerland. Biffy and Kenneth Cohen did not really see eye to eye. Cohen stayed with Biffy and June but felt himself an unwanted lodger – both on a domestic and professional level – as there were now effectively three stations operating in Paris and, although Biffy was Head of Station, the 'Z' organisation operated outside the normal chain of command.

Biffy's liaison work continued to develop and reap considerable benefits for SIS. Besides the ENIGMA programme, other high-level liaison was taking place. In December 1938, David Footman, of the SIS Political Section, went to Paris for talks on joint political intelligence operations against the Soviet Union, the Far East and in the Mediterranean. He reported to 'C' that his meetings with the French had passed off *'very happily'*, largely due *'to the excellent personal relations which 45000 (Dunderdale) has already established with his French friends'*. Biffy was also involved in a visit to Paris by Captain John Godfrey, the Director of Naval Intelligence, whom Biffy had first met in Nikolaev in 1919.

On the 12th of January, Godfrey visited Biffy's office to be briefed on counterintelligence, war planning and the Sidney Cotton aerial

Anthony Heath's permit to travel between SIS Paris Station and Château le Chêsne

Vice Admiral Godfrey DNI

photography operation. Godfrey was very happy with the visit, as were the French. *'Their impression of Capt. Godfrey was a very good one,'* Biffy reported, *'and I am sure that they will do everything for us after his visit.'* Godfrey visited again in August. Having embarked on a whirlwind tour of Copenhagen, Stockholm, Helsinki and The Hague he spent the last 24 hours of his trip in Le Zoute on the French/ Belgium border conferring with Biffy about war planning.[75] Biffy found him *'intelligent, persevering, original and far from typical, but he could be difficult and provocative'.*

During the spring of 1939, Biffy began to work with the French on joint war planning and arranged an invitation for Rivet to go to London for discussions about the deployment of a British Expeditionary Force to France in the build-up to war. During their visit, Rivet, Captain Henri Navarre of the German Section and Commandant Brun, their mobilisation officer, were extremely well looked after at the Dorchester Hotel and wined and dined at some of

---

75 John Godfrey became a lifelong friend of Biffy's. Godfrey was considered the most outstanding of all the military Directors of Intelligence. Ewan Montague, a distinguished barrister who served under him, stated that *'Godfrey was the only man to whom he would give the accolade genius.'* However, he was a difficult character and did not get on with the other service Directors of Intelligence. This led to his removal in 1942. Another reason given but unproved for his removal, was that he was found to have a German mistress.

the best restaurants in London. They had detailed discussions with key SIS officers.

It was very clear to 'C' that sending Biffy to Paris in 1926 had been an excellent move. He had made a success of both parts of his job, agent recruitment and liaison with the French. However, in the run-up to war, Sinclair was concerned that '*it was impossible for him to carry out all aspects of this liaison without interfering with his most important work, that of gathering intelligence*'. So, Biffy was relieved of dealing with the less glamorous parts of his remit such as '*counterintelligence, security censorship, passports and any kindred matters*'. This was passed to the other Paris station now being run by Major Geoffrey Courtney who had replaced Jeffes in 1937.

This allowed Biffy to devote all his time to the preparations for war, which now seemed inevitable. One task Biffy was glad to be relieved of was keeping an eye on the Duke of Windsor. A headache for the Paris SIS stations arrived in 1937 in the shape of the Duke and Duchess of Windsor, who came to live in Paris and Antibes soon after the Abdication. In Paris they rented a luxurious apartment at 24 Boulevard Suchet. MI5 already had them under surveillance due to their pro-Nazi sympathies. The French Police now took an interest, as did Biffy's friends in the Deuxième Bureau. The SIS station was told to keep a close eye on them. Luckily for Biffy this task was given to Geoffrey Courtney, but it would be surprising if Biffy did not get involved because he moved in the same social circles as the Windsors, both in Paris and on the Côte d'Azur. Biffy was also friendly with 'Fruity' Metcalf, the Duke's Equerry. As the Germans approached Paris, SIS tipped the Duke off and he and Wallis fled to Biarritz in a very unseemly manner, leaving their Equerry to fend for himself. Metcalf made his own way to England. Biffy would come across him again when Metcalf joined the Special Duties branch of the RAF. Metcalf always believed the Duke could have saved his reputation if he had remained in Paris until the last safe moment, assisting the various British missions to the French Government. '*This could have made him a hero, not a coward.*'

*

On the outbreak of war, one area of cooperation rapidly increased in tempo – the area of code-breaking and intercept. Biffy's SIS station at 1 Avenue Charles Floquet was given a public face on the outbreak of war as 'The Anglo-French Technical Cooperation Bureau'.

It became the clearing house for all communication between the SIS 'Y' intercept service and the intercept service of Bertrand's cryptographic department of the Deuxième Bureau. This was set out in a signal from the 'Y' service to their French counterparts dated the 2nd of March 1940:

> *I have seen a Note from Ministère de l'Air to Commandant DUNDERDALE dated 21st March, 1940. I have noted the description of your organisation and the respective functions of Commandant D'ALEXANDONY, Capitaine BAUDOUIN and Commandant de DAMPIERRE and will be guided by this in my correspondence to 'A' and (through 'A') to 'K'.*
>
> *This section too is aware of the great value to be obtained by close inter-allied collaboration, and is ready to work in the closest possible cooperation with yours.*
>
> *Here are my proposals for improved and more direct communication between your office and mine.*
>
> *The best means of communication is the daily courier service between our office in England and the office in the Avenue Charles Floquet. I therefore propose to send all correspondence for you to Commander Dunderdale, marked 'From Y for A'. Dunderdale will then send everything with this address direct to you (i.e. not through Capitaine B). For your part, will you please send correspondence for me to Avenue Charles Floquet, with the address 'From A for Y'. The letter 'Y' denotes the unified inter-service bureau, where all the British cryptographic sections work side by side, with a central registry for correspondence.*

Biffy was also putting in place some measures of his own.

Early in 1938, SIS decided to set up an organisation *'to plan, prepare and, when necessary, carry out sabotage and other clandestine operations, as opposed to the gathering of intelligence'*. This was designated Section 'IX' or Section 'D'. Much time was spent working at possible targets and operations in Germany and the already occupied territories, or those countries considered to be most prone to attack. Initially France did not fall into this category. However, Biffy and his friends in the Deuxième Bureau didn't agree and were in parallel discussions about a deployment of a British Expeditionary Force, the question of armed resistance, sabotage, the setting up of secret arms dumps or caches and the recruitment of suitable networks of French nationals. Although these were discussed, they were not implemented until the spring of 1940 when a team from Section 'D' under Leslie Humphreys[76] was deployed to France to work with Biffy's station and the French. The plan was *to create dumps and the organisation of parties to use them* and to circulate *false information within the German occupied territory*. The first of these tasks clearly needed considerable organisation in the short time at their disposal, while the second boiled down to creating the maximum amount of disturbance to the Germans with the minimum amount of retaliation on the civilian population.

This highlights the dilemma facing SIS from late 1940 onwards with the formation of SOE as a separate organisation not under SIS control, with the remit of taking the war to the enemy – 'setting Europe ablaze'. Sabotage and covert offensive action are not conducive to the gathering of strategic intelligence and the separation of the two functions under separate command did not make operational sense. It would have been much more realistic, pragmatic and successful if SIS had retained the offensive action capability to be used in conjunction with strategic intelligence-gathering and strategic objectives as and when appropriate.

Menzies would later in 1942 remark to Robert Bruce-Lockhart[77] that SOE *are bogus through and through, never achieving anything, compromising my agents, and are amateurs in political matters*.

---

76 Leslie Humphreys was the son of a diplomat. He was educated in Dijon and at Oxford and spoke fluent French. He had been an Assistant Commercial Attaché in Bucharest then transferred to SIS in 1939 and became the Section 'D' French Section Head. He was transferred to SOE in December 1940 and rejoined SIS at the end of the war, serving until 1964.
77 Sir Robert Bruce-Lockhart. Former SIS officer who ran the Political Warfare Executive responsible for propaganda operations.

This could be one of the reasons Maurice Buckmaster received scant recognition after the war for his command of 'F' and 'RF' sections of SOE.

As it turned out, in 1939 to 1940, not much was achieved, due in part to French military complacency about the security of the Maginot Line and the time needed to set these sorts of operations up. It was to become a mad scramble after the German attack in May. Biffy and his French friends were not convinced by the Maginot Line philosophy so did try and develop some of the Section 'D' plans.

One area where the French moved fast was in furtherance of the agreement struck with the Poles in Warsaw in July 1939. Once the Germans invaded Poland, it was essential to get the Polish cryptanalyst team working on ENIGMA to safety as soon as possible. Once the speed and success of the German Blitzkrieg became apparent, the Poles moved the cryptanalysts to Romania and then by train to Paris, arriving by early January where Bertrand took charge of them. He had set up a base for them – a Poste de Commandment or PC codenamed BRUNO at the Château de Vignoles in the village of Gretz-Armainvilliers, 25 miles northeast of Paris. They were

Left to right: Colonel Gwido Langer, Bertrand, Kenneth 'Pinky' MacFarlane

Peter Smithers

joined by a French team, a group of Spanish Republicans working on Spanish and Italian codes and British Liaison Officer Captain Kenneth MacFarlane, known as 'Pinky'. Here they continued to work in great secrecy on ENIGMA. They would be on the move again in a few months, this time to Algeria, but then back to France.

The French also restructured their intelligence service, creating a Cinquième Bureau which absorbed the Deuxième Bureau on the outbreak of war to oversee all clandestine intelligence operations.

Early in 1940, Biffy's team was boosted by the arrival on his staff of Peter Smithers, a Sub-Lieutenant in the RNVR, who had been languishing miserably in the Haslar Naval Hospital in Portsmouth with measles – alongside David Birkin.[78] A surprise telephone call from his friend Ian Fleming ended with him being interviewed by SIS and posted to Biffy's station. Although a late arrival, he would play an important role in the withdrawal of the station from Paris and its evacuation from Bordeaux a few months later.

One of the most important things Biffy did with an eye on future operations was to set up a clandestine safe house which was to become central to the operations of the JADE networks. Biffy's friend and loyal retainer Paul Kilesso had been talking about his need to move on from being Biffy's chauffeur and his interest in running a hotel. Paul Kilesso was born on the 15th August of 1897 at Dniepopetrovak and had fought and been wounded with the Russian

---

78 David Birkin – the navigating expert of the 15th Motor Gun Boat Flotilla. See, *A Dangerous Enterprise*.

Expeditionary Force at Verdun. After the war, he had no wish to return to a Bolshevik Russia and drifted to Istanbul where he met Biffy, who employed him as his chauffeur. He came to Paris with Biffy in November 1926 and continued to work for him as chauffeur and bodyguard.

At Biffy's suggestion, SIS funded the purchase of the Hotel de Havre at 37 Boulevard Montparnasse. Other than a career progression for Kilesso, Biffy's thinking was, with the future need to set up intelligence networks in an occupied France, what sort of establishment would not attract attention for the movement of people, stores and money, particularly with an established ownership and legitimate paper trail? A hotel fitted the bill perfectly. Once this purchase was complete, Kilesso was established as the legal proprietor. Biffy needed a new chauffeur and luckily had found another old friend of his in the émigré community in Paris – a former Captain in the Russian Imperial Guard who had fought for the Whites in the Civil War called Gressev, who had been at school with Biffy in Russia.

Tom Greene also helped in stay-behind preparation by agreeing with his friend Count Gerald O'Kelly de Gallagh et Tycooly, the Irish Special Plenipotentiary in Paris, that in the event of war he would assist SIS agents with Irish passports to facilitate movement or escape. O'Kelly also owned a very popular wine merchant, Vendôme Wine, in the Place Vendôme opposite the Ritz, which would continue to operate as a safe house and listening post throughout the war.

*

On the 10th of May the 'phoney war' came to an abrupt end with the German attack on the West. Holland, Belgium and Luxembourg had fallen quickly to the new form of warfare, the Blitzkrieg, fast-moving armoured columns, close air support and paratroops. British and French troops had advanced into Belgium to meet the Germans. They were quickly outflanked and pinned against the sea by a surprise and risky German attack codenamed FALL GELB (Case Yellow) which came out of the Ardennes, outflanking the Maginot Line and advancing along the valley of the Somme River to the French coast. This manoeuvre resulted in the Dunkirk evacuation of 140,000 British and about 200,000 French, Belgian and Polish troops.

On the 5th of June, the Germans launched FALL ROT (Case Red) the operation to encircle and capture Paris. The French Government and military descended into chaos, as did most of France.

Operating her ambulance in the north of France, Cornelia Grey had first-hand experience of the disintegration and terror in the face of the German advance.

Behind us we could hear the crash of bombs, and the roar of planes filled the air. The road leading south from St Quentin was just a solid line of traffic, such pathetic traffic, women walking carrying babies in their arms, tears streaming down their tragic faces, old men limping painfully along, and car after car filled to overflowing with human cargo and animals too, baby calves or new born goats and lambs and colts packed in with the people who wanted to save them!

On the 8th of June, the sound of distant artillery could be heard in the capital. Trains filled with refugees departed Gare d'Austerlitz with no announced destination. On the 10th of June, the French Government fled Paris, first to Tours and then to Bordeaux. Thousands of Parisians followed their example, filling the roads out of the city with cars, buses, trucks, wagons, carts, bicycles and on foot. The slow-moving river of refugees took 10 hours to cover 30km.

Geoffrey Cox,[79] the *Daily Express* correspondent, described the chaos:

All along the roadside cars were dotted, with families sleeping in or around them. As dawn came one after another gathered its belongings and started again on this seemingly endless journey. Traffic was as yet light, and the drivers drove at speed, with tired, set faces, racing to the next village to try to get petrol, to try to get

79 Geoffrey Cox worked for Claude Dansey in the 'Z' organisation.

food, housing, rest. On and on went this procession. We stopped ourselves to sleep for an hour. We fell asleep and woke to the roar of cars, leaving their stink of petrol over the fresh countryside. It was a nightmare of exhaustion, with people pressing on, uncertain where to go, leaderless, without news – for there were no car radios then – without advice, a nation disintegrating into a mass of squabbling, exhausted, desperate individuals at the one time when it needed cohesion in the face of an enemy.

Virginia Cowles, the exotic and pioneering correspondent for *The Sunday Times*, further described it:

Try to think in terms of millions. Try to think of noise and confusion, of the thick smell of petrol, of the scraping of automobile gears, of shouts, wails, curses and tears. Try to think of hot sun and underneath it an unbroken stream of humanity flowing southwards from Paris and you have the picture of the gigantic civilian exodus that presaged the German advance.

Cowles coincidentally was to be evacuated from Bordeaux on the same ship as the SIS station staff.

Biffy had sent June to London in early 1940 so as to be unencumbered when it came to direct war fighting. Others had chosen to keep their families with them. Biffy tried hard to maintain contact with his agents and with his French counterparts. It was almost impossible for him to gain any actionable intelligence from his agents, but Rivet, Bertrand and Paillole did their best to pass on what they knew. Biffy reported to London:

There were insurmountable difficulties in travelling across frontiers and in France itself due to the very severe control and complete disorganisation of certain traffic.

Biffy was instructed by Menzies to withdraw from Paris and to try and maintain contact with the French, but on no account was he or any of his team to be captured. Biffy gave his instruction for the evacuation of the station. Peter Smithers would be in charge of it, assisted by Charles Grey. The first fallback position would be the Château le Chêsne. Grey would ferry as many people and equipment as he could by air to Romorantin near the Château and Smithers would take the road party. Smithers described his mission:

As the German advance continued I was dispatched by Commander Dunderdale with a truck from the French Army and an armed escort to the Châtaeu le Chêne, near Salbris. In the truck were the records and archives of MI6 Paris. The Château belonged to Germaine Duchesse de Gantaut-Biron. I was to instal the archives and prepare the Château for the arrival of the MI6 staff from Paris. They arrived there in due course with their families and a number of 'attachments'. The nearest airfield was Romorantin to which Charlie flew at this point.

Once everyone was clear of Paris and at the Château, Charles Grey would take his Beechcraft to Romorantin and await further orders and, in the absence of Biffy, Smithers would develop a plan to evacuate via Le Verdon at the mouth of the Gironde near Bordeaux. If that didn't work he should head for Biarritz to evacuate by sea or overland via Spain and Portugal.

Biffy remained to close the station. For several days they had been destroying documents and preparing to leave. Fitzroy Maclean and Ian Fleming[80] visited the station in Avenue Charles Floquet where they found the staff working like dervishes to close down the station and prepare for their evacuation. Biffy had emptied his safe and booby trapped it to explode when opened by the Germans. Biffy, Fitzroy and Fleming made time to have a hurried lunch together before Biffy saw his team off with Peter Smithers in charge, with strict orders to get them all to safety. Ian Fleming resumed his pursuit of Admiral Darlan[81] and when he was unable to be of any further use at French Naval Headquarters moved to Le Verdon at the mouth

---

80 Both would be lifelong friends of Biffy's.
81 Fleming had been tasked by Admiral Godfrey, the DNI, to persuade Admiral Darlan to sail his ships to Britain.

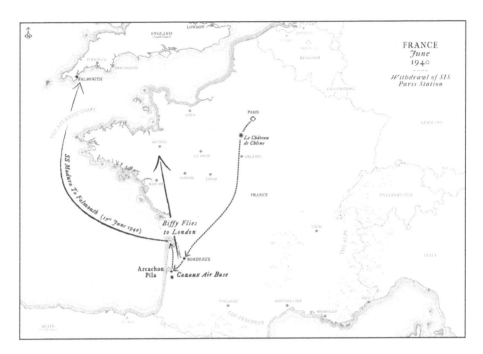

of the Gironde River to assist with the evacuation of essential personnel and equipment. He was joined in this by Steven McKenzie and
Patrick Whinney, both RNVR officers who were later to join SIS on
return to Britain.[82]

Tom Greene closed up his apartment, sealing it with a notice that
it was the property of an Irishman – a neutral – and under the protection of the Government of Eire. The ruse worked as on his return
in 1944 the apartment and its contents were dusty but untouched.
Tom took his wife, his younger daughter Lois and his niece, Doreen,
with him.

Sheelagh, the eldest, elected to stay in France with a view to setting
up networks in the future. Using her Irish passport as protection she
made her way to the Greene villa in Nice, where she got in touch with
Philip Keun who was staying at his father's villa in Antibes. Sheelagh
helped him start what was to become the JADE AMICOL network.
This was a brave decision as it was well known that she had worked

---

82 Both ended up working for Frank Slocum's clandestine naval operations.

Sheelagh Greene, 1937

for her father and Biffy in the SIS station. Later she became a full-time member of the JADE AMICOL network, where she coordinated air landing and parachute operations, ran the logistics and looked after the relatives of those executed or deported.

With all his staff safely en route to Britain and all final preparations made, Biffy left Paris amidst the increasing noise of German artillery fire before it was too late. He was intending to meet up with Grey and Smithers at the Château le Chêsne. He climbed into his Rolls Royce, the 1935 20/25, loaned to him by Sleator and driven by Pierre Rouat who had replaced Gressev, as he had decided to go underground to fight the Germans.[83] Biffy and Rouat made slow progress but eventually arrived at the Château.

The Château was situated next to the largest ammunition depot in France. Biffy reported to Menzies that if the dump blew up it would result in an '*instantaneous and painless death*'. Menzies decided enough was enough and called the team home.

At the Château, Biffy met up with Grey, Smithers, Humphreys of Section 'D' and his 2IC, Riley, still trying to organise equipment caches and saboteurs to train. Humphreys had lost contact with the French, but had made contact with Gressev, the driver, who told him he had a group of 21 men and five women who would be only too happy to get involved if they could be given weapons and explosives.

---

83 Gressev survived the war and was re-employed by Tom Greene in 1944. Gressev continued to work for the SIS station in Paris until 1964, driving their cars without a single scratch – a remarkable feat in Paris.

Humphreys had been on a trip to Switzerland probably to meet Martin Bachtold, Ash Acheson and Richard Straus.[84] He arrived back in Paris on the 11th of June to find the station and the military attaché's office evacuated. Humphreys waited seven hours in Paris while his various teams reported back in. Eventually they took off for the Château le Chêsne at 03:00 on the 12th in their cars, just ahead of the advancing Germans, arriving at 06:30. Hearing that Paris was not yet occupied, Humphreys, ever persistent, tried to go back there, taking a circuitous route via various airfields looking for dumps of stores that had supposedly been landed the day before – all to no avail. Eventually Humphreys went back to the Château le Chêsne, arriving on the 14th, where he found Biffy preparing to evacuate again in the face of a disintegrating situation and that Paris had been declared an open city on the 12th.

Biffy was ordered to leave and headed for Bordeaux. Biffy gave orders that the main SIS party must leave their beloved Château and head for Pyla sur Mer near Arcachon, on the Atlantic coast. Smithers had arranged a final jumping-off point of one of Baron Philippe de Rothschild's[85] houses, the Villa Don Cupi.

The intention was to evacuate with the rest of the Embassy on HMS ARETHUSA and, failing that, as the villa was on the beach, a final extraction could be arranged from there.[86] The SIS team were told to prepare to leave everything behind except two bags each. Most of them didn't have much anyway. Charles Grey had flown some of them to Cazaux, a military airfield southwest of Bordeaux. From there they went by road to join the others at Pyla. Humphreys's final effort was to go and see Rivet and Peruche to try and arrange for a liaison officer, Lieutenant Turck, to come back to London. This didn't work, unbelievably, for passport reasons. Humphrey's final act was to arrange

---

84 Swiss timber merchant and Section D agent. Straus was Section D's railway expert.

85 Philippe de Rothschild, a member of the Rothschild banking dynasty, racing driver and film producer, ran the family vineyards of Mouton Rothschild. He left France in 1940 and was arrested by Vichy authorities in North Africa. He eventually made his way to London, where he joined the Free French. He won a Croix de Guerre. His estranged wife died in Ravensbrook. He died in Paris in 1988.

86 Smithers did not join the evacuation, but he joined Ian Fleming and the 1st Sea Lord at Admiral Darlan's headquarters. Smithers flew back to England in a Sunderland Flying Boat with the 1st Sea Lord.

Baron Philippe de Rothschild   Villa Don Cupi, SIS evacuation assembly point

with Rivet a rendezvous in Lisbon at a later date. Humphreys and his Section D team then made their way to the evacuation point at Pyla.

Rivet and Bertrand had been busy themselves ensuring the Poles and Spanish at P.C. BRUNO were not captured by the advancing Germans. The situation in France was changing hourly. Biffy tried to help Bertrand get the code breakers out. In an exchange of signals with Bertrand between the 23rd and 28th of June, he offered to bring them all to Britain and told him that they could evacuate on a Royal Navy warship, *'apply to Lieutenant FLEMING or WHINNIE at Bayonne and embark there'*. Bertrand replied on the 26th thanking DOLINOFF (Biffy's codename) for the offer, informing him that the Poles had been evacuated by plane to Algiers.

He and his Deuxième Bureau officers had been told to stay put. On the 28th, Bertrand sent a final signal:

28.06.40 from Bertrand: *'For DOLINOFF. Are obliged to cease radio transmission by reason of Armistice conditions. We ask you to keep listening in each day in the same way as we hope to recommence soon clandestinely. You can count on me for security your work. Regards. Bertrand.'*

After the armistice, the Poles returned from Algeria to P.C. CADIX, the Château des Fouzes near Uzès in the Department of Gard. The story of the Poles and the French is continued in Chapter 11. During the chaos of May and June, Tiltman was busily trying to extract

Evacuees on SS MADURA, June 1940

the British team from P.C. BRUNO. Bertrand said to him, '*We value your party very much; we'd like to keep them, but you had better get them out while you can, and please tell Menzies that none of your secrets will get into enemy hands.*' Tiltman got his team out through Bordeaux just in time.

The last radio contact with SIS was on the 28th of June 1940. As Bertrand said later of this moment: '*Situation normale, pagaille partout*' or in English, '*Situation normal, all fucked up.*'

At 19:00 on the 18th Humphreys said goodbye to Rivet and Peruche in the driving rain and eventually reached Bordeaux at 06:00. They made their way to Le Verdon at the mouth of the Gironde where they joined the rest of the SIS evacuees, including Uncle Tom Greene, the station personnel and the Archibald brothers,[87] on board the SS MADURA[88] which sailed at 01:00 on the 20th and arrived at Falmouth on the morning of the 21st.

The last Peter Smithers saw of Charles Grey was him standing on

---

87 Both Archibald brothers were commissioned into the RAF with Biffy's support. In October 1942, Roy transferred to MI9 to work on the recovery of downed aircrew.
88 The plan to join HMS ARETHUSA didn't work – it was already full of Embassy staff and the Polish Government in exile. The SIS team was switched to the MADURA.

From left to right: Anthony Heath, Miss Watt (SIS Office Manager), Unknown, Tom Greene, Unknown

Charles Grey in RAF uniform

the quay beside a Talbot given to him by Tom Greene so that he could drive as fast as possible to join his family at the Château de Missery in Burgundy.

Charles waved to them, drew his revolver, fired three shots in the air and shouted, '*mission accomplished*'. He then sped away to join his family, but not before he had hatched a plan to continue working for Biffy in some way in the near future. Charles changed out of his RAF uniform into plain clothes, loaded the car with tinned food, water, fuel and several bottles of champagne and set off to find his family at Missery. It was very slow going. Eventually he ran into the Germans at Angoulême. A patrol ordered him to stop. With mounting fear, he realised that he still had on him all his military papers, both British and French. There was no time for him to do anything about it. They started to search him. So, you can imagine the state he was in as the search got closer to his inner pocket. In desperation he pulled out his American passport, together with a carton of British cigarettes which he had grabbed at the Villa Don Cupi. This little interruption saved him; his captors took the cigarettes and let him go. This narrow escape taught him a lesson and he wasted no time to find a place on the roadside where he could destroy his incriminating papers. He turned onto a small side road and there got rid of his identification papers, his radio equipment and his revolver, which was too dangerous to carry any further. It was lucky he took this precaution, for a little further on he was again stopped and systematically searched, but this time he was safe and his story of having become separated from his family and wanting to return to try and find them had a plausible ring to it. His American passport clinched matters. The Germans wanted to confiscate his fuel, but he stood up to them and eventually they let him go. It took him three days to get to Missery. He found his children safe, but Cornelia had gone to Paris, so he set off to join her, arriving two days later. As a last reminder of times past, they went to La Crémaillère for dinner before it became overrun by Germans.

As the MADURA left the French coast behind, Churchill was giving his 'Finest Hour' speech in the House of Commons. Biffy was about to join them on board when he received a signal from Menzies telling him an RAF Anson was coming to Cazaux airfield to get him out, so he about turned and Pierre Rouet drove him to the airfield. The Anson arrived, collected him and headed for England.

The Germans had marched into Paris at 06:00 on the 14th of June. By 09:45 a massive swastika flag was hanging over the Tomb of the Unknown Soldier under the Arc de Triomphe. Insult was complete. Biffy's 14 years in France were over.[89] Les Années Folles, the wild and exotic life of the 1920s and 1930s, was about to be followed by Les Années Noires.

89 For the subsequent fate of the Rolls, see Annex A.

CHAPTER 10 – LONDON 1940

'Success is not final, failure is not fatal,
it is the courage to continue that counts.'

Winston Churchill

'War changes the intelligence officer
from Cinderella to a Princess.'

Admiral John Godfrey DNI

Biffy got away in the nick of time. The Germans were not far behind him into Bordeaux and the whole of the west coast of France as far south as the Spanish border. This left SIS completely blind, except for their outposts on the periphery of occupied Europe, in Finland, Sweden, Switzerland and Portugal. All were to play a significant part in SIS operations for the next five years.

Once Biffy's plane landed, he drove straight to London to SIS Headquarters at Broadway Buildings. Here, he was ushered straight to the third-floor office of 'C' Stewart Menzies. There was a traffic light system over 'C''s door – 'red' not to be disturbed. The light changed from red to green and Biffy was ushered in to find Claude Dansey and Menzies. They listened to Biffy's report of the chaotic departure from Paris, the disintegration of the French and the status of any remaining assets left in France. It was a bleak picture, but not entirely without hope, as Biffy and his Deuxième Bureau friends had been working on contingency plans up to the last minute, as had Kenneth Cohen for the 'Z' organisation which was now fully absorbed into SIS. Menzies seemed completely calm over the disaster staring him in the face.[90] Biffy brought a message from General Maurice-Henri Gauché, the head of the newly constituted Vichy Intelligence Service which replaced the Cinquième and Deuxième Bureau.

---

90 Biffy liked Menzies, finding him '*charming, devious and highly capable but without the same dynamic personality as "Quex" Sinclair*'.

Broadway Buildings, SIS headquarters

As part of the Armistice settlement, the Germans had insisted the pre-war French Intelligence Services be dismantled and that no intelligence operations be carried out against the Germans, and that they must work against Great Britain. The newly appointed Vichy Defence Minister ordered the Secret Service to '*go underground*'. Gauché was soon to hand over to Louis Rivet, Biffy's old friend. The message for SIS was '*the fight goes on whatever happens*'. As we will see, they were as good as their word. Despite the disaster that had befallen France, French intelligence officers like Rivet, Paillole and Bertrand together with Biffy had realised the German threat long before the attack on Poland. The intelligence war had begun long before the hostilities and was to continue unbroken until the liberation.

Claude Dansey now explained that they had hoped the French would continue the fight from Vichy, but that now they had a problem with General de Gaulle who, as the Undersecretary of Defence, had refused to accept the Armistice and fled to London from where he broadcast to France on the 18th of June 1940. De Gaulle, after much soul searching, had flown to London with General Spears[91] landing

---

91 General Sir Edward Spears KBE, CB, MC. British Liaison Officer to the French in both world wars. He headed the British mission to de Gaulle and the Free French.

at Heston at midday on the 17th. The next day, Churchill gave his 'Finest Hour' speech and de Gaulle made his appeal to the French to fight on. The Armistice was signed on the 21st. De Gaulle broadcast to France again on the 22nd. On the 28th, the British Government recognised de Gaulle as Leader of the Free French. Friction between Britain and the Vichy Government with the Free French would continue until the liberation of France in 1944 and, in the case of Franco-British relations, much longer.

SIS needed to manage de Gaulle and support him, but also to continue to maintain contact with Biffy's friends in Vichy. To that end, it was decided to run two parallel departments within SIS. Biffy was to command 'A4', continuing to maintain and develop relations with Vichy, while Biffy's old rival, Kenneth Cohen, was given command of 'A5', working with de Gaulle and the Free French. Another complication was the question of the Poles. The Polish Intelligence Service, having evacuated to France, now had a large intelligence presence there which, as we will see, became effective immediately after the collapse of France. The Polish Intelligence Service had evacuated its command structure to London but were seen by de Gaulle as yet another way to usurp his position.

So, Biffy was also given responsibility for '*the Poles, Polish intelligence operations and certain French and other Special Lines*'. Both Menzies and Dansey realised that this structure was likely to cause friction between the sections and it was exacerbated by separate chains of command. Cohen reported to Dansey, for whom he had worked in the 'Z' Organisation and Biffy reported direct to Menzies. This friction was to continue until the end of 1943, but in some ways was quite healthy in that it tended to produce better intelligence. It was, however, to create for Biffy some difficult moments. Cohen was never a great fan of his, starting with their time in HMS IRON DUKE in Constantinople. He described Biffy as '*a genial expense account salesman*'.

'A4' and 'A5' sections each represented dramatically opposed French political opinion – many believing that Biffy's contacts with his old friends now in Vichy was the right approach. However, SIS and the British Government were stuck with de Gaulle and had

Victor Chatenay

positively encouraged a Free French Government and armed forces. Menzies and Dansey had to make it work, but it was going to be very tricky, and it was not to be until the run-up to the invasion of Europe that things would begin to settle down. In the beginning there was a great deal of friction and acrimony – the French accusing Biffy of recruiting Frenchmen arriving in England before they had the opportunity to join de Gaulle and Biffy accusing his opposite number, André Dewavrin (PASSY), the head of de Gaulle's embryonic intelligence service, of lack of cooperation. Dewavrin, in turn, would regularly complain to Dansey about Biffy and there is no doubt that Kenneth Cohen was not averse to a bit of pot stirring.

The maintenance of two French sections working in parallel and competing for resources, and France's 'third' service, further complicated by Polish intelligence operations in France, may have seemed totally impractical, but was the only pragmatic solution in the days following the fall of France. SIS faced some dire challenges in the late summer and autumn of 1940. The friction between Cohen and Biffy was nothing compared to the conflicting purposes and personal animosity between the British intelligence community as a whole and the Free French intelligence services. This marriage of inconvenience was only kept together by the fact that they needed each other. Victor Chatenay,[92] a resistance leader from Angers who escaped in 1943 and

92 Victor Chatenay, an early resister, set up the network 'Honneur et Patrie', which worked for SIS. He was married to a British wife, Barbara Sterling. He was arrested in 1943 but escaped and was flown to London where he joined Biffy. Later he switched to the Free French Intelligence Service the BCRA.

went to work for Biffy in London, was surprised by the level of vitriol. *'I had a conversation with [Tom] Greene about General de Gaulle and I was incredibly surprised to encounter such animosity...'*[93]

De Gaulle was a grudging guest. He would rail against his British hosts, complaining that he had been slighted by being given offices at 4 Carlton Gardens which could only be accessed by Waterloo Place and where, from his office, he could see Nelson's Column in Trafalgar Square. Difficulties with de Gaulle prompted Churchill's remark: *'I've had to bear many crosses in my life, but the heaviest has been the Cross of Lorraine.'* De Gaulle's overriding concern was that Frenchmen would play little or no part in the liberation of France, leaving a disillusioned population tainted by surrender and collaboration and lacking any self-respect. This would be a perfect breeding ground for the left, particularly as resistance led by communist networks was taking hold in France. De Gaulle was always concerned that post-war France should be a right-wing country led by him.

Dewavrin realised his power lay in his access to French speakers with which he could bargain with SIS for money, radios, false papers and delivery systems. He also worked out that he could exploit the demarcation between Cohen and Biffy by working closely with Biffy and the two were to build a working relationship out of mutual respect.

The greatest source of friction was the competition for agents. Rather than ask the French for manpower, Biffy would look elsewhere for agents who could work directly for SIS. He would recruit individuals he had known in France before the war, those whose names his Vichy contacts had given him and would recruit at MI5's clearing house for foreign refugees – the Royal Victoria Patriotic School on Wandsworth Common.

Any likely-looking potentials amongst those who passed the security screening, unless they were absolutely determined to join the Free French, were passed to an SIS officer on the staff called Jacolòt, a French naval officer who had been on the French naval staff in

93 Victor Chatenay, *Mon journal du temps du malheur.*

London before the war. He had joined Biffy's staff in 1940 and Biffy used him as a talent spotter when arrivals from France or the French Colonies were being screened. Likely recruits were given the opportunity of working direct for SIS – 'L'Intelligence Service', which still held an attraction for some Frenchmen who either believed in their 'aura' or as a way to properly help their country, being disillusioned with a collaborationist Vichy on the one hand and the blatant political opportunism of de Gaulle on the other.

*

Faced with increasing demands from the War Cabinet for detailed intelligence about what was happening across the channel, SIS had a lot of catching up to do. It was imperative to establish intelligence networks in occupied France as soon as possible. This required the recruitment and organisation of men and women in France, those who were prepared to take the risk and those with access to ports, railways, airfields and the German order of battle from which they could develop actionable intelligence. These individuals would need to be organised and supported by trained operators from SIS as well as money, radios and all the other equipment needed to gather and communicate their intelligence in a timely manner.

Frank Slocum, in charge of the newly created 'O' operations section, was charged with the delivery and extraction of agents and the recovery of classified material from occupied Europe. Slocum was a retired naval officer who had joined SIS in 1937.[94]

Initially he was responsible for all air and sea operations, parachute, air landing and maritime operations using submarines, civilian craft and motor gunboats. His remit covered the whole of occupied Europe from Norway to Greece. Given the scale of this remit, limited resources and competing interests of the different client services, responsibility for air operations was split off and put under the command of Air Commodore Payne in 1941.

Biffy galvanised his team into action. His priorities were to

---

94 For the full story of Slocum's clandestine naval operations, see *A Dangerous Enterprise*.

Captain Frank Slocum

Alliance House, Caxton Street

re-establish his links with Rivet, Bertrand and Paillole in unoccupied France and then to activate his 'stay behind' arrangements made before and during 'the phoney war'. He was also on the lookout for opportunities and new talent.

Having been given his mission, Biffy now had to set about creating his organisation and to start delivering. Biffy's inclination not to work in head office and the need to separate 'A4' and 'A5' sections played into his hands, so he found himself his own offices well away from Broadway but close enough to the intelligence and government hub. He set up shop at Alliance House, 12 Caxton Street, a comparatively modern Art Deco-style, small office block on the corner of Caxton Street and Palmer Street. Here, Biffy, relieved to be away from Broadway which he found *'run down, shabby, full of unnecessary paperwork and office intrigue'*, set himself up with his team on the first floor. The office was decorated with, in keeping with his style, both Russian and Ottoman Oriental rugs, a portrait of the King, a large autographed photo of the Tsar in a Fabergé frame, given to Biffy's father by the Tsar on the occasion of Biffy's birth on Christmas Eve 1899, and a large model of the Russian cruiser AURORA.[95] The exotic atmosphere was enhanced by wafts of frankincense and Turkish coffee.

95 Biffy was always keen on ship models. Anthony Fraser, his godson, recalled that there was an extensive collection at his house in Sussex and Biffy gave Anthony a large pond yacht called AURORA. The original cruiser, after which it was named, was completed in 1903. Many of its parts were supplied to the Russian Imperial Navy from Vickers by Richard Dunderdale. The AURORA fired the first shot of the Russian Revolution in 1917. Its captain was killed by Bolshevik mutineers and they then opened fire on the Winter Palace in St Petersburg.

At the beginning of the war, all SIS officers had to choose a military service cover. Biffy chose the Royal Navy as he had already held a commission in the RNVR during his time in the Crimea. Biffy was commissioned as a 'Temporary Commander (Special Branch) of the RNVR' backdated to the 2nd of September 1939. As such he was able to use either military or civilian status as appropriate but was mostly seen in naval uniform in Caxton Street and known as 'Chief' within his team and Commander Dunderdale to outsiders. Charles Grey chose the RAF and Anthony Heath the Army.

'A4' section occupied all three floors of Alliance House. Biffy was always very security-conscious. No one was allowed to visit without a specific appointment. Visitors were made to wait in a small anteroom on the ground floor where they were often locked in. The room was fitted with microphones and any conversation recorded. Biffy's rather imposing office was on the first floor, as was Tom Greene's, where Tom acted as gatekeeper for Biffy and as his deputy and Chief of Staff. On the two floors above were the main offices where Biffy's staff worked, consisting of some of the team from the Paris station, with a number of Russians and Frenchmen whom Biffy knew from Paris. Anthony Heath was sent to Stanmore to the Dower House to be Biffy's liaison officer with Polish intelligence. Smithers had initially gone to MI5 and was then posted to Washington. The Russians included Leonid de Narbevich, the French, Fernand Mercier, who ran the map room and Robert de Lesseps[96] (codename GOODFELLOW), who ran the secret registry. Phillip Schneidau (codename PHILLIPSON), who had been an early agent, ran the liaison with clandestine air and sea operations and was a conducting officer for outgoing or returning agents. Agents who had been blown or who had been captured and escaped were often employed at Caxton Street as they were unable to return to France. Victor Chatenay found himself in this position and was co-opted by Biffy, after a successful Lysander exfiltration operation, to help analyse the intelligence brought out every month.

Amongst them were reports from every prefecture in France sent to the Vichy Ministry of the Interior, described by Victor Chatenay:

---

96 Grandson of Ferdinand de Lesseps who built the Suez Canal.

Biffy at his desk at Alliance House

Each of these comprises a dozen chapters and each month, without fail this enormous dossier reaches us, which proves that we have extremely well-placed agents and that not all Vichy officials collaborate with the enemy.

Chatenay goes on to describe his specific work:

My job is to separate all information concerning military operations: bombings, protective measures and fortification, manpower, sabotage, requisitions, information concerning supplies, health, arrests, relations with the occupier, movements of Maréchal Pétain, mood of the population etc.

Biffy and Tom had evolved an effective modus operandi in Paris which they continued in London. Biffy remained the affable charmer, while 'Uncle' Tom ran the office with a rod of iron. Both were liked and respected. Tom moved his family into 66 Cranmer Court in Chelsea, a 20-minute walk from Caxton Street. With one daughter, Sheelagh, in France, his other daughter, Lois, joined the team in Caxton Street. They were supplemented by others including Dorothy Johns, the Canadian wife of Philip Johns, a formal naval officer, recruited into

SIS in 1939, who spoke fluent French. Charles Garton joined the team in 1941 after working in the SIS station in Madrid.

Charles Grey, L'ANGE BLEU, had eventually joined his family but, by July 1940, he realised that he must get them out of France, back to the United States. After a long, torturous car journey via Biarritz, Spain and Portugal they arrived in Lisbon on the 6th of August and set sail for New York. After he had settled his family, Charles returned straight to London and went to see Biffy. Charles was keen to continue his work for SIS and they hatched a plan which would put Charles in considerable danger. He would return to Paris, using his neutrality as a US citizen and the cover of working for the US Food Distribution Agency to continue his work gathering intelligence. Although he would work independently initially he would become part of the Polish 'F2' network from February 1941 until November 1942.[97]

Biffy also asked him to try and follow up on something he and Bertrand had been working on since the outbreak of the war. The Finns had been working on breaking Russian codes since the beginning of the Russo-Finnish war on the 30th of November 1939 and Biffy and Bertrand had been trying to persuade them to share their intelligence. The war ended in March 1940 just as Biffy and Bertrand were about to get very busy.

In anticipation of a full Soviet annexation of their country, Finnish code breakers had decamped to Sweden in what was called Operation STELLA POLARIS. The Finns had spent the previous 17 years working on Soviet codes and their methodology was invaluable to the Swedes but also to SIS and the Deuxième Bureau who had started to pay the Finns for codebooks and cipher systems. Biffy asked Charles Grey to reopen negotiations for them. Charles travelled to Finland on several occasions to have discussions on behalf of SIS. He would regularly travel via Berlin, putting himself at great personal risk. His cover was not 'official' and he was 'freelancing' for Biffy, regularly crossing into the unoccupied territory to deliver intelligence to the US Naval Attaché in Vichy who would include intelligence for Biffy

97 He worked from Paris until Pearl Harbor, then moved to the unoccupied zone.

in the diplomatic bag to London. This became known as the 'Vichy valise'. This unofficial intelligence activity came to the attention of Cordell Hull, the US Secretary of State, who insisted that it threatened US neutrality and must cease. He was ignored. After the US entry into the war, Grey got away from France and joined OSS, working in London and Lisbon. Biffy, always stylish and elegant, had not forgotten his old friend. On Charles's arrival in London in late 1940, he received a surprise package at his hotel room. Biffy had always been struck by his bravery and determination to help in Paris in 1939 and 1940. He arranged for Alfred Dunhill to make a silver cigarette case with the Royal Cypher on the lid; the inside was inscribed 'To the First Volunteer, L'Ange Bleu' and was signed by all the members of the SIS station in Paris in 1940. Grey was greatly moved by this gesture and it reaffirmed his view that SIS did things in style even when the chips were down. It further cemented his relationship with Biffy which was to continue well after the end of the war. The case remained in Biffy's office until Grey came back to London with OSS. To have taken it back to Europe would have been an automatic death sentence if it was found by the Germans.

Signatures of Bill (Biffy), Uncle Tom (Greene), Doreen and Sheelagh (Greene), B. Watt (Miss Watt, Office Manager) Pamela, Parky, Harry Achilley

CHAPTER 11 – VICHY

'La France a perdu une bataille!
Mais La France n'a pas perdu La Guerre.'

General de Gaulle's broadcast to France
from London 20th June 1940

'Every catastrophe is an opportunity.'

Thomas Shelby, *Peaky Blinders*

Across the channel, Biffy's friends in the Deuxième Bureau, Rivet, Ronin, Bertrand, Paillole and the others, were reeling from the disintegration of France. They found themselves in the dilemma that Victor Frankl, the Austrian psychiatrist, philosopher and Holocaust survivor, called *'Man's search for meaning'*.

The last of the human freedoms – to choose one's attitude in any given set of circumstances, to choose one's own way. And there were always choices to make, every day, every hour, offering the opportunity to make a decision, a decision which determined whether you would or would not submit to those powers which threatened to rob you of your very self, your inner freedom ...

After the French surrender on the 22nd of June 1940, this was the decision confronting Biffy's friends in the Deuxième Bureau. They chose a very courageous route, a route that was to test their integrity to the limit and that could have had them tried and executed at the end of the war.

As we have seen, Bertrand helped the Polish ENIGMA team to escape and set up at P.C. BRUNO. They were subsequently evacuated to Algiers and, after the French surrender, secretly brought back to P.C. CADIX, le Château des Fouzes at Uzès in July 1940. Before that, the Deuxième Bureau lost contact with Biffy in London on the 28th of June 1940 when their radio communications were cut. As Bertrand put it *'Le dernier lien avec le monde libre était rompu'* (The last link with the free world was broken).

Rivet had gathered his men at a temporary headquarters at Bajas and on the 21st addressed them, suggesting that they all escape to North Africa and, if unable to do so, *'to continue our fight clandestinely'*. Four days later they all gathered around the war memorial at Bon-Encontre where they swore to fight on. Paillole was given the responsibility of setting up a secret network within the military intelligence structure permitted by the Armistice. This would be known as the TR – Travaux Ruraux (Rural Engineer Works). Cells were set up in Limoges, Clermont-Ferrand, Lyon, Toulouse and Marseilles. Paillole used the alias of Philippe Perrier. *'Our mission was unequivocal: it determined the creation of our clandestine intelligence and counter-espionage networks in July 1940. We had to continue the fight...'* His orders were clear: continue the fight against Axis espionage services; penetrate pro-Nazi organisations such as the Milice; liaise with the British as soon as possible and support their networks; counterintelligence operations against the Germans in the Free Zone; and gather intelligence by developing agents in the occupied zone.

All these initiatives were secretly endorsed by General Weygand, the Vichy Defence Minister. They had the motivation and the structure, but one thing was missing – contact and communication with London. Paillole summoned Captain Jacques Abtey and told him to travel to Lisbon: *'Make contact with Biffy through the British embassy and find out how we can develop channels of communication.'*

Abtey was to travel under cover as part of Josephine Baker's retinue.[98] Abtey would take with him a massive amount of intelligence that had been gathered on the German order of battle, airfields, ports, the German preparations for the capture of Gibraltar and attempts to co-opt the IRA and Scottish and Welsh nationalist groups to carry out intelligence and sabotage operations in Britain.

Abtey reached Lisbon and sent his information to London, which arrived in November 1940. To Biffy and his team, this was exactly the news they had been waiting for. Although busy trying to set up networks in occupied France they had been waiting patiently for a sign from Rivet. Biffy immediately travelled to Lisbon on the 5th

98 Josephine Baker's work with the French and British Intelligence Services is recounted in detail in *The Flame of Resistance* by Damien Lewis.

Biffy's alias passport

Jerónimos Monastery, Lisbon

of September of 1940 to meet Abtey (VICTOR) using the alias John Green, flying from Bristol Whitchurch Airfield. They met in the Jerónimos Monastery,[99] where Biffy handed over the first of several radio transmitters and codes.

A further RV was fixed for March 1941. Rivet entrusted the second meeting to Bertrand who went by rail via Madrid to Lisbon where he checked into the Hotel Plaza du Rossio. Biffy had again travelled on his alias passport in the name of John Green. Biffy stayed with the SIS Head of Station as the hotel, as well as most of Lisbon, was crawling with German intelligence, the Portuguese Intelligence Service (PVDE) officers and paid informers. The pre-arranged RV with Biffy was set at the greenhouse of the Botanical Gardens which was unlikely to be heavily monitored by the Portuguese police or German informers. Biffy collected the bulky transmitter from the British embassy and, carrying out extensive counter-surveillance drills, drove to the Botanical Gardens. Bertrand did the same. Both were in cars with diplomatic plates so they could claim diplomatic immunity if stopped by the police. They parked side by side in the Botanical Gardens car park. Leaving an armed guard in each car, they walked separately to the front of the greenhouse where, despite the temptation to greet each other effusively, they maintained professionalism to put off anyone watching. They moved inside and were able to talk quite freely. Having caught up quickly, Biffy explained that when they went back

99 The Church of the Convento dos Jerónimos de Belém: Hieronymite Monastery founded in 1499 to commemorate Vasco da Gama's voyage of discovery.

Bertrand and his wife on
the run, 1944

to the cars, they would pass the radio in its sealed diplomatic bag from the boot of one car to the other while both drivers stood guard. Biffy handed over codes and schedules. Spare crystals for the radio were in a separate sealed bag. They returned to the cars and the switch took place without any problems. Biffy had also been asked by GC + CS to assure himself that Bertrand and his team were operating under conditions of complete secrecy and that ENIGMA was safe. Bertrand had expected to be asked and was able to reassure Biffy.

Bertrand drove straight to the Vichy embassy, repacked the radio in a French diplomatic bag and dispatched it by courier to Rivet in Vichy, where it was taken to P.C. CADIX and set up. Bertrand and Biffy were back in business. Between March 1941 and November 1942, Bertrand's team sent 2,748 messages to SIS and received 2,296 in return.

Although Biffy and his team at Alliance House had been working hard to establish networks in the occupied zone, this clandestine link with Vichy was real progress and was to continue to provide excellent intelligence until after the German occupation of Vichy in November 1943. Rivet, Ronin and Paillole were forced to flee to Algiers and then London, eventually burying the hatchet with the Free French. Bertrand remained in France. The volume of signal traffic mentioned above was to be his undoing.

Most importantly they had re-established the link to P.C. CADIX which was able to send a total of 4,679 decrypted ENIGMA messages before it had to close down and leave France in a hurry. Bertrand also

View of the area around Le Trident

had an excellent network within the PTT, the French long-distance telephone system, who monitored all telecommunication between France and Germany.

He also established links with the 'F2' network, a Polish network working jointly for both SIS (Biffy) and the Polish Intelligence Service in London. The 'F2' network, which we will have a detailed look at in Chapter 14, eventually worked across the whole of France.

The German detector service, the 'Funkabwehr', eventually tracked down P.C. CADIX. Bertrand moved his team to his hometown of Théoule-sur-Mer on the south coast, just to the west of Cannes and La Napoule. Here, Bertrand arranged the use of a villa, 'Le Trident'.[100] Le Trident is named after the three rocky outcrops projecting into the sea which drop off into deep water – deep enough for a submarine to get relatively close and for a dinghy to ferry passengers in or for a felucca from Gibraltar to get nearby to the villa. This plan, Operation CRICKET, was scheduled for the night of the 2nd/3rd of December. The operation was postponed twice, first to the 10th and then to the 25th. When London was told that the Italians had occupied Le Trident and the adjoining coastline, the operation was cancelled.

Le Trident had previously been used as a pick-up point on the 2nd of September 1942 when the felucca SEA DOG on an SIS operation VAGRANT, picked up 10 Polish members of the 'F2' network. When

100 Le Trident, designed and owned by Barry Dierks and Frank Sawyer, the same team that designed George Keun's villa, Tana Merah.

that attempt failed, Bertrand contemplated exfiltrating his wife, himself and the Poles in a French military aircraft leaving an airfield near Marseilles, but these planes left without Bertrand on November the 11th with parties of French intelligence officers. He then considered sending the Poles out into Switzerland, but again that proved impossible.

Bertrand returned to Cannes where the party remained in great danger until January the 14th when the first party of Poles left Cannes for the Franco-Spanish frontier at Perpignan. They were followed by the second party on February the 4th. On February the 5th, however, the Poles were betrayed to the French or German border guards by their Spanish guide. Two of them, Fonk and Lenoire, were captured by the Germans. Both died in German hands without revealing their secret to the Germans. The rest – and these included the people who knew the most – were captured by the Spaniards but were rescued by SIS who exfiltrated them to England. Meanwhile, Bertrand and his wife returned to their home at Théoule where Bertrand placed himself at the disposal of an SIS intelligence network KLEBER, resuming contact with Biffy via KLEBER's wireless. Bertrand remained with KLEBER for a year until January 1944. Then, he too was captured by the Germans.

After his capture on the 5th of January at the Basilique du Sacre-Coeur de Montmartre, Bertrand was taken to the headquarters of the Abwehr in Paris. There he found himself confronted by Christian Masuy, a well-known interrogator, torturer and executioner, also known to be corrupt.[101] To establish his moral domination over Masuy, Bertrand announced who he was: Colonel Gustave Bertrand of the Deuxième Bureau of France. Impressed by the stature and reputation of his captive, for Bertrand was one of the most famous names in the French secret service and one of the most wanted, Masuy arranged for Bertrand's incarceration at the five-star Hotel Continental near the Place Vendôme. There he was offered a deal by Colonel Friedrich

---

101 Masuy: (real name Georges Delfanne). His team were very dangerous for the Resistance and SIS. He was obsessed with torture – electricity, pliers, finger presses and the full spectrum of medieval torture. However, his speciality was water torture – 'La Baignoire' – where victims were held under water until they nearly drowned.

Rudolf, chief of the Abwehr in France. If Bertrand would help in a *tauschmaneuver*, a radio deception with the British, calculated to establish the time and place of the invasion, Bertrand would receive '*a heated house in Neuilly and a salary of 200,000 francs a month (against the 6,800 francs he was receiving at the time of his arrest), plus a percentage of the profits of intercepted parachutes*'. He would also receive an identity card showing that he was a member of the Abwehr, a document that would have made him '*untouchable even to the Gestapo*'.

Bertrand accepted this deal. Then, about a week after his capture and after he had been reunited with his wife, he vanished. He managed to get a message to Biffy that he was free.

He and his wife were on the run until April the 27th, when they received a message from an agent codenamed FAN FAN. SIS was sending an aircraft to collect them in the vicinity of Orléans. But, owing to the intensity of German activity, they missed that plane and another that came in May. It was not until May the 31st that they received instructions from London that led to their escape. On that evening they heard their message from the BBC: '*Les lilas blancs sont fleuris*' – the white lilac is flowering. The aircraft would land on a lilac field at a farm at Charmont, 15 kilometres northeast of Pithiviers. On the night of the 2nd/3rd of June they were successfully picked up. Bertrand described their first night in Britain as follows.

3rd of June. Rest until 10 A.M. Real breakfast. The departure for London in a car 150 kilometres. The airfield is near Cambridge. Ouf! What a curious feeling to still be alive. Arrive in London towards 12:30. All the way military convoys marked with the white star which are going to the invasion. Alliance House on Caxton Street where Biffy Dunderdale and 'Uncle' Tom (Greene) are waiting for us. The two principals of this special operation. Hugs, congratulations. I give my report of my arrest and escape to Biffy. Biffy gives it to his photographer, Ptitchkin, who will copy it and give it back to me at 5:30 P.M., the time at which (the chief of French counterespionage) Paillole will come and see me at Biffy's. Lunch at St James's Court. Then we are installed at St Ermin's Hotel in Caxton Street in a comfortable room, flowers everywhere, and a battery radio on a table to enable us to follow events. Later on I will go to see General Menzies, chief of the IS. This evening the third message from BBC during three broadcasts will tell our friends in the whole world 'Michael a rasé sa moustache' (Michael has shaved his moustache). Which is true. This I did the moment I arrived and before they took my pictures for my identity card.

Bertrand's joy at his arrival was not shared by his French colleagues in London, who shunned him then and for years afterwards for having provided 'C', not de Gaulle, with his technical intelligence and for having been 'a British secret agent'. Such indeed was the feeling against Bertrand that not until 1967, 23 years later, did Bertrand receive any form of recognition from the French Government. Even then, when he was awarded the Légion d'honneur from President de Gaulle, it was for his post-war secret service work, not for anything he had done during World War II.

On the evening of the 5th of June, 'C', Biffy, June and the Bertrands dined together at the Dunderdales' home in Wilton Place. Bertrand was to record of that event:

5th June. General Menzies invited to dinner at Biffy and June's ... He congratulated me on my brilliant conduct during the course of my resistance, during the course of my arrest and escape. He told me that he was proposing me for a British decoration as a reward for the services I had rendered. A DSO!

Bertrand's Distinguished Service Order, given for 'distinguished services under fire, under conditions equivalent to service in actual combat with the enemy', was gazetted at the end of the war. Others, of course, were to remember that day for different reasons. As Biffy and Bertrand dined, one of the most important moments in the war was unfolding. Allied invasion fleets – 5,000 ships of all sizes carrying the troops and their equipment, with an escort of 600 warships – were approaching France.

CHAPTER 12
EARLY FRENCH NETWORKS

'Harsh combats still await us, but peace will return to this torn earth and to hearts tortured by hopes and memories.'

Albert Camus

'Robert envoie ses amitiés à Jean de la Lune.'

BBC message for the JOHNNY network

'It will be alright in the end, and, if it isn't alright, it isn't the end.'

John Lennon

Between 1940 and 1944, Biffy sent 57 agents to France in addition to those already in place. By the time of the liberation, Biffy, in parallel with Cohen and the Free French, had very extensive intelligence-gathering networks across the whole of France. There were to be many setbacks and disasters along the route, but operations began almost as soon as Biffy and his team had settled into Caxton Street.

As the Germans tore into France, many French men and women set sail from the west coast of France, heading for southwest England. The fishing industry on the west coast of Brittany was substantial, with many small and medium-size vessels operating from the numerous little harbours between Ushant and the Loire. In 1940, many of these boats were still working under sail, though mechanisation had begun during the 1930s. As von Kluge's 4th Army occupied Brittany almost unopposed, vessels of all shapes and sizes were put to sea carrying refugees, both civilian and military.

Among the first to arrive in Cornwall was a young cavalry officer named Hubert Moreau, son of a French admiral.

He had escaped when being moved to Germany as a prisoner-of-war. He commandeered a small sailing boat at Beg-Meil, arriving at Polperro in Cornwall a week later on the 1st of July 1940. He was

FRANCE
- to the -
MEDITERRANEAN
SEA

1940-1944

IRELAND

ENGLAND

THE
NORTH
SEA

THE
NETHERLANDS

GERMANY

WALES

TEMPSFORD

London   MANSTON

Southampton   TANGMERE   Dunkirk

Brussels   Cologne

BELGIUM

Clandestine
Air Operations

FALMOUTH   DARTMOUTH   CHERBOURG
-EN-COTENTIN

LUXEMBURG

Clandestine
Naval Operations

Rouen

Jimmy
Phil
Groupe 31
Felix

Paris
Jade Networks

German
Occupied Zone

BREST

MONTOIRE

F₂

Nantes

FRANCE

SWIZERLAND

THE
ATLANTIC OCEAN
SEA

Free Zone
Nov. 1940

Vichy

Lyon

ITALY

THE ALPS

Bordeaux

The Bay Of Biscay

PC Cadix

Avignon

Nîmes   Aix-en-
Montpellier   Provence

Cannes

Marseille

HENDAYE

Clandestine
Border Crossing

THE PYRENEES

ANDORA

PORTUGAL

Porto

SPAIN

Madrid

ALIBI Network
Georges Charadeau

Barcelona

Palma

SIS Station including
Walter Sleator

Billy Delivers radios to
Bertrand

Valencia

THE
MEDITERRANEAN
SEA

Lisbon

Seville

ALGERIA

Scale

0   100   200 km

MOROCCO

Contemporary sketch of Moreau arriving in Falmouth   Hubert Moreau

taken to Falmouth and after several drinks and an excellent dinner, the intelligence officer who debriefed him introduced him to his wife who was French and friends with the Moreau family. During the dinner their host probed Moreau about conditions in France. *'We are completely without information about the present situation'*, he told them, *'and I know that up-to-date intelligence would be very much appreciated in London. It would be really useful to be able to follow from day to day what the Germans are doing in occupied France.'* Moreau gradually agreed that he would be interested in a clandestine return to France. The debriefing officer was Anthony Heath – on temporary detachment from Biffy's team as a Port Security Officer. In reality, he was a talent spotter for Biffy.

It was suggested that when he travelled to London the next day, he should make his way to Biffy's office in Caxton Street. Here he spent a few minutes locked in the waiting room until Tom Greene took him to meet Biffy. Biffy was delighted to see Hubert as he'd known his father, an admiral in the French Navy, from Paris. Moreau agreed to return to France by fishing boat. Biffy's staff were already developing the idea of using the fishing boats that had left Brittany as a clandestine method for infiltrating agents back into France and recovering intelligence. They had set up a small operating base in Mylor Creek, near Falmouth, drawing on the facilities of the Royal Naval base nearby for operational and logistic support. Needing a crew, Moreau went to Olympia, which was being used as a barracks for the Free French, and in the corner where the Breton fishermen were congregated, found a tough young boy he liked the look of, Raymond Le Corre.

On the 10th of July, they went down to Falmouth and found a suitable fishing boat, the *Rouanez-ar-Peoc'h* (Queen of Peace), whose crew of five immediately volunteered for the job. However, when Moreau learned that the crew had left 26 children behind in France, he decided he could not accept their help on such a dangerous mission.

He and Le Corre then decided on another boat, a Douarnenez sardine pinnace, despite it having several problems. It had a small leak and the engine had been under water, but a mechanic promised to have it back in running order within 24 hours. Moreau left the repairs to be carried out by a small boatyard under Le Corre and the RN's Base Engineer Officer and went back to London to look for a crew. Armed with a letter of authority from Biffy, he went down to Portsmouth where he interviewed a number of fishermen co-opted into the Free French Navy and serving on the battleship COURBET. He picked three men from Le-Guilvinec, who already knew Le Corre as they had all escaped to Cornwall on the same fishing boat.

Moreau returned to Falmouth with his team. Work on the boat had almost finished and Uncle Tom Greene was there to lend a hand and oversee their departure. Moreau and his crew found him more like '*a father, rather than an uncle*'.

The crew took on board 2,000 litres of petrol, while Moreau and Uncle Tom set off on a foraging expedition. They returned with a small barrel of Algerian red wine which Uncle Tom had 'liberated' from the French hydrographic vessel, *Président-Théodore-Tissier*. Tins of bully beef and biscuits were also found and stowed away on board.

On the 26th of July, they were ready. They decided to leave in the afternoon to take advantage of the good weather and make maximum use of the short hours of darkness so that they would be close to the French coast at daybreak. Available intelligence indicated that French fishing boats were obliged to only operate within four miles of the coast. They had to fly a white flag over the French flag; and had to return to port before sunset.

Uncle Tom and Mills, the Port Engineer Officer, came to have a farewell lunch with them. The stock of red wine they had liberated failed to perk them up and everyone felt rather flat when, at 15:30, the time came for them to set off. Uncle Tom became quite emotional and was obliged to blow his nose frequently. At 16:00 they sailed, and from the harbour mouth, Moreau could still see Tom waving his handkerchief.

The crossing was uneventful and at first light next day they were some miles west of Ushant, having decided not to attempt the Chenal-du-Four passage inside the island, which had many rocks and one of the most vicious tidal streams on the whole French coast. At about 08:00, they were 'buzzed' by a Dornier bomber which unnerved them as they didn't know if this was a prelude to interception by the German navy. In his briefing from Biffy and Uncle Tom, Moreau had been given a lot of latitude to land where he liked and to bring back whatever background intelligence he was able to gather, including general information on conditions in towns and villages, identity cards, movement restrictions and other details useful for future agent insertion, as well as details of defences and military units.

They landed by dinghy near Le Guilvinec and made for Le Corre's parents' house, where they spent two days gathering useful information including details of identity documents and permits, travel restrictions and the state of morale in Le Guilvinec and the surrounding villages. They also gathered a complete collection of the local newspapers since the beginning of the Occupation which included, among other things, all the directives put out by the local German Headquarters.

At one point Moreau was detained by a gendarme who took him to see the local French maritime administrator Monsieur Québriac to explain his presence. This could have gone badly but luck was with him. Moreau took Québriac into his confidence, explaining to him that he was from England and needed his help. Completely fortuitously, Québriac had served under Moreau's father in the French Navy and hated the Germans and offered to help in any way he could.

Moreau spent more than two hours with Québriac, who gave him a full overview of the area including the mood of the population and details of local military installations. The Germans often used him to promulgate administrative instructions from Kommandantur and as a local liaison officer. Moreau could not have found a better source of intelligence.

In addition, Québriac's official duties allowed him to travel to Quimper, Rennes and Lorient, so he was able to inform Moreau in great detail about regulations concerning navigation and the possibilities for landings in different ports or on local beaches. He also gave him a stack of blank forms necessary for coastal movement, including blank crew lists and customs clearance forms, ready stamped and signed. Moreau couldn't believe his luck. Biffy had his first recruit in occupied France and the beginnings of what was to grow into a vital group of port-watching networks. Moreau and his crew quickly set sail for Falmouth.

That evening, while they were off Ushant, Moreau woke up suddenly to complete silence. The engine had broken down. Luckily it was only a dirty fuel line. It took an hour to clean it and by next morning they were within sight of the English coast. One last excitement awaited them on arrival: when they failed to reply to a challenge from the signal station on Pendennis Castle at the entrance of Falmouth Harbour, a shot was fired across their bows to convey the order to heave to. They were soon boarded. Moreau produced his secret 'Laissez Passer' and they were allowed to proceed, while Mills, the Base Engineer Officer, was warned by telephone of their arrival. Mills was so excited that he was unable to wait. He jumped into a boat and came to meet them, relieved that they returned safe and sound.

Moreau's first job was to telephone Caxton Street, where he spoke to Tom Greene who was in a state of excitement at the successful mission and safe return. Moreau was told to get a good night's sleep and come up to London first thing in the morning.

Before leaving, Moreau instructed Mills to look for a better boat for future operations – they settled on a fishing boat which was a sailboat but with a powerful auxiliary engine – the sails would make them inconspicuous as there was little or no fuel in Brittany for fishing boats, but the engine could be useful in a tight spot.

Moreau caught the 7:00 train to London. He was met by Biffy and Uncle Tom, who were extremely pleased to see him. The intelligence brought back was not of great strategic importance, but it did give an idea of the conditions of life and, more particularly, of the ability to travel to and around Brittany. The documents Québriac had given to Moreau were of real value in that they opened up the possibility of future operations to the Brittany coast. While the newspapers were being studied in detail, Moreau was put to work writing a full report.

Biffy also agreed to him going to see the Free French, where he gave a short report to de Gaulle, Admiral Muselier and Colonel Dewavrin (PASSY). Moreau was unimpressed with what he found at the Free French headquarters in Carlton Gardens and it reinforced his view that working for SIS was the right decision.

Having written his report, Moreau started planning a second mission. Mills telephoned to say the new boat was ready and Moreau and Tom Greene left for Falmouth. Another agent, Michel Coulomb (COURTOIS), who was going to set up the SIS CARTWRIGHT network, would join them just before they sailed.

Moreau was given complete freedom of movement in France. It was agreed that, after landing, the boat would return to England, then return to France around the 17th of August to pick them up. During the 12 days they would have ashore, Coulomb was to go to Paris and Moreau was to both recruit additional agents and find out what he could about the Germans' preparation for invasion of Britain. To this end, he planned to see Théry, an engineer at Lorient, whom he had met on his first mission. Hopefully he would be able to give Moreau some useful information.

They sailed as planned on the 5th of August 1940 and reached Douarnenez the next day where they entered the harbour, hidden amongst the fishing fleet. They were not stopped and did not arouse suspicion by hiding in plain sight. Moreau and Coulomb went ashore and made their way to the Ty-Mad pension, a safe house which Moreau had set up on his first trip.

By 07:00 the next morning their fishing boat was on her way back to Falmouth, again without incident. Moreau and Coulomb took the train to Quimper where Coulomb left for Paris, while Moreau headed off to tour the Breton coast. They were to rendezvous at Ty-Mad on the evening of the 17th.

Moreau first went to call on the maritime administrator Québriac. He had been called away to Lorient but had left the intelligence he had collected in the care of his wife. He spent the morning gathering information from friends about what was going on in the dockyard, telling them that he had been away in Paris for some time. Large-scale building works were being carried out for the Germans, but he concluded that they could not be connected with a planned invasion of Britain which would have to take place before the end of September, if at all. It seemed clear that Brest was to become a base for U-boats and capital ships.

Moreau arranged for two of his former schoolmates to make a reconnaissance along the north coast of Brittany, looking for any signs of German invasion preparations while he conducted a reconnaissance towards Saint Malo and in the Cotentin Peninsula.

There were no signs of any suspicious concentration of shipping at Saint-Brieuc. Moreau was able to collect some information from shopkeepers and from the owner of the bistro. A certain amount of maritime activity had been seen but nothing on the scale of invasion preparations.

When he stepped off the train at Brest the next day, French and German police were checking identity documents of passengers as they left the platform. His papers were genuine, but his date of birth showed that he was old enough to be called up for military service and therefore might have been arrested. Using his local knowledge, he quickly slipped up a small staircase leading to the station restaurant where he had often been a customer. His arrival there attracted no attention and when he had finished his drink, he went down into the station concourse by the main stairs. The gendarmes had gone.

The next day, the 14th of August, he debriefed his two schoolfriends who had bicycled to Aber-Wrac'h and Morlaix without seeing anything significant. He then took the train to Quimper, where he was due to meet his friend Monsieur Québriac in front of the cathedral the next day. Québriac was on time at the RV. While they were lunching at a nearby *crêperie*, Québriac brought Moreau up to date on events at Le Guilvinec. The Germans, having picked up rumours of clandestine landings, had fortified the port, making future landings more difficult or even impossible.

Moreau needed to contact one further source of intelligence, Théry, the Chief Engineer at Lorient. Moreau caught a train there that same evening and spent part of the next day watching the port and a secondary airbase near the town. That evening, he slipped discreetly into Théry's garden. Théry promised to get him a detailed plan of the naval base, showing the new installations built by the Germans and full details of the ships and U-boats.

Moreau spent the afternoon of the 17th of August on a jetty in the fishing port, from which he could watch the entrance to the naval dockyard and take some discreet photographs. That evening, Théry handed over his detailed plan and a full report. Moreau told him to do everything possible to ensure that German workmen and sailors were segregated from the French dockyard personnel as the RAF were likely to carry out a bombing raid as a consequence of this intelligence.

On the afternoon of August the 18th, Moreau was back at Tréboul where Coulomb had already arrived from Paris. Their pick-up was due in before nightfall and Moreau kept watch at the window with a view of the bay. After dinner, having still seen nothing, he could not resist making a visit to the port in Douarnenez. As he reached the quay, he saw his three men landing. They had only just arrived and were on their way to the local bar for a few drinks. They arranged to meet at 07:00 next morning and Moreau, much relieved, went back to Ty-Mad. The next day they returned safely to Falmouth.

The CARTWRIGHT network based in Paris had outstations in Beauvais and Rheims as well as contacts with Biffy's Vichy friends who ran two courier routes for them, one through Spain, the other through Marseilles. Like many of the early networks, CARTWRIGHT did not last long. A series of arrests on the 7th and 9th of July 1941 effectively finished it off, although survivors went on to join more effective networks like the JADE networks and 'F2'. Coulomb had been betrayed by Mathilde Carré, a young French woman who was

Buvette-du-Rosmeur

responsible for the betrayal of the INTERALLIE network, whom we will meet later in Chapter 14.

For his third mission, Moreau was landed at Douarnenez where he was using a bar, the Buvette-du-Rosmeur, as their safe house and 'post box'. The bar was run by Marie Nouy, known as 'Mimi La Blonde', and her two sisters. It was conveniently close to the port, but not frequented by Germans. The three sisters were happy to use their bar to provide support to the emerging network and lodgings for the crew on their overnight visits to the port, though their readiness to do so caused some unnecessary tittle tattle.

The pick-up was fixed for a month's time. However, Moreau returned to the Buvette-du-Rosmeur from a week-long intelligence-collecting foray, during which he had obtained important German plans from Lorient, to find that in his absence a fishing boat named *Ma-Gondole*, which had sailed to England during the exodus, had returned to Douarnenez. He thought her crew had recognised him and he decided to leave as soon as possible without waiting for his own boat to pick him up. The sisters put him in touch with the skipper of a fishing boat from Etel, which was anchored outside the harbour, who agreed to get him back to England.

As Moreau was now considered compromised as a result of *Ma-Gondole*'s return to France, his usefulness to Biffy was at an end.

He went on a course at the Royal Naval College at Dartmouth and was commissioned into the Free French Navy. Moreau's operations were considered a success by Biffy and his team. He had proved the possibility of clandestine landing by boat, gathered basic intelligence on conditions in France, put together the basis of a network and started to gather more strategic intelligence on preparations for the invasion of Britain and the all-important U-boat threat.

*

While Moreau was concluding his third operation, a young 19-year-old Breton named Daniel Lomenech was arranging his own escape onboard the unfortunately named *Lusitania* – a Concarneau-based tuna fishing boat. Lomenech's parents, Odette and Louis, owned a fish and vegetable cannery at Pont-Aran between Concarneau and Lorient.

When Lomenech arrived in England on the 20th of September 1940, he was interviewed by Biffy's talent spotter François Jacalòt[102] at the Royal Patriotic School who recommended Lomenech to Biffy as someone with exceptional knowledge of the Brittany coast. Biffy took him on as Moreau's replacement. His parents had similar attitudes and outlook and were to become part of what developed into Biffy's JOHNNY network. His parents and sister were eventually captured and deported to concentration camps, as was Mimi La Blonde. The parents were executed, his sister survived but died soon after returning to France. Mimi La Blonde survived.

In November 1940, Daniel Lomenech began what was to be a long involvement in intelligence operations in Brittany. He was put ashore on a beach at Rospico between Raguénès and Port-Manech from a trawler originally named *Le-Grec*, which had been added to Biffy's Mylor flotilla. It was decided to use the name and registration number of the *Rouanez-ar-Peoc'h* because the Germans might find it more difficult to remember a Breton name accurately. He was accompanied by another agent working for Biffy, Jean Milon. They were to be picked up a month later. Milon had been recruited

---

102 Jacalòt had been the naval attaché at the French Embassy in London before the war. Biffy knew him via the Deuxième Bureau. In 1940 he stayed in London to work with Biffy.

Daniel Lomenech (right)   *L'Emigrant*

by Biffy after escaping from Brittany to the unoccupied zone then across the Pyrenees into Spain where he went to the British embassy in Madrid who got him to Gibraltar and then to England. The mission passed off without incident and, after problems with the initial pick-up, Lemenech and Milon got away on the appropriately named *L'Emigrant* with 10 Frenchmen and some British and Polish military evaders. *L'Emigrant* was subsequently added to Biffy's fleet.

During December 1940 and the early part of 1941, the Germans not only tightened fishing regulations, but the Abwehr made serious inroads into the embryonic networks being set up in France. Despite this, two operations undertaken in March by Biffy's Mylor flotilla were successful. On the 18th of March, a mission codenamed ALLAH, in support of Biffy's JOHNNY network, was led by Robert Alaterre, who had been an archivist at the French embassy in London. The second-in-command and radio operator was Jean Le Roux, who had escaped from Camaret on this same boat in December with Daniel Lomenech and Jean Milon.

They were due to be landed on the west coast of Brittany, but the Breton crew got drunk on rum, lost their way and made a landfall on the north coast near Île Vierge. The ALLAH team were put ashore near Lampaul-Ploudalmézeau. Daniel Lomenech contacted his father at Pont-Aven who came to collect them and the all-important radio in his car.

Their task was to set up an intelligence-collecting network for Biffy covering the ports of northwest France, and particularly Brest, which

Photograph taken by LIÉNART, Biffy's agent, of SCHARNHORST under camouflage netting in Brest

had become a high-priority intelligence target after the arrival of the German battle-cruisers SCHARNHORST and GNEISENAU. The ships were being frequently bombed by the RAF and there was an urgent need to find a source in the dockyard to make a battle damage assessment and find out how long it would take to repair and ready them for sea. That source was the engineering inspector of the Brest dockyard, Monsieur Hubert (LIÉNART). For nearly a year, many of Le Roux's transmissions concerned these ships.

On the 19th of April 1941, *L'Emigrant*, bearing the name *Le-Petit-Marcel* for this operation, was sent to pick up Jean Milon from a beach at Bréhec-en-Lanloup between Paimpol and Plouha. She was intercepted by two German patrol boats six miles offshore and towed into Cherbourg. Raymond Le Corre, Marcel Guénolé and Jules Kerloc'h, the Breton members of the crew, were imprisoned and eventually deported to Buchenwald.

The loss of *L'Emigrant* was a severe setback for Biffy and was compounded by the loss of Jean Milon while trying to get back to England on his own after the failed pick-up. He stole a heavy, open, six-metre-long sailing boat from a small harbour for the crossing. Jacques Mansion, de Gaulle's first emissary who should have been picked up by *L'Emigrant* at the same time as Milon, had gone off on his own and a man named Chemine, who was the third passenger, declined to join Milon because he thought the risks involved in Milon's open boat were too great. Milon put to sea on his own. He was never seen again.

*

By the end of 1940, Biffy was in difficulties over his relations with the Free French. His was not an easy hand to play; he needed them to supply manpower for his operations, but his section was supposed to operate in France independently of them, leaving close relations with them to Kenneth Cohen. He also had to attempt to re-establish contact with his friends in the Vichy administration, which in August had tried de Gaulle *in absentia* and condemned him to death. Moreover, Biffy's French friends in London, including the former French Consul-General, who subsequently returned to Vichy, tended to be strong anti-Gaullists and the Free French became convinced that Biffy shared these anti-Gaullist views, which may well have been true. Biffy, on the other hand, felt that de Gaulle's intelligence service, the BCRA, was interfering with his networks in France. This was complicated when Free French operational security came under scrutiny following the abortive Dakar expedition of October 1940.

Matters came to a head over Christmas 1940 when Churchill had Admiral Muselier,[103] de Gaulle's deputy, arrested and put into Brixton Prison on the basis of some letters passed to MI5 by a man called Meffre, appointed by PASSY to tighten up Free French security. The letters were forgeries concocted by Meffre. De Gaulle was furious: his worst suspicions about the British Government had been confirmed. He believed that Muselier's arrest had been contrived by SIS to discredit the Free French and that Meffre was a plant of Biffy in PASSY's organisation. This was not true: General Spears had recommended Meffre to PASSY, not Biffy. Biffy was exonerated by a Foreign Office investigation which found that *'the British Security Services were in no way involved'*. In fact, the Muselier affair probably suited de Gaulle quite well. Muselier and de Gaulle hated each other, Muselier

---

103 Muselier, a native of Marseilles, had given the Free French their emblem the Cross of Lorraine.

believing that he, not de Gaulle, should lead the Free French. PASSY did not have the strength of character or experience to keep Muselier in check and Muselier eventually split from de Gaulle in 1941.

The friction between Biffy and the Free French is also illustrated by the case of Jean Le Roux, 2IC and radio operator of the ALLAH mission. Originally, he had been recruited by Biffy's talent spotter because he was a radio technician and Biffy was in need of a radio operator for the JOHNNY network. Le Roux agreed provided he was a member of the Free French forces. This was agreed, but Biffy much preferred to employ individual Frenchmen without the knowledge of the Free French, if he could get away with it. On the eve of his departure for France with the ALLAH mission, having not yet joined the Free French forces, Le Roux refused to leave unless he was allowed to do so. He was quickly taken to 4 Carlton Gardens and signed a voluntary engagement. He went to France, assuming that all his signals would be shared with the Free French. He was not amused when he returned to London and found that this had not happened and that it had never been intended.

This inevitably led to friction within SIS, between Biffy's section and Cohen's. Cohen had the direct support from Claude Dansey, Assistant Chief of SIS, whose deputy he had been in the 'Z' organisation. Biffy, on the other hand, was strongly supported by Menzies. In spite of the friction between Biffy and Cohen, they remained friends, but it was nothing in comparison to the friction between SIS and the Free French and between SIS and SOE.

In February 1941, Dewavrin again complained to Dansey about Biffy's hostility to de Gaulle. Menzies smoothed things over by explaining Biffy's role to Dewavrin, primarily that of collecting strategic intelligence from the ports in France. Menzies did not mention his links to Vichy. It was agreed that Biffy was authorised to ask the Free French for manpower, but it was also made clear to Dewavrin that his 'A4' agents *need not of necessity join de Gaulle, but if they can be persuaded to do so, the less bother will occur*'. As we have already seen, having two parallel SIS French sections seemed completely inefficient, but it was the only practical solution to the split between Vichy and de Gaulle after the fall of France. It was not without potential risks. As one SIS station warned Broadway in May 1942, 'any suspicion that [the] British were in contact with Bertrand would sow the deepest seed of distrust in the heart of even our best friends among the Free French'. Biffy's work with the Poles continued to exacerbate the situation. The Free French complained that the Poles were not only allowed to operate much more independently than they were but were also permitted to recruit French agents of their own. Biffy's work with the Poles and particularly their 'F2' network are covered in Chapter 14.

Despite his difficulties with the Free French, Biffy would have a hand in the rapprochement of the various competing factors in the French hierarchy. In late 1942, Paul Paillole had escaped from France in the aftermath of the German invasion of Vichy. Some of his colleagues headed for Algiers to join Admiral Darlan, others like Paillole, Rivet and Ronin headed to London to meet SIS with whom they had been working closely via Biffy. Ronin and Paillole escaped via Gibraltar and eventually landed at Hendon at 11:00 on the 19th of December 1942. Tom Greene was there to meet them and took them to Biffy's office. That night they had dinner with Tom and Biffy before collapsing exhausted. Having been bought a new wardrobe by SIS, a meeting with Menzies took place the next morning. Both Dansey and Menzies, with Biffy and Kenneth Cohen in attendance, stressed the need for various French factions to work together. Paillole needed someone exceptional to send to France as his personal envoy to explain what was happening in London and Algiers. Biffy found him Michel Thorval. On January the 19th 1943 at 02:30, he was parachuted into France near Issoire. Within hours he was in radio contact with London and Algiers. He returned to London via Lysander pick-up on February the 18th, having successfully completed his mission. Within weeks, all the French factions were talking to each other despite a significant setback with the assassination of Admiral Darlan. Biffy, his team and Kenneth Cohen can take significant credit for this rapprochement.

During 1940 and the early part of 1941, Biffy's intelligence-gathering efforts were beginning to pay off. He had mounted five missions from Mylor Creek to Brittany before the capture of *L'Emigrant* put an end to these operations. The arrival of Daniel Lomenech sig-nalled the start of other maritime operations using French trawlers, an idea that had already occurred to Biffy:

What you want is one of the local trawlers that are working and behaving like a Frenchman … these little trawlers have permission to stay out three or four days at a time and if we could get another one of them we can lurk about and instead of the agent ashore having to fit in with our plans entirely, we can fit in with when he can deliver.

By early 1941, Biffy had several networks in both occupied France and with his contacts in Vichy. On the 15th of November 1940 one of the most successful early networks was established in Paris, the INTERALLIE network set up by the Poles. The INTERALLIE story eventually ended in disaster and the fallout would preoccupy both Biffy and Tom Greene throughout the rest of the war.

*

The JOHNNY network, meanwhile, was providing good intelligence from Brittany. JOHNNY was set up in early 1941 by Daniel Lomenech, his parents Louis and Odette, Robert Alaterre, Jean Le Roux and Jean Milon and began operations on the 18th of March 1941.

The network operated in all the key towns and ports of Brittany and elsewhere including Quimper, Brest, Paris, Nantes, Rennes, Rouen, Bordeaux, Lorient and Morlaix and excellent intelligence on ports and maritime operations, including battle damage assessments of the bombing of the German battle-cruisers SCHARNHORST and GNEISENAU as to their seaworthiness and likely movements. They had also set up clandestine courier lines into Spain. It had the first wireless set operating from Brittany to London, with its first success-ful transmission on the 26th of March 1941.

The network was commanded by Robert Alaterre until the 1st of December 1941 when he escaped to England following a betrayal and penetration of the network by the Gestapo.

Robert Alaterre

He was succeeded briefly by André Malavoux, but in February 1942 he was also betrayed and arrested. The network was then taken over by Jean Le Roux who ran it until June 1942 when, following its betrayal by Jean Pierre Lamandé,[104] a wave of arrests broke up the network. Of its 180 agents, 60 were sent to concentration camps where 35 of them died, and 53 were executed, including Daniel Lomenech's father Louis.

Daniel Lomenech escaped to England after going on the run. He spent the rest of 1942 and 1943 running covert fishing boats from Dartmouth and Falmouth to the coast of Brittany, delivering and recovering agents for SIS, installing dead letterboxes and bringing out classified mail containing valuable intelligence. Lomenech was awarded the DSC and bar for *'distinguished service on hazardous special duties in French waters'*.

As a footnote to the JOHNNY story, François Jacalòt, in his capacity as Biffy's recruiter amongst the French in London, met André Pajot in the French House pub in Soho. Pajot outlined to Jacalòt a scheme to return to France and set himself up in Paris selling cocaine in nightclubs to German officers. Extraordinarily, Jacalòt was able to sell this scheme to Biffy on the basis that if Pajot could get himself to Paris, Biffy would find a means get him the cocaine. Pajot with the codename SOSTHÈNE got himself to Paris, via Portugal, Spain and the unoccupied zone. On the night of the 27th of June 1941, in

104 One of the network radio operators, who was turned by the Gestapo in exchange for the release from prison of his fiancée Lisette Pastor.

an operation codenamed VALISE, the fishing boat *Vincent Michelle* rendezvoused with the submarine HMS SEALION, five kilometres from the French coast in the Bay of Bréhec. Six escapees were put on the submarine. Two radios, money and clothing were transferred to the *Vincent Michelle* as well as several kilos of cocaine for Pajot. The cocaine was later taken by Jean le Roux to Paris and dropped for Pajot at a pre-arranged RV with a cut-out called George Crosnier at 21 Rue de la Villette. History doesn't relate how successful the addiction operation was or what happened to Pajot and the money he earnt by selling the cocaine! The cocaine plot may seem unusual to us today, but in the 1920s and 1930s in Paris, at the height of Les Années Folles, cocaine use was not only very widespread, but considered normal, even being sold freely as Vin Marini à la Coca du Pérou and Pastilles Marini au Chlorhydrate de Cocaine. A French National Intelligence report of the 1920s highlighted German production of morphine and cocaine for deliberate marketing in France to create a climate of addiction. The German Army was no stranger to drugs. Tablets of Pervitin were given to all troops taking part in the invasion of Holland, Belgium and France. Pervitin is crystal meth. The 1st Panzer Division consumed 20,000 tablets in May and June 1940 leading to the description of '*Petrol and Pervitin equals Blitzkreig.*' There would have been a ready market for drugs amongst the Germans in France.

*

In addition to establishing clandestine maritime routes into and out of France, SIS made use of the RAF's newly established Special Duties squadrons 138 and 161. These were set up to airland and recover agents, to bring back intelligence using Lysander aircraft and to parachute agents and equipment using Hudson, Halifax, Stirling and Whitley.

The Lysander was the workhorse used extensively to ferry agents into and out of enemy territory at night, as well as recover Allied airmen who had been shot down and were on the run. The aircraft

Special Duties, Lysander

were modified for the role. The undersides were painted matt black to make the aircraft harder to spot from the ground. Normal camouflage paint was retained on the sides of the body and tops of the wings to make it harder to see against the ground. A 150-gallon fuel tank was fitted to the belly of the aircraft to increase its range and a ladder was fitted to the port side of the fuselage to give passengers faster access in and out of the aircraft.

The aircraft were stripped down to the bare essentials to save weight and make additional space. The Special Duty pilots had to navigate by moonlight, using just a map and compass. Usually, they were looking for an improvised landing strip in a field marked out with fires or torches by an SIS or SOE agent or the local Resistance network, although they were advised not to rely on only spotting these lights and to ensure the proper security recognition signals were used. Pilots were told not to land if the recognition signal was incorrect, the layout of the flares was not as specified or if the indicated field was not the one they expected. Once on the ground, a fast turnaround was essential to avoid any German reaction.

If the mission involved both the insertion and extraction of agents, the outgoing agent would hand out his own luggage and take in the luggage of the homecoming agent before disembarking. In extremis up to four passengers could be carried in the Lysander,

Philip Schneidau's hockey team, 1939

jammed into the rear cockpit in extreme discomfort. Once loaded the Lysander would quickly get airborne again, climbing away as fast as possible.

The first operation carried out by the newly formed Special Duties Squadron was carried out for Biffy. On October the 9th 1940, Flying Officer Jacky Oettle, flying a Whitley, dropped Philip Schneidau (PHILLIPSON, FELIX) by parachute into the Fontainebleau area. He was to be picked up by Lysander 10 days later, the night of the 19th/20th of October. This was to be the first Lysander pick-up of the war.

Philip Schneidau – short, stocky and irrepressible – was born in the Channel Islands in 1903. As a young man he lived with his parents in Paris in the 1930s. His parents were wealthy and Biffy got to know them socially. Philip played international hockey for France before the war. Although he grew up in Paris, when he was 21, he chose British citizenship. When war broke out, he volunteered for the RAF. He became driver and interpreter to Air Marshal 'Ugly' Barratt, the commander of the British Air Forces in France. After the fall of France, Philip was evacuated to England by warship along with Barratt and the British Ambassador. His parents, wife Simone and young son remained in France. In the autumn of 1940, he responded to an appeal throughout the Armed Forces for bi-lingual French

Philip Schneidau   Philip in disguise

speakers for special operations and was interviewed by SIS. Biffy saw his name and immediately took him on before anyone else could get their hands on him.

After training, they hatched a plan for him to return to France to set up a network in the Paris area codenamed FELIX. He would be parachuted to a drop zone close to his family home at Montigny-sur-Loing near Fontainebleau. He would first visit his wife and son and then continue to Paris to see his parents. The whole family would be doubly at risk because, not only were they to be involved in SIS work, they were Jewish.

Philip was scheduled to be dropped on the night of the 9th/10th of October 1940, but because of bad weather the drop was cancelled five times in a row, by which time Philip was becoming increasingly frustrated.

In preparation for this trip to France, Philip had to do three things: change his appearance, learn about carrier pigeons and arrange for his return journey. He changed his appearance by growing a modest beard and wearing spectacles. He was afraid that his clean-shaven face might be too well known from the days when he had been a hockey international. The pigeons were to be his only means of transmitting a message from France. In those days clandestine radios were in their infancy. He would need to be able to send a message if there were any problems with his pre-planned pick-up. The only alternatives would be a pick-up by a motor gunboat on the coast of Brittany or a long hike over the Pyrenees.

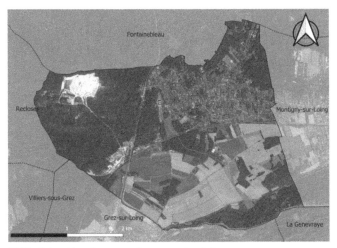

Philip Schneidau drop zone in quarry, top left

Philip was briefed to keep his pigeon inside a sock and carry it in his rucksack. As instructed, he cut off the toe of a pair of socks and carefully put his pigeon, 'Kemley Lass' code number NURP.36.JH, into a sock so that her head stuck out of the hole at the toe.

Philip landed by parachute in a sand quarry near Bourron-Marlotte, about two kilometres from his wife's family villa Les Troènes.

The drop zone was selected because of its visibility from the air, even at night. There was to be no reception team on the ground. The drop was made successfully and Philip reached the villa at 06:00. He made a stealthy approach to the back door and, seeing the housekeeper in the kitchen, was about to enter when the housekeeper saw him and warned him off, indicating that there were Germans in the house.

He withdrew through the forest at the back of the house and circled round to a house across the road from Les Troènes, which was owned by Henri Glépin. Glépin confirmed that the Germans had requisitioned the villa and that Simone and their son, Pierre, were living in Paris with her parents Paul and Evéline Schiffmacher. Leaving his pigeon and his parachute with Glépin,[105] Philip travelled to Paris and

---

105 Henri Glépin joined the FELIX network and went on to assist with parachute and air landing receptions and other resistance work throughout the war. He was never caught and his work was recognised by a certificate signed by Field Marshal Montgomery in May 1946.

Les Troènes

together the family set about interviewing close friends and business contacts. By the time Philip returned to Fontainebleau for his Lysander pick-up, he had created the nucleus of Biffy's FELIX network. Paul (NAPOLEON) and Simone would expand the network in Philip's absence.

However, the Lysander failed to make the pick-up rendezvous again due to very bad weather. Philip encoded a message saying that he had established the basis of the network and was awaiting pick-up. The message was dispatched by pigeon at 08:00 on a Sunday morning. At 16:30 the same day the pigeon arrived at its owner's pigeon loft at East Grinstead; 15 minutes later, the owner telephoned for a despatch rider who took the message to the Air Ministry in London. The message arrived at 18:30, just over 12 hours from the release of the pigeon in France. It took another 13 hours before there was anybody on duty with the necessary clearance to open the message and telephone Caxton Street.[106]

Meanwhile, on the 19th of October 1940, Flight Lieutenant Farley, frustrated by the bad weather and aware of how anxiously Philip

[106] The story of the use of pigeons was to have a sequel in 1982. Biffy's neighbours in Surrey, David and Anne Martin, were renovating a fireplace in their 17th-century house when they found the skeleton of a bird with a ring on its leg and a red plastic capsule – the usual mark of a military carrier pigeon from World War II. When they unscrewed the capsule they found a coded message, 27 groups of letters and numbers written on very thin paper. Biffy immediately told them to forget about it and certainly not publish anything. The message also contained the pigeon's personal identity code NURP 37 DK 76. Sadly, not Philip's pigeon which got their message through identity code NURP 36 JH 190. Eventually in 2010 Bletchley Park took an interest in this message and there is now a permanent exhibition, 'Pigeons at War'.

would be waiting for his pick-up, persuaded his Squadron Leader to let him try the operation. It was agreed on the condition that, if the weather was still bad over the French coast, he would abort. He took off from Tangmere in marginal conditions.

The weather improved over France and Farley found the field south of Fontainebleau on the Plateau des Trembleaux. As arranged, Philip switched on the inverted 'L'-shaped pattern of lights which he had designed with Farley on a tablecloth in Oddenino's restaurant – the basic flarepath design for a Lysander pick-up landing which never needed to be improved throughout the war.

Farley landed at 01:17. Philip clambered in and Farley immediately took off. After take-off, he noticed something was jamming the free movement of the elevator. He throttled back until he could clear it, losing a little height. At this moment a bullet, fired by a German sentry in the nearby village of Marlotte, came up between Farley's knees and went through the compass. They were lucky. For some time, Farley could see to map-read by moonlight, but then the cloud built up. Climbing to 16,000 feet, they were still in cloud with no navigation aid at all, having lost the compass. The radio was out of action due to intense rain and the rear cockpit, with no canopy, was bitterly cold. Over the French coast, the weather was just as foul as it had been when Farley had taken off from Tangmere. There was a strong south-westerly gale blowing and Farley was afraid that they might be drifting back over enemy territory. They were completely lost. Farley told Philip to look out for any sight of land and somewhere where they might make a forced landing.

At about 06:30 Farley said that the petrol tanks were empty and that they were flying on 'fresh air'. Luckily at that moment Philip reported seeing a place on the top of some cliffs where they could land. Farley was worried that they still might be over enemy territory. At this point the fuel finally ran out. They glided down and, when about 50 feet up, they saw that the ground above the cliffs had been planted with wooden anti-glider posts. Farley told Philip to get on the floor of the cockpit prior to landing because of the danger of a wing snapping off and decapitating him.

When they hit the ground, the wings came off as predicted. As

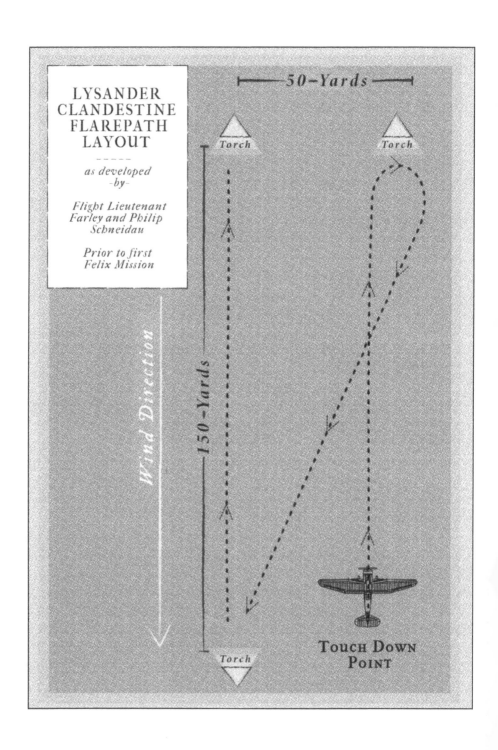

LYSANDER
CLANDESTINE
FLAREPATH
LAYOUT

- - - - -

as developed
-by-

Flight Lieutenant
Farley and Philip
Schneidau

Prior to first
Felix Mission

50-Yards

Torch

Torch

Wind Direction

150-Yards

Torch

Torch

TOUCH DOWN
POINT

they might still have been in enemy territory, Philip took off his civilian clothes and stuffed them into a rucksack together with other compromising material. In his underwear, he jumped out of the wreck of the Lysander and shouted at Farley: *'Wally, get out! It will catch fire.'* Farley replied: *'If there's one thing it won't do it's catch fire. There's no fucking petrol.'* Farley climbed out and set off to look for help. If he came back with friendly help, he would raise his right arm. Otherwise, Philip should throw everything incriminating over the cliff.

Ten minutes later Farley reappeared escorted by two soldiers. Farley had his right arm raised and the soldiers' rifles were slung over their shoulders. Philip hastily got dressed and went to meet them. They had landed in Scotland. The pair were taken to nearby RAF Connel, near Oban, where they were brought before the station commander, who quizzed them as to who they were and what their mission was. Farley gave his name, rank and number. Philip said that they had been doing a special recce over the Atlantic, but that he was not allowed to give his name or any further details. This did not amuse the station commander who placed them under close arrest. Eventually word came through from London that they were to be released immediately and sent to London without further questioning.

Philip made another trip into France on the 10th of March 1941. The drop zone was 700 yards from his house in a clearing on the edge of the Forest of Fontainebleau. The purpose of the operation was to deliver a radio, codes and cash to the FELIX network in Paris. There was a strong easterly wind and Philip's parachute was blown into the forest and he hit a tree. It remained open and dragged Philip up the tree swinging him hard against it, knocking out two teeth and damaging one leg so that he walked with a slight limp. It took him an hour and a half to get everything down, including the all-important radio which had been damaged in the drop.

Philip found a reliable dentist in Paris to repair his teeth and someone to repair the radio. He discovered that this dentist had another 'patient' who was a German colonel. Under threats, the dentist had agreed to help this officer smuggle gold back to Germany every time

Paul Schiffmacher (Philip Schneidau's father-in-law) and Henri Glépin

he went home on leave. A thick layer of no doubt stolen gold had to be attached to the back of his front teeth. After this routine had been in progress for some time, the German colonel was so well disposed to the French dentist that he made him an honorary member of his officers' mess. Subsequently, Philip was invited to dine there as the dentist's guest. In conversation with senior German officers, he was able to gather useful intelligence.

The FELIX network would survive for almost two years. It worked closely with the INTERALLIE network, which would be its undoing. Philip's father-in-law was eventually betrayed by Mathilde Carré and he was arrested on the 12th of January 1942. He was deported to Buchenwald but survived. Felix Jond (JULES, MOULIN), who had been the 2IC, took over the network which continued to operate till 1944. Simone and her mother continued to help escapees by hiding them in their Paris flat.

Philip was picked up from a field not far from his house on the 10th of May 1941, the pick-up being 'covered' by small bombing raids in the area to keep German defences busy. Despite this, the Lysander was chased by German night fighters, which they managed to evade by some expert flying.

Biffy felt Philip had done quite enough in France and might also have been blown along with his father-in-law, so kept him on the staff of Caxton Street as an agent handler, conducting officer for departing agents and liaison officer with the SIS naval department[107] and the Special Duties Air Squadrons. For these early missions, Philip was awarded the DSO, gazetted on the 25th of May 1943 with no citation or unit, normal procedure for an SIS decoration, but in itself a breach of security.

His was to be the friendly face that stepped out of the darkness at Tangmere, Tempsford, Falmouth or Dartmouth to welcome returning agents. On road or rail trips to London he would remind the agents of their tradecraft in spite of their relief at being back on British soil, regularly reminding them not to speak French.

*

Alice Marguerite was a former Deuxième Bureau operator, with links to Rivet and Paillole, having worked for them from 1925–37 on anti-Bolshevik operations. Because of Biffy's close relations with the Deuxième Bureau and their operations against the Russians in the 1920s and 1930s, he would have certainly known about her, or could well have met her. Alice was one of the true members of 'La Résistance de la Première heure'.[108] She began by helping French and Allied servicemen escape to Spain. She herself made her way to Spain accompanied by Pierre Goutier. On arrival in San Sebastian, she arranged a meeting at the British Consulate and, after initial discussions with Harold Goodman, the Consul and his deputy Alan Hillgarth,[109] she and Goutier were taken to the Hotel Continental to meet the newly arrived SIS team, Leonard Hamilton-Stokes and David 'Togo' Maclaren. They had been sent by Biffy to work with Walter Sleator, setting up cross-border networks from northern Spain into France. They were already in touch with four Frenchmen, Robert Urbain, Jean Paloc, André Nodon and Jean Richard, who were keen to get back into France and had agreed to work for SIS. This

---

107 See *A Dangerous Enterprise*.
108 Resister from the beginning – a designation separating those who began their resistance activities immediately as opposed to others who waited to see which way the wind was blowing.
109 Alan Hillgarth had provided high-grade intelligence to SIS during the Spanish Civil War. He was a close friend of Winston Churchill and had direct access to Stewart Menzies.

Alice Marguerite

embryonic network was given the codename GEORGES – FRANCE/
GROUPE 31.[110]

Alice and Goutier were immediately co-opted, Alice returned
to France on the 30th of August 1940 whilst Goutier was sent to
England for training. Her first network was set up in Paris inside the
Prefecture of Police. This cell was run by Sarah Rosieu and Roger
Bertrand. They had been recruited by Jaime de Lavsende Reichasch,
a professional French intelligence officer, who knew Goodman and
Hillgarth from the Spanish Civil War. Alice returned to Spain to meet
Goutier when he returned from England. Together they crossed the
Spanish border at Hendaye on the 3rd of December 1940; Goutier
became Alice's deputy in GROUPE 31. Alice took on the *nom de
guerre* Madame Louis. Together they posed as a married couple
under the aliases of Mr and Mrs Georges and Mr and Mrs Perrin.

GROUPE 31 acted as an umbrella organisation, absorbing many
'homegrown' spontaneous resistance networks or other SIS networks that had been disrupted by enemy activity, such as LA BANDE
À SIDONIE and the remnants of JOHNNY. It was to become one of
Biffy's success stories, eventually operating 45 cells in five countries including Rostock in Germany. Operating centres included
35 in France (five in Vichy, one in Corsica, one in Monaco), four
in Germany, three in Italy and two in Spain, managing some 263
agents together with a network of 53 couriers run directly by Alice

110 GROUPE 31: SIS code 23031 – 23 being the country code for Spain.

to coordinate the activities of the individual cells. Intelligence gathered included details of coastal fortifications, naval and merchant shipping, oil deliveries from Spain, U-boat operations and aircraft production in Germany.

At the end of the war, the SIS mission to France run by Tom Greene and designated the 'Anglo-French Communications Bureau'[111] summed up the activities of GROUPE 31:

> *The '31' Group provided extremely valuable military and economic information from all over France with ramifications into Corsica, Italy, Belgium and Germany. The information supplied on ship and submarine movements from Bordeaux and the Brittany coast was particularly useful, and was transmitted with the minimum of delay by wireless from its headquarters. The Group also specialised in reporting on submarine base and aircraft construction. There was a regular courier service to Spain.*

However, things were not always going to be easy, as a result of the treachery of Madeleine Téry Vicomtesse de la Villeaucomte, who had become the mistress of a German officer, a fact not known to GROUPE 31 when she was approached to join the network. Her betrayal was to lead ultimately to the execution or deportation of most of the leadership of GROUPE 31. Fifteen, including Pierre Goutier, were shot on the 27th of November 1942 at Mont Valérien. Alice[112] and her sister Madeleine were deported to concentration camps but survived the war.

As a result of the arrests of their GROUPE 31 leaders in October 1941, André Peulevey and his network leader Louis Turban, who had been running the Rennes section of GROUPE 31, had to lie low. No wireless transmissions and minimal contact with other agents. The first surge of arrests ended on the 20th of November. After that they

---

111 Anglo-French Communications Bureau: Established in Paris in 1944 to discover what had happened to their agents, to recover money and equipment and to process honours and awards. Based at 8 Avenue des Tilleuls Villa Montmorency.

112 Alice was supposedly awarded the Military Cross by SIS, but there is no official record of this. It is also believed that she held the rank of Sub Lieutenant in the RNVR which would have made the award of the MC possible as opposed to a George Cross.

André Peulevey

very cautiously made contact in Rennes with the JOHNNY network. Turban and André got a message back to London when the head of JOHNNY, Robert Alaterre, returned to London by boat on the 28th of November. Turban wanted to get André to London for training, to discuss plans for restructuring and to get him away from the German round-ups, including not only their penetration of GROUPE 31 but also the destruction of the INTERALLIE network, betrayed by Mathilde Carré (See Chapter 12). Arrangements were made with Biffy in London to extract him using the SIS gunboat route from Brittany to Dartmouth and he left on the night of the 6th/7th of January 1942, on MGB 314 from the Guenioc Island Pinpoint.

André was met at Dartmouth by Phillip Schneidau and immediately taken to London to meet Biffy. He was asked if he would go back and continue to work for 'A4' and rebuild a network coopting the remains of JOHNNY into GROUPE 31. He agreed and was then put through a concentrated three-week training course – it had to be short as if he was away too long from his railway job the Germans would notice. He could only be away from his post for 15 days, arranging sick leave due to rectal bleeding.

He returned to France on the night of the 1st of February again on MGB 314 to the Guenioc Pinpoint, on an SIS operation code-named TURQUOISE.[113] Unfortunately the Germans had continued their disruption of GROUPE 31. Turban had been arrested a few

---

113 For a full account see *A Dangerous Enterprise*.

days previously as had their radio operator Alain de Kergolay, who broke under torture and gave André away. André returned to his SNFC office in Rennes. He dropped into the office of the German Head of Railway Operations for a cup of coffee. The German covered his surprise and made an excuse to leave for a minute; 15 minutes later André was in the hands of the Gestapo. He was interrogated and tortured for 18 months, 11 of which he was kept in solitary confinement. Eventually he was deported to Natzweiler and Dachau. He survived and was able to report to Tom Greene at the Anglo-French Communications Bureau, delivering the 50,000 francs operating funds and his radio, which he was able to hide before being arrested.

When Walter Sleator fled Paris in June 1940, he evacuated his staff and some of the Rolls Royce cars to the Franco depot in Biarritz. One of these was Biffy's personal Rolls, Silver Ghost, which he had sent south in 1939. Sleator had lent him the Rolls 20–25 'for official duties'. Biffy's own car was quickly appropriated by the Germans and disappeared. The 'loan' Rolls story is at Annex A.

Sleator left Paris in two cars, a Simca and a Rolls Royce 1935 Phantom II Continental.[114] It is believed that one of his passengers in the Rolls was Kenneth Cohen, the commander of the 'Z' team in Paris, who had been ordered home by Dansey. He was to fly out of Le Bourget airport. Sleator offered him a lift, but rather embarrassingly the Rolls broke down en route. Eventually repaired, Cohen made his flight. Sleator nursed the car to his family home at Oysonville 79 kilometres from Paris, where it was left hidden until the end of the war. Sleator made it to Madrid. He had already agreed to join SIS and help with operations from Spain back into France. On the 15th of June 1940, he flew to London for briefing and some hurried training. He was also given a temporary commission in the RAF Reserve. By the end of the month, he was back in Madrid and given diplomatic cover so he could work out of the embassy. While in London he coincided briefly with Biffy and they spent a few days together planning how to set up their first network which was to be called ALIBI. In time its

---

114 Sold at Bonhams during the 2021 Goodwood Festival of Speed for £117,300.

Jacques Kellner   Georges Paulin

first sub-network would be set up in Paris known as Réseau PHILL. ALIBI would continue to operate for SIS under Biffy's control until the end of the war. PHILL was not so lucky.

Before the war, in his capacity as Managing Director of 'La Franco', Walter Sleator had become very good friends with some of those he worked with in the luxury car and coach-building business. Notable amongst these were Georges Paulin, Jacques Kellner and Jean Schoofs, who had married Sleator's sister Aileen. Together they would form the nucleus of Réseau PHILL.

Georges Charadeau (CHAMBON or CHOBIÈRE) had been recruited by Biffy's friends in the Deuxième Bureau to carry out intelligence-gathering in Spain during the Spanish Civil War. He

Pau Grand Prix 1930, Georges Charadeau is the man with glasses, fourth from the left

made many contacts and honed his skills as a clandestine intelligence officer. When the war ended, he returned to France but kept up with his contacts in Spain, as did SIS. On June the 23rd 1940, he left his home in Pau, heading for Madrid with the intention of joining the Free French. It took him two days to get to Madrid. Arriving at the British Embassy he was immediately put in touch with Walter Sleator, newly returned from London with a mandate to set up cross-border networks.

Sleator persuaded Charadeau that working for SIS was the most effective way forward. Sleator gave him Biffy's directive and agreed to fund a network; ALIBI was born. It was certainly one of the first SIS réseaux and remained active until August the 30th 1944, when it was no longer needed. In mid-July, Charadeau brought his family to Madrid for security reasons – to prevent them being taken prisoner and tortured in order to put pressure on Charadeau if he was ever captured. His wife Yvonne opened an haute couture boutique to act as a cover for the ALIBI 'letterbox' and later 'A5's' network ALLIANCE.[115] The boutique was both an excellent cover but also a commercial success, counting both Franco's wife and the German Ambassador's wife as clients who would gossip and drop small pieces of intelligence.

ALIBI's mission, as directed by Biffy in London, was to gather military, industrial and political strategic intelligence. Sleator had got his mistress, Georgette Jaguenau, known as 'Zette', out of France and she acted as courier and liaison officer between the boutique and Walter's office in the British Embassy.

In August 1940, Biffy directed Georges Charadeau to cross into France to contact Commander Abel Savalot, the US Naval Attaché to the Vichy Government. Savalot was one of Biffy's contacts from his Paris days. Between them, Sleator, Charadeau and Savalot were able to support deliveries to ALIBI cells in France including funds, real and forged documents, radio sets, codes and weapons.

Between 1940 and 1942 they carried out 50 border crossings. As

---

115 ALLIANCE was run by Kenneth Cohen. Marie-Madelaine Fourcarde was the organiser and leader in the field. She had replaced Georges Loustanau-Lacau (NAVARRE) who had been betrayed to the Gestapo. Loustanau-Lacau had been talent-spotted by Biffy in Paris in 1938.

Georgette Jaguenau, 'Zette'

ALIBI grew, it spread its network across the whole of France and beyond. Its purpose was only to gather intelligence and it steered well clear of SOE networks whose aim was offensive action. At its height, ALIBI had 423 operators and 20 sub-networks. One of these sub-networks was PHILL, which was set up in Paris to gather intelligence on the armaments industry, aircraft production and jet fighter developments.

After the mass exodus of the summer of 1940, people gradually returned to Paris, including Jacques Kellner and many of his workers, including Georges Paulin and Jean Schoofs. Schoofs became the recruiter for Réseau PHILL. Sleator and Charadeau had already visited Paulin in the south of France and asked him to be on standby. Now back in Paris, it was the time to become operational. Jacques Kellner's company was gradually incorporated into the development of German aircraft, including the embryonic Messerschmitt 262 Jetfighter, clearly of great interest to SIS. Paulin could have joined Kellner's company but could not bring himself to be directly involved with the enemy, so got himself a job as a dentist. He went to work at the practice of Emile Dürenberger. Dürenberger was a high-society dentist who had had connections with the Deuxième Bureau before the war and was still in contact with them through their Vichy organisation. His exact allegiance was questionable – agent, double agent or triple agent? His clients included senior Nazis in Paris, among them General Stülpnagel, the military Commander of Paris. Ostensibly he reported to Rivet and Perruche in Vichy, who in turn passed on intelligence to Biffy in London. However, Paulin also used the practice as a cover for PHILL activities and as a live letterbox. Members of the PHILL network were properly registered as patients so that they could deliver information to him. Documents were hidden in a hollow statue of the Goddess Diana on the mantelpiece of Paulin's office.

The PHILL network gradually took shape over the early months of 1941. Jean Schoofs approached Jacques Kellner to see if he was interested in working with him, for Sleator and for SIS in London. He agreed immediately. Paulin was activated separately but at the same time. In turn, Kellner recruited his factory foreman Robert Etienne. PHILL was taking shape; in time it would have 14 key operators including Roger Raven, a metal worker at Kellner, Fernand Fenzy and Marius Roubille. Jean Schoofs became the courier between Paris and Madrid. His wife Aileen was the cell liaison officer in Paris. Marius Roubille, a train conductor on the route between Paris and Toulouse, was recruited to manage the courier service between Paris and Madrid. Roubille would go to Paulin's dental practice to receive messages for carriage to Spain. While Roubille was seated in the treatment chair, Paulin would extract the documents written in minuscule handwriting from the statue of Diana and during treatment slip them into Roubille's hand who in turn slipped them into his jacket lining.

As well as treating his fellow agents of PHILL, Paulin also treated Karl Bömelburg, the Head of the Gestapo. High stakes indeed.

Now that PHILL was established, it needed a radio to transmit its intelligence to London. Biffy arranged for Sleator to get a radio to Marius Roubille in Toulouse. He in turn took it to Paris and delivered it to Paulin. Paulin took the radio to Kellner in his office at his factory in Billancourt, where, after showing it to Robert Etienne, he locked it in a filing cabinet, later moving it to a purpose-built 'hide', behind the skirting board in his office.

Unfortunately, the Paris – Toulouse courier route had come under German suspicion and had been blown when one of Roubille's fellow railway workers caved in after being threatened with torture and the firing squad. A hidden container with aircraft drawings intended for SIS had been found. It also contained some of Roubille's

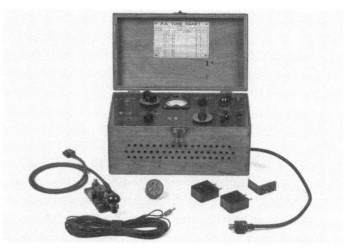

SIS clandestine radio, c. 1942

personal correspondence. He was put under surveillance and they observed his meetings with Jean Schoofs at the Grand Hotel Regina in Toulouse. The Gestapo used the Bonny Lafont gang[116] to carry out the surveillance and ultimately the arrest of the PHILL operators. Not only did the demise of PHILL stem from the discoveries of the courier route, there was another source of intelligence for the Germans – an informer who had been working for them since before the war called Mauser – a Swiss German electrical engineer who knew both Paulin and Fernand Fenzy. He was also a patient at the Dürenberger dental practice and had somehow worked out that the PHILL network was using the practice at 3 Place de Rennes as a clearing house for the high-grade intelligence it was delivering to London and that Paulin's 'patients' were in fact members of the network. This was passed to the Gestapo. So, two lines of intelligence were developing about PHILL and not only was Roubille under surveillance, Paulin was being watched as well. It was not only Mauser who fingered the dental clinic. Henri Lafont had questioned a Frenchman who he suspected was ostensibly working for Vichy, but in reality was working

116 The Bonny Lafont gang – The Carlingue or French Gestapo, jointly run by Pierre Bonny, a corrupt policeman and Henri Lafont, a criminal. Based at 93 Rue Lauriston in Paris, it worked for the Gestapo and was renowned for its brutality and corruption. Bonny and Lafont were executed in December 1944.

for Biffy's friends and passing information to London. In any event a suspicious picture was developing. Paulin had a strange collection of patients – a railway worker, a former army signals officer, an architect and a woman who seemed to spend an inordinate amount of time in the dentist's chair. Their surveillance also noticed the link between the dentist surgery and the Kellner factory at Boulogne-Billancourt which was producing parts for Messerschmitt. Between the Abwehr, the Gestapo and their French acolytes and the Bonny Lafont gang, a comprehensive surveillance and penetration operation sealed the fate of the PHILL network.

On Friday October the 31st – the same day the radio set was delivered – Aileen Schoofs, Georges Paulin, Jacques Kellner and Joseph Figoni were arrested. The complicated journey of the radio set started with Biffy in Caxton Street, then by diplomatic bag to Sleator in the embassy in Madrid, then to Georges Charadeau across the French border to Toulouse before it arrived in Paris. From the time the set was handed over in Toulouse, moved to Paris, delivered to Paulin at the dental practice and then taken by him to the Kellner factory, they had been under surveillance. The Germans also had Paulin's patient list supplied by Dürenberger with little or no coercion.

Further arrests followed, Robert Etienne on the 2nd of November and Marius Roubille on the 3rd. Both had been left to 'run' to see if they would expose anyone else the Germans did not know about. Roger Raven and Fernand Fenzy were arrested on the 6th. PHILL was effectively finished in the space of a week. The only one to get away was Jean Schoofs. He was warned by Georges Charadeau about the roll-up of PHILL and told to disappear. This was the one stroke of luck in the whole debacle as he knew the whole structure of ALIBI, Sleator's and Georges Charadeau's work in Madrid and the link back to Biffy in London. Jean went on the run to Toulon where he tried to disappear, but the Germans were still on his trail. He eventually escaped to Spain and after a period lying low resumed work for SIS – this time for Marie-Madeleine Fourcade and the ALLIANCE network, controlled in London by Kenneth Cohen.

The Germans tried the PHILL team by military tribunal. Of the 14 members of the network, five were sentenced to death, five were deported to concentration camps and four escaped and went underground.

On the 21st of March 1942 at 16:00 the five were taken to the execution ground at Mont-Valérian and tied to posts. Paulin's shoulder and arm were in a plaster cast due to the extreme torture he had suffered – as they all had. None of them said a word. Jacques Kellner and Robert Etienne were shot first at 16:01, Fernand Fenzy at 16:05, Roger Raven at 16:15 and finally Georges Paulin at 16:23. The Germans were in no hurry and as a final act of torture had made Paulin wait and watch his comrades being shot for 25 minutes, a very long time when you know the final bullet is for you.

Marius Roubille was lucky to escape execution and was deported to Mauthausen where he was murdered by lethal injection on the 11th of April 1945. Aileen Schoofs survived and was liberated in Germany in May 1945 and returned to Paris.

Did PHILL achieve anything in its short life? It proved the concept that networks could be run by Biffy in Caxton Street via Sleator in Madrid then, using Georges Charadeau as a cut-out, across the border into France. The ALIBI network continued to run effectively until the liberation of France, as did ALLIANCE. ALIBI would eventually have 20 subgroups communicating through 15 wireless sets. The PHILL network had delivered vital intelligence on the development of the Messerschmitt ME262 Jetfighter at the Kellner works and had mapped out in detail the vast Renault armaments factory next door to the Kellner works in Boulogne-Billancourt. On March the 3rd 1942, the RAF bombed the Renault factory with limited success, but the Kellner works were completely destroyed, setting back the development of the ME262 by some time.

Although an undoubted setback, the destruction of PHILL taught SIS and their other networks a great deal about operational security, counter-surveillance and compartmentalisation using cut-outs. This was to be put to good use by other networks in the future, not least the 'Imperial Gem' – the JADE network that was to prove crucial to the war's outcome.

CHAPTER 13 – THE 'IMPERIAL GEM'
LE RÉSEAU JADE (THE JADE NETWORK)

'Le trois chattes Mimi, Minou et Minette
vont très bien.'[117]

'On the other side of the firing line, in those
occupied regions where, in spite of nameless
sufferings, they have not for one single instance
permitted their hope and endurance to falter.'

Adrian Carton de Wiart

By 1941, Biffy was a highly experienced intelligence officer beginning to learn the reality of establishing networks and running agents in a non-permissive environment. Biffy and his team in Caxton Street would pass requests for specific intelligence to his networks in the field, sifting the material that came back by radio or courier via the air and sea clandestine lines of communication and passing it on to the relevant customers, knowing that many life-or-death decisions would be made on the back of it. All the while, they were living in a state of tension and concern about what was happening across the channel and the fate of the men and women of their networks at the hands of a ruthless enemy, helped by many French traitors and collaborators. The fate of JOHNNY and PHILL were a case in point.

Given the expediency of getting back into France to gather intelligence, the speed with which this was done, particularly by Biffy's 'A4' team, was remarkable. However, this expediency had its penalties. In clandestine intelligence work, enthusiasm is no substitute for training or thorough, watertight procedures, particularly in the face of a professional enemy well versed in counterintelligence operations. Running any sort of network in occupied France was a tall

---

117 '*The three cats Mimi, Minou and Minette are very well.*' BBC message broadcast periodically to inform Claude Arnould's wife that he was okay. He had sensibly sent her into hiding in the Deux-Sèvres. She did not see him for four years. Mimi, Minou and Minette were their three daughters.

order at any time, faced with the Abwehr and Gestapo. The Germans also held an ace in the shape of the French 'Gestapo' and their many collaborators and informers, who did for the PHILL network.

Combine a formidable and ruthless enemy with a lack of training and situational awareness and it is no surprise that networks like PHILL and JOHNNY were short-lived. They were not well versed in compartmentalisation and cut-outs, counterintelligence and disciplined procedures. On the other hand, Biffy's friends in Vichy, collectively working for SIS, were intelligence professionals, fully trained, careful and able to operate in a hostile environment.

ALIBI was able to survive the destruction of PHILL largely because Georges Charadeau was an experienced intelligence professional and operated on Biffy's behalf as a sponsor of many sub-networks, providing support and a clearing house for intelligence recovered. If a sub-network went down it was closed off, the others were protected where possible and new ones were recruited and activated, enabling ALIBI to operate and survive until the liberation. ALIBI became an independent routing for the backlog of intelligence reports that were beginning to develop by 1943.

The JADE networks – AMICOL and FITZROY, also relatively early starters – were much better organised and structured, able to withstand setbacks and enemy successes. They rolled with the punches and survived, delivering a very effective operation from 1940–44. Initially, both networks were linked together under the overall network name JADE. The two parts were started separately to improve operational security. After a series of arrests during 1943, the remnants of both came together. Six months later, following more arrests when FITZROY was badly hit, they separated again, with AMICOL proving to be one of the most successful of the SIS networks. It survived until September 1944 and had a significant role in the liberation of Paris, saving it from destruction. By the end of the war in France, both parts of JADE had hundreds of agents, many of whom did not survive. Four individuals – the founders and driving force – stand out: Claude Lamirault, Pierre Hentic, Claude Arnould and Philip Keun. Three out of the four had direct links to Biffy. Pierre Hentic was to become close to Biffy later. A fifth member of the network was Paul

Claude Lamirault

Kilesso, who had direct ties to Biffy and was to play a vital role until his arrest in January 1944.

Claude Lamirault, a fervent Catholic and a member of the extreme right group Action Française, had spent his adolescent years in Maison-Lafitte, an affluent suburb of western Paris, 11 miles from the centre. His parents had a grand house at 27 Rue Étienne-Péroux called Le Castel Saint-Yves. They also happened to let out two rooms to the Archibald brothers, close friends of Biffy, lawyers and free-lance operators for SIS in Paris. The reader will recall that they helped Biffy take the ENIGMA machine to London in August 1939. They introduced Claude to Biffy, who may also have been aware of him through his Deuxième Bureau friends.

Lamirault joined the French Army in 1938, serving in the Chasseurs Alpins. He took part in the short-lived Norwegian campaign and, after the French surrender in 1940, escaped to Britain via Tangier and Gibraltar. On arrival in Liverpool, he immediately contacted the Archibald brothers in London, who had escaped Paris with the SIS station. Roy Archibald took him to see Biffy in Caxton Street, who recruited him on the spot. Bill Cordeaux of SIS described him '*as tough as any gangster and rather an ugly customer*'.

Pierre Hentic, the only one not known to Biffy before the war, had served with Claude Lamirault in the Chasseurs Alpins. Hentic could not have been more different to Lamirault. A working-class upbring-ing in the 1920s and 1930s had led him to become a communist with a keen desire to fight on the Republican side in the Civil War. However,

Pierre Hentic (MAHO)

he became disenchanted with the communist ideal when a friend of his returned from Russia and told him what communism was really like. Pierre Hentic fought in Norway alongside Lamirault, returned to France and then tried to get to Britain or North Africa, failing to do so. Eventually, demobilised after the Armistice and disillusioned, he went back to work as a laboratory technician. He tried multiple times to escape via Brittany, but each attempt was foiled. Lucky not to be caught, he eventually met up with Denise Lamirault who quizzed him on his attitude towards the war. Satisfied with what she heard, she introduced him to her husband and he was recruited in February 1941.

After fighting in World War I, Claude Arnould spent the inter-war years as, amongst other things, French Military Attaché in Denmark

Claude Arnould's false driving licence

Claude Arnould disguised as a gendarme

Philip Keun's personal file
ID photograph, SIS London

and as a businessman, travelling widely. In fact, he worked for the Deuxième Bureau and had met Biffy in this capacity. In 1940 he had decided to carry on the fight and founded what was to become JADE AMICOL in October 1940. He quickly established contact with his old Deuxième Bureau comrades, now operating under the cover of Traveaux Régionaux ('TR') and, in particular, TR117 in Toulouse. Arnould was to be put in touch directly with Biffy in Caxton Street by Philip Keun.

Philip Keun was a long-time family friend of Biffy's, tall, athletic, energetic, irrepressible, usually taciturn but given to bursts of gaiety and very tough.

Philip's father George had known Biffy and Biffy's father Richard in Constantinople. When George moved to France, he built the Villa Tanah Merah in Antibes, where Biffy was a regular guest before the war. Philip's genealogy was exotic, being related to Princess Flavio Borghese. His father was Anglo-Dutch, a descendant of Bernard Keun, a Lutheran pastor, chaplain of the Dutch consulate in Smyrna in the late 18th century. George's father, Philip's grandfather Alfred, was a shipowner. George would also join JADE AMICOL. His mother, Germaine Tarbierre, was Anglo-French and both were very close friends of Biffy's. Philip attended Blundell's School in Tiverton, Devon from 1925–30. Described by Bill Cordeaux as an '*international adventurer with more than his fair share of charm and cunning*', he was recruited by SIS and worked on several missions for them in

Turkey, Hungary and Bulgaria. By 1940, he was in Paris and Biffy asked him to stay there to set up an intelligence network.

While mulling over Biffy's offer, he had joined the Foreign Legion and fought in the 1940 campaign. He was lightly wounded, then captured, but managed to escape. He went to recuperate at his father's villa in Antibes in the unoccupied zone. He thought a lot about Biffy's discussion with him about setting up a network in France. After recuperating for several weeks, he escaped by fishing boat to Gibraltar and on to Britain where Biffy's team met him and arranged for him to be trained.[118] He was given the codename DEUX or AMIRAL and he was parachuted back into the unoccupied zone. He set himself up in Marseilles and quickly began his work infiltrating the Vichy Maritime Intelligence Bureau in the Marseilles/Toulon area. In January 1941, Keun made contact with Arnould who was already well established in the Bordeaux area. Keun offered to join forces and ensure that the new network JADE AMICOL[119] would have the full support of SIS and be under the control of Biffy's 'A4' section.[120]

By 1942, Biffy had two circuits under the JADE umbrella covering almost the whole of France. By 1943, together with the intelligence derived from his Vichy connection and his Polish networks covered in Chapter 14 and ALIBI, Biffy was getting a vast amount of intelligence.

One day in late January 1942, Biffy was sitting at his desk when the phone rang: '*Biffy, it's Pat Southby, can I come over and see you?*' Lieutenant Commander Pat Southby worked for the Director of Naval Intelligence but was seconded to Combined Operation Headquarters[121] working on Admiral Mountbatten's planning staff. He and Biffy knew each other from the 1930s; Biffy knew better than to ask what he wanted.

118 There is a misconception that Keun first joined SOE, which came about because he was trained as quickly as possible using the SOE training schools. He appears in Peter Churchill's book *Of Their Own Choice* as a student on an SOE course.
119 AMICOL came from an amalgamation of Keun's codename AMIRAL and Arnould's COL or COLONEL.
120 Philip Keun's first cousin was Prince Junio Valerio Borghese, who became notorious as the Black Prince – a combat swimmer for the Italian Navy and a committed fascist. His other cousin worked in the Greek Resistance.
121 Combined Operations was a tri-service organisation commanded by Admiral Louis Mountbatten, charged with conducting strategic raids into occupied Europe as a precursor to the invasion of France. Among its successes was both the Bruneval and St Nazaire raids. It was not so successful at Dieppe, which was a disaster.

Normandie dry dock, St Nazaire, 1942

An hour later Southby was shown into Biffy's office.

'*What's cooking Pat?*'

'*Well, we want to blow up some lock gates in France. Can you help?*'

'*Which lock gates in particular?*'

'*The Normandie dry dock in St Nazaire.*'

Biffy was fully aware that the number-one strategic intelligence priority, since the end of 1940, concerned German U-boats operating out of French ports. His networks, particularly the JADE networks, were heavily engaged in gathering this intelligence and had agents in all the ports in western France from Bordeaux to Le Havre.

Pat Southby went on to explain that the Navy was equally concerned about large and powerful surface raider battleships such as the BISMARCK, TIRPITZ, SCHARNHORST and GNEISENAU which, operating together with the U-boats, posed a very serious threat to the Atlantic convoys and could sever Britain's lifeline. The previous May, the BISMARCK had been engaged by the Royal Navy and badly damaged. The BISMARCK then made a dash for St Nazaire to carry out repairs but was attacked by the Fleet Air Arm which further damaged the ship's steering gear. Rather than be boarded and captured, the captain scuttled his ship. This made the Navy rethink the strategic value of the Forme Joubert, one of the largest dry docks in the

HMS CAMPBELTOWN

world and the only one within reach of the Atlantic that could carry out repairs on the BISMARCK's sister ship the TIRPITZ and the other large surface raiders. The Forme Joubert was colloquially known as the Normandie Dock as it had been specifically built in 1937 for the Blue Riband liner *Normandie*.

On Wednesday the 14th of January, the TIRPITZ passed through the Kiel Canal and headed for Norway. The Royal Navy was very concerned that she would join the battle cruisers SCHARNHORST and GNEISENAU in Brest, forming a powerful surface battle group to operate in conjunction with the U-boats. If any of these surface ships was to be engaged and damaged, she would either head back to Germany or to St Nazaire. If she headed for Germany, it would give the Navy the chance to intercept her. A plan was needed immediately to deny the use of the Normandie dock.

This had come as a direct order from Churchill. Southby explained that the plan being worked up involved a daring Commando raid up the Loire River to the port facilities, ramming a destroyer filled with explosives into the dock gates and blowing them up. Simultaneously, Commandos would attack and destroy port facilities, U-boat pens and shipping. Combined Operations planners needed every scrap of intelligence available.

Southby asked Biffy what he had. Biffy thought for a moment, then rang a bell on his desk. Someone came in and Biffy asked him to bring the 'Bertie' files. The file was brought in. Biffy looked through it and said, *'Has anything come in since last Thursday?'* The person who had brought the file, standing behind Southby, replied *'No'*. Southby recognised the voice and turned to greet his cousin Charles Garton. Biffy grinned and said, *'I thought you two might know each other.'*

As it turned out, Biffy's section of SIS was able to provide much valuable intelligence including a detailed plan of the port and its defences as well as street maps of the town which were reproduced for the Commando Force. Much of this intelligence was provided by the GROUPE 31 network.[122]

Ultimately, the raid was a success, the dock being completely put out of action until 1947, but it was at considerable cost to the Commandos and Royal Navy.[123] This success prompted Churchill to say *'March closed for us with the brilliant and heroic exploit of St Nazaire. Here was a deed of glory intimately involved in high strategy.'* Biffy and the brave men and women of his networks in France can take some credit for this.

*

Two other people who played a significant role in the JADE operation had a direct connection with Biffy.

We have already met Paul Kilesso who had started working for Biffy as his chauffeur in 1921 in Constantinople, continuing to do so in Paris until such time as he was installed as the owner/manager of the Hotel du Havre at 37 Boulevard Montparnasse. From the outset he became a very important part of the JADE team, acting as network financial controller, as well as operating the hotel as a safe house, a clearing house for intelligence, a storage for materials and other essential tasks. There was a visual code known to those who might visit – one of the shutters would be partially closed if it was

122 Of the 15 members of GROUPE 31 shot on the 27th of November 1942 at Mont Valérien, six were residents of St Nazaire.
123 The Command ship for the raid was MGB 314, commanded by Dunstan Curtis detailed from the 15th Motor Gun Boat Flotilla – see *A Dangerous Enterprise*. Dunstan Curtis went on to join Ian Fleming's 30 Assault Unit.

not safe. Just before he was arrested on the 24th of January 1944, as the Gestapo stormed into the hotel, he was able to set the danger signal, thus ensuring that George Tournon, a key operator in Paris for FITZROY and AMICOL, did not walk into a trap, enabling him to rally both networks after Pierre Hentic and Philip Keun were arrested in 1944. Kilesso had also emptied the safe of all SIS funds and details of agents who had been staying at the hotel. Despite being extensively tortured, he gave nothing away.

Sheelagh Greene, Tom's eldest daughter who had worked in the SIS station in Paris, was 26 when Biffy and her father left France in 1940. She elected to stay in France and go underground, emerging to work for AMICOL as a full-time agent. Initially from June 1940 to December 1941 she worked with Philip Keun, setting up the operating headquarters in the south of France and then Paris. Then, in January 1942, she was put in charge of all parachute operations and logistics for the network as well as taking care of the families of members of the network who were killed, imprisoned or deported. She did this for two and a half years. After the war she was awarded the Croix de Guerre. Her citation said that she showed courage and composure in all circumstances ... *'faisant preuve en toutes circonstances de courage et de sang froid'.*

JADE FITZROY began operations in January 1941 after Claude Lamirault parachuted into France with a radio set and money to fund the network and continued to operate until the liberation. Its primary

Sheelagh Greene

Couvent de la Sainte-Agonie interior

Entrance to the Couvent de la Sainte-Agonie

mission was to gather military intelligence. The first year was spent organising and recruiting across the whole of France, setting up a dozen sub-networks geographically organised into two zones, Zone North and Zone South, with cells in Paris, Brittany, the Pas de Calais, Somme, Chateauroux, Bordeaux, Marseilles and Lyon, with radio posts in Paris and Sartrouville.

Its intelligence requirements included German military order of battle and dispositions, aircraft production, maritime activity (particularly U-boats and capital ships), telecommunications, coastal defences and eventually V1 and V2 rockets and launch sites.

By the liberation, it had a total of 525 agents of whom 70 were killed and 172 were deported.

JADE AMICOL's initial focus was on southwest France, centred around Bordeaux. Recruits were largely from the Catholic and ecclesiastical circles. In the summer of 1942, a headquarters was established at the Couvent de la Sainte-Agonie at 127 Rue de la Santé in Paris. Here, the Mother Superior, Henriette Frede, allowed them the use of a set of rooms above the chapel. She and three of her nuns, Mère Jean, Sister Marie-Vianney (Jeanne Assmat) and Sister Edwige (Lucie Gand), acted as collators of intelligence collected by the network and as couriers between the network radio sets that were dispersed in safe houses in the area around the convent.

The use of the convent was to remain secret at all costs and was only known to Arnould and Keun; they were both fanatical about its security. Despite the convent being on the same street as the

The Mother Superior,
Henriette Frede

infamous La Santé prison where many resisters were incarcerated and executions carried out, the convent was never discovered as an SIS centre of operations.[124]

Gradually, Zone headquarters were established in Bordeaux at the Jesuit Lycée St Joseph de Tivoli, Lyon, Nancy and Nantes, with 13 sub-networks connected by a separate network of 18 couriers, one for each of the 18 radio posts that the network eventually established across the whole of France. Time-sensitive intelligence was transmitted by radio, other classified material was sent out by air and sea, as well as overland to Spain. The network was resupplied with money, radios, food and weapons by parachute drop. These were the responsibility of Sheelagh Greene. The scale of funding from Biffy's office in London started at 250,000 francs per month at the outset in 1940. By 1944, it was running at three million francs per month.[125]

Whilst these two networks worked as one initially, Philip Keun did not get on with Claude Lamirault, for some reason feeling that Lamirault would betray him.[126] After a wave of arrests in February 1942 that badly damaged FITZROY, the two networks split. Not only did Keun not trust Lamirault, he also believed their arrests were due to a lack of security, so he was determined to separate AMICOL. Biffy and Tom Greene had been concerned for some time

---

124 The convent is seen briefly in the film *Is Paris Burning?*. It was demolished in the 1960s.
125 Three million francs in 1944 roughly equated to £390,000.
126 Reported in a conversation by Victor Chatenay with Philip Keun in Biffy's office in Caxton Street.

that Lamirault was pushing his luck and should be brought out to London. Lamirault refused, so Biffy sanctioned the split of the two parts of the JADE networks, with Paul Kilesso running the finances of both and Pierre Hentic running clandestine transportation with a stand-alone network.

This initial wave of arrests in April 1942 was directed at the FITZROY headquarters in Sartrouville where they captured the network radio operator and his set. Lamirault was back in England at this time, conferring with Biffy. He insisted on returning to France immediately, parachuting blind. He was able to contact the remnants of the group and arranged for six key operators including his wife to escape to Britain via Spain. Denise Lamirault later parachuted back into France to regroup FITZROY after a second wave of arrests including that of her husband in rather dramatic circumstances.

One of Lamirault's most impressive achievements was the acquisition of an official identity card and badge used by French police. Both card and badge were sent to London by courier, faithfully copied by SIS's counterfeiting section and returned to France. The false badges allowed Lamirault and a few chosen members of the JADE group to pass through police cordons. In the end, however, it was the fake identity card that caused his downfall.

On the 15th of December, Paul Fortier had a planned meeting with Claude. Claude wanted Fortier to go with him to the Hotel Moynton in the Rue Moynton to try and track down an agent from Marseilles who had failed to turn up at a meet. They went to the hotel to make enquiries, posing as policemen with Claude using his police badge. Claude asked to see the register. The proprietor was suspicious and signalled to a chambermaid who slipped out of the hotel. Fortier noticed and warned Claude that they should leave. Walking away from the hotel they saw the chambermaid accompanied by a police officer, Mohamed Djellou. Djellou challenged Claude, who immediately drew his pistol and shot him dead. Claude and Fortier ran for it, splitting up in the process. Fortier escaped but Claude was cornered outside the Richelieu-Drouot Metro Station. A shootout followed and Claude was wounded in the arm and captured. He was handed over to the Gestapo who, after patching up his arm, wasted no time in applying the usual medieval interrogation techniques.[127] Paul Kilesso had warned him to be very careful in using the false police identity card. He was transferred to Fresnes prison. Attempts were made to rescue him, but they failed. He was eventually deported to Dachau on the 2nd of July 1944 but survived the war only to be killed in a road accident in France in May 1945. After his arrest his wife Denise parachuted into France to try and re-establish the network but she in turn was arrested in early 1944.

Also in December 1943, Claude Arnould was shot twice in a Gestapo ambush but escaped, to be hidden and treated for two months in a clinic in the Rue Violet. Arnould had a rendezvous with a contact at the home of Maria Errazuriz, Philip Keun's aunt by marriage, at 1 Avenue Président Wilson. She was a member of JADE AMICOL. He was accompanied by his secretary Mireille Froge. They were unaware that the Gestapo had taken over the apartment as a speculative trap for anyone who turned up, having arrested Maria the day before. They entered the building unseen by the Milicien who was supposed to be concealed in the concierge's room but had decided to steal some wine from the cellars of the owners in the basement. Claude led the way up to the first-floor apartment. He rang the bell. The door opened and the butler indicated trouble. Claude ran down the stairs, being fired at by Bernard Fallot.[128] He was shot in the arm and heel but made his escape by Metro and taxi to Mireille's flat in the Rue de Sèvres. Claude got in touch with a friendly doctor who took him to the Clinic Violet in the Rue du Violet, where he was patched up and hidden for three months until he recovered. He flew to London by Lysander on the 5th/6th of April to consult with Biffy, returning on the night of the 11th/12th.

In the space of a month both FITZROY and AMICOL were leaderless. Luckily, Pierre Hentic was back in England working with Biffy in Caxton Street. He immediately returned to France to set up an

---

127 His torture included the infamous Baignoire where he was repeatedly almost drowned in a bath of ice-cold water. He refused to speak and his interrogators, with grudging admiration, called him 'The Chevalier de la Baignoire'.

128 Bernard Fallot: Member of the Carlingue or French Gestapo, based at 93 Rue Lauriston. Tried and executed on the 1st of October 1947.

Maria Errazuriz,
Philip Keun's aunt

Entrance to Maria Errazuriz's
apartment at 1 Avenue Président
Wilson. Scene of shootout with Gestapo

independent courier network to bring out agents and intelligence. He pulled together the remnants of FITZROY into his new group as well as working closely with Philip Keun and the still functioning AMICOL network.

*

Pierre Hentic, alias MAHO, was the only key player in FITZROY/ AMICOL not known personally to Biffy before the war. He was soon to form a close friendship with both Biffy and Tom Greene, who treated their agents with a great deal of friendship and empathy.

Pierre Hentic had initially come out by Lysander to be briefed at Caxton Street. He was flown to Tempsford, then taken by Philip Schneidau to a hotel in Bayswater. There he met one of Biffy's staff, Mr Oxley, who was to be his conducting officer. Arriving at Caxton Street, he was met by Tom Greene and taken immediately to see Biffy. Initially, Hentic wanted to join the Free French in North Africa, but Biffy talked him into going back to France as the 'Chef de Terrain', charged with the setting up of a separate network to support both the remnants of FITZROY and AMICOL using the clandestine air and sea lines to France.

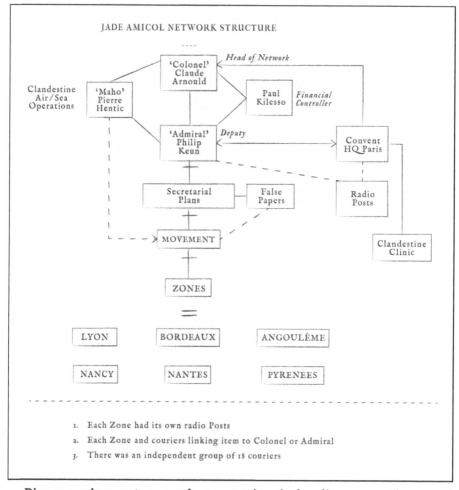

JADE AMICOL NETWORK STRUCTURE

1. Each Zone had its own radio Posts
2. Each Zone and couriers linking item to Colonel or Admiral
3. There was an independent group of 18 couriers

Pierre underwent a crash course in air landing operations and a shortened parachute course at Ringway. In spite of his intense training, he did have time to notice the ravishing Mia, who worked for Biffy in charge of aliases and false documents. Mia was lusted after by all; she ignored it gracefully. No one knew anything about her personal life, but everyone used any excuse to visit her office. She seemed totally oblivious and maintained she was married to an officer deployed to North Africa. There is more than a suspicion that Hentic and Mia had a sly dalliance. On the 27th of May 1942, Pierre Hentic parachuted back into France to set up his new operation.

Eventually he was responsible for more than 20 parachute operations, 10 air landings and six maritime pick-ups, involving many agents and several tons of classified mail destined for Biffy.

Victor Chatenay's[129] pick-up is typical of how an operation was conducted. Instructed to meet MAHO at 16:15 in the Trocadero Aquarium, MAHO gives him the next RV and tells him to buy a torch. The next RV is at the Câfé d' L'Université at 20:00. MAHO meets them and tells them to follow him. They walk very quickly a few 100 metres to a parked lorry. MAHO gets in the front with the driver, the others are in the back which is full of sacks of charcoal. The lorry moves slowly past the dreaded Fresnes prison towards Orléans. Things get very tense when they are stopped at a German roadblock. Papers are in order, no search and all is well. Eventually they stop in a farmyard where the charcoal is exchanged for lots of packages for London – mostly Swiss precision instruments and radio components, weighing more than 200 kilos. They get out of the truck and walk through several villages leaving false tracks, doubling back, practising all the techniques of counter-surveillance. Eventually, near the village of Chanay they stop in a large field of close-cut stubble. The packages are collected from them and stacked in a pile. Torches are set out in the 'L' shape. There is no wind. The truck is driven away and hidden in a copse. Things are tense, no smoking.

After 30 minutes the faint noise of a plane. It appears to go away. MAHO gives a signal to switch on the torches. Suddenly the plane is there and rolling to a stop. No talking. Move to the ladder on the left-hand side of the fuselage. Remember the pilot is covering you with his pistol with the safety catch off. MAHO speaks to the pilot. He gives the signal to get in. Three people squeeze into the small compartment. A second Lysander takes the stores. The Lysander accelerates away climbing steeply. It has been on the ground for 90 seconds. The journey is tense but luckily uneventful. Flying low they cross the channel. Gradually they gain height and can hear the pilot calling

129 Victor Chatenay had set up a network for Biffy in Anjou consisting of 296 members. In 1943 the network was betrayed, 107 were arrested. Victor escaped and Biffy arranged an exfiltration by Lysander. He then worked in Caxton Street on preparations for D-Day. He was a great motoring enthusiast and rather amusingly his driving licence was number 007!

on the radio. Suddenly on their right the airfield is illuminated. The Lysander turns sharply and lands. Immediately the landing lights go out. Two figures approach the aircraft and Philip Schneidau greets them in French. A car whisks them to the officers' mess for breakfast and by mid-morning they are with Biffy in Caxton Street.

Hentic returned to France and was most effective in setting up his network, working with Philip Keun, sending out a great deal of intelligence and rescuing both agents and escaped aircrew.[130] Both Hentic and Keun were subsequently betrayed and arrested.

Hentic was arrested on the 6th of January 1944. He was due to meet a contact in a café near the Saint-Placide Metro station in Paris. As usual, he arrived early to check out the local area for signs of surveillance of the RV. He checked the surrounding streets for telltale signs of the Gestapo – Rue du Renard, Rue Saint-Placide, Rue de Fleurus – nothing. He chained his bicycle to a railing and went to back room of the café to meet his contact. As he ordered a coffee, there was a sudden commotion behind him – five men in long leather coats all with pistols in their hands. 'Hands up', followed by a knee in the stomach. Hentic then saw his friend Aubertin, PRALINE, his face badly beaten, wearing a coat over his shoulders to disguise the handcuffs. He had clearly given away the RV under torture. Aubertin tried to protest that it was not him who had blown the meeting. Unfortunately, he used Hentic's codename MAHO, which made things worse, as the Gestapo had been looking for him for some time. This was not helped by the discovery of two Michelin maps in his coat pocket, a clear indicator of his involvement in air landing and parachute operations.

Hentic soon found himself at 101 Avenue Henri-Martin, the headquarters of the Gestapo torturer Masuy. After a severe beating an SS colonel intervened to stop the torture; no explanation was ever forthcoming as to why, but it saved him from a great deal of suffering. Eventually he was deported to Dachau but survived.

Philip Keun had returned from London where Biffy had been briefing him on the role of JADE AMICOL in the forthcoming invasion.

---

130 For a full account of this, see *A Dangerous Enterprise*, Chapters 7 and 8.

Philip Keun in disguise

He came back by parachute on the 6th of February 1944 and was accompanied by three other members of AMICOL, Jeanson, Lorient and Tissier, landing near Boisseaux. He was already aware of the wave of arrests that was hurting his network and that Arnould was in hiding, recuperating in the clinic on Rue Violet. Keun badly injured his back on landing. His first concern was to get to Paris to put things back together and re-establish their radio link to London. Having done this and making sure their headquarters at the Sainte-Agonie Convent was safe, he decided to get out of Paris to somewhere where the Gestapo activity would be less intense. Initially he moved to Orléans, to the Hotel du Petit Caporal, a nondescript hotel in the suburbs where the owner Yvonne Pétinay was a very reliable agent. His local radio operator had a large amount of intelligence to transmit and they needed to change transmission location often. One day they had a close call. Lorient the radio operator heard a suspicious crackling in his earpiece. He quickly looked outside. In the distance, a car was approaching along a dirt road. Quick as a flash, the young man gathered up his equipment and slipped his documents into a satchel. Afterwards, he looked out of the window. He smiled; the car had got stuck in the mud. He would not be taken away that day.

Philip Keun was preoccupied with getting his network back in shape ready for D-Day. He spent his time well away from Paris and he was careful, having heard that his description had been circulated to every Gestapo unit in France. He changed his appearance and got new identity papers.

On the night of the 2nd/3rd of June, Pierre Tissier carried out AMICOL's final air operation at Outarville, north of Orléans. Joseph Camara landed by Lysander, bringing further instructions for Philip from Biffy. Philip was still in Orléans when the D-Day landings took place three days later. He was busy gathering intelligence useful to the progress of operations in Normandy and transmitting them to Biffy in London. One early success was the identification of a fuel delivery operation for German units in Normandy. The fuel was stored in a very large, camouflaged and heavily defended depot at Sens. The fuel was moved in tankers to Montargis Railway Station and then loaded onto trains and taken north. This information was transmitted to London and the next day the depot and railyards were bombed and destroyed. JADE AMICOL was getting extremely busy gathering and transmitting intelligence but also countering mounting pressure from the Gestapo.

Philip decided to move his headquarters out into the country. Tissier knew of an abandoned farm at Gué de la Thas that they could use, located between Vienne-en-Val and Marcilly-en-Villette that belonged to René Bergé, a member of the network, which was already being used as a safe house.

Their cover was that they were a group of refugees. They had genuine papers and permission to use the house thanks to the Mayor of Vienne, Monsieur Cathelineau, who was also a member of JADE AMICOL. The move to the farm completed, Keun continued to move back and forwards to Paris and Bordeaux. Between his trips, a supposed leader of the local Samatha Maquis, GERARD (Guy Eymer), came to the farm to ask for help getting a message to London requesting an arms drop. While they waited for a response from London the Maquis leader left. In fact, he was a Gestapo plant. On the evening of the 28th of June, Keun returned from a trip to Bordeaux. As he arrived, he thought he saw unusual movements of German vehicles in the area. He gave orders that they would move the next day. There were seven people on the farm. Four from AMICOL: Pierre Tissier, Céline Mory, Marcel Petit, Philip Keun, and three from outside the network: the friend of the alleged maquisard, the farmer, Léger, who introduced him to Keun, not knowing that he was a traitor and Aimé Dechez, a local resister. Marcel Petit described the raid:

Gué de la Thas, where Philip Keun was captured

It was a peaceful night, and we were all sound asleep when at around 6 a.m., we were woken suddenly by the sound of doors being broken and windows smashing. Then guttural voices, whose echoes reached us, left us in no doubt as to the identity of these morning visitors.

'Oh no! We are done for... It's the "Boches"!!'

We were up and dressed in the blink of an eye. Mémée headed for the attic door while Philippe [Keun] and I looked out through the gaps in the roof tiles. Our P.C. was completely surrounded by Germans and militiamen who were armed to the teeth. We counted dozens of them. There were too many of them and any kind of resistance was impossible. Philippe told us to abandon our weapons, which we buried under the straw. I quickly took a few papers out of my wallet that might secretly interest the Boches. I hid everything between two tiles, while Philippe tore several documents into tiny pieces and also slipped them into a hiding place.

Keun realised soldiers were itching to shoot and any attempt to fight would have been futile. If he had been alone, he would not have hesitated, but not wanting to compromise the others, he resigned himself to doing nothing. The search of the farm was completed quickly.

Those captured were handcuffed and lined up facing the brick wall of one of the farm buildings. Petit again:

> ... *I convinced myself we were all going to die in a few moments. Philippe was on my left, Céline was on my right. Nobody flinched, and when our assassins would fire (we heard them preparing for the execution behind us), we would not give them the satisfaction of having extracted a complaint from us, a word of grace ...*
>
> *'I beg your pardon, Émile, for having dragged you into this dirty trap. I'm truly sorry...,' Philippe said to me.*
>
> *This admirable man, who was going to die with us, was not thinking of himself, but still of us! The time seemed to drag. Won't they just finish us off?*
>
> *'It's all over, my poor Émile,' Céline tells me in a low voice. 'Soon it would be over...' I thought about my little Nicole, of my mum.*

A flurry of bullets were fired over their heads to frighten them. They were questioned. Philip was quickly identified and insisted that the others were of no importance in an attempt to save them. They were then loaded onto a truck and taken to Orléans.

Jean Lorient, the radio operator, arrived at the farm a little later. Just in time he saw the German patrol that had been left behind to catch anyone else. He was the only one to escape. The others were held in Orléans for a few hours and were briefly interrogated before being taken to Paris. There was no chance of escape from the truck. They were under heavy escort handcuffed to the benches. During the journey, Philip and Pierre said to Céline, the only woman arrested with them: *'We'll do everything to prevent you from being beaten. All we ask is that you say nothing for 48 hours.'* Upon their arrival in Paris, Philip and Pierre were held at Avenue Foch and the others, Céline, Marcel Petit, Aimé Dechez and Léger, were taken to the French Gestapo on Rue Lauriston. Céline, faithful to her instructions, denied everything, but on Saturday the 12th of July, Pierrot spoke to her and said: *'You can admit that you are from the network; they found the memorandum with your name on it, which was to be telegraphed that evening to London.'*

Once at 84 Avenue Foch, Keun and Tissier were immediately separated. The traitor had disclosed enough for the Gestapo to know immediately that they were an important catch. Philip Keun was severely tortured. All he would say was that his name was Kane, Gerald George Philip Kane, British subject and army officer. He was in France for strictly military purposes. The torture went on until the 1st of July. He said nothing. The Germans eventually deported him to Buchenwald on the last transport out of Paris on the 15th of August. Keun had been looking forward to deportation as it meant an end to torture and he could go with a clear conscience as he had not cracked. He was also concerned that, as the Allies approached Paris, all prisoners would be massacred. As it turned out Paris was liberated on the 25th and all prisoners freed. Less than a month later on the 9th of September, he was gruesomely executed by slow strangulation with wire, along with a group of other British agents.[131]

Philip was held in very high personal and professional regard in SIS Head Office. Biffy wrote him a letter for transmission to the field just days before he was arrested but due to his arrest it was never sent. Part of it read *'you have really done a good job of work. One day I will be able to tell you how much that means to us. Meantime, I'm afraid silence is golden.'* It went on to say how well his present of 'Chanel dim-bash' (Turkish for Chanel No. 5) went down with *'the young lady in question'*, in all likelihood Sheelagh Greene, who may well have been back in London from France at the time. The letter ended *'... everyone using your material is praying for you, and I can assure you that they are many'*.

Marcel Petit was the last to see Philip at Buchenwald:

On 9th September, I went to see him for the last time ... He was surprisingly calm ... 'Whatever happens to us,' said Philippe to me, 'we will at least have felt the satisfaction of having fulfilled our duty without a fuss, but not without results, and we will not

---

131 On Armistice Day 2021, the current Chief of SIS issued a photograph of Philip Keun on his Twitter account with a message: *'Today we remember the bravery and sacrifices of all those who defended our democracy including Philip Keun an MI6 agent who ran a highly successful intelligence gathering-network in occupied France.'*

face any reproach. Despite everything, it would be a shame to end up so stupidly here. What do you expect Emile, we have caused a lot of damage to the Germans, and they are making us pay for it! We can still but hope ...'[132]

Philip

---

132 The JADE network eventually had 1,200 operators, 68 were arrested, 42 were deported, 20 were shot, hanged or beheaded and six escaped from captivity.

CHAPTER 14 – 'WILSKI'

'The soul of Poland is indestructible.'

Winston Churchill, 1939

As well as its responsibility for Vichy and independent networks, Biffy's section of SIS, initially designated 'A4' (July 1940–April 1942), then renamed 'P5' (May 1942–December 1943) and ultimately Special Liaison Controllerate from December 1943 onwards, had direct liaison with the Free Polish Intelligence Service. Biffy formed an excellent working relationship with them and in return they liked and respected him. He was always referred to by them as 'Wilski'.

The Polish military tradition dates back centuries but is different to the military development of most other countries, due to long periods of occupation and partition and domination by Russians, Austrians and eventually Germans. Poland had not existed as a nation since 1795 until its emergence as a nation again at the end of World War I. The new Polish military structure was modelled on France who had a prominent military mission based in Warsaw. Because of their history, the Poles had a deep understanding of the value of intelligence and the methodology of intelligence-gathering and clandestine warfare. Within their new military structure created in 1918 was a large intelligence organisation – Oddzial II – the second division of the General Staff. This department had seven sections, or 'Sekcja' with the following responsibilities:

Sekcja I   Reconnaissance.
Sekcja II   Offensive intelligence in Eastern Russia, Lithuania, Belarus, Ukraine and Galicia, Austria, Germany, France and Great Britain.
Sekcja III   General intelligence and surveillance overseas.
Sekcja IV   Psychological operations and propaganda.
Sekcja V   Liaison with overseas services.
Sekcja VI   Special operations.
Sekcja VII   Ciphers and encryption.

An extensive network of agents and networks was set up amongst the Polish émigré communities that developed across Europe after World War I. There were over a million Poles living overseas, with large groups living and working in the German Ruhr Valley and in the coal mines of northern France. The Polish attitude to intelligence can be summed up as: *'The knowledge of how a potential enemy was developing and deploying his military might make one's own limited forces that much more effective. It was not a weapon that a newly reborn nation, especially one as vulnerable as Poland, could afford to neglect'* and, as we have already seen, the Poles were way ahead of both France and Britain in the field of cryptoanalysis.

With a better understanding of the effectiveness of Polish intelligence work and in light of the rising threat from Germany, the French and British gradually woke up to the fact that all three intelligence services needed to work together. Eventually the degree of British–Polish collaboration on intelligence-gathering would be unprecedented. This was largely due to Biffy, but it would take some time to become effective.

On the 1st of September 1939, 20 years after regaining its sovereignty, Poland was invaded again. The Polish Army was no match for the Germans. France and Britain, in spite of their tripartite defence agreement, were unable to render any effective military assistance. On the 17th of September, the Polish Government moved to Romania and subsequently to France and then to London. In Poland, many soldiers went underground and the Polish resistance, the Polish Home Army, was born. In 1940, Polish troops were involved in the Narvik campaign who ended up in France and Britain. In France alone there were 100,000 Polish troops as well as many Polish civilian expatriates. After the collapse of France, the Polish Government and 25,000 Polish troops were evacuated to London to join those of the Polish Army, Air Force and Navy already there. By June 1940, Britain was Poland's key ally. On the 19th of June 1940, just as Biffy and his station were escaping France, Churchill assured General Sikorski *'we are comrades in life and death. We shall conquer together or we shall die together.'* He went on to say that *'we will keep faith with the Poles'* and thus began a very close political and military cooperation that was to last throughout the war. In the field of intelligence cooperation, this relationship was managed by Biffy and his team.

As we know, Biffy's relationship with Polish Intelligence began with the 1939 meetings about ENIGMA, but Biffy had been developing additional relationships with the Poles, initially through his friends in the Deuxième Bureau. It helped that Biffy spoke fluent Polish.

One early event that Biffy is likely to have had a hand in was the evacuation of the Polish National Gold Reserves. The Polish Government went into exile in Romania and took the decision to evacuate the National Gold Reserve with them. On the night of the 4th/5th of September 1939, the gold, weighing 80 tonnes,[133] along with bank notes and bank note printing plates were loaded onto trucks and railway wagons and assembled in the town of Sniatyn near the Romanian border. The intention was to move them to France via Romania as arranged between Polish Intelligence and the Deuxième Bureau. Biffy was aware of the plan and in touch with 'C' who had offered support if necessary. The gold was transported to the Romanian Black Sea port of Constanta. The Romanian Government was under extreme pressure from the Nazis to join the war on their side or at least remain neutral. Either of which would have resulted in the gold being impounded. A decree was issued by the Romanian Government on the 15th of September, sealing all borders.

Two weeks prior to this, Captain Robert Brett RNVR in command of the tanker SS EOCENE, which had been taken up from trade, was heading for Batumi to collect a cargo of oil. EOCENE was owned by Richard Dunderdale. Brett received a 'flash' signal from London to sail direct to Constanta and take on a very important and secret cargo, the Polish gold, and get it away to safety in Istanbul where it would be transported to Beirut. A French warship would then take it to France. Late at night on the 15th of September, the gold was secretly loaded aboard the EOCENE. Nazi agents were busy at work in Constanta trying to persuade the Romanians to seize the ship.

---

133 Worth approximately US$1.8 billion today.

Captain Brett, not wishing to be interned for the duration of the war and not willing to give up without a fight, darkened ship, silently slipped out of the harbour and set course for Istanbul. Hugging the coast, the EOCENE eventually made it to Istanbul on September the 19th 1939. There the gold was transferred to the Turkish authorities who then made arrangements for its onward movement to Beirut where French warships were waiting to take it to France. The long odyssey of the Polish gold had begun. From Beirut, the gold went to France but was evacuated to Senegal before the collapse of France and then eventually on to London and New York.[134]

*

Biffy's relationship with the Poles was to be one of the most success-ful relationships between Britain and her Allies of the war. It was essentially a liaison relationship. Biffy didn't 'run' any of the Polish networks but facilitated their operations with training equipment and funding. His 'A4'/'P5' section was also the 'post box' through which all requests for intelligence and the responses from the Poles were passed. Inevitably, Biffy and his team did become involved in some aspects of the functioning of the Polish contribution to the intelli-gence war, as we will see.

Polish Intelligence initially set up shop in their military headquar-ters at the Reubens Hotel at 39 Buckingham Palace Road in London, a 10-minute walk from Biffy's office in Caxton Street. From July 1940, the head of Polish Intelligence was Colonel Leon Mitkiewicz, who had limited experience as an intelligence officer. Most of the detailed work was done by his 2IC, Stanislaw Gano, who replaced Mitkiewicz in December 1941. Biffy knew Gano well, having met him in Paris before the war. On the 6th of August 1940, Biffy told 'C' that 'liai-son with all sections of the Polish intelligence service is now working smoothly...'

134 The gold that was moved to London was returned to Poland in 2019: 8,000 gold bars, each weighing 12.5kg, were transported on eight aircraft over several months.

On the 24th of August 1940, Biffy set out a list of duties with regard to the Poles:

- *Handling correspondence to and from the naval, military and air sections of the Polish General Staff Intelligence.*
- *Summarising and distributing information from Polish sources to the General Staff for information, comment and subsequent action.*
- *Drafting and distributing requests from the Poles to SIS representatives and their Polish opposite numbers abroad.*
- *Arranging meetings between SIS experts and their Polish opposite numbers in London.*
- *Contacting Polish naval and military liaison officers on matters relating to administration e.g. facilities for W/T communication and collaborating with them in operational plans regarding their European network of agents and contacts.*
- *Summarising and distributing questionnaires concerning subjects on which SIS wished action to be taken by Polish Intelligence.*
- *Consulting SIS HQ with regard to special requirements and conveying instructions to the Poles for action.*

All reports emanating from Polish sources were marked 'JX'. The Poles were unique amongst the governments in exile in London in that they were allowed to run their intelligence service independently, with their own communications base, training, radio communications and codes until just before the Normandy landings when all communications with Europe were heavily controlled. The Polish base at the Dower House in Stanmore was administered by Anthony Heath and his wife. The Poles also developed their own radio sets which were subsequently adopted by SIS. At Stanmore, the Poles had set up a small electronics factory. It was staffed by experts in telecommunications, who built radio transceivers for their networks. The Poles had soon developed the best, most technologically advanced sets, which '*pushed all other existing devices down to the status of museum pieces*'.

Polish intelligence officers at Stanmore

Between 1941 and 1944, about 10 models were manufactured in substantial quantities. SIS used the Polish sets (B.P.3 and A.P.4) to equip networks in Paris, Lyons, Bordeaux and Rheims. A total of 24 Polish sets ensured constant communication between SIS agents and their British home station. The Polish sets were not only the best, but also the most compact. The A.P.4 could be considered the model of the genre. Equipped with some miniaturised components, an excellent receiver housed in a very small box, a transmitter of adequate power and using a 110/120-volt external power supply, this set was certainly one of the best for any clandestine network. An additional advantage was that it could be hidden in a deep hide and operated by remote control.

Biffy's brief to Anthony Heath was to ensure that the Poles at Stanmore had everything they needed and that, for security reasons, they must be kept independent from the War Office. Heath was given a free hand by Biffy in all matters including housing, food, transport, welfare, arms and ammunition as well as operational security. Biffy wrote to Gano, setting out how he thought cooperation should work:

19th March 1941
Dear Gano,

Reference our conference, I would like to confirm that for the sake of satisfactory liaison it is most essential that we should run both our services more or less on parallel lines. That is to say – everything to do with clandestine stations abroad controlled by agents I think should belong to your 2nd Bureau.

The question of your workshops, taking our system as a precedent and in view of the particular type of material they produce, I am sure you will agree with me should also be under the control of your 2nd Bureau.

As regards the interception station, that appears to me to be also an entirely Secret Service responsibility.

Everything concerning official communications, such as between your Foreign Office and your Embassies abroad, should certainly be under some other official establishment.

It would appear to me that with this analogy between our two services we will be able to develop the excellent results already obtained, through the close collaboration of our services on parallel lines.

Yours ever,
Wilski

The Polish intercept service was based at a house called 'The Arches' (designated camp 235) at Feldon, just outside Hemel Hempstead, a 20-minute drive from Stanmore. It consisted of a Radio Intercept Company commanded by Captain Kazimierz Zielinski and included a section dedicated to intercepting U-boat signals run by Boatswain Madez, who had worked on U-boat intercepts since 1931. Biffy reported to Menzies that the Polish intercept team would '*work under our instructions wherever we may desire*'. The Polish intercept and intelligence services were particularly highly regarded for their expertise, not only on Germany but also on Russia. Their Russian intercept department was run by Czeslaw Kuras who had been intercepting Russian communications since 1923, being encouraged to share material on the Soviet Union even after Bletchley's Russian section was shut down in July 1941. In communicating this decision to the independent Polish signals intelligence operation at Stanmore, Bletchley indicated their continued interest in receiving information on Russia. In short, the direction not to spy on Russia after their entry to the war in July 1941 did not prevent SIS from asking the Poles to do the job for them: *'I asked Commander Dunderdale for his opinion and possible requirements. He said he was especially interested in intelligence focused on Russia. Since the [Polish] Radio Intelligence Company at Feldon was the only source of information about Russia for [SIS]'*.[135]

From the summer of 1940, the Poles started to establish networks in both occupied and unoccupied territory. Intelligence gathered was either passed through Polish channels to 'A4' or given to local SIS operatives for onward passage to 'A4'.

In France, the network was set up in July 1940 by a group of three Polish officers in Toulouse. Wincenty Zarembeski (TUDOR), Mieczyslaw Slowikowski (RYGOR) and Roman Czemiawski (ARMAND/WALENTY) had all been intelligence officers in the Polish Army. They had no money, codes, radio or any contact with London. Initially, their organisation helped Poles escape France to England. Messages sent with escapees found their way to Colonel Gano and to Biffy. A wireless set, codes and money were sent out to Marseilles in August 1940, with Tadeusz Jekiel (DOCTOR) who was to be their first radio operator to help TUDOR set up the network which would eventually be known as 'F2'.

By the end of 1940, four different cells making up the 'F2' network had been set up: TUDOR in Marseilles, PANHARD in Lyon, RAB at Toulouse and another cell in Paris run by ARMAND/WALENTY known as INTERALLIE which covered most of occupied France. Messages were sent from Paris via the wagon-lits attendant on the Paris Marseilles Express for TUDOR to transmit to London.

DOCTOR was based in Bordeaux where his sub-network specialised in information concerning U-boats and other shipping. It also

135 Polish Intelligence Department internal minutes from the 23rd of July 1943.

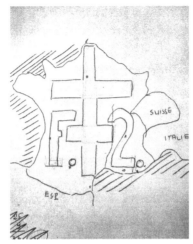
'F2' network logo

reported on German troop movements on the Italian rail network. It was the reporting of a German armoured division heading south by train through Italy that provided the first combat indicator of a German invasion of North Africa.

*

The setting up of INTERALLIE as a separate network from the rest of 'F2' was to ultimately prove the value of a cellular or compartmental- ised structure. Whilst disaster struck INTERALLIE after its betrayal by Mathilde Carré and its subsequent destruction, some elements of the network were able to escape capture and rejoin 'F2'. Although

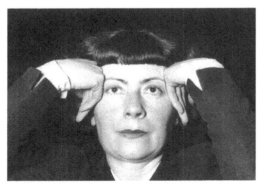
Mathilde Carré

'F2' had its own setbacks, it continued to expand, providing excellent intelligence until after the liberation of France. Mathilde Carré also betrayed the SNCF railway employees. Those who survived formed a new network, Réseau ZERO, and got in touch with the ALIBI network to pass on vital important intelligence on rail movements. It too was eventually penetrated and destroyed. The leader of the network, Germain Bleuet, the station master at Arras, was shot in June 1944.

The INTERALLIE network was run by Roman Czerniawski (WALENTY). During January 1941, the first objective of INTERALLIE was to create a cell structure of 13 isolated compartments covering the whole of occupied France, linked by a separate courier system. Their task was to collect military intelligence and transmit it to London via courier to the radio post in Marseilles, until later in 1941 they set up their own radios with a direct link to London. Carré (VICTOIRE) collated the intelligence, producing excellent intelligence summaries. She also did much of the recruitment and was therefore in an extremely important position in the network – too important. Throughout 1941, INTERALLIE flourished, sending to London a steady stream of excellent reports. VICTOIRE and WALENTY were living together and all was going well until WALENTY made the mistake of importing Renée Borni, another of his mistresses, letting her into the network, giving her the codename VIOLETTE and employing her as a cipher clerk. In October 1941, WALENTY made a trip to London. In his absence, relations between VICTOIRE and VIOLETTE reached rock bottom due both to sexual jealousy and professional rivalry. On the 16th of November 1941, the network had been functioning for a year and, in breach of all operational security rules, the network headquarter staff decided to have a 'birthday' party. Two days later the network ceased to exist.

On the 18th of November 1941, at 05:30 in the morning, the Gestapo broke into the flat where VIOLETTE and WALENTY were asleep and arrested them. MAURICE, one of the radio operators, and a friend, who were sleeping above, heard the noise and escaped over the rooftops; MAURICE eventually got to the unoccupied zone and then on to Britain. This arrest started a chain of events which in the end took out nearly every member of INTERALLIE. VICTOIRE was the architect. The disaster did not stop there, it led to the break-up of the SIS networks JOHNNY, OVERCLOUD and FELIX and the penetration of the SOE network AUTOGIRO.

However, the first break-in was not the fault of VICTOIRE. The chain of events started when DENISE (Madame Buffet) got into conversation with a near neighbour of hers in Cherbourg, a docker, and asked for information. This man repeated details of the approach to a German corporal in a pub, who duly reported the story as '*a case of suspected espionage*' to his superiors.

The Abwehr in Paris was notified and Captain Erich Borchers was sent to Cherbourg to investigate. He needed someone local to act as an interpreter as his French was poor. To help him make the necessary enquiries and arrests, he took a Field Security Police sergeant, Hugo Bleicher, who happened to be on duty that afternoon. The two Germans found, arrested and interrogated the docker who was able to give them further information: Madame Buffet, he said, was undoubtedly working for an important Allied intelligence network. He believed her immediate boss was a man he knew only as KIKI, who came down by train from Paris once a month to collect the information Buffet had collected; this man was not due until the beginning of next month (November). Meanwhile, while waiting for KIKI's arrival, Borchers and Bleicher arrested Buffet and in her possession found a complete list of the network. VICTOIRE was arrested in Paris. Bleicher was able to turn her with ease and she continued to betray many other members of the network, The network lost all five radio posts and 100 agents. Having helped Bleicher penetrate the SOE network AUTOGIRO, she then concocted a fantastic plan with Philippe de Vomécourt (LUCAS) to escape to Britain with the connivance of the Abwehr.[136]

The Mathilde Carré story and her developing role as a triple agent continued to involve Biffy and Tom Greene throughout the rest of the war. They had to attend numerous meetings with MI5 and the Double Cross committee to decide whether to play VICTOIRE back to the Germans. The initial meeting to discuss Carré's future was

---

136 For the full story – see *A Dangerous Enterprise*, Chapter 5.

held in Biffy's office at Caxton Street at 17:00 on the 5th of March 1942, a week after her controlled escape to Britain on SIS's MGB 314 on the 27th of February. Present at the meeting were Biffy, Tom Greene and Philip Schneidau, Gubbins and Buckmaster from SOE, 'Tar' Robertson and Christopher Harmer from MI5 and Colonel Gano from Polish Intelligence. Biffy made a long statement supported by Gano that:

> *Speaking for himself and the Head of the Polish Secret Service,*
> *as soon as a source of information was tainted they washed*
> *their hands of the case and were prepared to hand it over to the*
> *Security Service. This was the position in the case of VICTOIRE*
> *as they did not believe that any further useful information could*
> *be gained.*

Biffy also cast doubts on parts of VICTOIRE's story but agreed that there should be no hostile interrogation in order to retain VICTOIRE's confidence in case there was an opportunity to play her back to the Germans.

Shortly after these preliminary meetings Biffy declared no further interest in the future use of VICTOIRE or her future in this country. He was happy to hand over responsibility for her to SOE. However, throughout the rest of the war SIS had to attend many tedious meetings about her – which Biffy usually delegated to Tom Greene or Charles Garton.

Biffy also made it very clear to SOE that LUCAS on his return to France was not to contact any SIS circuit except the remnants of INTERALLIE.

WALENTY was also turned by the Germans and dispatched to London as a double. On arrival he immediately declared his position to Colonel Gano. Eventually, he was given the new codename BRUTUS, and took part in the D-Day deception programme Operation FORTITUDE. VICTOIRE's fate was soon decided, she was imprisoned and handed over to the French in 1945. She was sentenced to death. The sentence was later commuted to life in prison. In the end she served seven years, was released and died in obscurity in 1974.

The destruction of INTERALLIE had a knock-on effect with 'F2'. TUDOR was burnt and escaped to London and command of the network was taken over by Leon Sliwinski (JEAN-BOL) who pulled the remnants together, reactivating those who had been lying low or on the run, as well as recruiting new agents. It had almost fully recovered by the summer of 1942.

By now, 'F2' had spread across France and was involved in running courier routes across the Franco-Swiss border as well as to Gibraltar from the south of France using Polish-crewed feluccas. When the Germans occupied the whole of France after the Allied invasion of North Africa, 'F2' was hit by further arrests but recovered again. In January 1944, Biffy reported to 'C' that during 1943 his section had issued 1,161 intelligence reports based on the collection plan of 'F2'. Biffy had also been able to put the leaders of 'F2' in touch with his friends in Vichy who assisted 'F2' with tip-offs, logistic support, facilitation of courier routes and on occasion, radio transmissions via their secret radio interception post-CADIX.

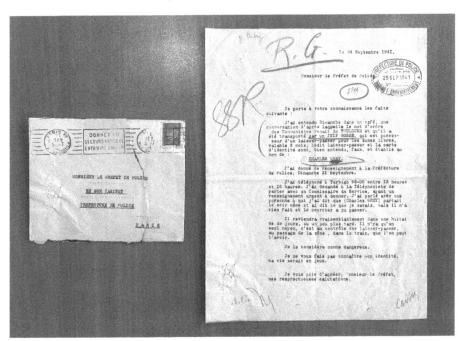

Charles Grey denunciation letter

Catherine Dior

Biffy was also able to activate another route for the transmission of intelligence to London. His old friend from Paris, Charles Grey, had returned to Paris at the end of 1940. He had maintained his links with the US Embassy and with SIS, posing as a neutral American. He joined 'F2' on the 1st of April 1941 and stayed active as a full-time agent until the 31st of December 1941 when he escaped via Spain to join the newly formed OSS. Grey (codenamed GRIS) was able to act as courier into the unoccupied zone, delivering intelligence to the US Naval Attaché in Vichy who arranged for its onward transmission by diplomatic bag or radio. Grey was never caught despite being denounced by an anonymous informer in September 1941.

Arrests continued throughout the spring of 1944, but despite this 'F2' contributed significant intelligence on German order of battle and fortifications both in northwest and southern France prior to the Allied landings in these regions. In July a further 16 agents were arrested, among them the chief of the Normandy sector. Among the arrests in Paris was that of Catherine Dior, sister of the fashion designer Christian Dior. She was arrested by the Bonny Lafont gang working for the Gestapo. Horribly tortured, she gave nothing away and was eventually deported to Ravensbrook on the last deportation train from Paris. She survived and returned to Paris to work with her brother.

In 1940, while Zarembeski, Slowikowski and Czemiawski were putting together 'F2', another valuable Polish source was already supplying information to London. Following the German invasion of Poland, the Polish cryptographers, responsible for breaking the ENIGMA code and building a replica of the ENIGMA machine, had escaped to France via Romania with SIS help. By October 1939 they were integrated into the Deuxième Bureau's cryptography department, *Le Section d'Examen* (SE), run by Colonel Gustave Bertrand ('Bertie', known to the Poles as Col. Bolek). Bertrand's close relations with the Polish cryptographers pre-dated the outbreak of war when he had facilitated their liaison with SIS over ENIGMA. He was to work indefatigably on their behalf throughout the war.

This group of 18 Polish cryptographers formed a centre of radio interception known as Équipe 300 or Cell Z. Following their escape to France, they worked from November 1939 until June 1940 at P.C.[137] BRUNO, at the Château de Vignolles at Gretz-Armainvilliers, near Paris. On the 10th of June 1940, Bertrand and his aides requisitioned several buses and drove the Poles and their machines south, near Brive. From there they were flown to safety in Algiers in July. Bertrand, however, was determined to continue his own work – contriving, with the help of Colonel Rivet, to remain employed by the Vichy intelligence service and to ensure that the work of the Polish cryptographers should continue.

By October 1940, the Poles had been brought back from Algiers and were settled in the Château des Fouzes, near Nimes (P.C. CADIX), which had been secured for Bertrand by General Weygand himself. There, together with a group of Spanish Republican cryptographers and five Frenchmen, they continued until November 1942 to work on ENIGMA and to send out immensely valuable messages dealing with all aspects of enemy activity, Abwehr agents in France and intelligence acquired from Rivet's Réseau KLEBER. Bertrand also managed to set up ENIGMA cells in Algiers and Rabat.

Bertrand had established independent contact between Équipe 300 and London through a colleague in Geneva, Commandant Perruche. Communication continued to be channelled through Geneva until March 1941, when Bertrand travelled to Madrid to meet Biffy who

---

137 P.C. – Poste de Commandment.

handed him a W/T set for future use. From November 1940, Équipe 300 was also in touch with TUDOR in Marseilles and remained in close contact with the 'F2' network until November 1942. It appears that both Bertrand and 'F2' used the 'Vichy Valise' – i.e. diplomatic bag – to communicate with Spain, Switzerland and London and also used the Deuxième Bureau radio transmitter at Clermont-Ferrand.

Following the Allied landings in North Africa, Bertrand again managed to smuggle the members of Équipe 300 out of France. Some went to North Africa to join the intelligence cell there, but the principal Polish cryptographers were smuggled over the Pyrenees to Spain, whence their evacuation to the UK was facilitated by SIS. Bertrand himself remained in France working with the KLEBER network until he was arrested in Paris in January 1944. He managed to escape and evade recapture until he was rescued by SIS in June 1944 and taken to London.

The work of Équipe 300 was both specialised and important. Its staff were expert cryptographers and had the most modern equipment. Most importantly, its interests and communications were protected constantly by the ingenious Col. Bertrand who arranged for them to be funded first by the Deuxième Bureau and later by the Vichy authorities. Through his efforts the work on ENIGMA was able to continue undiscovered, passing on to London critical strategic intelligence from its intercepts.

In July 1941, Slowikowski (RYGOR) was given instructions to set up an intelligence network in Vichy-controlled French North Africa, a huge area stretching from the Libyan border to Senegal. Effectively he was a one-man band, starting from scratch without any support or much guidance. The first thing he needed was a good cover story for his network AGENCY AFRICA. Like all good covers it had to be plausible and withstand detailed scrutiny. He also had to recruit a network, instruct them in what intelligence they needed to collect and how to do it. His final problem was how to forward the intelligence to London. Luckily, he had great qualities of tenacity, resistance and resourcefulness.

RYGOR hit on a brilliant idea for his network's cover. He founded a porridge factory – the Floc-Av Company. The product was only sold in chemists, safeguarding it from the restrictions on the sale of food introduced by the Vichy authorities. In fact, the porridge became the only food product which could be purchased without restrictions. It was exported to France and even sent to the French POW camps in Germany.

The sales organisation consisted of RYGOR's outpost commanders and agents. This would, of course, greatly facilitate the agency's work, especially as road and rail travel had been further curtailed by the authorities. As representatives of the firm, they would inevitably receive priority for unrestricted use of transport. Moreover, as salesmen of porridge they would, in their new capacity, have fairly easy access to military units, airfields, naval bases and ports.

RYGOR produced detailed instructions for his agents on what intelligence to look for and how to format it into reports. By the 15th of May 1941, Biffy's section reported that AGENCY AFRICA had established itself in Algiers and was in the process of establishing network outposts in Tunis, Oran, Casablanca and Dakar. Initially, time-sensitive intelligence was passed to London by radio from Algiers to the secret Polish/Vichy ENIGMA station, P.C. CADIX in the south of France and then on to London, eventually finding its way to Biffy's team for collation and distribution. Written reports, documents and plans were sent to the outpost in Tangiers where RYGOR had arranged with Colonel Eddy, the US Naval Attaché and OSS station chief, to have them sent to London by diplomatic bag.

Between May 1941 and the Allied landings in North Africa (Operation TORCH) in November 1942, AGENCY AFRICA had become a massive operation with its network of intelligence officers and agents stretching across the whole of North Africa. It had two principal radio stations directly in touch with London and its own counterintelligence team which successfully prevented the network from bring penetrated. Its survival was also helped by the close friendship between RYGOR and Marcel Dubois, a staunch anti-Nazi and Head of the DST,[138] in Morocco from 1941–43. The network provided all forms of key intelligence: strategic, operational and tactical,

---

138 DST – Direction Surveillance du Territoire. The Vichy counterintelligence service.

Mieczyslaw Slowikowski
(RYGOR)

to enable the TORCH landings to take place. In all, RYGOR sent 1,244 reports to London which were disseminated through Biffy's office in Caxton Street. Biffy arranged with 'C' to have RYGOR awarded the OBE for which the citation written by Biffy read:

> *He supplied consistently accurate information in connection with a certain major military operation which proved of inestimable value to the War Office and contributed in no small way to the success of the operation.*

Colonel John Knox, the OSS station chief in Algiers stated:

> *The Polish network under RYGOR's expert guidance and constant supervision were, by all odds, the most efficient and professional in their field, supplying the Allies with a wealth of valuable and proven material.*

After the TORCH landings, AGENCY AFRICA was wound down. RYGOR was summoned to London for debriefing, arriving in Greenock on the 1st of January 1943. Biffy had him met and looked after on his trip to London, arranging for him to stay at the Rembrandt Hotel in Knightsbridge. He was greeted warmly at the Polish Headquarters at the Rubens Hotel in Buckingham Gate, but not as warmly as at his initial meeting with Biffy on the 5th of January 1943. Arriving at Caxton Street he was immediately taken up to Biffy's office where Biffy expressed his delight at meeting him, commenting on the excellent work of AGENCY AFRICA and telling RYGOR that he had recommended him for the OBE. Meanwhile, Tom Greene was assembling Biffy's staff as well as representatives from the AGENCY AFRICA 'customers' in the briefing room. Biffy introduced RYGOR and started: '*Gentlemen! I am privileged to introduce RYGOR, whose work is very familiar to you.*' There was considerable applause and then Biffy introduced his team and the officers from the War Office.

After the meeting, Biffy took RYGOR back to his office and they had a long discussion. Biffy started by saying: '*Sir, you were brought to London at the insistence of General Menzies, the head of the British Secret Service, who wishes to have your report on the internal situation in French North Africa. Our officers there lack your experience in these matters, and most of their estimates are obviously second-hand.*'

Biffy then told him that Menzies would like to have this assessment for inclusion in his next brief for the Prime Minister, who needed it for his impending meeting with President Roosevelt. The situation in North Africa was on the agenda. Time was short and they needed to get down to work immediately. RYGOR spoke in Polish, Biffy translated and his secretary took notes in shorthand. The report included a general outline of internal policies in French North Africa prior to the Allied landings on the 8th of November 1942 and how the dynamics had changed, the role played by Darlan and other French leaders, the detail and background to Darlan's assassination on the 24th of December 1942 and the focus and politics of political parties and factions such as 'La Résistance', 'Combat' and the French Royalist Party.

RYGOR also answered Biffy's questions regarding who should be considered for senior positions with the Free French. Their conversation was interrupted by a telephone call from Menzies inquiring whether the report was ready. Biffy assured him that it would be ready shortly and that, in his opinion, '*it was interesting, detailed and incisive*'.

Although they were pressed for time, Biffy did not want their meeting to end abruptly. Biffy promised to take RYGOR to see the huge map of North Africa hanging at the War Office with all AGENCY AFRICA's intelligence information marked on it, from which Operation TORCH was planned. Biffy escorted him to the door. Shaking his hand, he added, *'I'm sorry that you are not British – for what you have done for Britain, you wouldn't have to work again for the rest of your life!'*

*

By the end of 1942, Biffy's section, now renamed 'P5', was continuing to run three lines of operations: his ongoing Vichy networks, his other French networks and his liaison with and management of Polish networks in Europe. Since the United States' entry into war, December 1941, a fourth responsibility was developing rapidly with the arrival in London of the newly formed Office of Strategic Services. 'P5' was beginning to receive such a large volume of intelligence that Menzies asked Biffy to filter what he sent him by producing a fortnightly summary, highlighting *'items of outstanding interest. Where there are no such items, I would prefer the paragraph to be as short as possible.'*

Prior to the North African landing, 'P5' product included extensive reports from Bertrand in Vichy covering details of all Vichy armed forces order of battle and intelligence activity in France and North Africa as well as topographical intelligence on ports and beaches in preparation for the landings in North Africa, as well as confirming intelligence on the Germans.

From occupied France, Biffy was getting excellent intelligence on coastal defences from the Pas de Calais to Brittany, ongoing U-boat activity and other maritime activity. In the south of France, networks reported on coastal defences in Toulon and Marseilles, shipping and reports on the deployment and order of battle of the Italian Piave and Legano divisions in France. German troop deployments and defences on the Mediterranean were also reported. From Germany and Poland, reports came to Biffy on shipbuilding in the shipyards at Ebling, Kiel, Stettin, Pillau, Konigsberg and Lübeck, on U-boat bases at Danzig and submarine construction at Gdyna and Katowice. The development of chemical warfare came from Bialystok in Poland together with details of German troop reinforcements for the Eastern Front.

Most importantly and with increasing frequency, Biffy's section was reporting on the development and deployment of the V1 and V2 rockets from networks in France, Poland and Germany. These were corroborated by intelligence from the Polish agent in Switzerland, Halina Szymanska.

As well as France and North Africa, Polish intelligence activities covered Spain, Portugal, Latin America, the Balkans, Scandinavia and the Baltic states, the Middle East as well as, most importantly, Germany and Poland. The Poles were able to maintain communications and courier lines between Warsaw and London, using Paris as a staging post. One of Biffy's reports to 'C' describes the various concealment devices used by the couriers:

> *Valuable articles were never used, as liable to be stolen. Backs of pocket mirrors, backs of hairbrushes, backs of nailbrushes, hollow toothbrushes, shaving brushes, shaving sticks, cakes of soap, fountain pens, pencils (Eversharp type), suitcases with false bottoms, soles of shoes.*

Critical information coming out of Germany and Poland on V1 and V2 rockets was corroborated by information coming from Polish and French networks in France. A great deal of this information was

Concealment devices

passed through Biffy's section, in parallel with Kenneth Cohen's networks, ALLIANCE and AGIR. The earliest reports on V weapons came from Biffy's team in February 1941. The next series of reports began in June 1943, starting with information from slave labourers on the Peenemunde testing site. When received in Biffy's office, they immediately knew what it was and put out an order that anything further on V weapons and their development was to be marked for 'Most Immediate' transmission. By November 1943, there were continuous reports coming to Biffy from networks in Poland and Germany, including photographs. In the spring of 1944, a V2 rocket fell into the bank of the River Bug near the testing ground at Sarnacki. The rocket was quickly hidden by the Resistance and later, with some considerable difficulty, smuggled into Warsaw where it was examined by a Polish scientist who extracted its fuel and sent a sample, via Brindisi, to London in May 1944. SIS asked to see the whole rocket and it took until July 1944 for them to arrange, together with SOE and Polish Intelligence, for an air pick-up. Sending the whole V2 by air was impractical as it was 14 metres (47 feet) long and weighed 13,000 kilos (29,000 lbs). Only key components could be sent.

The Poles stipulated that one of their technical experts must accompany the chassis of the rocket. A note from Biffy's section stated that: *'The Polish agent who brought this information and material (i.e. photos, plans and sketches) has made a study of the subject and is well versed in the latest V2 developments in Poland.'*

The flight was scheduled for the 25th of July under command of S.G. Calliford. The mission was uneventful until the landing in Poland where the DC3 aircraft bogged in on landing and the brakes seized. Matters were not helped by the heavy load. Eventually, the brakes were fixed and the wheels freed for take-off which was effected using full throttle and the DC3 staggered into the air.

With only one stop at Bari (where SIS/SOE had a base) the precious cargo arrived safely in London on the 28th of July 1944. One of the passengers, Dr Rettinger, a prominent Polish politician, sent a telegram to Anthony Eden, British Foreign Secretary, paying tribute to the *'efficiency of all British services concerned in this enterprise'*, which was codenamed Operation WILDHORN III.

From mid-1944 onwards, Biffy's intelligence enabled the RAF to attack and destroy launch sites. Some reports in early 1945 gave the location of V-weapon manufacture inside Germany, including V2 factories at Ebensbach, Leitmeritz and Frankfurt-am-Main. Biffy later said that he regarded the work on the V-weapons as one of the most important carried out by his section.

*

The final part of just how important the Polish contribution to strategic intelligence was involves the story of Agent KNOPF and Biffy's JADE AMICOL network. The story is surrounded by considerable mythology. Either just before or at the outbreak of war, Polish Intelligence had been able to recruit a very significant agent with excellent access to the highest levels of German military and political planning. This agent was codenamed KNOPF with the code number 594. KNOPF's identity still remains unknown. What is known is that KNOPF himself, and probably a network of agents that he ran, had high-level access to the Oberkommando der Wehrmacht (OKW), to Hitler's inner planning circle within OKW and the High Command of the German Armed Forces. KNOPF's reports were passed to Biffy along with the other intelligence gathered by the Poles. Reports included German plans for the invasion of Malta in 1942, German strategy and operational plans on the Eastern Front (including the order of battle and date of Operation BARBAROSSA) and German plans for the Mediterranean and North Africa. KNOPF also reported the location of Hitler's headquarters in East Prussia and his obsession with the capture of Stalingrad. Biffy reported that:

> the source of whom the Poles think very highly is not a Pole. He has not specified his informants but state that they are highly placed and in touch with the German High Command.

In April 1943 another report written for General[139] Alan Brooke, the Chief of the Imperial General Staff, stated:

'KNOPF' forecast very closely the general outline of the German summer campaign in Russia. Many of his reports were clear and factual and showed an accuracy of detail which precludes the possibility that he was indulging in intelligence guessing.

KNOPF's reports were certainly read by Winston Churchill. The intelligence he provided would have underpinned the Prime Minister's overall war strategy and would have acted as the 'HUMINT' equivalent of ENIGMA. KNOPF's reports would have enhanced and confirmed ENIGMA intercepts and vice versa. It was noted that: *'KNOPF's information on the position of Hitler's HQ is confirmed by Most Secret Sources'.*[140] KNOPF sent his reports by wireless, since a report on his work refers to 'errors in transmission' such as misspelled names. SIS was able to confirm KNOPF's information and ensure he was not a 'plant'.

There has been much speculation about who KNOPF was. Candidates have included General Hans Oster, Colonel Alexis van Rohne, Lieutenant Colonel Kurt Jahnke and Admiral Wilhelm Canaris. All of whom have well documented anti-Nazi credentials and were executed in the aftermath of the plot to assassinate Hitler. It is possible that they were all part of the KNOPF network and were swept up in the post-bomb plot purge.

The case for Canaris is quite plausible. He certainly had a Polish mistress, Halima Szymanska, the wife of Colonel Anthony Szymanska who had been Polish Military Attaché in Berlin in 1939. On August the 22nd 1939, Canaris tipped him off that Poland would be invaded on the 1st of September. Colonel Szymanska left for Warsaw the next morning to warn the Polish High Command and was never seen again – rather convenient for Canaris. Halima was in close touch with Polish Intelligence in Switzerland and London and

---

139 Later Field Marshal 1st Viscount Alan Brooke.
140 Most Secret Sources intelligence was the designated term for *'highly secret information obtained by intercept'* i.e. ENIGMA.

Admiral Canaris   Halina Szymanska

via them, reported to Biffy. She was issued with a Polish diplomatic passport and a French ID card forged by SIS to enable her to travel to meet Canaris. Canaris had arranged for her to live in Switzerland, as both a personal convenience and as an avenue to pass information to SIS via the Abwehr Head of Station, Hans-Bernd Gisevius, including a warning of the German attack on the Low Countries, passed to Szymanska by Canaris on a stopover to Lausanne railway station on his way to Rome. The report was passed on by SIS but not acted on.

One of Canaris's possible motivations would have been his horror at how prisoners and Jews were being murdered by the SS Einsatzgruppen on the Eastern Front. He had complained to General Keitel, Chief of the OKW, who warned him not to take his protest to Hitler, '*the matter has already been decided*'. Canaris's attitude was also noted by Heydrich.

Increasingly disillusioned with Hitler, the Nazis and the war, it is entirely possible that he used his military intelligence organisation, the Abwehr, as a platform and cover for his own intelligence activities. It is well known that he did pass information via Halima Szymanska including a warning about the invasion of Russia and a plan to capture Gibraltar – both pieces of intelligence attributed to KNOPF. After 1942, Canaris visited Spain on several occasions using the alias Juan Guillermo and again it was possible that he was in contact with the Poles, or directly with SIS.

As well as passing intelligence, he used the Abwehr to save the lives of a considerable number of Jews. As early as 1938, Canaris had become involved with an anti-Hitler group of senior ranking military officers and Foreign Ministry officials including General Ludwig von Beck and Ernst von Weizsäcker. There is speculation that Canaris was directly in touch with Stewart Menzies, 'C', but this is unlikely. What is more likely is that he used a 'cut-out', Ewald von Kleist-Schmerzin, who did visit Britain and was in touch with SIS. Canaris was also fully aware and probably instigated an approach by the Abwehr to the British Government as early as 1940, via the Vatican. Later in the war Stewart Menzies was keen to develop contact with Canaris with a view to arranging a meeting. Unfortunately, this became known to Kim Philby who told the Russians. A story was leaked to the British press that Canaris was a disaffected anti-Nazi. Menzies was disappointed, *'Every time we build something up, something like this happens and destroys what we have built.'*

It is also highly unlikely that Canaris was the KNOPF wireless operator himself, but it would not have been at all difficult for him to find one in the Abwehr, using codes and a set supplied by the Poles via Switzerland.

It is also possible that the wireless operator was provided by General Reinhard Gehlen,[141] Chief of Intelligence at Fremde Heere Ost, the German Eastern Front Command Centre, who was also reportedly in touch with the Allies by radio.

It is clear that Biffy in his Polish liaison capacity handled KNOPF's material. What is not clear is the truth surrounding Canaris's meetings with Philip Keun and Claude Arnould who ran Biffy's JADE AMICOL network in Paris. By the spring of 1944, JADE AMICOL had survived many attempts by the Gestapo to destroy it. It had become Biffy's most important network in France. Not only was it collecting military intelligence but also high-level political intelligence. It was also in touch with disaffected Germans in General von Stülpnagel's headquarters in Paris. As we know, Keun did not survive the war, being betrayed by an informer on the 29th of June 1944 and executed in September. Arnould survived and was awarded a DSO for his work. Arnould maintained that Keun, at Menzies's request, delivered

---

141 Gehlen became Head of the Bundes Nachrichten Dienst (BND), the German Foreign Intelligence Services, after the war.

via Biffy, had been in touch directly with Canaris in April and May 1944. Arnould was concerned as he thought that it was a set-up:

Because I feared that the whole matter might be a trick by the Germans to find our headquarters. But Keun assured me it was not a trick and that Canaris was representing a group of high-ranking Germans who were anxious to get in touch with the Allied high command in London. He told me he must get this information to London without delay.

Arnould maintained that Keun immediately arranged a Lysander pick-up and went to London to consult with Biffy and Menzies. The records of all Lysander pick-ups are meticulous – no such flight took place. Anthony Cave Brown, in his book *Bodyguard of Lies*, also maintained that there were several meetings between Canaris, Keun and Arnould in the forest of Fointainebleau at Longchamp racecourse, in the Place Donfert-Rochaeu and in the JADE AMICOL headquarters at the Convent of Sainte-Agonie.

All of this is pure fantasy. To quote Biffy:

It seems inconceivable that it happened this way if it happened at all. In the first place, Canaris was far too wily an old bird to commit himself under circumstances where the messenger might very easily be captured. And Keun himself would have thought twice about carrying any message.

This rings true. It is highly unlikely that an experienced intelligence operator like Canaris would expose himself in this way, particularly as he was very distinctive-looking, without any attempt at disguise. Also, by February 1944, Canaris was under suspicion and under surveillance and had been moved from his post as Chief of the Abwehr. Philip Keun had moved away from Paris to what he thought was a safe house in an isolated farm at Gué de la Thas, south of Orléans. His last recorded trip to London was on the 25th of December 1943 by MGB 318 in order to see Biffy and get instructions for JADE AMICOL's role in the invasion. He returned by parachute, damaging his back on landing. Also, Arnould who had successfully run his network throughout the war and evaded capture is also unlikely to have allowed Canaris to go to his secret headquarters at the convent.

Whoever it was, KNOPF's intelligence was accurate and of great strategic value and it would have passed through Biffy's office on its way from the Poles, to where it was most needed. It reinforced the ENIGMA intelligence and was in turn verified by ENIGMA, thus enabling the Allied strategic planners to have two impeccable sources.

*

At the end of the war, Biffy was asked to write a full appraisal of the contribution of Polish Intelligence for Winston Churchill. He stated that the Poles were among the best, if not the best at the intelligence game. Between the outbreak of war and the 8th of May 1945, Biffy's section (Sequentially 'A4', 'P5' and 'SLC') produced 45,770 intelligence reports, of which 22,047 were received from Polish sources supplied by 1,500 French and British agents in Biffy's networks, and 600 Polish agents. He concluded by saying:

> It will thus be seen that Polish agents have worked unceasingly and well in Europe during the last five years, and that they have provided, often at great danger to themselves and to their relatives, a vast amount of material of all kinds on a wide range of subjects. The Polish IS has made an invaluable contribution to the planning and the successful execution of the invasion of France, and to the ultimate victory of the Allied forces in Europe.

And in a personal letter to Colonel Gano dated the 30th of June 1945:

> It would be impossible for me to finish this letter without saying how much we have appreciated your close collaboration with our Service and the great contribution you have made towards winning the war against Germany and Italy. I would like also to convey to you on behalf of our organisation best wishes for the future. Yours Wilski.

Biffy with Polish intelligence officers, prior to D-Day

Towards the end of 1943, Biffy was made an Officer of the Order of Polonia Restituta (Order of the Rebirth of Poland) for his outstanding work for 'National Defence and fostering good relations between countries'. At the same time, 130 Poles were decorated by the British Government for their intelligence work. These covered all the changing strategic imperatives of the Allied war aims. Sequentially: the U-boat threat, advanced warning of Operation BARBAROSSA, Operation TORCH, the Normandy landings and the V-weapon threat. The Poles also played a significant part in ENIGMA and the Double Cross project and strategic deception for the Normandy landings; 48 per cent of all reports received by SIS from occupied Europe came from Polish sources. Biffy again:

We cannot overstate the importance and meaning we attach to the outstanding services rendered by this magnificent organisation.

CHAPTER 15 – THE AMERICANS AND THE END IN FRANCE

'A date which will live in infamy.'

President Roosevelt describing Pearl Harbor

Although the Japanese surprise attack on Pearl Harbor on Sunday the 7th of December 1941 marked the formal entry of the United States into World War II, on the intelligence front, much had been going on for 18 months before that. After the outbreak of war in September 1939, the US Government was debating two alternative courses of action. One was to support Britain and keep her in the war by supplying her with the material assistance which was desperately needed. The other was to give Britain up as lost, retreat into isolationism and to concentrate exclusively on American rearmament to counter the German threat. That America decided to support Britain was due in large part to the efforts of one man, Colonel 'Wild Bill' Donovan.

Donovan was an eminently successful corporate lawyer from New York and a close friend of President Roosevelt. He also happened to be a World War I hero who held America's three highest military decorations.[142] Donovan had also served in the 1916 Pancho Villa Campaign in Mexico where he had met the young Charles Gossage Grey, who, as well as working for Biffy in Paris and later in the 'F2' network, would be an early recruit to Donovan's OSS.

Immediately after the fall of France in 1940, Britain's future did not look too bright. Roosevelt did not feel assured that aid to Britain would not be wasted. This negative view was compounded by the dispatches of the US ambassador in London, Joseph Kennedy. Kennedy desperately wanted to keep the US out of the war, briefing consistently against Britain. He was also seen as an appeaser, a friend of Germany and an anti-Semite. Luckily his dispatches did not cut much

---

142 Congressional Medal of Honor, Distinguished Service Cross, Distinguished Service Medal, Silver Star, Three Purple Hearts, National Security Medal.

William Joseph 'Wild Bill' Donovan, Head of the OSS

ice with Roosevelt who was more inclined to support Britain in its fight for survival and dispatched Donovan on a fact-finding mission.

Between the wars, when the US had no formal intelligence service, a group of Anglophiles had set up what amounted to a private intelligence service known as 'The Room'. Members included Donovan, Vincent Astor, Kermit Roosevelt, David Bruce (Andrew Mellon's son-in-law) and Nelson Doubleday, the publisher. They met monthly in an apartment at 34 East 62nd Street in Manhattan with '*an unlisted telephone number and no apparent occupant*'. The Room later changed its name to 'The Walrus Club'. The Walrus Club had close links to SIS via two similar organisations in London, 'The Ends of the Earth Club' and the '1b Club'. Stewart Menzies was a member of both. There was also interaction in France via 'The Travellers Club' in the Champs-Élysées – a regular haunt of the Deuxième Bureau officers and of Biffy and Charles Grey before the war. At Churchill's behest, SIS had dispatched William Stephenson, a Scots-Canadian businessman, to the US to lobby for support for Britain. Stephenson left for New York in mid-June 1940. He established himself on the 33rd and 34th floor of the Rockefeller Center, given to him for free by Nelson Rockefeller, a member of The Room. Stephenson lobbied hard and was eventually introduced to Roosevelt by Bill Donovan.

Donovan arrived in London by Pan-Am Clipper in July 1940. As directed by Churchill he was given complete access, except for

Bletchley. His visit started with a meeting with Lord Gort, Chief of the Imperial General Staff, on the 24th of July, set up by Stewart Menzies. During his visit, which lasted until the 3rd of August, he became friendly with Admiral Godfrey the DNI, his principal staff officer Ian Fleming and key members of SIS including Biffy. Donovan returned to the US with a completely different message for Roosevelt – if Britain was supported, they would fight and win. This ultimately led to the Lend-Lease deal in which US military equipment was made available in exchange for long-term lease on British bases in the Caribbean.

On July the 11th 1941, Roosevelt signed an order naming Donovan Coordinator of Information (COI), effectively setting up the beginnings of a formal intelligence agency. Donovan set up shop on the 35th floor of the Rockefeller Center, immediately above SIS. After Pearl Harbor, Donovan got into top gear. COI changed its name to the Office of Strategic Services (OSS). Donovan recruited agents, selecting individuals from all walks of life – from intellectuals and artists to people with criminal backgrounds. He hired a great many women, dismissing criticism by those who felt they were unsuited to such work. Among his prominent recruits were film director John Ford, actor Sterling Hayden, author Stephen Vincent Benét and Eve Curie, daughter of the scientists Marie and Pierre Curie. Other OSS recruits included poet Archibald MacLeish, banker Paul Mellon, businessman Alfred V. du Pont (son of industrialist Alfred I. du Pont), psychologist Carl Jung (who helped with the effort to analyse the psyches of Hitler and other Nazi leaders) and members of the Auchincloss and Vanderbilt families. There were so many 'aristocrats' in the agency, a joke went round that the OSS stood for 'Oh So Social'.

'*Woe to the officer,*' wrote OSS Colonel (and later ambassador) David Bruce, '*who turned down a project because, on its face, it seemed ridiculous, or at least unusual.*' Every hare-brained plan for secret operations (from phosphorescent foxes to incendiary bats) would find a sympathetic ear in Donovan's office. Questioning orders became a way of life for OSS officers. Donovan was unconcerned. He often said, '*I'd rather have a young lieutenant with guts enough to disobey an order than a Colonel too regimented to think and act for himself.*'

David Bruce, Head of
OSS London

OSS was soon to encounter scepticism in London and it was the same in Washington. Donovan firmly defended his new creation. On one occasion, at a Georgetown dinner party, he overheard disparaging remarks made about OSS by senior naval officer, Admiral Horace Schmahl. Donovan challenged him – *'My "Tonka Toy" outfit as you describe them could get all the secret files from your office and blow up the naval ammunition depot before midnight.'* Donovan slipped away, made a phone call and by midnight his hastily activated covert methods of entry team had delivered the entire contents of the Admiral's safe to Donovan at the dinner party. Donovan also told the suitably chastened Admiral where to find the dummy charges in his ammunition depot.

In early 1941, before the formation of COI, Ian Fleming, assistant to Admiral Godfrey in British Naval Intelligence, suggested to Donovan that he should select, as intelligence officers, men who possessed the qualities of *'absolute discretion, sobriety, devotion to duty, languages, and wide experience'*. Their age, Fleming added, should be *'about 40 to 50'*. Donovan declined Fleming's advice. Instead, he promised Franklin Roosevelt an international Secret Service staffed by young officers who were *'calculatingly reckless'* with *'disciplined daring'* who were *'trained for aggressive action'*.

This difference in approach and culture was going to bring about a serious clash with SIS and, in particular, Claude Dansey who viewed OSS as amateurs *'playing Cowboys and Indians'*. *'Ah, those first OSS arrivals in London! How well I remember them,'* reminisced the

British author Malcolm Muggeridge, '*arriving like jeune filles en fleur straight from a finishing school, all fresh and innocent, to start work in our frowsty old intelligence brothel. All too soon they were ravished and corrupted, becoming indistinguishable from seasoned pros who had been in the game for a quarter century or more.*'

The first herculean task of these OSS newcomers was to find their way through the complicated structure of British intelligence: SIS, MI5, SOE, GC + CS, MI9 and learn how to convince the British to teach them the tricks of the trade. General Donovan's first requirement was for an OSS commander who would be accepted by the class-conscious elite who ran the British Intelligence Community. His selection of David Kirkpatrick Bruce was inspired. The 41-year-old multi-millionaire was a handsome, cultured representative of the American upper class.[143]

Bruce ticked all the social and political boxes. He had been a member of 'The Room', his father had been a prominent United States senator and his wife, the daughter of Andrew Mellon the steel magnate, was the world's richest woman. Although there was much opposition to OSS within SIS, led largely by Claude Dansey, the 'gentlemen' of the OSS headquarters at 70 Grosvenor Street largely came from the same social circle that Biffy had frequented before the war. Many had lived in Paris or come from families that Biffy knew well, like the Vanderbilts and Hydes, including Henry Hyde,[144] son of James Hyde. In part, Dansey's professional antipathy stemmed from jealousy. OSS had got a grip of the differing requirements of intelligence-gathering and special operations under a unified command, unlike the differences between SIS and SOE that were to dog the British intelligence community until the end of the war.

The Americans found a friend and champion in Biffy, who added liaison with OSS to his already full portfolio of Vichy, special French networks and Poles, in the aptly named Special Liaison Controllerate.

143 Bruce's distinguished career included service as Chief of the Marshall Plan mission to France, 1948–49; he was US Ambassador to France, 1949–52; Ambassador to Germany, 1957–59; Ambassador to Britain 1961–69; and American delegate to the Vietnam Peace Conference in Paris 1970–71.

144 Henry Hyde. Educated at Cambridge and Bonn University. Law degree from Harvard. Fluent in French and German. Lifelong friend of Biffy.

He was a regular visitor to OSS Headquarters. He was no doubt helped by June who came from the same background as many of the OSS officers in London and by friends from his Paris days like Charles Gossage Grey and Henry Hyde, who was the OSS liaison with General Giraud in Algiers. Hyde was a fervent anti-Gaullist whose sympathies echoed those of Biffy and his Vichy network.

In May 1943, after a long series of meetings between Bruce and Stewart Menzies, the British offered OSS an equal partnership in European intelligence operations in preparation for the invasion of France, to be known as Plan SUSSEX, designed to radically improve relations with the Americans and the Free French. It involved the dispatch of 50 two-man intelligence teams throughout France in advance of the OVERLORD landings. The teams would consist of a Frenchman and either a British SIS agent or an American from OSS. They would parachute 40 to 60 miles inland from the English Channel, covering the operational area that stretched from Brittany to the Belgian border and as far inland as Strasburg on the French-German border, collecting military tactical and operational intelligence of immediate value to Allied ground commanders. OSS was delighted with this plan, but Dansey was still not happy and he ensured that his 'man', Kenneth Cohen, was the British coordinator. Weeks after SUSSEX was first proposed, it had become *'increasingly and painfully clear'* that some British intelligence officials were still exerting *'power and influence'* to prevent the establishment of an *'equal, independent and coordinated'* American intelligence service.[145] While many MI6 officers were friendly to OSS, in particular Biffy who was singled out as the most friendly and helpful, a few like Dansey sought to maintain the *'omnipotence'* of SIS in Europe, feeling that OSS would always be a *'distinctly junior partner'* and an anathema.

Plan SUSSEX suffered not only from British and American friction but also the ever-present friction between Gaullists and non-Gaullists.

---

145 Dansey's antipathy for the Americans is difficult to explain. He had been part of the British mission to the US, in 1917, to help the US Army set up an intelligence capability to assist the British and French. This capability was abandoned after World War I and Dansey must have felt that his efforts had been in vain and that America could never take intelligence seriously. He had also been married to an American.

Overall, coordination was given to Kenneth Cohen, supported by Colonel 'RÉMY' Gilbert Renault,[146] of the Free French, and Colonel Francis Pickens-Miller from OSS. Biffy helped to smooth many ruffled feathers and force through the selection of French agents from the French armed forces. Biffy's good relations and friendly attitude towards OSS was to stand him in good stead, not only for the rest of the war, but on into the Cold War and beyond the supposed end of his career in 1959.

*

In no small part due to the efforts of Biffy and many others in the business of intelligence-gathering and clandestine operations, the D-Day landings were able to take place successfully on the 6th of June 1944.

Between July 1940 and June 1944, SIS set up a total of 33 networks in France. Of these, 15 survived. By D-Day, SIS had a total of 12,299 agents working in France. In addition, they had worked extensively with the Vichy Intelligence Service who had set up three separate structures to work with SIS: Service Renseignement (SR) KLEBER run by Louis Rivet, SR Air run by Georges Ronin and Traveaux Régionaux run by Paul Paillole.

SIS Special Liaison Units, Special Communication Units and Special Counterintelligence Units had been deployed to support the ground battle in France. They were attached to military formations and headquarters and supplemented the SUSSEX teams. Their jobs respectively were to handle the distribution of ENIGMA material, provide SIS's own separate channel of communications, develop counterintelligence operations and connect with SIS networks as they were liberated. In the counterintelligence field, SIS was already on the lookout for German intelligence officers who had specialised in operations against the Russians. Although the war in Europe was not yet over, some in Broadway, including Biffy, had seen the writing

---

146 Gilbert Renault escaped to England from Brittany in 1940. He set up the very successful Confer de Notre Dame intelligence network. He was awarded the DSO and OBE by the British as well as the Légion d'honneur, Croix de Guerre and Liberation Medal from France and the Legion of Merit from the US.

on the wall and were not going to allow a repeat of the 1930s. The Allied breakout from Normandy in mid-August 1944 soon overran the SUSSEX teams and most of Biffy's and other SIS networks, as well as the Polish 'F2' network. Following the liberation of Paris on the 15th of August, in which the JADE AMICOL network played a significant part, and the landings in the south of France, by late August, France was effectively liberated. On the 23rd of October, after all the mistrust and factional infighting of the war, the Allies recognised General de Gaulle's administration as the provisional government of France. The SIS role in France soon wound down. Priorities were closing down operational networks, settling outstanding obligations to agents and tracing agents who had disappeared like Philip Keun, Pierre Hentic and André Peulevey. SIS also needed to establish its structure in France and the basis for liaison with the French intelligence services. Biffy and Tom Greene also made it their business to ensure that de Gaulle understood the role played by the likes of Bertrand, Rivet and Paillole.

Soon familiar faces gathered in Paris. Paul Paillole returned to take up counterintelligence duties. Charles Gossage Grey returned as an intelligence officer at the US embassy, Tom Greene was posted from London to set up the Anglo-French Communications Bureau in the Avenue des Tilleuls where his job was to set up a temporary SIS station and to track down agents, recover SIS equipment, close down networks and provide proof of agents' work for SIS during the war to the French authorities who were busily trying to sort real resisters from 'also-rans' and collaborators. One of these agents was André Peulevey who was liberated from the Natzweiler concentration camp. André had gone to London in January 1942 on one of the 15th MGB Flotilla exfiltration operations (Codename OVERCLOUD III), been trained by SIS and returned by gunboat on the 2nd of February 1942 (OVERCLOUD IV). Unfortunately, he walked straight into a Gestapo trap because of the treachery of Mathilde Carré. He was immediately arrested, but not before he had been able to hide his 50,000 francs of operational funds. After 40 months of torture and prison, he re-established contact with Uncle Tom on his liberation, promptly recovered his money and handed it over to Tom in Paris.

Tom returned to his old apartment at 69 Avenue Victor Hugo which he had sealed up, claiming it was the property of a 'neutral' Irishman. The apartment and all his possessions that he had left four years earlier were untouched, if very dusty. The apartment became a port of call for SIS officers visiting Paris or on their way to their appointment in Europe, including Nicholas Elliott and his family en route to take up a post in Bern. Once France was liberated and JADE AMICOL was closed down, Sheelagh Greene went back to work for her father as his private secretary. She was also given authority to follow the advancing Allied armies to try to find out what happened to SIS agents and recover those still alive.

Charles Grey, ever the adventurer, had spent the war working for the 'F2' network, then OSS. He returned to the US embassy as Head of Counterintelligence. He did not get on well with the US Ambassador, Jefferson Caffery, a rather stiff, formal type. The charming Grey, having had had a 'good war', found very little in common with his ambassador. On return to Paris, Grey had reactivated his membership of both the Travellers and Jockey Club. One day in the Travellers, after a good lunch, Grey looked up from the backgammon board to find two members of the Jockey Club in white gloves,

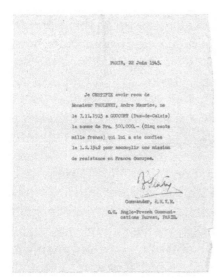

André Peulevey's receipt for returned secret funds

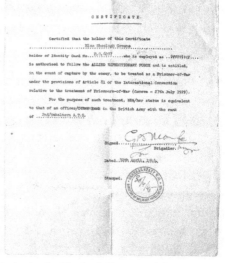

Authority for Sheelagh Greene to follow Allied forces to locate missing SIS agents

standing to attention. They had come to deliver a challenge to a duel on behalf of a friend, who felt that Grey had insulted him. Monsieur Grey has the choice of weapons. Would he please communicate his answer later?

News of the challenge spread so rapidly that Charles Grey found on his return to the embassy a message summoning him to the ambassador's office. Caffrey told him in the severest terms that any member of his staff involved in a duel would have to resign on the spot. Grey was despondent. He loved his job, but if he declined to fight, he would never again be able to hold up his head in Parisian society. The solution came to him just in time. He wrote a note accepting the challenge and informed the seconds that his choice of weapons was tanks – at any range they cared to select. Problem solved. Sadly, this amusing story is yet another part of the mythology surrounding Biffy and his friends. What really happened was, at the Travellers annual ball, a non-member arrived trying to crash the party. Charles Grey was informed and confronted the Frenchman, telling him that it was a private club and that he must leave. The man responded by saying that his integrity had been called into question and promptly challenged Charles to a duel. The dilemma concerning the reaction of the US Ambassador was overcome by a close friend of Charles's, Jimmy, Duc de Cadaval[147] offering to fight the duel on his behalf – apparently allowed under the rules of duelling. The duel was fought in the Bois de Boulogne using blunted rapiers. By 1944 duelling was not to the death but was conceded once the first 'hit' was made. Jimmy de Cadaval struck the first blow and won on behalf of Charles Grey.[148]

*

As the war in Europe wound down, changes were afoot in SIS. There was also about to be a significant change in Biffy's personal life. Before the war, in 1937, June had joined the board of the Société de secours aux blessés militaires – wounded World War I Veterans, under the auspices of the French Red Cross, giving her address as care of 1 Avenue Charles Floquet – Biffy's office.

147 Jaime Alvares Pereira de Melo, 10th Duc of Cadaval.
148 Related to the author by Charles Grey's son, Jimmy Grey.

When war broke out, she worked every day at the American Hospital. At some point, prior to the invasion of Holland and Belgium on the 10th of May 1940, Biffy sent June to London, for safety and to get her out of the way so he could concentrate on his agent-running and liaison duties with the French in preparation for war. June moved into 16 Wilton Place, the house that Biffy had bought just before the war. When Biffy escaped from France in June 1940, he immersed himself in the urgent task of getting networks set up and agents back into France. June quickly got herself involved in war work with the British War Relief Fund, of which she eventually became Deputy Vice Chairman.

The fund was set up to raise money in the US to fund relief projects in Britain. Her first trip to the US was by ship from Liverpool on the 17th of August 1940, returning again by ship to Liverpool on the 6th of September. Atlantic crossings by ship at this point in the war were increasingly hazardous and Biffy promptly put a stop to it, ensuring that she travelled by air via the Pan Am Clipper flying boat service from Lisbon, via Bermuda to New York. Using her considerable connections with wealthy families in the US, she was very successful in fundraising. She also used the fact she was living in London and could tell people first-hand about life in the Blitz, regularly giving interviews to US newspapers, which were carefully managed to ensure that they made the point about the horrors of the Blitz without giving away bomb damage assessment information to the enemy.

Two of her early successes were the funding of a canteen for factory workers in Taunton and the delivery of a baby bath unit to the Prince of Wales Hospital, Plymouth:

A 'Novel and Practical Gift' from the people of Plymouth, Massachusetts, United States of America, through the British War Relief Society of Americas to the people of Plymouth, England, was presented to the Devon Red Cross in London on Thursday December 18th 1941.

The bath, the first of its kind to be constructed, came with a two-tonne van containing two 100-gallon water tanks, two boilers and stoves and other equipment. It was presented by Mrs W. A.

Dunderdale, a representative of the War Relief Society to Mrs L. Sayers, of Alston Hall, Holbeton, Devon, Vice-President of the Devon Red Cross. Alongside the stoves, which could heat 60 gallons of water at the same time, was a coal bin. The van also featured a sink and a wringer to enable babies' clothes to be washed as well as a dozen of the collapsible white baths with their wooden frames and under a seat was a nest of 10 zinc baths for adults. A medicine cupboard, folding ward screens, chairs and kettles, completed the equipment.

There has been speculation about whether June had any involvement in Biffy's intelligence work, but it is very unlikely that June had any operational function. Given Biffy's position, his work with Vichy and his independent networks, the Poles and increasingly OSS, any involvement of Biffy's wife where she could be exposed to capture would have been madness. They seemed to have stayed together until at least June 1944 when, as mentioned earlier, they were recorded hosting a dinner at home on the 5th of June 1944 with Menzies and Bertrand to celebrate Bertrand's safe arrival in London and, presumably, the invasion scheduled for the next day.

Gradually their marriage was to fall apart. It had begun to unravel in Paris before the war. They had no children and, after the first flush of marriage had worn off, found their characters were quite different. Biffy, always with an eye on pretty women, gradually became interested in other people. June became disillusioned. Their age

Medal awarded to June by the French Government for her wartime medical work

difference didn't help; June was 17 and Biffy 29 when they got married. June moved out to live at 35 Lower Belgrave Street in 1945. Eventually their marriage was dissolved by an annulment in Paris on the 30th of April 1947 as June was underage when they got married. The annulment process probably suited both of them as it was quicker than a divorce.

After the end of his marriage to June in 1947, Biffy was introduced to Dorothy Hyde, the ex-wife of Montgomery Hyde, also an SIS officer. Hyde began the war working for SIS in Bermuda where he ran the censorship operation. This was a cover for a team of SIS personnel whose job was to open all the diplomatic mail passing through Bermuda from the Americas to Europe, Bermuda being the Atlantic 'hub' for the Clipper Flying Boat Service between New York and Lisbon. Dorothy Hyde was one of the team of women who worked in the basement of the Hamilton Princess Hotel, opening the diplomatic bags, extracting and copying anything of intelligence value and then resealing the bags. The resealing was the tricky part. Most bags had complicated knots and lead or wax seals, which had to be replaced exactly so as to prevent the recipients knowing that their mail had been tampered with. Dorothy became very adept at this. Biffy had been introduced to Dorothy by Ingram Fraser. Fraser was a close friend of Biffy's and an SIS officer. Dorothy was divorced from Montgomery Hyde in 1952 and the same year married Biffy.

Dorothy Dunderdale

*

At the end of the war, an event took place in France on the 26th of June 1945 which reunited Biffy's wartime team. A memorial service for Philip Keun was held at 11:00 in the Chapel of Le Couvent de la Sainte-Agonie in the Rue de la Santé, the JADE AMICOL head-quarters. Those attending included Biffy, Tom Greene, Charles Grey, Stewart Menzies, Bertrand, Paillole and many others from SIS and the Deuxième Bureau, as well as survivors of both JADE AMICOL and FITZROY. The coming together felt like a moment not just to remember Philip, but all those who had made sacrifices in the pursuit of victory.

But as much as those present would have hoped for an end to war, the next conflict was about to begin, with an enemy Biffy knew all too well.

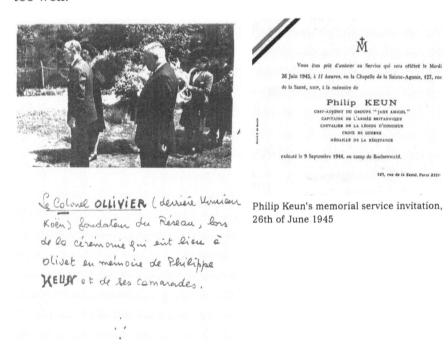

Philip Keun's memorial service invitation, 26th of June 1945

Claude Arnould and Philip Keun's father, George, at Philip's memorial service

CHAPTER 16
CONTROLLER SPECIAL LIAISON

'From Stettin in the Baltic to Trieste in the Adriatic, an iron
curtain has descended across the continent. Behind that line
lie all the capitals of the ancient States of Central and Eastern
Europe. Warsaw, Berlin, Prague, Vienna, Budapest, Belgrade,
Bucharest and Sofia, all these famous cities and the popula-
tions around them lie in the Soviet sphere, and all are subject,
in one form or another, not only to Soviet influence, but to a
very high, and in some cases, increasing measure of control
from Moscow.'

Winston Churchill, Fulton Missouri, March 5th 1946

George Keenan, the US State Department Russian expert, watching the 1945 victory celebrations in Moscow, was overheard by
British journalist Ralph Parker saying: '*They are cheering. They think
the war is over, but it has only just begun.*'

Discussions surrounding the post-war structure of Britain's intelligence services, '*the future organisation of intelligence relating to
foreign countries*', had begun by the end of 1943. In October, a three-
man committee under Nevile Bland was set up to report on '*the future
organisation of the SIS*'. '*The Bland report – future organisation of
the SIS*' was finished in October 1944. In this 38-page document the
future of SIS was set out, covering all aspects of its structure and
methodology from recruitment to cover organisations. It also set out
the parameters for liaison with friendly or Allied intelligence services – a large part of Biffy's work during the war. The report also
addressed the issue of Special Operations and the friction that had
permeated relations between SIS and SOE throughout the war. In
future, the Special Operations function would be part of SIS, paving
the way for the disbandment of SOE at the end of the war and the
absorption of its function and its best operators into SIS. The report
also identified the future threat from Russia:

In general we can count on the NKVD and other Soviet organisations pursuing covert aims and activities in contradiction to the overt policy of the Soviet government, but with the latter's blessing.

Russia was soon to become the enemy once more.

SIS was to be reorganised into four departments:

- Requirements, responsible for identifying and defining intelligence requirements.
- Production, responsible for gathering intelligence.
- Finance and Administration.
- Technical Services.

In turn, the production department was to have five regional controllers: Western Europe, Northern Area, Eastern Mediterranean, Far East and the Americas, and Controller Production Research which was *'responsible for all agents controlled direct from Head Office'*.

The one anomaly was Biffy, always a free spirit and liking his independence of action, albeit within the structure of the service. Given his track record, including the delivery of the ENIGMA machine and his wartime operations, he was allowed to retain his unique position as Controller Special Liaison. He was to continue to carry out his carefully developed liaison arrangements with the French, Poles and Americans. It also included his team of émigré linguists – mostly Russians and Poles – his *'highly specialised staff of Russian speakers ...'* Biffy knew the threat posed by the Russians better than most, except those of fellow officers like 'Gibbie' Gibson who had also worked against them in the 1920s and 1930s. He relied not only on his experience, but also on his instinct. As his godson Anthony Fraser told the author, he had a habit of tapping the side of his nose with his forefinger... *'I can smell it'*. He was well aware that the Soviets, from the time of the Revolution, were experts at deploying a wide range of overt and covert subversive actions, the full sophistication of which would take the West a long time to work out. The Russians played a long game – the recruitment of Philby, Maclean, Burgess, Cairncross and Blunt is a case in point. Recruited in the 1930s, they only began to come into their own in the 1950s.

At the end of the war, Biffy's team at Caxton Street started to move on. Uncle Tom went to Paris to set up the Anglo-French Communications Bureau to help dismantle networks, recover money and equipment and award decorations. Delicate decisions had to be made involving recommendations for awards and decorations. There were security considerations, too. Former agents had to be trusted or paid (or a combination of the two) not to publish their memoirs and tell tales at the pub. Widows and orphans also had to be taken care of. Winding up JADE AMICOL for example cost millions of francs.

Anthony Heath left his Poles at Stanmore and headed for Italy. Biffy wrote him a letter on the 13th of April 1945 which was a masterpiece of cryptic veiled speech.[149]

PERSONAL

London. S.W.1
13th April 1945

Dear Heath,
I am glad to know that the final arrangements have been made for
your return to the land of sunshine, and I would like to take this
opportunity of asking you if it would be possible to call and give
my personal greetings to our mutual friends. If you can, please tell
them that I hope we shall meet again very shortly and that if there
is anything I can do for them at this end, to let me know.

Incidentally, as you already know, a letter has been sent to them
mentioning that you were likely to be in their part of the world and
I am sure that they will do everything possible to help you.

Don't forget that I would like to hear from you from time to time
and I suggest that if you have any urgent messages or papers,
you entrust them to our friends who will know what to do with

---

149 Veiled speech: A means by which two people can discuss openly something they both know about and understand in front of others without directly referring to the detail as subject matter directly.

them. Don't miss any opportunity of doing the things we discussed generally.

Wishing you the best of luck,
Yours ever,
Biffy

Heath played a significant role in Italy working behind enemy lines, running SIS networks with the Italian Partisans. In April 1945, it was Heath who tipped off the Partisans as to Mussolini's whereabouts. He and his mistress Clara Petacci were summarily executed.

Biffy moved from Alliance House on Caxton Street to 2 Ryder Street, the old Section D offices. He was delighted to stay out of Head Office in Broadway because of his general independence of mind and lack of conformity, or did he smell something, somewhere wasn't quite right?

By July 1945, his Special Liaison Controllerate was established at Ryder Street. It consisted of two sections: Atlantic and Non-Atlantic. The Atlantic Section, counter-intuitively, targeted Russia, collecting intelligence radio traffic intercepted by the Poles at their stations in Stanmore and Scotland and decrypted at Boxmoor; radio telegraph messages transmitted in clear, telephone intercepts; and open sources such as the Soviet press. The traffic was read by a team working with the General Post Office and telegraph companies. The intercepted material was passed to Captain Eddie Hastings at GCHQ and then returned to Biffy's operations centre in a house called Firbanks in Roehampton. This operations centre was run by Major Arthur Allen[150] and Squadron Leader Macdonald. The radio intercepts were supervised by another of Biffy's White Russians named Bunakov, who collected material from all over the Soviet Union to be analysed by an office on the first floor of Biffy's old office in Caxton Street and another team based in Artillery Mansions in Victoria Street. The Atlantic Section was subdivided into:

Department A, the coordination department, run by Mr Shelley, who was responsible for communications interception units, analysts and customer departments.

---

150 Russian linguist. Father of Gillian who was a secretary in SIS and would marry George Blake.

Department B, headed by Sandy McKibbin, which dealt with economic and social conditions.

Department C, under Major Rikovsky, the military section dealing with the Red Army and NKVD and some strategic industries and infrastructure.

Department D, led by Major Leonard de Narkevich, the naval section.

Department E, under General Baranov, the aviation section.

Both Narkevich and Baranov had worked for Biffy from the early days in Paris. The departments collated all incoming intelligence to analyse it in detail. It was then entered into a comprehensive filing system. The intelligence was then sent to the relevant SIS section for a decision as to whether it should be sent on to the relevant 'customer'.

Individual pieces of intelligence did not make much sense, until compared with other reports and put into an intelligence summary. Biffy was convinced that Russia was so tightly controlled that the old way of setting up networks that he had used in the past would be very difficult in Russia after the war and that intercept was the way ahead, but he also believed that highly placed agents operating on their own were needed to complement the intercept material.

The Non-Atlantic Section was based in Ryder Street and was run on a day-to-day basis by Squadron Leader Macdonald, who was Biffy's deputy, replacing Uncle Tom. Charles Garton moved with Biffy from Caxton Street.

Charles came from yet another long-serving SIS family. His father and uncle had been in SIS from the early days with Mansfield Cumming. During the war he had worked for Biffy in the SIS station in Madrid and later in both Caxton Street and Ryder Street. He met Sheelagh Greene after the war and, in April 1948, put in an application to SIS to marry her. The application makes interesting reading; signed off by Biffy in pencil in the top right-hand corner, it is annotated on the bottom:

Vetting unnecessary as Miss Greene was a member of our staff, therefore approved. SLC to inform applicant.

Charles Garton outside Biffy's office on Ryder Street

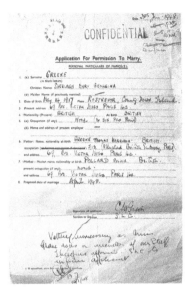

The task of the Non-Atlantic Section was a continuation of Biffy's wartime work, liaison with the emerging French Intelligence Service and the Americans, initially OSS, then the SSU and eventually the CIA. Biffy's first task was to go to Paris, where he stayed with Tom Greene at 69 Avenue Victor Hugo. His visit was to reaffirm SIS connection with the emerging French Intelligence Service and the rapprochement between the Vichy Operation – Paillole, Ronin, Bertrand and Rivet and the Free French, (PASSY) André Dewavrin and (RÉMY) Gilbert Renault[151] that had begun in 1944 with PLAN SUSSEX. Biffy also took time to visit his domestic staff from his pre-war apartment and ensure that they had enough funds to begin a new life.

He also went to see his old friend Charles Gossage Grey, L'ANGE BLEU, who was running counterintelligence operations at the US embassy. After much celebration and laughing over the duel story, Grey introduced Biffy to Phil Horton who was running the OSS Station in Paris. Charles Grey briefed Biffy on his counterintelligence priorities in terms of captured Germans. First, those working in the anti-Nazi resistance, second, those with intelligence experience

---

151 Colonel André Dewavrin DSO, MC. Gilbert Renault DSO, OBE.

working against the Russians, third, those involved with special weapons projects – V1 and V2 rockets and jet fighters and fourth, war criminals. It was clear to both of them which way the wind was blowing with regard to the future enemy.

Before he left Paris, Biffy went to see Bertrand to discuss reactivating their conversation with the Finns regarding Russian codes that had petered out in 1940 and 1941, despite the efforts of Charles Grey. In late 1945 they arranged an operation whereby, with the agreement of the Finns and the Swedes, four of the Finnish codebreakers who had fled to Sweden, in Operation STELLAR POLARIS, were taken to France. Their cover story was that they were joining the French Foreign Legion, even travelling via the Foreign Legion's training depot at Sidi Bel Abbès in Algeria. They were based in the Château de Belloy just outside Paris, producing detailed reports from their archives on the Soviet order of battle. Known as Source-267, the reports were passed on to the British code breakers via the SIS station in Paris and shared with both the French and the Americans. Collecting intelligence on Russia was still highly sensitive, but Biffy's operations did much to put SIS in a good light with the Americans.

Before Biffy had left for Paris, he had also made an astute move with regard to the Poles and the future of Poland. By 1944 it was clear that Poland would not be a free country. Yet again, one occupier would be replaced by another. The vast Polish intelligence archive assembled in London after five and a half years of war would be of immense value to the Soviets. The Polish Intelligence Service in London, together with Biffy, determined that it should not under any circumstances be returned to Poland. On the 30th of June 1945, he wrote to Gano:

Dear Gano,
I must refer you to our agreement of 1940 by which, at the cessation of hostilities in Europe, any records, official documents, wireless sets, account books and correspondence dealing with our mutual activities, should be handed over to my representative who will bring this letter. As you will appreciate, there is no further necessity for keeping those records in view of the fact that the liquidation of our mutual organisations is being completed.

I should be glad if you would let me know when you can receive my representative for this purpose.

It would be impossible for me to finish this letter without saying how much we have appreciated your close collaboration with our Service and the great contribution you have made towards winning the war against Germany and Italy. I would like also to convey to you on behalf of our organisation our best wishes for the future.

Yours,
Wilski

On the 6th of July 1945, the same day the British Government recognised the Polish Government in Warsaw, instructions were issued to Major Stanislaw Paproki in charge of the Polish/British liaison office as follows:

Following your departure to Scotland with your team, certain developments took place which oblige us to provide you with new instructions as to the selection criteria with regard to our archives.

1. *The documents which earlier had been considered as valuable and were to be kept in the Archives in Scotland – are now to be taken to London and deposited in the agreed place under special protection.*
2. *Everything else is to be burnt immediately and in situ. This applies without exception and in particular to all the documents pertaining to:*
   - *Information on the USSR.*
   - *Cooperation with the British, Americans, etc.*
   - *Personnel records, accounts, etc.*
3. *This work is to be carried out as soon as possible, sacrificing accuracy if necessary. The point here is not to be overtaken by events, which are developing faster than we anticipated. There will be no recriminations if you, Major, order the destruction of material which individual commanders here would consider necessary. You have complete discretion in meeting this objective: to quickly*

secure the documents you consider of value and to destroy every-
thing else.

4. *As quickly as is possible, please bring the crated documents men-*
tioned under 1) above to London and deposit these at the secret
location.

This location was the cellar of Biffy's office at 2 Ryder Street.

Biffy also retained responsibility for liaison with the Americans, not least because they liked him very much.

On the 15th of October 1945, the OSS was disbanded to be succeeded by the Strategic Services Unit (SSU). Donovan did not retain his job and returned to his law practice. His replacement as the First Commander of the SSU was General John Magruder. When Biffy went to Paris in 1945 and met Phil Horton he discussed the Soviet problem at length, teasing him by revealing the outlines of ideas he had for various operations while clearly also trying to work out what material Horton might have to offer in an exchange. He reiterated the Menzies message that the uncertainty over the future of the OSS was the only thing delaying full cooperation and suggested he should go to Washington in October to discuss the issue with Horton's bosses, flattering his host by suggesting that it might be helpful if he were also there. '*He is extremely interested of course in the problem of intelligence work on Russia, both from the positive viewpoint of the procurement of intelligence and the counter-espionage viewpoint of the protection of the British and American services against agents provocateurs and penetration,*' Horton told Washington. '*He is convinced that it will not be possible to produce any regular and reliable flow of intelligence on Russia by agent penetration. He feels that the only technique which will produce results is that supplied by the technical services.*'

Biffy also stated that, in his discussion with his French friends, they had come to the same conclusion. The shared view was that '*we have all but given up on trying to run agents inside the Soviet Union, we have no HUMINT, no aerial reconnaissance and no POWs to debrief*'.

Just how bad this intelligence gap was is shown when the Russians exploded their first atomic bomb on the 29th of August 1949, way ahead of estimate. Bill Donovan reacted by sending John Bross, a clever and sophisticated lawyer, to London to run the OSS office and liaise directly with Biffy's SLC. OSS needed help from SIS, whose reports on the Soviet Union were highly valued, in order to survive in Washington.

However, it was not to be, but in replacing OSS with the SSU nothing really changed in London. Biffy's office continued a seamless liaison and whilst there was uncertainty as to the future of the US intelligence community, the volume of SIS reports increased.

Soon after his trip to France in October 1946, Biffy set sail on the *Queen Elizabeth* from Southampton to New York and then onwards to Washington for a series of liaison meetings with intelligence officers and with General Hoyt Vandenberg, who was Director of the Central Intelligence Group (CIG). Biffy knew Vandenberg from London when he had commanded the air component for D-Day. OSS was gone and the SSU closed in September 1946 to be replaced by the CIG. However, Biffy spent over a month in the US cementing relationships begun in the war. On the 14th of November 1946, Hoyt Vandenberg gave a lunch in Biffy's honour at the Army and Navy Club, which was attended by many of Biffy's old OSS friends as well as the new crop of US intelligence officers. On the 27th of November, Biffy took his leave of the US intelligence community with an office call to Vandenberg, returning to London to brief 'C' on his findings. Soon after his visit in February 1947, Congress passed the enabling legislation under the National Security Act, thus creating the Central Intelligence Agency (CIA). Biffy's friend Hoyt Vandenberg remained in post until May 1947, being replaced by Admiral Roscoe Hillenkoetter.

One thing the newly formed CIA inherited from OSS was the crucial Donovan principle of merging Secret Intelligence and Special Operations in the same organisation. The functional titles changed to Foreign Intelligence and Covert Action, thus avoiding SIS's persistent problem with SOE, but the theory was the same: to centralise all clandestine operations under one command.

In 1948, SIS and the newly created CIA held the London Conference on War Planning. This was attended by senior CIA officials and the agenda covered a range of practical issues in the event of war with the Soviet Union. These included joint handling of tactical intelligence, stay-behind projects, special operations planning and common training. The conference led to long-term liaison and a further meeting in 1949 in Washington cemented these close relations.

Biffy took a high-profile role both in the 1948 conference and the follow-up meetings in Washington in 1949. The 1949 meetings led to an exchange of letters between Admiral Roscoe Hillenkoetter, Director of the CIA, and Stewart Menzies, 'C'.

Hillenkoetter:

> *I am convinced of the necessity for a close working relationship between our services, particularly with regard to our relatively new responsibilities on the operations side. For our part, we are fully prepared to designate a resident liaison officer in London to facilitate the relationship in this field and would welcome the early designation of a representative of your office in Washington who would be particularly qualified to deal with these activities.*

And:

> *May I express appreciation for the opportunity which you have afforded us for discussion of our mutual interests and may I also express the appreciation both of myself and of my Assistant Directors for the exceedingly competent representation which you provided.*

Menzies replied in kind:

> *I deeply appreciated your letter... mainly because your reactions so fully endorse my own, but also for its cordial tone, which augurs well for our joint undertakings... No doubt, snags will arise, but I am confident that our firm realisation of a common purpose and a common gain will enable us to iron them out.*

This mutually agreeable outcome to future relations between SIS and CIA was due in no little part to the personal relations that Biffy forged with OSS in the war and the SSU afterwards. Biffy was to go on working closely with the Americans for the rest of his life – well past his supposed retirement date, as we will see. John Tiltman of GC + CS/GCHQ would also have a long working relationship with the NSA. Tiltman first met Pres Currier and his team of US code breakers when they arrived at Sheerness in 1941; 40 years later in 1981 he was still working at the NSA cracking Soviet codes. These long and personal relationships would cement what was to become known as the Special Relationship.

*

Biffy's long Russian experience stretching from his early days in Crimea, through his anti-Bolshevik operations in Constantinople and subsequently Paris, along with his stable of émigrés in London and his linguistic fluency made him an obvious choice when it came to debriefing Soviet defectors. As we know, Biffy had debriefed two important defectors in Paris before the war – Boris Bazhanov, one of Stalin's Secretaries and Grigory Bessadovsky, the Chargé d'Affaires at the Soviet embassy in Paris. Therefore, the debriefing of defectors was added to his already extensive remit as Controller Special Liaison.

At the end of the war, there was a mad scramble between the West and Russia to track down and recruit German scientists voluntarily, or in the case of the Russians, by kidnap and coercion. In particular, those who had worked on the Nazi V1 and V2 rocket development, as well as those working on atomic weapons and jet fighters. During October 1946, they instigated Operation OSVAKIN. Soviet targeting teams systematically searched for and arrested numerous scientists and technicians who were then taken to Moscow and put to work under duress. This programme had a two-fold effect: many scientists fled to the West as word of the kidnappings got out and the Americans instigated their own kidnapping programmes through dissident émigrés.

Lieutenant Colonel Grigori Tokaev

Lieutenant Colonel Grigori Tokaev, a highly respected aeronautical engineer, had been a lecturer in jet engine technology and rocket propulsion at the Zhukovsky Air Force Academy in Moscow and had enjoyed a long career at the elite Institute of Engineers and Geodesics.

At the end of the war, he had been transferred on the orders of Stalin to Berlin with instructions to help in the kidnapping of German scientists who might assist the Soviet missile research programme. As the senior scientific adviser to General Ivan Serov, Russian Commander in Berlin, Tokaev was ordered to contact Professor Kurt Tank, Focke-Wulf's chief aircraft designer, and Dr Eugen Sanger, a jet propulsion expert. If they refused to go voluntarily to the East, they would be kidnapped. *'Nobody will interfere with you,'* Serov told him. *'But remember, Comrade Stalin relies on you to produce results.'* Tokaev was unable to recruit either specialist, which did not go down well in Moscow, incurring Stalin's displeasure – not a good position to be in.

Tokaev had often thought of defection to the West as he was inherently anti-Soviet. He was a native Ossetian from the Caucasus and maintained contact with dissident groups there. He became a target of the émigrés working for the Americans who tried on at least one occasion to kidnap him. The attempt failed, but Tokaev was worried that the NKVD would arrest him because of his contacts with dissident groups and his failure to get Tank and Sanger to defect. In October 1947, he decided to defect to the British. He crossed into the British Zone in Berlin with his wife Aza and daughter Bella. He went straight to the British Berlin Sector Military Headquarters and requested asylum. He was quickly passed to the SIS station at the Olympic Stadium headed by John Bruce Lockhart. The Tokaevs, now codenamed STORK/EXCISE, were flown by the RAF to Northolt where Biffy's SLC took charge of them, setting them up in a safe house protected by MI5 and the Metropolitan Police. Soon after their arrival, a suspected assassin was detected outside the house which prompted a rapid evacuation to Frittiscombe, a very remote farmhouse at Chillington near Kingsbridge in Devon, then owned by Fred Winterbotham, who had, by this time, retired. The Tokaev defection was extremely valuable for SIS, for Biffy's new department and for the Foreign Office's Information Research Department who wanted to exploit him as a *genuine ideological defector*.

Biffy's team, joined by aeronautical and rocketry experts from the RAF and the Royal Aircraft Establishment Farnborough Research Institute, started an extensive debrief at the SLC office in Ryder Street. Tokaev would produce a great deal of intelligence during the course of his debrief, some of it of varying quality, but nevertheless an excellent haul for SIS. It included details of the Soviet guided missile programme, including its mission, structure and scientific progress. He told Biffy that *'Stalin demands the production of larger rockets with a range of up to 6,000 kilometres.'* His intelligence was to have a significant impact on SIS intelligence estimates of the Soviet strategic rocket threat. It would also lead to some very risky operations to confirm Tokaev's information, including the RAF flying a Canberra bomber from West Germany to the River Volga to photograph the missile centre at Kapustin Yav and then exfiltrating to Persia. The mission was a success, but the RAF vowed *'never again'* – they had already lost one aircraft over the Soviet Union and the US had lost five.

Encouraged by the Tokaev defection, Biffy forwarded a plan to use Tokaev to persuade others to defect and an 'outstation' of SLC was created at Bad Salzuflen in the British Zone in Germany to coordinate policy and attempts to persuade Russians to defect. This didn't always go according to plan. An embarrassing incident took place in the spring of 1948. Tokaev had identified Colonel Jason Davidovich Tasoev, Head of the Soviet Reparations Committee in Bremen on the north German coast, as a potential defector. He was given the codename CAPULET. A period of cultivation followed, codenamed Operation HOUSE PARTY. Not only did this identify a potential defector but it helped in the management of Tokaev (EXCISE) who had a propensity to be quite difficult, as this letter from 'C' to the Foreign Secretary illustrates.

TOP SECRET
SECRETARY OF STATE

EXCISE's information about the Soviet Airforce was of very great value to us. However one of the difficulties in handling him is that he looks upon himself as the architect of a great anti-communist underground movement which will some day come into the open and free Russia from her present masters (and incidentally his own part of the Caucasus from the Russians). His ideas on the subject are not very sound and he has not been encouraged to believe that SIS would back him. EXCISE naturally takes a different view and fails to understand why we do not give more active support to his 'movement' and treat him personally as a V.I.P. When in this mood of depression, he refuses to talk and the flow of valuable technical information about the Soviet Airforce dries up.

In order to loosen EXCISE's tongue during a recent spell of silence, Biffy Dunderdale arranged for him to meet a friend and fellow-countryman called Colonel Tasoev, the officer in charge of the Soviet Repatriation Mission in the United States enclave at Bremen, who EXCISE had identified as a possible defector. The meeting was successful in that EXCISE is now talking again freely, but it has on the other hand created an extremely embarrassing muddle.

Contact with Tasoev had been established initially through an American intermediary, with the approval of the US Director of Military Intelligence in Germany, General Robert Walsh. The final meeting took place on April the 23rd at the home of the director of

Bremen's US Port Operations, Stanley A. Clem, when Tasoev, against Tokaev's advice, decided to defect there and then. They spent a night in Hamburg and then after lunch drove to a British Air Force Station and boarded a plane for London. The aircraft, borrowed by SIS, was the personal transport of the Chief of the Imperial General Staff, Field Marshal Montgomery, and had flown Tokaev to Bremen the previous day.

Tasoev's meeting with Tokaev had been arranged to demonstrate SIS's capacity to attract and protect defectors. It was also hoped that the operation would *'loosen Tokaev's tongue'* as he had become increasingly erratic. However, the meeting was not a success and each accused the other of being a traitor. While Tokaev appeared very shaken by the episode, Tasoev's confidence was completely undermined and on May the 7th, at the first opportunity, he fled his safe house, a flat on Bishop King's Road, Kensington, and asked a patrolling policeman to take him to the Soviet embassy. Tasoev was then escorted to Hammersmith police station where he was locked up while frantic Foreign Office staff tried to sort out the muddle with both the Russians and the Americans. SIS concluded that CAPULET's change of heart had been prompted by his fear of retribution against his 20-year-old son Vasili, who was living in Moscow.

The Tasoev shambles proved extremely awkward, especially when the matter was raised in the House of Commons on the 17th of June 1948. The exchange was reported in Hansard:

59. Mr. Emrys Hughes asked the Secretary of State for the Home Department in which police station Colonel Tasoev of the Soviet Army was confined when in London; what were the circumstances of his detention; the reasons of his interrogation; who conducted it; and whether he will make a full statement explaining the occurrence.

63. Mr. Gallacher asked the Secretary of State for the Home Department where Colonel Tasoev stayed while he was in this country.

Mr. Eden: The circumstances in which Colonel Tasoev came to this country were explained by my right hon. Friend, the Secretary of State for Foreign Affairs on Wednesday of last week. Pending clarification of Colonel Tasoev's position formal leave to land was withheld and as an alien who had not been given leave to land he was liable to be detained under the provisions of the Aliens Order. He was temporarily accommodated in a flat, but he left this flat and got himself into difficulties owing to his lack of acquaintance with this country. For instance, he was rejected from a bus by a firm-minded conductor as a passenger unable to pay his fare. He was then lodged temporarily in Hammersmith Police Station – a modern station with quite suitable accommodation. He was not subjected to any interrogation, and I am satisfied that he was well treated and that due consideration was shown to him. As my right hon. Friend explained, when Colonel Tasoev changed his mind and expressed a desire to return to the Soviet authorities, effect was given to his request.

What was not reported in Parliament was that some in SIS suggested that Tasoev should 'disappear' by being drugged and thrown out of an aircraft over the North Sea. This idea was swiftly dismissed and on May the 20th Tasoev was flown to RAF Gatow in Berlin arriving at 11:00. He was driven to the Soviet military headquarters in Luisenstrasse and at 17:00 he was handed over to the Russians. As far as Biffy was concerned, he had carried out the attempt to get CAPULET to defect as part of his brief. He was caught on the hop by CAPULET's request to defect immediately, but it is hardly surprising he took the decision to fly him to London.

'C' agreed with Biffy and wrote to the Foreign Secretary on the 19th of May:

On EXCISE's advice we attempted to recruit the man as an agent in Germany to help in following up the operational leads provided by EXCISE. Unfortunately, at our final meeting with him, he refused to work in this way and applied for asylum in England as a political refugee. We had to accept him as a defector on these terms. After his arrival in London, he went back on his decision to defect and asked to be put in touch with the Soviet Embassy in London for immediate repatriation to Russia. It is not clear whether this change of mind was due to the fact that he has a son in the Soviet Union or whether he intended to double cross us from the start. From the legal point of view he is entitled to demand his repatriation and the Home Office, which has been burdened with his care subsequent to his change of mind, is not prepared to retain him in detention.

Tokaev still retained some intelligence value, being 'loaned' to other government departments by Biffy's SLC. He continued to give insights into Soviet attitudes of mind, their strategic fears and anxieties. He could interpret political developments in the Kremlin and insights into the key players. He was also involved in setting up deception operations which were planned and executed from Biffy's Ryder Street office as Biffy had formed a strong bond with EXCISE and was the only person who understood him. One of these operations was ANTONOV, the objective being *'to shake the confidence of the Soviet leaders by convincing them that a powerful subversive movement was well established'*. The plan was approved by 'C' and implemented as Operation FLITTER. The operation ran until 1955 with some success.

Defectors would continue to be a vital source of intelligence throughout the Cold War, but their real value came from those such as Oleg Gordievsky when they were kept in place as agents.

Tokaev proved to be the last valuable defector for many years. In the early 1950s the flow to the British was limited to low-level officials and soldiers; 83 Russians came into the hands of Biffy's SLC in 1948, in 1949 it dropped to 28 and by 1950, 17. This general failure to attract high-level defection was described as *'heart-breaking'* by one young SIS officer who worked on the defector programme in the Bad Salzuflen Station.

Biffy's SLC, considered an anomaly in the post-war SIS, but somewhat untouchable due to Biffy's formidable reputation and track record, had a wide-ranging remit. His large team of émigrés was not only useful in debriefing defectors and identifying potential agents to recruit, but it also provided an excellent translation and interpretation service for both SIS, MI5, the War Office and other government ministries and departments.

CHAPTER 17 – SILVER AND GOLD

'If speaking is silver, then listening is gold.'

Turkish proverb

After the end of the war, SIS officers stationed behind the Iron Curtain found it difficult, but not impossible, to operate. However, their main focus – recruiting and running agents – was proving to be as difficult as Biffy had predicted. Two outposts, Berlin and Vienna, created out of the anomaly of the wartime alliance between the USA, Britain, Russia and later France, became scenes of extensive intelligence activity and the front line in the emerging Cold War. Both cities were divided into zones, each run by one of the four Allied Powers. Biffy's SLC was interested in both cities from the perspective of defectors and the possibility of technical intercept. In 1947, the Vienna station had recruited as an agent a former Nazi officer who was involved in the black market, codenamed SUBALTERN. He arranged the defection of three Russian soldiers, a lieutenant and two NCOs, but no one of significant intelligence interest. His real job was to identify and recruit a high-level defector. This was likely to be '*a slow and wearying undertaking*'. Biffy travelled regularly to Vienna on SLC business using his wartime alias John Green.

In 1949, Peter Lunn had arrived in Vienna as Head of Station. He was the son of Sir Arnold Lunn, founder of the Lunn Poly travel agency, and had links to SIS. Peter was an expert skier who had represented Britain in the 1936 Winter Olympics at Garmisch.

Peter Lunn was reviewing reports from a source in the Austrian Post, Telegraphs and Telephone Administration. The report identified the routing of telephone cables linking the Soviet Army HQ with its field units. It ran underground through the British and French sectors, presenting an opportunity for technical intercept. Lunn got in touch with the Post Office Technical Department at Dollis Hill, where he had a contact, Peter Taylor, whom he knew from the war.

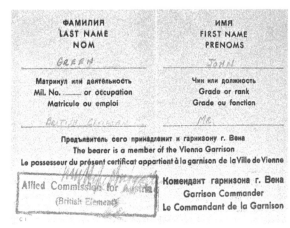

Biffy's alias identity card, Vienna

He asked him to review the reports and work out if it was possible to tap these cables. Taylor confirmed it was possible if an access tunnel could be dug. Lunn then got in touch with another of his contacts, an experienced private mining engineer well known to SIS, who agreed to design and oversee the construction of a tunnel from the cellar of a police station to the main telephone cable running between the Soviet headquarters at the Imperial Hotel and their military airfield at Schwechat. Lunn got the go-ahead from SIS headquarters and they developed an operation which was to be one of SIS's most successful technical operations. The CIA were brought into the operation in 1951.

The operation was so successful that Lunn decided that it could be repeated. So, in 1951, in conjunction with the CIA, he set up two more tunnelling operations codenamed SUGAR and LORD. Operation SUGAR ran from the cellar of a commercial cover, a costume jewellery shop called Gablons, which was run by a locally recruited Austrian SIS agent. The shop was a commercial success and SIS were able to fund the operation from the sales profits. Operation LORD was also run under commercial cover from the cellar of a villa in the French sector by John Wyke, SIS's leading technical expert. The cover was a business selling Harris Tweed. The intercepts were collected each day by a laundry van – a cover

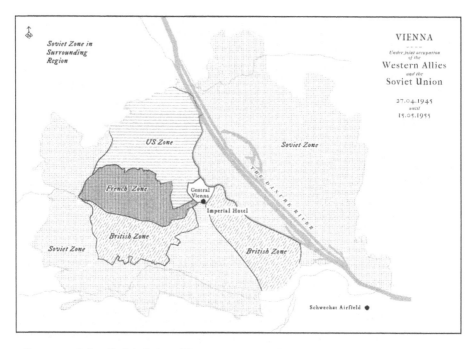

VIENNA

Under joint occupation
of the
Western Allies
and the
Soviet Union

27.04.1945
until
15.05.1955

often used for British intelligence operations.[152] The operation nearly ended in disaster. Before the advent of the laundry collection service, an SIS officer was collecting the tapes from a schoolgirl walking in Schönbrunn Park when he was arrested on suspicion of being a paedophile.

SILVER, LORD and SUGAR produced a vast amount of raw material which needed to be processed. The RAF ran a regular shuttle service to London to deliver the recordings. On arrival in London, Biffy's transcription service processed the 'take'. Biffy insisted on direct access to 'C', avoiding Assistant Chief Jack Easton in order *'to protect his operation'*. To deal with the enormous output from the operation, SIS created a new Y Section based in Carlton Gardens, run by Tom Grimson, a former Irish Guards officer who had joined SIS after the war. His personal assistant was an old friend of Biffy's, Pamela Peniakoff, widow of Colonel 'Popski', the legendary White Russian, who had commanded the No. 1 Long-Range Demolition

---

152 Twenty years later, a similar cover was used, 'The 4 Square Laundry', for undercover intelligence operations in Northern Ireland.

Squadron or 'Popski's Private Army'. This special Y service team included several former members of the Free Polish Intelligence Service, who Biffy had arranged to stay in London after the war. Biffy also arranged for the recruitment of daughters of White Russian émigrés, whom he knew, as translators. Once transcribed, the material was passed on to a section of 12 Russian-speaking Army and RAF officers for collation and interpretation. It was then distributed to the appropriate customer departments and to the CIA.

The three tunnel operations ran successfully until 1955 when the Allies withdrew from Austria. The intelligence was excellent, including both details of the Soviet order of battle and strategic intelligence on Soviet intentions. Much of the monitoring work was extremely dull but with the occasional light relief for the young serviceman monitoring the tapes, when the female telephonists would discuss their sex lives in explicit detail.

The success of SILVER gave rise to a second tunnelling intercept operation in Berlin, codenamed GOLD/STOPWATCH. Lunn had been posted from Vienna to Berlin and, along with his CIA counterpart, Bill Harvey, and John Wyke, also now posted to Berlin, wanted to repeat the success of the Vienna operations. A site was picked for the tunnel and the work began. It was decided the project would hide in plain sight and a large warehouse should be constructed over the tunnelling site to absorb the spoil and conceal the bank of monitoring equipment. The warehouse roof was covered in genuine intercept antennas to give the impression it was an intercept facility targeting Russian communications but disguising its real purpose. The construction was a major undertaking, carried out by a team from the Royal Engineers who had conducted a 'rehearsal' by working out tunnelling techniques at a secret location in Britain which had similar sandy soil as the Berlin site.

The most difficult part of the whole enterprise was excavating the vertical shaft to reach the cables, which were just two inches in diameter and barely two feet below the surface of the main road leading to East Berlin's Schönefeld airport. This required very precise engineering, with the busy road likely to collapse into the hole at any moment. *'This was the most delicate and tedious job in the entire process,'* one of the CIA officers involved recalled. *'The vertical shaft was carved out using a "window blind" shield. A slot was opened and about an inch of soil was removed; then that slot was closed and the next one opened. This was repeated until the target cables were reached, a process that required extreme patience and skill.'*

The SIS technical team placed wiretaps on the three target cables in May 1955. The 'tap chamber' was sealed off from the tunnel by a heavy steel door with a sign reading: *'Entry is forbidden by order of the Commanding General'* in both Russian and German to make the tapping operation look like an official Soviet or East German facility and make anyone who stumbled across it hesitate before entering. A microphone linked to the warehouse enabled those on duty to monitor any activity inside the tap chamber. A four-man intelligence section was maintained on site to monitor the conversations as they came through, to report any flash intelligence and provide daily round-ups of what had been heard. The tapes of the voice conversations were flown back to London to be transcribed by Biffy's Russian émigré team, assembled to deal with the 'take' from the Vienna tunnel. The encrypted tapes were sent to Washington for decoding.

Unfortunately for Operation GOLD, the initial Anglo-American planning team assembled in London included George Blake, who had volunteered his services to the KGB when he was captured during the Korean War. Luckily Blake's treachery dated from 1951 or 1952. He was not released until July 1953, so was not a party to Operation SILVER. Blake's treachery caused very significant damage to SIS networks and, when eventually caught in 1961 and tried for espionage, he was found guilty and sentenced to 42 years.

Although the Russians knew of the GOLD tunnel, they chose to leave it in place so as to protect Blake who was much more valuable in place in London. The Soviets 'discovered' the tunnel in April 1956, when heavy rains had caused damage to the underground cables necessitating repair. Engineers went out in force to carry out repairs and it was decided that this was the time to expose the tunnel and close down the operation.

Although the tunnel was blown, there was so much material to be processed by Biffy's team of Russians that this part of the operation continued up until September 1958. The tunnel taps produced a staggering amount of data: 50,000 reels of tape, 443,000 fully transcribed conversations, 40,000 recorded telephone conversations, six million hours of teletape traffic and 1,750 high-grade intelligence reports. GOLD provided a very significant haul, supplying intelligence on the Soviet nuclear programme, the entire order of battle of the Group of Soviet Forces Germany, Soviet Naval deployment in the Baltic, early warning of the creation of the Warsaw Pact, KGB and GRU structure, operation and tradecraft, as well as Khrushchev's denunciation of Stalin at the 20th Communist Party Conference.

Biffy's team played an invaluable part in both SILVER and GOLD, proving yet again Biffy's case for the value of intercept operations. Conversely it also proved the value of having high-grade agents in place, something which was to haunt SIS for the rest of Biffy's career and beyond.

Russian officer examining recording
equipment in Berlin tunnel

CHAPTER 18 – SEMPER OCCULTUS –
THE CHANGING OF THE GUARD

'MI6, a department known in the Foreign Office,
politely, but not very sincerely, as The Friends.'

The Hon Monty Woodhouse. SIS Head of Station, Tehran 1951–55

'Once you have entered the secret world,
you may think you can leave it, but it never leaves you.'

William Stevenson

Other than 1940, 1956 can be described as one of the worst years for SIS since its beginning in 1909 – probably its Annus Horribilis. Anglo-Russian relations were deeply strained, with the 'Crabb affair' incident in Portsmouth Harbour, the Baltic Resistance movement – 'The Forest Brotherhood' – exposed as a Soviet deception and the 'discovery' of the Berlin tunnel all occurring in the same year. All the while, ticking away in the background, there was the ongoing mole hunt for the 'third man'. Finally came the Suez Crisis and an ill-fated coup attempt in Syria, Operation STRAGGLE.

In July, following the disasters in the early part of the year, Sinclair had been dismissed and Sir Dick White, the Director-General of MI5, was appointed to '*whip SIS back into shape*'. Biffy would survive all this up until 1959 when he would be 60 and due to retire anyway, but he would see an increasing curtailment of his independence of action and the direct access to 'C' that he had enjoyed with Menzies and Sinclair. The culture of the service was about to change. The days of the independence and freedom of action of the 'Robber Barons', including Biffy, Harry Carr and 'Gibbie' Gibson, were numbered.

The British intelligence community began to bow to American pressure to investigate the possibility of moles in their own structure after the disappearance of Burgess and Maclean in May 1951. Dick White, the Deputy Director of MI5, was put in charge of the mole hunt. His pursuit of traitors was to continue when he was appointed

Director of SIS the next year. Whilst suspicion began to centre on Kim Philby, MI5 cast its net wide across government in general and SIS in particular. The atmosphere of the investigation brought morale to a low ebb in SIS. Much time and effort were expended on the belief that the 'third man' had something Russian in his background. This description fitted many of the now senior SIS officers who had long connections with Russia and had spent a lifetime fighting Bolshevism. These included Leo Stevani, the Gibson brothers, the Whittalls, the La Fontaines and of course, Biffy.

However, they were all eventually exonerated as suspicion homed in on Philby, although he had resigned from SIS in 1951, maintaining his cool and strongly protesting his innocence. In 1955, with no tangible proof against him and a strong SIS lobby supporting him, he was officially exonerated by a Parliamentary statement given by the Foreign Secretary, Harold Macmillan. Philby had been told of Macmillan's statement in advance and he called a press conference at his mother's flat where he delivered an impressively confident performance of bare-faced lying, stating categorically that he was not the 'third man'. This was to seriously affect Dick White and his future management of SIS which he was to take over the following year, by which time Philby was in Beirut working as a journalist for the *Economist* and the *Observer*. He was also back on the SIS books as a freelance.

In Washington, Philby's exoneration was greeted with disbelief and fury. Many in the CIA wanted to sever links with SIS but were overruled. SIS needed the CIA as much as the CIA needed SIS. When Philby disappeared from Beirut in 1963, the CIA believed that SIS had tipped Philby off and allowed him to slip away. Dick White was always convinced that Philby was guilty and felt that many in SIS deliberately obstructed his investigations. The Philby affair was to have a serious knock-on effect to how he managed, reformed and restructured SIS during the first seven years of his tenure. He would regularly stress to his officers '... *if proof were needed, this operation has demonstrated beyond all doubt, the prime importance of the human intelligence source, handled with professional skill and expertise*'.

As the Cold War took shape, SIS started to reactivate World War II-style support operations for resistance or partisan movements. In the Baltic states, the Controller Northern Area, Harry Carr, approached 'C' with plans to provide support for anti-communist groups and the infiltration of clandestine operators into Russian-occupied territory as early as late 1945. This was to consist firstly of training and infiltrating radio operators to groups of partisans reportedly fighting against the Soviet occupying forces and, secondly, of working with émigré opposition groups to recruit and train agents to be infiltrated into the Baltic states. 'C' agreed and it was decided that, as Biffy's Special Liaison Controllerate was responsible for émigré operations, this operation was to be run by Carr out of the SLC office in Ryder Street. Alex 'Sandy' McKibbin, who was already working at SLC, would oversee the day-to-day operations.

Carr and McKibbin, like Biffy, were also born and brought up in Russia. Carr was born in 1899 near St Petersburg and took part in the British Army campaign in support of the White Russians in 1919. McKibbin had run a timber business in Estonia before World War II. Likewise, the officer running the US end of this operation, George Belic, was born in Russia in 1911. His father was a colonel in General Denikin's army and may well have known Biffy in the Crimea. The Belic family was evacuated from Odessa in 1920 and George Belic and his mother arrived in the US in 1923. His father died in one of the last battles. George worked in Naval Intelligence in World War II and in 1947 joined what was to become the CIA.

SIS needed a means of infiltrating agents without using a parachute drop that came with the high risk of detection. Biffy reminded Harry Carr of both his own Helford Flotilla and Frank Slocum's 15th Motor Gunboat Flotilla[153] used for very successfully inserting agents clandestinely on the Brittany coast during World War II. Many officers of Slocum's 'Private Navy' had remained in SIS after the war including Slocum himself who was now Head of Station in Stockholm. A command structure was set up in Hamburg consisting of Commander Anthony Courtney, attached from Naval Intelligence, David Wheeler,

---

153 See *A Dangerous Enterprise*.

Hans-Helmut Klose | S-boats at HMS ROYAL CHARLOTTE, Kiel

a Baltic specialist, and John Harvey-Jones.[154] Courtney recruited a former German E-boat captain Hans-Helmut Klose, with a fanatical hatred of communism, who had undertaken similar operations for the Abwehr in the closing years of the war.

He picked a crew of like-minded former E-boat sailors and a German E-boat was found and refurbished for use on the operation. The E-boat had been taken to a small discreet shipyard near Portsmouth and rebuilt. It was stripped of armaments and torpedo tubes, and its twin Mercedes-Benz 518 diesel engines were thoroughly overhauled by Royal Navy mechanics who assured SIS of a guaranteed speed of 45 knots, one of the fastest ships afloat. It was also the most silent due to the fitting of underwater exhausts. The radio and radar equipment, fitted by the Admiralty's Signal and Radar Establishment, would be operated by a single British officer serving on board. The cover story was that the E-boat was part of the British Government 'Baltic Fishery Protection Service' and the mission, codenamed Operation JUNGLE, was launched in May 1949. Operation JUNGLE was set up along the lines of a World War II SIS/ SOE operation. A training base for agents was set up at 111 Old Church Street in Chelsea, a four-storey house rented from a British officer posted overseas. A trusted married couple, Eddie and Mavis Flowers, managed the domestic side of the project. George Collier taught the agents coding and communication and John Crofton

154 Future Chairman of ICI and television personality.

Fort Monckton, Portsmouth

supervised all aspects of tradecraft. Fieldcraft training was conducted on Dartmoor and in the Scottish Highlands and weapons training, unarmed combat and boating skills were taught at the SIS training base, Fort Monckton, near Portsmouth.

When ready for operations, agents were flown to Germany and held in a safe house in Hamburg until the deployment date when they were transferred to Kiel to the former Naval Air Station at Holtenau. This barracks housed HMS ROYAL CHARLOTTE – the cover name for a naval intelligence operation – and a number of British Army units. Here they were met by their conducting officer Lieutenant Commander David Ramsey DSC.[155] They were quietly embarked on Klose's souped-up E-boat which was moored at the end of the jetty of what was the British Kiel Yacht Club. The agents, carrying rucksacks and Schmeisser submachine guns, boarded and went below. Once hidden below decks, Klose slipped his mooring and headed for the Danish island of Bornholm. The operation relied on stealth and speed. The E-boat was to dash from Bornholm to the drop-off and return as fast as possible. Klose was used to this. In 1944/5 he had captained a similar E-boat in the Baltic, dropping German agents behind Russian lines. His answer to the inevitable question,

155 David Ramsey had won his DSC at Anzio where he also lost a leg. Subsequently he was employed in intelligence duties.

'*What happens if we're caught?*' was a reassuring '*We're faster than anyone else, and trust me, the Russians never sank my boat during the war.*'

In Bornholm, Klose anchored in a small cove used by the Danish Navy while he waited for the final weather report. The message from Hamburg forecast storms. There was no alternative but to wait for an improvement. The next day, the weather cleared and Klose set a course at full speed directly towards Palanga in Lithuania. Two kilometres offshore, the radar screen was clear and he ordered the engines to be cut. At 02:00, the six men lowered themselves into rubber boats and were rowed to the shore. Their landing was successful. However, within hours, the group were ambushed and all were killed. Back in London SIS received a mission successful message and Carr breathed a sigh of relief. The message was sent by the Russians and this set the tone for almost all future operations.

Unfortunately, Biffy and Harry Carr had been obliged to keep SIS 'R5' section, the counterintelligence section, informed for counterintelligence input into the operation. 'R5' was run by Kim Philby. Unsurprisingly Operation JUNGLE was blown from the outset. Over 100 agents were landed in Poland and the Baltic states. All were ensnared in an elaborate Soviet network of hoax guerrillas and either turned to be played back against SIS or were killed. All Carr's operations had been controlled from Moscow from the outset thanks to Philby.

However, whilst Philby was undoubtedly responsible for the overall betrayal, it was not the only problem in London. In setting up 'The Trust' in 1921, the initial Bolshevik sting operation against the White Russians and SIS, Feliks Dzerzhinsky was told by Lenin: '*Tell them what they want to hear…*' In other words, play to their preconceived ideas and aspirations. SIS wanted to hear that a strong, effective armed resistance existed in the Baltics and Poland, particularly the group of vehemently anti-Bolshevik officers born in Russia – Carr, McKibbin, Gibson and Biffy. Whilst Biffy understood the complexity and weaknesses of the émigrés, he didn't really want to believe what was becoming increasingly obvious. However, he was not directly responsible and was able to avoid the punishment meted out to Carr and McKibbin.

It was the same story in Ukraine with SIS's support for the organisation of Ukrainian nationalists – Operation SHRAPNEL. The Americans were suspicious but went along with it. However, in the wake of Harry Carr's humiliation, John Bruce Lockhart became suspicious. His investigation confirmed that the whole operation had been under control of Soviet intelligence since the first group had been captured after landing by parachute in 1950. When Dick White took over, he *'decided to resist American pressure to become involved in further clandestine warfare'*. Biffy avoided much of the fallout of these disasters as they were not directly his operations and Philby's treachery was seen to be behind all of it, but it was clear that Biffy's status as an independent and a law unto himself was about to be curtailed.

The other event that did not go well for SIS was the Lionel 'Buster' Crabb affair. On the evening of the 19th of April 1956, White, still at MI5, had been told about an SIS operation in Portsmouth Harbour that had gone badly wrong.

In the early 1950s, Russians had begun deploying a new class of warship, the *Sverdlov* class of cruiser mounting a formidable armament of medium-calibre guns. They were the largest and most powerful ships built by the Russians since the end of the war. When the *Sverdlov* had passed through the straits of Dover, the Navy took hundreds of photographs and recorded her radar and sonar signatures.[156] Several clandestine diving operations were targeted against the *Sverdlov* during the 1953 Spithead Naval Review without incident. Biffy was involved in the oversight of these operations. Amongst Biffy's private papers examined by the author, is a dark blue leather-bound photograph album with the ER II Royal Cypher on the cover, inscribed in gold lettering to Biffy. The album is an official photographic record of the 1953 Coronation. The first part of the album consists of about 20 immaculate black and white photos of the coronation. At the end of these is a photo of Biffy in full dress uniform at the Spithead Naval Review, in which 193 Royal Naval ships took part, together with 13 Commonwealth warships and 16

---

156 HMS ROYAL CHARLOTTE, the naval intelligence operation in Kiel, included an intercept station and was closely involved in monitoring the *Sverdlov* (callsign CHOYT 22).

Biffy's Queen Elizabeth II
Coronation album

Biffy, Miss Watt and Dorothy at Spithead Review

foreign warships including the *Sverdlov*. After Biffy's photograph in the album there are 16 photos of the *Sverdlov*. One suspects that it was the new Queen, the Duke of Edinburgh and John Sinclair's way of sharing a private joke and expressing thanks for a job well done.

Three years later, in April 1956, a state visit by Nikita Khrushchev[157] and Marshal Nikolai Bulganin was due to take place. The Soviet delegation would visit Britain on the *Sverdlov* class cruiser ORDJONIKIDZE which would moor in Portsmouth Harbour. SIS, knowing about the visit well in advance, had planned an operation on behalf of the Admiralty to examine the hull of the ORDJONIKIDZE, in particular the sonar sensors, the propellers and any sound signature reduction devices. The operation was planned and executed by Nicholas Elliott, the Head of London Station, a protégé and close friend of Biffy.

Nicholas Elliott decided to use Lionel Crabb for the operation. Crabb, a former Royal Navy diver awarded the George Medal in the war for underwater bomb disposal work, had worked for the Admiralty since 1948 as an advisor on underwater salvage and driving matters.

He had also undertaken some SIS work on the side including the dive to examine the *Sverdlov* the previous year. The involvement of SIS, which at the time did not 'officially' exist theoretically, helped the Admiralty to ensure 'deniability' if the operation was discovered.

---

157 First Secretary of the Communist Party, Minister of Defence.

Russian cruiser, *Sverdlov*, at Spithead Review

Ten days before the visit, John Bruce Lockhart, SIS's Controller Western Europe, presented a file containing six proposed operations to Michael Williams, the Foreign Office official responsible for liaison with SIS. Among them was a request by the Admiralty that a frogman should examine the ORDJONIKIDZE. The Admiralty wanted to know the dimensions of the propeller, because the craft was faster than originally estimated by Naval Intelligence and its features were important for setting homing torpedoes. That day, Williams was distracted by his father's death early that morning. Without comment, he returned the file to Bruce Lockhart, who assumed that the Admiralty's request had been approved. SIS had followed its standard operating procedures, but Williams had failed to inform his own chain of command of the details of SIS proposed operations. The Prime Minister Anthony Eden later insisted that he had forbidden all intelligence operations during the visit, but if he gave that order, it was not received by SIS.

On the 16th of April the day before the cruiser was due to arrive, Crabb arrived in Portsmouth with his SIS Conducting Officer, Ted Davis.[158] They checked into the Sally Port Hotel that evening.

[158] Commander Ted Davis had run Frank Slocum's 15th MGB Flotilla and had remained with SIS after the war. He had been Head of Station in Norway, then Head of 'R3' Section – the Naval liaison section in the London station.

Lionel 'Buster' Crabb   Nicholas Elliott

Contrary to the fundamental rules of diving, Crabb drank at least five double whiskeys and smoked numerous cigarettes. The matter was not helped by Ted Davis having a minor heart attack. Davis carried on. On the 19th at 07:00, Crabb commenced his first dive and then surfaced near the Russian cruiser. After resubmerging, he returned to the shore for some adjustments to his equipment and dived again. He never returned. Davis raised the alarm and by 11:30 had cleared their rooms. An MI5 officer tore out the page with Crabb's and Davis's names from the hotel register. The hotel's owner was given a receipt for the page by the police and a stern warning not to mention the incident.

It is not known exactly what happened, but the ORDJONIKIDZE's commander had alerted his superiors that the crew had spotted a frogman surfacing between their ship and an escorting destroyer. No formal protest was lodged initially but during a reception the incident was mentioned by the commander to his British hosts. The Commander-in-Chief Portsmouth, denying knowledge of any frogman, assured the Russians there would be an inquiry and hoped that was the end of it.

The Prime Minister was not told of Crabb's disappearance until the 3rd of May. Furious that this might interfere with his diplomatic initiatives and conveniently ignoring the fact that similar operations were carried out by the Soviets against the Royal Navy, Eden told the Commons the next day that Crabb was 'presumed' dead and added an unprecedented rider: *'I think it is necessary, in the special*

Sally Port Hotel, Portsmouth   Ted Davis, Crabb's
                                conducting officer

circumstances of this case, to make it clear that what was done was done without the authority or the knowledge of Her Majesty's ministers. Appropriate disciplinary steps are being taken.'

Eden was apoplectic. He told the Cabinet Secretary, Sir Norman Brook, that SIS was *'incompetent and inadequate and its future could not be trusted under the present management'*. He ordered that Sinclair's retirement should be accelerated and Dick White's appointment as 'C' brought forward in spite of strong opposition within SIS.

However furious Eden was and however incompetent the operation may have been, the way it was handled diplomatically was masterful. Official announcements were some time in coming. Rather than panic and rush to respond, the response was piecemeal. First there was an announcement of the mysterious disappearance of a man staying in a hotel in Portsmouth. Then there was a pause before a name was given. A newspaper reporter found out that the man had arrived in Portsmouth with scuba gear. Then there was an official announcement naming Crabb as a decorated war hero and saying that he occasionally did underwater research for the Admiralty as a contractor. A few days later a denial was issued that he was on official business and that was the last official comment. Throughout, there was an air of vagueness. This was clearly the right tactic as the story did not gain traction and the Soviet visit went ahead and, following a single protest, the Russians dropped the matter.

Quite what Biffy had to do with the Crabb operation, if anything, is unclear. However, on the 17th of October 1955, Biffy and Dorothy hosted a dinner at Walton Street for Lord Louis Mountbatten, the First Sea Lord, Sir John Sinclair, Head of SIS, Donald McLachlan, a former Naval Intelligence Officer and Ian Fleming. They would have most certainly discussed the *Sverdlov* class cruiser and intelligence operations against them. Mountbatten was a keen diver and had a penchant for clandestine operations. He also maintained close links with SIS. It is possible that they discussed a dive on the ORDJONIKIDZE, as at that time they would have known about the forthcoming state visit. Whilst it has never been suggested that Biffy planned and directed the operation, it was just his style. Furthermore, Nicholas Elliott was a protégé, colleague and close friend of both Biffy and Ian Fleming.

*

When Dick White took up his post on the 14th of July 1956, barely three months after the Crabb affair, it heralded a change in style within SIS – a less aggressive approach to operations, focusing on systematic intelligence-gathering rather than the adventurous, buccaneering approach of the 'Great Game'. The guard was changing.

White possessed great personal charm and modesty, but in spite of being a member of the lively Garrick Club, he was reserved and was regarded as isolated and standoffish by his staff. This was in complete contrast to Menzies who had enjoyed frequent informal chats over a few drinks in the evening with his senior staff. Biffy was almost always present and also had a habit of walking into Menzies's office for a chat, often saying: '"C", *these operations are too secret to be put on paper.*' This relaxed relationship between White's predecessors and their senior officers confused the chain of command to outsiders. Biffy loved this loose structure. '*The Russians could never understand our service because of the muddle of command. Much better than military organisation.*' Biffy understood that Russians disliked uncertainty and feel threatened by ambiguity. Biffy assumed that this informal relationship and direct access to 'C' would continue. Jack Easton told White that '*Biffy is cagey and won't talk to others involved in his anti-Russian operations.*' Biffy was rightly suspicious and security-conscious. Gibbie Gibson was of a similar view.

White wanted to change the old culture of SIS and get rid of the 'Robber Barons' – *'not only are the cowboy operations to end, but the cowboys must be removed'*. The 'Witch Finder General' was John Briance, White's personal assistant, who quickly earned the nickname the 'Undertaker'. He took White's directive seriously and spent a great deal of time and effort looking for officers to be given early retirement and paid off with 'golden handshakes' or found sinecure jobs outside SIS. Biffy was certainly in the frame. However, his track record, experience and standing within SIS meant that it would be hard to justify pushing him out early. Of all the Great Game 'Robber Barons', he was probably the best and most effective. For SIS officers like Biffy who operated on the front line, White's appointment as Chief was absurd. He doubted whether a security service officer had the experience, commitment and courage for offensive operations. *'He'd never run field agents. He'd never run risks. Our operations aren't like MI5's. If something goes wrong in Tripoli you can't telephone the local friendly police chief for help.'* Biffy was right, White had no interest in the old style of operations and there was a creeping fear in SIS that life would be dull and no longer *'the capital sport'* described by Mansfield Cumming.

However, 12 days after White took over, on the 26th of July 1945, President Gamal Abdel Nasser announced the nationalisation of the Suez Canal. Any discussion of Biffy's early retirement was immediately put on hold. White needed Biffy's experience. The Prime Minister Anthony Eden was adamant that Nasser would not be allowed to get away with it. *'I want him removed and I don't give a damn if there is anarchy and chaos in Egypt.'* A considerable change of heart after the Buster Crabb affair.

Back in March, Anthony Eden had given SIS a general mandate to *'pursue Nasser's destruction'*. Julian Amery, the Conservative MP for Preston North, was no stranger to the world of intelligence and covert action and his network in the Egyptian opposition and his friends in SIS made him a natural selection to support Eden's directive to SIS.

He had had an interesting career – he had worked as a war correspondent in the Spanish civil war, for the Foreign Office in Belgrade and during the war joined SOE, working in the Eastern

Mediterranean, Yugoslavia and later in Albania with David Smiley. He had a very extensive network of contacts in the Egyptian dissident community and in SIS. He also happened to be son-in-law of Harold Macmillan,[159] the then Chancellor of the Exchequer.

He also was adept at overt political pressure from the Suez Group in Parliament which sought to shape political attitudes to Nasser's decision to nationalise the Suez Canal company. The Suez Group had been formed in the early 1950s in response to Iranian Prime Minister Mosaddegh's nationalisation of British oil interests. Mosaddegh was removed from office in 1953 by a coup organised by SIS and the CIA (Operation AJAX). Under the 1954 Anglo-Egyptian agreement, British troops were to be withdrawn from the Canal Zone by June 1956. The Suez Group opposed this erosion of British power in the Middle East. Amery energetically used all his influence and contacts, operating in a freebooting style that Biffy would have recognised. He was described as *'being born with a silver grenade in his mouth'*.

From the beginning of 1954, Amery had been involved in Egyptian dissident planning for a coup to remove Nasser, but these plans fizzled out after the signing of the Anglo-Egyptian agreement. Early in 1956, Amery revived his Egyptian contacts – members of the Egyptian Royal Family, exiled politicians and military officers and King Zog of Albania now living in the south of France, Zog being related to the Egyptian Royals and having his own network in Egypt. Amery's plan was to assist in the overthrow of Nasser and put in place a pro-British government which would accept a renewed British military presence in the Canal Zone. When Eden gave the nod to SIS to remove Nasser, Amery's clandestine activities started to mirror SIS's own brief. By the beginning of July, they were working closely together.

Although Amery had many close contacts in SIS, it was Biffy as Controller Special Liaison who was charged with liaising with Amery's networks. They were old friends and shared a similar style. At a meeting at the Foreign Office on the 1st of August 1956, it was agreed *'that we should tell our Egyptian friends there was no longer any substantial difference between the government and ourselves'*.

159 Harold Macmillan became Prime Minister in 1957. Julian Amery served in his Government as Undersecretary for War 1957–58, the Colonies 1958–60, Minister of Aviation 1960–64.

Amery then held a series of meetings with his Egyptians in Geneva, Cannes and Paris. Planning continued between SIS and Amery and his private network.

On the 27th of August, Amery flew to Cannes with Biffy to introduce him to his contacts and finalise planning for the coup. They met with Amery's key contact Ismaddine Mahmoud Khalil, Deputy Chief of the Egyptian Intelligence Service, who was already known to SIS, at King Zog's villa. In outline, the plan involved a coup by a group of dissident officers who would kill Nasser. Khalil was so excited to meet a genuine SIS officer, even asking Biffy for his address *'in case I want to send you a Christmas card'*. This involvement with Amery's network became all the more important when, a few days later, the Egyptian General Intelligence Directorate the Mukhabarat rolled up SIS's own network in Egypt, raiding the Head of Station's house and arresting 20 members.

Amery was also close to the French Prime Minister Guy Mollet and the Defence Minister Maurice Bourgès-Maunoury. Both had been very active in the Resistance during the war and were known to both Amery and Biffy. Biffy also kept his friends in the French intelligence services briefed on developments. What was shaping up was an Anglo-French-Israeli operation. On the 29th of October the Israelis invaded the Sinai. As part of the pre-arranged plan, Britain and France issued a joint ultimatum, which, as agreed with the Israelis, was ignored and paved the way for a joint British-French airborne assault operation on the Suez Canal. Before the Egyptians were defeated, they blocked the Canal by sinking 40 ships in it, thus rendering it impassable for shipping. Ultimately heavy political pressure from the US and Russia forced a withdrawal of British and French forces.

Ironically Amery and SIS's aspirations were scuppered by his father-in-law Harold MacMillan, who had secretly been in touch with the Eisenhower administration. The US insisted on a full British and French withdrawal from Suez. This put pressure on Eden to resign. Eden's mistake was not to strike in July when public opinion was very supportive, and against Nasser. Despite a wave of outrage after the invasion, public opinion was still supportive. An opinion poll held on the 10th/11th of November found that 53 per cent supported Eden with 32 per cent against. Eden was also very ill. He spent a month at Goldeneye, Ian Fleming's house in Jamaica. He never recovered medically or politically and resigned on the 9th of January 1957.

Within SIS the fallout was predictable. Dick White had supported the SIS role in Eden's volte-face, supporting an assassination operation and deploying SIS teams with the invasion force, but it was not his style or how he wanted to run SIS. In fact, it was exactly the sort of thing he wished to eradicate. Subsequently he was to instigate a policy that SIS would never again be involved in assassinations, even though he had proved himself willing to implement government policy even if he didn't agree with it. He recognised that this operation was just the sort of thing that the 'Robber Barons' were good at, which may well be why he put Biffy in charge of liaison with the Egyptian dissidents. He may also have put him in place knowing that, as Biffy was due to retire in two years' time, it would not be hard to get rid of him early if he had to.

*

Before he retired from SIS three years later, Biffy may have managed one other important operation. At the end of the war, Polish politics again became complicated. The Poles had fought hard for the Allies in every major engagement from the Battle of Britain onwards. They had produced the first ENIGMA machine for the GC + CS, delivered by Biffy. Throughout the war they had conducted exceptionally professional intelligence operations on behalf of SIS, with Biffy as their liaison, controller and processor of the intelligence produced. In July 1945, the British, French and US government had withdrawn their recognition of the wartime Polish Government in Exile, in favour of the newly created Soviet-backed government in Warsaw. The Free Polish armed forces had been disbanded in 1945. Their members were unable or unwilling to return to the newly communist Poland and either stayed in Britain or emigrated to other Western countries. In Britain, due to their immense contribution to the war effort, the Poles were seen in Whitehall as deserving of special support and assistance. Churchill singled the Poles out as 'special' when, in a House of Commons speech, he declared that:

> Her Majesty's government will never forget the debt they owe to the Polish troops who have served them so valiantly and for all those who have fought under our command ...

The Polish Resettlement Act was passed in 1947. It was known as the 'Winston Churchill promise' and enabled qualifying Poles and their dependants to remain in Britain and made the then Assistance Board responsible for meeting the needs of qualifying Poles and their dependants. A total of 45 resettlement camps were set up across Great Britain. Most of Biffy's wartime Poles were resettled here and many joined SIS in Biffy's SLC émigré translation service. Others like Stephan Mayer, the pre-war Director of Polish Intelligence, were given a job for life within SIS.

As well as moving quickly to secure the Polish intelligence files in the basement of Ryder Street, there is little doubt that Biffy would have made every effort to recruit anyone returning to Poland, perhaps even persuading some to return to Poland as 'sleepers', or with a view to recruiting and establishing networks there. This may have resulted in SIS having three highly placed agents with the Polish Intelligence Service, the Urzad Bezpieczeństwa (UB) by 1958. The CIA described the information received from these Polish agents as 'some of the most valuable intelligence ever collected' and contributed US$20 million to help SIS expand their Polish operations. If Biffy had initiated and run this operation, it would be an excellent end to his career.

*

SLC was officially wound up in 1957 and Biffy oversaw the closure and destruction of its files. Biffy reported that he was 'fully embarked on the destruction of his sections records, including Polish records'. Biffy retired from SIS in 1959, aged 60, the normal age for retirement from SIS. In spite of Dick White's reforms of the service and his stated desire to remove the Old Guard – the 'Robber Barons' – Biffy

Biffy at Alces Place

served out a full career. He was not eased out and given a 'golden handshake'. Nor was he found a sinecure job, as is often written, as Honorary Consul in Chicago. A simple check of the Foreign Office diplomatic lists for the years 1960 onwards makes no mention of Biffy in Chicago or anywhere else.

Biffy had married Dorothy Hyde, former wife of Montgomery Hyde, a wartime SIS officer, in 1952. When in London they lived at 44 Walton Street, where they employed a butler named James Pullen, who according to Anthony Fraser, Biffy's godson, was the caricature of the butler who helped himself to his employer's brandy. In the country they lived at Alces Place in Sussex. Alces Place was a U-shaped terrace of cottages knocked into one house. The core of the building was medieval, complete with resident ghost. Biffy sold Alces Place on the 17th of August 1956 and he and Dorothy moved to 'Castlefield' in Bletchingley on the North Downs in Surrey where they were to live until Dorothy's death in 1978.

In trying to unravel what Biffy did after 1959, one inevitably runs up against the wall of secrecy surrounding SIS operations and personnel after 1949 when the published history closes. Therefore, for the last 10 years of Biffy's career, we enter the realm of speculation.

However, there are some clues. Anthony Cavendish, who had left SIS in 1956 to become a journalist, complained that his fellow journalist, Chapman Pincher, '*did us no favours*' when he highlighted the fact that '*SIS officers never lose contact with their organisation when they retire.*' It is well known that SIS regularly calls on those who have retired to either help out with something that requires their specialist expertise or asks them to remain working in a discreet capacity at arm's length.

Did Biffy fully retire in 1959 after leaving SIS? There are a number of things that point to the fact that he didn't. Biffy was well liked by the US intelligence community and at the end of the war they had gone out of their way to ensure that he was rewarded with the Legion of Merit. In the late 1940s, Biffy made many liaison visits to the US and maintained his strong links with the CIA. On the 28th of August 1965, six years after Biffy retired, Admiral John Godfrey, the former Director of Naval Intelligence and long-term friend of Biffy's, wrote to him as follows.[160]

28th August 1965

Dear Biffy,
In 1939 a combatant rank was needed to enable you properly to carry out your work in Paris, and I am glad you chose the dark blue rather than the khaki or light blue thus perpetuating an affiliation with the Royal Navy which began in the Black Sea in 1918. One snag about the Navy is that it is not very good at saying 'Thank you', a handicap which it shares with the profession you have so ably served for so long. We are inclined to take things for granted and to overdo the theory that work brings its own reward and that gratitude is a bonus.

Starting in a humble capacity you have become an elder states-man, continuing to work almost full time after official retirement on most inadequate remuneration.

In this respect the country has been fortunate in being able to retain your services, and make use of your unique gifts,

160 Reproduced courtesy of the Paul Biddle Archive.

specialised knowledge and wisdom over a period of nearly half a century, an achievement which you share with very few and those only Admirals of the Fleet.

It has been my good fortune to enjoy your friendship for more than twenty-seven years including four years of close collaboration during World War II.

You have had to put up with many stresses and strains, but these are inseparable from a long career in public service and on the whole there are more ups than downs. The solid fact is that you alone have survived these vicissitudes, and are still actively employed on the retired list, enjoying your work and the esteem and confidence of your Chief and colleagues. They have acquired the habit, after years of experience, of leaning heavily on your shoulder – and, of course, a shoulder cannot be leant on unless it is offered.

Added to this you have found time to run the Thirty-six Club[161] and thereby to perpetuate the sense of tradition and goodwill created during the War.

Yours ever,
John Godfrey

The important part of this letter is '*you … are still actively employed on the retired list, enjoying your work and the esteem and confidence of your Chief and colleagues.*'

The most plausible theory is that Dick White asked Biffy to continue to work with the Americans to 'steady the ship' after the difficulties and scepticism of the 1950s which was further exacerbated by the final defection of Philby from Beirut to Moscow in January 1963. No one in SIS could quite believe that someone at the heart of their counterintelligence operations who controlled everything SIS knew about the Russians could be a traitor. '*If he was the "third man" there was no tooth fairy, no Santa Claus and Dumbo would never fly. If it really was Kim, it was the end of the world as we knew it.*' Biffy's long

---

161 The Thirty-six Club – a dining club of former NID officers named after DNI's official residence at 36 Curzon Street. Members included Ian Fleming, Peter Smithers and Nicholas Elliott.

Debbie Dunderdale

experience with the Soviets going back to 1918, together with his pro-America leanings, would have made him an invaluable resource at the height of the Cold War as the man charged with helping to keep the relations with the US intelligence community alive.

Dorothy died on the 24th of October 1978 when Biffy was approaching his 79th birthday. Biffy, for the first time in his life, found himself at a loose end and lonely. An old friend, Deborah Jackson, the widow of Henry McIntosh Mcleod who had died of cancer, invited Biffy to New York and to stay in her apartment. They had been 'set up' by Henry Hyde, son of James Hazen Hyde, Biffy's old friend from his OSS days who had kept in touch with Biffy, like Charles Grey, since the war. Early on after Biffy's arrival she took him to lunch at the Knickerbocker Club[162] where she held widow's privileges and which has a reciprocal arrangement with Boodles, Biffy's London club. Deborah suggested that if Biffy was going to come and live in New York, he should become a member and gave him the list of members to look through to see whom he knew and who would help him get in. Amongst many members that he knew, one name triggered a long dormant memory, Mark Sevastopolu.

A few days later Biffy telephoned Mark, introduced himself and asked if he was the same Mark Sevastopolu who had worked for Charles Heidsieck, the champagne house in Paris in the 1930s. Mark confirmed that this was indeed the case. Biffy then told him that he had signed Mark's exit papers from Biarritz allowing him to head for

162 The Knickerbocker Club – 2 East 62nd Street, founded in 1871 and considered one of the most exclusive clubs in the US.

London in 1940. What had stuck in Biffy's mind was Mark's place of birth filled in on the form – Odessa. Several years later after Mark's death, when Biffy was established in New York having married Deborah in 1980,[163] he called Dimitri, Mark's son, and invited him to lunch at the Knickerbocker Club where he told him the story. Dimitri is among those who befriended Biffy in his old age, attesting to his charm, manners and bonhomie, but always with the Biffy caveat in conversations making clear that he had signed the Official Secrets Act and could not discuss any aspect of his life and adventures covered by it.

Andrew Fulton, posted as SIS Head of Station in New York for the last few years of Biffy's life and charged with keeping in touch, also attested to Biffy's charm and avuncular nature and that he retained all his faculties until the end. As to Biffy's career, Andrew Fulton knew nothing specific but agreed that Biffy may well have been asked to 'steady the ship' after Philby and Suez as a well-liked and respected friend of the US. Certainly, the US intelligence services knew he was there and he regularly entertained them.

For some time before his death, he suffered from Trigeminal Neuralgia, an extremely painful condition affecting the nerves in the head and face. Biffy Dunderdale died of natural causes at the New York Hospital[164] on the afternoon of November the 13th 1990 with Debbie at his bedside, attended by Staff Physician Doctor James Hoffman. He had been admitted on the 8th of November after Debbie had noticed him beginning to weaken. He was 91.

Biffy was cremated at the Garden State Crematorium in Bergan New Jersey and his ashes were taken to Bletchingley where they were scattered. He was a much-loved character in the village. A memorial service was held at St Mary the Virgin Church in Bletchingley attended not only by his family but many past and present SIS and CIA officers. A plaque to his memory was installed in the church.

Six days after he died, Andrew Fulton, the Head of Station in New York, wrote a condolence letter to Debbie. Enclosed was a letter from the then 'C' Colin McColl, not only offering her condolences and

---

163 They lived in a luxurious apartment 13F, at One East 66 Street and 5th Avenue where they were looked after by a Jamaican maid, the wonderfully named Hyacinth Lightbody.
164 Now the Weill Cornell Medical Centre.

Biffy's memorial plaque at Bletchingly

Silver bowl presented by Debbie to SIS in memory of Biffy

those of the service, but also highlighting Biffy's contribution to SIS and his outstanding career as an intelligence officer.

Biffy's cosmopolitan upbringing and early life undoubtedly prepared him for life as an intelligence officer. He was quick-witted, highly intelligent and resourceful, well-educated and a multi-linguist. His father, Richard, gave him a great deal of responsibility at an early age. All attributes which, when combined with confidence and charm, made him a natural candidate for recruitment into the world of intelligence. He was able to readily recognise in others the key motivators of agents: money, patriotism, ideology, revenge and probably quick to learn other tricks of the trade such as entrapment and blackmail.

Biffy certainly left his mark on SIS and, in his will, left money to the Century Benevolent Fund of 100 Westminster Bridge Road, London SE1 – the address of Century House, SIS headquarters from 1964–94. His worldly knowledge, experience of operations, achievements, his '*40 years of licensed thuggery*' and his affable demeanour were of great profit to young officers in SIS and his exploits were regularly used in instruction on the Intelligence Officers' Induction Course. His sense of humour, courage, acumen, bravery, audacity and presence of mind – the essentials for success – were an example to all. Russians would describe him as having '*a fine structure of soul*'.

He was, in the words of John le Carré, '*built by the same firm that built Stonehenge*'.

EPILOGUE – 007

'Is he in hell, or is he in Heaven.
That damned elusive 007.'

Kingsley Amis, The James Bond Dossiers

'*Some myths are never put to bed*,' wrote John Scarlett, the Head of SIS from 2004–09, '*... the best thing is not to argue about it but to put facts on the table*'. There are many myths surrounding Biffy's legendary career, but the enduring one seems to be that he was the model for James Bond.

Biffy became friends with Ian Fleming in 1940 and remained close to him throughout his life. Both were also close friends with Fitzroy Maclean who is also touted as another model for Bond. Fleming was keen for his novels to be as accurate as possible and would look for anecdotes and technical advice from friends and acquaintances: '*My plots are fantastic, while often being based on truth*' and '*everything I write has a precedent in truth*'. Fleming's rather aimless life had been given direction and focus by the war. Although Bond was a post-war figure, he had many echoes of the pre-war and wartime worlds of espionage. The likes of Biffy, Fitzroy Maclean and John Godfrey gave him models to work from.

There is no doubt that Biffy helped him. The best example is *From Russia with Love*. In a copy of *Diamonds are Forever* inscribed to Biffy it says on the flyleaf, '*To Bill, who has helped me with the next one, with affection from Ian.*' The 'next one' was *From Russia with Love*, published on the 8th of April 1957. Fleming thought it was his best Bond book, a view shared by President John F. Kennedy, who listed it amongst his 10 favourite books.

Biffy's fingerprints are all over *From Russia with Love*, starting with the book's basic building blocks of Istanbul, the Orient Express and a coding machine. The Author's Note at the beginning, which sets the tone for the rest of the novel:

Inscription from Ian Fleming to Biffy in his presentation
copy of *Diamonds are Forever*

NOT that it matters, but a great deal of the background to this story is accurate. SMERSH, a contraction of Smert Shpiónam – Death to Spies – exists and remains today the most secret department of the Soviet government. At the beginning of 1956, when this book was written, the strength of SMERSH at home and abroad was about 40,000 and General Grubozaboyschikov was its chief. My description of his appearance is correct. Today, the headquarters of SMERSH are where, in Chapter 4, I have placed them – at No. 13 Sretenka Ulitsa, Moscow. The Conference Room is faithfully described and the Intelligence chiefs who meet round the table are real officials who are frequently summoned to that room for purposes similar to those I have recounted.

I.F.
March 1956

Fleming confirmed that the information came from Colonel Grigori Tokaev, one of the defectors handled by Biffy. Biffy would have suggested that Fleming talked to Tokaev, which he did at length. Fleming's own copy of *From Russia with Love* is annotated 'The Russian background comes mostly from a Soviet refugee spy called Tokaev ...' Unfortunately, Tokaev had the last laugh, as 13 Sretenka Ulitsa was nothing more than a drab block of shops. SMERSH however did exist – born out of the Special Division of the Cheka. It was an execution service charged with the pursuit and murder of enemies of the state, hence the name 'Smert Shpiónam' – Death to Spies. Its first head, Vyacheslav Rudolfovich Menzhinsky, was just the sort of macabre villain that would have appealed to Fleming.

The plot turns on obtaining '"*the brand new Spektor*[165] *machine. The thing we'd give our eyes to have." "God," said Bond softly… "The Spektor! The machine that would allow them to decipher the Top Secret traffic of all." "The Spektor itself is a grey japanned metal case with three rows of squat keys, rather like a typewriter."*' This is a direct reference to the ENIGMA machine – the first example of which Biffy brought to London in August 1939, as described in Chapter 8. The general concept for *From Russia with Love* – the collection of a top-secret coding machine from Istanbul and delivery to London via a train journey – no doubt had its origins in the trip made by Biffy and his team on the Golden Arrow in 1939 to deliver the ENIGMA machine from Paris to London.

When Darko Kerim, the Istanbul Head of Station, is telling Bond his life story, he describes his upbringing in Trebizond on the Black Sea coast of northeast Turkey. His father was '*a great fisherman and his fame spread all over the Black Sea. He went after the swordfish.*' Darko is summoned to a meeting with his father.

There was another man with my father, a tall quiet Englishman with a black patch over one eye. They were talking about the Russians. The Englishman wanted to know what they were doing along the frontier, about what was going in at Batoum, their big oil and naval base only fifty miles away from Trebizond. He would pay good money for information. I knew English and I knew Russian. I had good eyes and ears. I had a boat. My father had decided that I would work for the Englishman. And that Englishman, my dear friend, was Major Dansey, my predecessor as Head of this Station. And the rest, Kerim made a wide gesture with his cigarette holder, "you can imagine". "But what about this training to be a professional strong man?" "Ah," said Kerim slyly, "that was only a sideline. Our travelling circuses were almost the

---

165 Renamed Lektor in the film to avoid confusion with SPECTRE.

only Turks allowed through the frontier. The Russians cannot live without circuses. It is as simple as that. I was the man who broke chains and lifted weights by a rope between the teeth. I wrestled against the local strong men in the Russian villages. And some of those Georgians are giants. Fortunately they are stupid giants and I nearly always won. Afterwards, at the drinking, there was always much talk and gossip. I would look foolish and pretend not to understand. Every now and then I would ask an innocent question and they would laugh at my stupidity and tell me the answer."

Besides the description of Claude Dansey, whom Fleming would have known from his days at NID, this is a direct reference to Biffy's offensive action operations in Transcaucasia run out of Trebizond using Turkish fishing boats, as described in Chapter 4.

The attempt to kill Bond on the Orient Express is based on the death of Captain Eugene Karpe, a US Naval Attaché who was pushed from the Arlberg Express on February the 23rd 1950 – a case Biffy would have been fully aware of. Karpe was the Naval Attaché in Romania and was leaving Romania in a hurry after being tipped off that he was about to be arrested for espionage. He had with him papers relating to a blown US network in Russia, incriminating him and other agents. Karpe was also a Russian expert with extensive knowledge of Russia's Black Sea and Danube River fleets.

Two years later in February 1952, Ryan Parescu, a 25-year-old Romanian, confessed he helped push Karpe to his death from the train. The Swiss Federal Police said, *'The crime was committed on orders from a foreign organisation.'* Karpe's mutilated body was found on February the 23rd 1950 in the Lueg Pass tunnel, 12 miles south of Salzburg, Austria. He was travelling between Bucharest and Paris. The police statement said Parescu confessed *'with the aid of two accomplices he pushed Capt. Karpe from the train after stealing important documents in his possession'*. In the course of the journey, Karpe had stayed over in Vienna for a few days and visited the wife of his friend, Robert Vogeler, an American businessman sentenced a few days before in Budapest to 13 years in jail for spying and sabotage. After Karpe's body was found, Mrs Vogeler told a reporter she had a mysterious telephone call warning her to let the fate of *'your friend be a lesson for you'*.

There are other references in the book that originated from Biffy. The gun used by Grant the KGB assassin, for example, was based on a KGB cigarette case gun developed for use by their highly successful assassin Nikolai Khokhlov, who had defected to the US in 1954.[166] There are also several other 'Biffyisms' in the book. Darko Kerim, the SIS Head of Station in Istanbul, is described as an Oxford-educated former shipowner – Richard Dunderdale? Fleming describes Kerim's office:

> *in the centre of the room the big desk winked with polished brass handles. On the littered desk were three silver photograph frames, and Bond caught a sideways view of copperplate script of two Mentions in Dispatches and the Military Division of the O.B.E.*

These are exactly the same as Biffy's first three awards for his work in the Crimea. Three pages later, Kerim looks at Bond and says:

> *"There is something going on in the enemy camp, my friend. It is not only this attempt to get rid of me. There are comings and goings. I have few facts," he reached up a big index finger and laid it alongside his nose, "but I have this." He tapped the side of his nose as if he was patting a dog. "But this is a good friend of mine and I trust him."*

The nose-tapping gesture is pure Biffy, as related to the author by all those who knew him.

Biffy's experience with defectors also comes out when Bond speculates what will happen to Tatiana Romanova:

> *Probably at Dover she would be taken away to "The Cage", that well-sentried private house near Guildford, where she would be*

---

166 He was later hunted down by the Russians and poisoned with Thallium but survived. This is the first documented use of this type of poisoning – which now seems to be used regularly by the direct descendant of SMERSH – Unit 29155 of the GRU.

put in a comfortable but oh so well-wired room. And the efficient men in plain clothes would come one by one and sit and talk with her, and the recorder would spin in the room below and the records would be transcribed and sifted for their grains of new fact – and, of course, for the contradictions they would trap her into.

There is another little twist in the book that certainly came from Biffy. The SMERSH assassin sent to kill Bond is called 'Nash'. Some KGB/SMERSH files were stamped on their cover 'Nash' – the description for 'one of ours' – a sympathiser, informant or defector. The character Nash in the book is a former IRA killer called Red Grant. His chosen cover name is Captain Norman Nash.

It is unlikely that the Bond character is wholly fictional. Fleming's inspiration often came from the people he worked with or admired and this gave his novels a sense of realism and intimacy. There are a group of people who have characteristics that contribute to make up the Bond pastiche: among them are Fitzroy Maclean, diplomat, soldier, SOE operator and Fleming and Biffy's lifelong friend. He often 'pooh-poohed' the intelligence business, but it was probably a case of me thinks he doth protest too much. Other candidates include Patrick Dalzel-Job and Dunstan Curtis,[167] both of whom served in Fleming's 'Private Army' 30 Assault Unit during the war. Whilst Curtis and Dalzel-Job are often mentioned in the list of 'Bonds', they are less likely as Fleming had little or no field time with them.

Undoubtedly there are parts of Biffy in the Bond character. Like Bond, Biffy was a *bon vivant* who was always immaculately dressed, liked champagne and excellent food. The period of Biffy's life that is closest to the Bond image is his time in Paris from 1926–40. Biffy was a connoisseur of vodka, from his upbringing in Russia and years spent in the company of Russian émigrés. He certainly liked dry martinis, usually at the bar of the George V Hotel. He smoked Turkish cigarettes specially made for him which he would smoke in a long black ivory cigarette holder. They may or may not have had three gold bands embossed on each. This is more likely to

---

167 Skipper of MGB 314 of the 15th Motor Gun Boat Flotilla. See *A Dangerous Enterprise*.

Conrad O'Brien-ffrench

be an embellishment of Fleming's. Three gold rings denotes the rank of Commander in the Royal Navy, a rank which both Fleming and Biffy held.

Biffy loved the company of women – you only have to look at the photographs taken on his motor yacht of his wife June, Lily Greene, Coosie Hottinguer and Simone Heath. Amorous adventures outside his marriage are not documented but it would not be surprising if he had a number of lady friends. He remained a great flirt until the end of his life, regularly embarrassing his step-grandson by chatting up his glamorous girlfriend.

So much of Biffy's persona fits the Bond make-up, except that of the physical. That is more likely based on another candidate, Conrad O'Brien-ffrench. He was another adventurer with an exotic profile like Biffy. Born in 1893, brought up in Italy, he had joined the Royal Canadian Mounted Police aged 17.

He returned to Britain to serve in World War I. In 1918, he was recruited into SIS. He served in Russia during the Civil War, then India where he became a fanatical mountaineer and then an expert skier. In the 1930s he rejoined SIS, joining Claude Dansey's 'Z' parallel organisation working under commercial cover, having established 'Tyrolese Tours' offering package tours to Austria and Bavaria. It was here that he became friends with Fleming. His intelligence work earned him a place alongside Biffy in the Gestapo's 'Black Book', marked for arrest and execution. He certainly had all the physical characteristics of Bond.

There is another fundamental difference between Biffy and Bond. Biffy was an outstanding intelligence officer who, as far as we know, didn't kill anyone. Bond did not gather intelligence but spent his time hunting down and killing Her Majesty's enemies. Of course, a large part of the Bond character is Ian Fleming's fantasy aspirations. As John le Carré wrote in *Tinker Tailor Soldier Spy*:

Few men can resist expressing their appetites when they are making a fantasy about themselves.

Evidence that Ian Fleming was indeed exercising his imagination along these lines not long after the war comes from an account of an early 'Thirty-six Club' dinner at the Junior Carlton. A group of men who had all been in the wartime secret services were deploring the bland efficiencies of the modern intelligence business and regretting that real-life agents lacked the glamour and dash of those in novels:

Ian said the whole organisation wanted revolutionising and he still saw a use for the traditional spy of fiction. Whereupon he imaginatively pictured the adventures he might have had in the last war given complete freedom and unlimited money. The exploits were not all that dissimilar to those of Bond …

Peter Fleming referred to this change of attitude as '*a nation of weaklings flouncing in a bureaucratic soup*'.

Biffy was the Secretary of the 'Thirty-six Club'.

Fleming also once alleged that he had had a one-night stand on a European train with Diana Napier, wife of the operatic tenor Richard Tauber. According to Lady Mary Pakenham, this never happened. It was a story of Fleming's inspired by the tale of a young Biffy translating for a Russian general and an English Lady whom the general was trying to seduce on the Trans-Siberian Railway.

As Ian Fleming said himself:

James Bond came out of thin air really … he was a compound of all the secret agents and commando types that I met during the

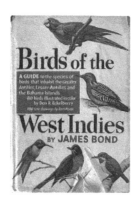

Second World War when I was Personal Assistant to the Director of Naval Intelligence. The thing was, my job got me to the heart of things ... and it was all the things that I heard and learned about secret operations that finally led me to write about them in a disguised way with James Bond the central character.

In spite of all his wartime influences, Fleming took the name for his character from that of the American ornithologist, James Bond, author of the definitive field guide *Birds of the West Indies*:

It struck me that this brief, unromantic Anglo-Saxon and yet very masculine name was just what I needed, and so a second James Bond was born.

There is one other oblique reference to Biffy that came much later than *From Russia with Love* in 1964 in *You Only Live Twice*, when Bond supposedly dies on a mission to Japan. 'M' feels obliged to issue an obituary in *The Times* which includes a reference to Richard Dunderdale '*... his father being a foreign representative of the Vickers Armaments firm*', Biffy's language skills '*... his early education from which he inherited a first-class command of French and German, was entirely abroad*' and his ability to box '*he had twice fought for the school as a lightweight ...*' There is much of Biffy in Bond but the resemblance is not exclusive.

APPENDIX – DRAMATIS PERSONAE

> 'The years have passed, my friends have died, but their spirit is still alive. They rejected the invader, the occupier, the profaners of our liberties, and their fight weighs heavily on my conscience.'
>
> Marie-Madeleine Fourcade
> Leader of the ALLIANCE SIS network

So often, at the end of a book, the reader is left thinking, '*I wonder what happened to them?*' There was such a range of characters involved in Biffy's life that I have tried to answer that question about those closest to him.

Richard Dunderdale: Moved to South Africa from Istanbul after contracting TB. He died in the Moltan Nursing Home, Pietermaritzburg, Kwazulu-Natal, South Africa on the 13th of February 1945.

Sophie Dunderdale: After Richard's death, moved to London and lived with Biffy at 44 Walton Street. Biffy then bought her a flat at 92 Radcliffe Gardens where she died on the 8th of September 1955 and is buried in Putney Vale cemetery.

Lilly Dunderdale: Married Arthur Whittall on the 25th of August 1928. Whittall continued to serve in SIS until 1955. Lilly died on the 13th of February 1968. Arthur died on the 17th of January 1978.

June Dunderdale: Returned to Paris after the war. Her marriage to Biffy was annulled in 1947. She remarried John Taylor, a US Army colonel, in 1948 and they moved to Long Island in 1951. June worked for the fashion house Balmain until her early death in February 1967 at the age of 56.

Dorothy Dunderdale: Married Biffy in 1952 and lived with him very happily in Alces Place and then Bletchingley in Sussex. Dorothy died after a short illness in 1978.

Debbie Dunderdale: Biffy remarried his third wife Debbie in 1980 and they lived between Bletchingley and New York. Debbie died in 1994.

Tom and Sylvia Greene: Returned to Paris in 1944. Tom served there with SIS until 1948 when he retired to Estoril in Portugal aged 58. He was awarded the OBE, Legion of Merit and Croix de Guerre. He died in 1965 aged 73. When Tom died, Sylvia returned to England.

Lois Greene 'Lola': Married Roderick Sheridan in 1940. He worked for the Foreign Office. They had a nomadic lifestyle living all over the world, including in Zanzibar. She died in 2004.

Sheelagh Greene: Having helped her father Tom wind up the JADE network, she married Charles Garton, one of the SIS officers who had worked for Biffy during the war. They were married first at a civil ceremony in London and later at a church service in Paris conducted by Abbé Vorage, who had been one of Bertrand and Biffy's prize agents. The service was held in the Couvent de la Sainte-Agonie, the wartime headquarters of JADE AMICOL. They lived first in Surrey, then in Wadeford House near Chard in Somerset and had

Sheelagh Greene and Charles Garton on their wedding day in Paris

Wedding present given by JADE AMICOL
veterans to Sheelagh Greene

three children. Charles left SIS after the war as he was due to be posted to Korea. Sheelagh had had enough of operational living, so he decided to retire and become a gentleman farmer. In writing this book, all the Woods/Greene/Garton family have been extremely helpful but had no idea their mother was such an effective and brave agent, who had worked behind enemy lines from 1940–44. They finally understood some of their mother's seemingly eccentric habits – never having the wireless on so that she could hear any noise out of the ordinary and often looking out of the window so she could watch all the approaches to Wadeford House. Virginia Hall, one of SIS's most effective agents, pointed out that agents working in France '*age quickly out here … we'll never be quite the same again*'. Sheelagh died in 1999.

Doreen Greene: Continued to work for SIS after the war, helping her uncle wind up the wartime SIS operations in France. She met and married an American journalist, Herbert Richardson, in Paris in 1953 and went to live in Cascais in Portugal. Tom Greene did not want to live in Britain, so on retirement followed Doreen to Portugal. Richardson died in 1963. Doreen remained in Cascais until she died in 1999.

Anthony Heath: After serving as Biffy's liaison officer with the Poles at Stanmore, he was posted to Italy where he spent the rest of the war. From 1946–52 he was attached to the British Embassy in Rome,

Buenos Aires 1953–55, London 1956–58, Milan 1958–60 and Saigon 1960–62. He retired in 1963. He had two sons, Philip and Sebastian. Biffy was godfather to Philip. Heath died in 1995.

Pierre-Louis Rivet: He retired from the French Intelligence Service on the 15th of April 1947 with the rank of general. He died on the 12th of December 1958.

Georges Ronin: Having worked for Biffy from 1940–42 he escaped with Louis Rivet to North Africa where he worked for the Free French. He was awarded the Légion d'honneur. After the war he remained in French intelligence until his retirement. He died in 1954 aged 60.

Gustave Bertrand: Honoured by the British, Poles and Americans. Was not recognised by General de Gaulle at the end of the war even though he was immediately reintegrated into the new French Intelligence Service in 1944. Eventually recognised but only for his post-war work. He was awarded the Légion d'honneur on his retirement from the French Intelligence Service in 1950. He retired to his hometown of Théoule-sur-Mer where he became a Mayor. In 1973 he published his book, *ENIGMA ou la plus grand ènigme de la Guerre 1939–1945*. This was the first public exposure of ENIGMA. He died in 1976. His wartime awards were the Croix de Guerre, Resistance Medal, Escapers Medal, DSO (UK), Legion of Merit (US), Polish Cross of Valour + bar and Golden Cross of Merit + bar, in addition to French campaign medals. Bertrand is sometimes dismissed as an unpleasant egomaniac. The truth is far from that. He was an effective intelligence officer and recognised the importance of ENIGMA very early on. He never broke the secrecy pact about ENIGMA and he had the wit to bamboozle the Germans when captured and go on the run and escape. British DSOs are not given to foreign recipients lightly.

Paul Paillole: He remained with the French Intelligence Service until 1953. In retirement he fought to get recognition for his work in Vichy working for the British. He had limited success with de Gaulle. He became Mayor of La Queue-les-Yvelines, a suburb of Paris, between 1965 and 1983. He died in 2002.

Charles Gossage Grey: After joining the OSS in 1942 he served in London, Lisbon, where his family joined him, Italy and finally Paris in 1944. Once France was liberated the family moved back home. Charles transitioned to the CIA, retiring in 1961. He lived in Paris but travelled regularly on CIA business. He was hit by a car in Palm Beach, Florida and died on the 6th of March 1987. Having been initially buried in the Passy cemetery behind the Trocadero at the insistence of the Alumni of the French Resistance, he was later reburied in the Cimetière de Montparnasse alongside his wife Ivanka. His tally of medals included the Distinguished Service Cross (US), Légion d'honneur and Resistance Medal (France), the King's Medal for Courage (UK), the Golden Cross of Merit (Poland) and the Order of the White Rose (Finland).

Coosie Hottinguer: Spent the war working in Biffy's JADE AMICOL network. She was picked up by the Gestapo, imprisoned in Fresne but was not deported. After the war she was instrumental in setting up the Association Nationale des Anciennes Déportées et Internées de la Résistance (ADIR) in July 1945 for the dual purpose of providing material and moral support for the survivors of the camps and honouring the memory of those who did not return. Composed exclusively of women who had been imprisoned in concentration camps or French prisons because of their wartime resistance, the ADIR became the principal cornerstone on which most female deportees or prisoners rebuilt their lives. For this work she was awarded the Légion d'honneur. After her divorce from Philippe Hottinguer, Coosie lived with Ingram Fraser in Paris. She died in 1988.

Josephine Baker: Ended the war a heroine of the Resistance, being awarded the Resistance Medal, Croix de Guerre and Légion d'honneur. After the war she continued her musical career and became active in the civil rights movement in America where she fell foul of the McCarthy era witch hunt. She later lived in Roquebrune in the south of France. She died in Paris of cerebral haemorrhage on the 12th of April 1975. She received a full military funeral and was buried in Monaco. In 2021 she was interred in the Panthéon in Paris.

Walter Sleator: Returned to Paris after the war, where he took control of the Rolls Royce franchise – some say by questionable means. However, he went from strength to strength, becoming a very successful businessman. He had been awarded the OBE for his wartime work with SIS. He died in 1964 aged 61 and is buried in Neuilly-sur-Seine.

Ian Fleming: After the war he worked for the Kemsley newspaper group until 1961. He carried on numerous affairs, eventually marrying Ann Rothermere in 1951. The marriage was not a happy one, both of them continuing to have affairs. Fleming had bought a house in Jamaica, Goldeneye, where he wrote 14 James Bond novels. He was a heavy smoker and drinker. He died of a heart attack on the 12th of August 1964. He remained a lifelong friend of Biffy and Charles Grey.

Fitzroy Maclean: Remained lifelong friends with Biffy and Ian Fleming. After working in the Paris embassy, he was posted to Moscow and travelled extensively in Russia and central Asia. He joined the SAS and fought in North Africa throughout 1941–42. In 1943 he was chosen by Churchill to lead a strategically important SOE mission to Tito's partisans in Yugoslavia. His success earned him a CBE, the Russian Order of Kutuzov, the French Croix de Guerre and the Yugoslavian Partisan Star. He ended the war as a brigadier. After the war he became a Conservative MP and was knighted in 1957. He lived between Strachur in Argyll and the Palazzo Boschi in Korčula. He died on the 15th of June 1996 aged 85.

Peter Smithers: Having organised the evacuation of the SIS Station on the SS MADURA he was involved in counter-espionage, then posted to Washington where he worked with OSS on behalf of SIS. It is strongly suspected he ran agent CYNTHIA …

After Washington he went on to work in Peru and Mexico. After the war he entered politics, becoming a Conservative MP for Winchester in 1950. From 1962–64 he was permanent Undersecretary of State at the Foreign Office. In 1964 he became Secretary General of the Council of Europe. He was knighted in 1970, his life peerage having been vetoed by Edward Heath. He became a Swiss citizen and spent the rest of his life indulging his passion for horticulture. He died at Vico Morcote in Switzerland in June 2006.

Kenneth Cohen: Continued in SIS until his retirement in 1953. He was widely expected to be promoted Head of SIS but was probably not chosen because he was Jewish, at a time when relations with the Arab world were becoming all-important. After retirement he worked in the steel industry and for Euratom. He was awarded the CMG in 1946 and the CB in 1954. He also held the Légion d'honneur, Croix de Guerre, Legion of Merit (US), Officier de la Couronne (Belgium) and Order of the White Lion (Czechoslovakia). He died in September 1984.

Paul Kilesso: After his capture and torture, he was deported to Mauthausen. He survived and was liberated by the Americans. In very bad shape, he was sent by the International Red Cross to a clinic in Switzerland. Fully recovered he returned to France in 1948. He was subsequently awarded the Resistance Medal, Croix de Guerre with Palm and Chevalier of Légion d'honneur and the British Military Cross. He died on the 1st of December 1985 and is buried in Odessa.

Claude Lamirault: Survived Dachau and resumed his work for the French Intelligence Service. He was killed in a car crash in France on the 27th of May 1945. He was made a Companion of the Liberation on the 13th of May 1945.

Pierre Hentic: Was sent to Dachau after his arrest and imprisonment in France, from where he was liberated in 1945. After the war, in a letter to the head of MI9 dated the 1st of September 1945, Tom Greene wrote, '*Of all the agents I have come into contact with during this war, none took more risks, had more successes, was more honest, and certainly less assuming, than Hentic.*' He joined the

French Army Parachute Troops and went to Indochina with the 1er Bataillon de Choc, conducting commando operations. In his second tour he became a captain, leading a team of indigenous troops in the Groupement de Commandos Mixtes Aéroportés, a parachute unit working on the Plateaux Hrés. After Indochina he went to Algeria with the action service of the French foreign intelligence service, SDECE, forerunner of the DGSE, on Operation OISEAU BLUE. This was designed to train up a force of locals, the Clan Kabyle, to fight against the FLN, but having already been penetrated, they turned against the French after being armed and trained. Hentic was sent to sort out the mess, which ended with 11e Regiment Parachutist de Choc and the 3e Regiment Parachutistes Coloniaux attacking them between the 9th and 12th of October 1956; 122 rebels were killed and 19 French. Hentic was promoted to colonel in 1960 and returned to France in 1961. He was a fanatical skier and set up a combination of parachuting, skiing and shooting competitions. He left the army in 1966. Among many decorations he was awarded the Commander of the Légion d'honneur, a British MBE (many believed an MBE did not reflect his bravery and contribution and that a DSO would have been more appropriate), the US Medal of Freedom, the Resistance Medal and Croix de Guerre (with 13 bars). He died on the 9th of March 2004.

Claude Arnould: Continued to work as intelligence officer for the French and also for the Vatican. He carried out missions in China, Vietnam, Israel, South Africa, Latin America and the US. He was awarded the Légion d'honneur, Croix de Guerre, the Resistance Medal and the British DSO. He was not made a Companion of the Liberation, a gross omission considering his contribution, including saving Paris. He died in Paris in December 1978.

Philip Keun: Executed at Buchenwald on the 9th of September 1944. He is remembered at Blundell's, not only for his wartime heroism, but for his physical prowess and natural leadership. He was head of house of Francis House and captained the first XV. There is a Keun trophy presented every year for athletics.

Claude Arnould's DSO

The 'Keun Cup', Blundell's school

Frederick Winterbotham: After his involvement with SIS work when Biffy was Head of Station in Paris, Winterbotham spent the war working on the management of the dissemination of ULTRA, the codename for intelligence, derived from reading ENIGMA. After the war he published several books including *The Ultra Secret* in 1974, following close on the heels of Gustave Bertrand's book. This caused some excitement in the intelligence community as ULTRA/ENIGMA had remained a closely guarded secret for over 30 years. Winterbotham returned to Devon and died in 1990 aged 92.

Nicholas Elliott: Remained with SIS after the war. He retired after Kim Philby's escape to Moscow in 1963. He worked for Lonroh from 1963 to 1969. He was also an advisor to Margret Thatcher on intelligence matters. He died in London in 1994.

Bapsy Cursetji Pavry: Continued to provide useful access and intelligence to the British government. She was invited to attend the Paris Peace Conference in 1946 and was helpful behind the scenes in negotiation of Indian independence. In 1952 she married the 90-year-old Henry Paulet, 16th Marquess of Winchester. Within weeks of

Schneidau (top right) with hockey team, 1947

the marriage, Paulet left Bapsy for his former fiancé Eve Fleming, mother of Ian. For the rest of her life Bapsy used the title Lady Bapsy Marchioness of Winchester. She died in 1995.

Philip Schneidau: Remained with SIS until 1947, working for three years from 1944–47 in the embassy in Paris. On his retirement he returned to being a chartered accountant. He died in January 1984.

Hans-Thilo Schmidt: Captured by the Gestapo in 1943. It is unknown what happened to him during his incarceration. In September 1943 he committed suicide using a cyanide capsule procured for him by his daughter Gisela. He is buried in an unmarked grave in a forest cemetery south of Berlin.

Rodolphe Lemoine: Captured by the Germans in 1945 when already very ill. He died on the 3rd of October 1946, aged 75.

ANNEX A – THE ROLLS ROYCE

Walter Sleator, who ran Franco-Britannic Autos Ltd and was a friend of Biffy's and had agreed to run what became the PHILL network, loaned Biffy a Rolls Royce 20–25 registration number 2521 RJ5 in 1939 for official duties. Biffy's personal Rolls Royce, a silver Ghost 45PK, was sent to the Franco-Britannic auto depot at Biarritz where it was eventually commandeered by the Germans. When Biffy left Bordeaux by air on the 20th of June 1940, he instructed his driver, Pierre Rouat, to hide the Rolls from the Germans and, when he could, hand it to the US Embassy in Paris for safe keeping. The US being neutral at this stage of the war and being designated the 'protecting power' for all British related matters.

Due to the chaos in France and his inability to get back to Paris, Rouat drove the car to central France where he hid it until the situation calmed down. Rouat was only able to reach Paris in August. He called at the US Embassy and spoke to the Consul General Sam Wiley. He wanted to avoid the car being requisitioned by the Germans who had ordered that all civilian cars be presented for inspection at the Parc de Vincennes. He asked Wiley to *'undertake to keep it in safe custody as the property of an officer attached to the British Embassy Paris'*. Wiley agreed and sent his driver to collect the car. He then issued Rouat a receipt:

Je soussigné, Samuel Hamilton Wiley, Consul-Général des
États-Unis d'Amérique, certifie que j'ai pris possession pour
Mr. W. Dunderdale de Monsieur Pierre Pierre Rouat, 71, Avenue Victor Hugo, Paris,
de la voiture Rolls-Royce No. 2521 RJ 5.
Paris, le 20 Septembre 1940
(Signed) Samuel Hamilton Wiley
Consul Général des États-Unis

Wiley informed Rouat that he was being posted to Lisbon and that he would get the car to Portugal. Wiley left Paris at the end of August and had a fellow diplomat, possibly Charles Grey, drive the car to Portugal in November 1940. Wiley kept the car in Portugal until November 1941 when he was transferred to Algiers.

In 1943, the Rolls was shipped to Tangiers and later driven to Casablanca by an American Vice Consul and finally driven on to Algiers. Wiley kept the car until early 1944 when he was to return to Washington. He sold the car to a Frenchman resident in Algiers for 60,000 francs which he kept to return to Biffy. So far so good, however, the official investigation into the matter by the Foreign Office (which had been instigated by a report from Tom Greene, by this time back in Paris) stated:

It is evident that Mr. Wiley made use of the car in his official capacity in France, Portugal and Africa. Mr. Wiley may have stored the car in a garage in Algiers and no doubt there are British officials who were in Algiers at the time who remember the Rolls-Royce in which the United States Consul-General used to ride.

Although the car had been left in the care of the American embassy on behalf of a British embassy official, Mr. Wiley made no attempt whatsoever, either in

Portugal or in North Africa, to get into touch with British Consular or Diplomatic Authorities to ask for instructions concerning its disposal, and this at a time when any Consular or Diplomatic Officer would have been glad to have an addition to his car-pool.

The statement that Mr. Wiley disposed of the car for 60,000 francs to some Frenchman, whose name he did not remember and that he held that sum at Commander Dunderdale's disposal, is rather unusual.

The sale of an expensive car at a price which anyone who was in Algiers at the time knew was far from the usual prices prevailing, and to a person concerning whom no details were given to help to trace him, is surprising as also the fact that the sale was effected without consulting the British Consular Authorities on the spot and that the proceeds of the sale were not handed to the latter or deposited in an American official account.

TRACING OF THE CAR

It was reported to this Department in June 1946 that the Franco-Britannic Autos Ltd. had received a letter, dated 6th June 1946, from the Comptoir Colonial, 4, rue Villegaignon, Algiers asking for a starting handle for a Rolls-Royce car which had broken down in South Algeria, this being the very same car which forms the object of this report.

RESULTS OF ENQUIRIES MADE BY THE CONSULATE GENERAL AT ALGIERS

The Consul-General at Algiers was requested to enquire into the matter and has reported as follows in his letter DOLO/DT/1503 of 20th November 1946:-

"The car.......... was sold by Mr. Hamilton Wiley to a certain Mr. Edouard E. Salles, Villa El Bresson, Chemin Laperlier, El Biar, Algiers, in December 1943. We assume that the price at this stage was 60,000 francs, Mr. Salles being the Frenchman living near Algiers, mentioned in your letter of the 29th June, whose name Mr. Wiley cannot remember.

On the 4th December 1945, the car was bought from a M. Sire, a business associate of M. Salles, by one Abdelaziz Brahim, who is the proprietor of the Comptoir Colonial, and from whom the request for a new starting handle came. M. Abdelaziz Brahim possesses the necessary documents showing that he bought the vehicle from M. Sire, who was selling it on behalf of M. Salles, and has, moreover, the necessary 'carte grise' showing that the car is registered locally under No. 1508 AL.17. His papers are, therefore, quite in order. He informs us that he bought the car for 225,000 francs, since when he has bought various spare parts and made improvements to it, and has already received an offer of 350,000 francs for it. He further avers that he is confident that he could now get 500,000 francs for the car. In any case he is definitely unwilling to sell it for 60,000 francs, and, moreover, now that he has learnt something of the car's history, we have gathered the impression that he intends to sell it very quickly. This, then, is the position."

Mr. WILEY'S PRESENT ADDRESS

The American Consulate-General at Algiers have informed the British Consulate-General there that Mr. Wiley is at present with the United States War Shipping Administration in Naples.

The American Consul-General at Algiers has written to Mr. Wiley, but has had no reply. The American Vice-Consul suggested that Mr. Wiley could be officially contacted, if necessary, through the Department of State or War Shipping Administration in Washington.

Mr. WILEY'S SUGGESTED SETTLEMENT AND PRESENT VALUE OF CAR

Mr. Wiley states that he sold the car in 1944 when he was leaving Algiers for Washington. As he took the 60,000 francs with him he must have converted them into dollars at the time. His offer to pay 60,000 devaluated francs in settlement is therefore quite absurd.

A second-hand Rolls-Royce car of the type in question is said to fetch nowadays in Paris somewhere about 500,000 to 600,000 francs.

CONCLUSION

There is no doubt whatsoever that the car was handed over to the Protecting Power, i.e. to the United States embassy, that an official receipt signed by the Consul-General of the United States is in the hands of the owners of the car, that the car was used for official purposes for some years and that in the circumstances it is for the Protecting Power to restore the car to its rightful owners.

H.L. Rabino.
3rd March, 1947

After considerable discussion within the Foreign Office, it was decided not to make an official complaint but to inform the State Department:

Even if it leads to nothing, I think the State Department would like to know about the dishonest action of one of its employees.

Sadly, the trail of the Rolls then turns cold. It may still be in Algeria or sold to an international collector.

ANNEX B – HONOURS AND AWARDS

Biffy left SIS with an impressive tally of Honours and Awards from Britain as well as other Allied countries:

GREAT BRITAIN
The Companion of St Michael and St George (CMG)
Member of the Order of the British Empire (Military) (MBE)
Two Mentions in Despatches (MID)
World War I Victory and War Medals
World War II Victory and Defence Medals
1939–45 Star

FRANCE
Légion d'honneur
Croix de Guerre avec Facture

IMPERIAL RUSSIA
The Order of St Anne
The Order of St Olav

POLAND
The Restituta Polona

USA
Legion of Merit

Biffy's work earned him the gratitude of the Americans in the shape of the award of Officer of the Legion of Merit 'For Special Services to the Allied Cause' gazetted in the *London Gazette* of the 29th of November 1946. Biffy's citation for the award sums up his relations with OSS. It reads:

1. *The entire service of Commander Dunderdale has been honourable since the rendition by him of service upon which this recommendation is based. A similar recommendation for this individual has not been submitted.*
2. *The officer recommending this award has personal knowledge of the service upon which this recommendation is based.*
3. *Commander Wilfred Albert Dunderdale, British R.N.V.R., while serving in close collaboration with the Armed Forces of the United States, distinguished himself by exceptionally meritorious conduct in the performance of outstanding services. Detailed narrative of the services for which this award is recommended:-*
   For many years commander W. A. Dunderdale has been an important member of the British Intelligence Service. Before the war he was in charge of the British Intelligence French Section and in 1940 moved his staff from Paris to London where he has since been located.
   When the Secret Intelligence Branch of the United States Office of Strategic Services began to function in London in 1942, Commander Dunderdale fully realised the importance of this counterpart of his own service and was indefatigable in his efforts to give it every assistance. A close personal relationship

developed between him and Major (now Lt Colonel) William P. Maddox, Chief of the Office of Strategic Services Intelligence Branch, as a result of which Commander Dunderdale's long experience in the complex methods and techniques of Intelligence were put at the disposal of the American organisation. This proved of incalculable value in expediting the efficient implementation and activation of the secret intelligence operations envisaged and in procuring and relaying vitally important information to the Joint Chiefs of Staff in Washington and to the Theatre Commander. In addition, Commander Dunderdale was completely cognizant from the beginning of the need for the closest possible cooperation between the American and British Intelligence Services; and, to this end, he most effectively used his influence with his organisation. To him is due a large share of the credit for the important results obtained on an operational level. The most outstanding example of this is the SUSSEX plan conceived and executed jointly by the two services, under which approximately 50 2-men agent teams were parachuted into France before D-Day and relayed to headquarters information of immense value to the United States and Allied armed forces.

From December 1944 onwards Commander Dunderdale was Liaison Officer for the British Intelligence Service with the Office of Strategic Services Secret Intelligence Branch; and, by making available to the latter for all the resources of his own office and its experienced staff, consisting of some 50 persons, he strengthened even more the bonds between the two organisations. The exchange of intelligence material and discussion and comments upon it increased so that the experts in both services were utilised to the full, to the great benefit of our armed forces in the crucial last six months of the war with Germany.

By his superior cooperation, by his unfailing desire to be of assistance in every possible way, and by his constant support in the councils of the British Intelligence Service, Commander Dunderdale has earned the deep esteem and gratitude of his American colleagues.

Commander Dunderdale was not wounded while performing the above services.

The accomplishment of the service for which the award is recommended extended from August 1942 to May 1945 and has been completed. The service was performed in London.

4. Proposed Citation: For the LEGION OF MERIT with rank of OFFICER.

Commander W.A. DUNDERDALE, R.N.V.R., in recognition of his material contribution to the successful operations of a special unit in the European Theatre. The unfailing support, interest, and wholehearted cooperation of Commander Dunderdale greatly aided the implementation and accomplishment of important operations, the results of which proved exceptionally valuable to the United States Armies in the defeat of Germany.

5. In order to support this recommendation, it has been necessary to divulge in the preceding paragraphs information classified as Secret. However, the proposed citation has been made sufficiently general to permit publication of it separately with the classification restricted.

J.R. FORGAN
Colonel, GSC
Commanding

SOURCES AND BIBLIOGRAPHY

'The life of spies is to know, not to be known.'
George Herbert, 1651

The research for this book took three years. As I said in the introduction, writing the biography of an intelligence officer is a challenge, as the very nature of his life and work is secret. It is akin to gathering a full and accurate intelligence picture on a specific target. However, with detailed research and analysis of all available sources, a lot of detective work, cross referencing, some educated guessing and considerable luck, it was possible to produce a pretty accurate picture of Biffy's life and work.

I was extremely lucky to find Biffy's surviving family and close friends and be given access to their private papers, photographs and memorabilia. Biffy kept many of his personal documents, as did his friends: Tom Greene, Sheelagh Greene, Charles Grey and Anthony Heath. These personal papers formed a solid foundation on which to build.

I next went to the SIS Official History: 'MI6 1909–49' by Keith Jeffrey and used it throughout as my 'Baedeker' guide. It was very useful. The book would have been very difficult to write without it.

Subsequently, much time was spent scouring archives in Britain, France and the US which yielded a surprising number of nuggets.

Finally, I trawled the extensive literature about the secret world and its associated history including the fictional works by Ian Fleming.

One source led to another, but intelligence target folders can seldom provide 100 per cent accuracy and this book is similar.

PRIVATE PAPERS

Chris Perowne
Anthony Johnson and Danielle Golden
Anthony Fraser
Sebastian Allaby and Philip Heath
Georgina and Robert Woods
Jane Garton
Jimmy Grey
Pascal Sandevoir and Eric Le Roux
Diana Mara Henry
Alan Bryden
Micheline Billard
André Kervella
Charles Schaefer
Paul Biddle
Michael and Giles Keun
Colin Cohen
General Jonathan Riley and the Trustees of the Royal Welch Fusiliers Museum

THE NATIONAL ARCHIVES, KEW

Robert Andrew Fulton, UN, 1990	**Diplomatic Service List, 1990**
French proposal re cooperation on Bolshevism (1924)	**FO 371/10480**
Muselier Case FO file	**FO 1093/221**
Refugee arrivals numbers 1940	**HO 213/556**
CX on German Gas Warfare including P5 & Polish reports	**WO 208/4322**
CX from P5 French Org II & Deuxième Bureau Algiers	**SOURCE NOT RECORDED**
P5 report on German W/T Station	**ADM 199/2489**
P5 reports from Blanc and Baculan, Ariel & Puck	**ADM 199/2489**
P5 report U-boats at Lorient	**ADM 199/2467**
Ariel & Puck reports Anti-invasion precautions	**ADM 199/2468**
P5 reports Construction at Meulan	**ADM 199/2470**
P5 report Shipping activities Cherbourg & St Malo	**ADM 199/465**
How news was brought from Warsaw (end of July 1939)	**HW 25/12**
Black Sea defences 1921 report	**ADM 137/1735**
Crimea reports 1921	**ADM 137/1752**
Dunderdale senior Miocene & Minhla registrations	**BT 110/1258 & BT 110/1094**
Situation in Constantinople 1920	**ADM 137/1769**
Report from Southern Caucasus 1921	**ADM 137/1770**
Dunderdale senior sale of LOTCO ship Miocene	**FO 371/24113**
Evacuation from Bordeaux	**FO 371/24316**
ISIS Corsica report	**ADM 239/767**
Poles & Deuxième Bureau N Africa 1942	**FO 1093/211**
Bodyline (V Weapon) targets	**AIR 20/8199**
Crossbow (V weapon) reports	**AIR 40/3009**
Vichy French intelligence	**WO 193/182**
Franco-Russian relations 1922 CX from Constantinople sources	**FO 371/8184**

Russian Black Sea fleet 1922 CX from Constantinople sources	**FO 371/9384**
SIS Eastern Summary 22-01-1923	**FO 371/9290**
SIS Eastern Summary 26-09-1922	**FO 371/7896**
CX Soviet mission to Afghanistan 1922 (Constantinople report)	**FO 371/8083**
Int reports 1920 including Dunderdale	**ADM 137/2501**
Report on Russian Trade Delegation, Constantinople 1922	**FO 371/8167**
CX on Russian Trade Delegation, Constantinople 1922	**FO 371/8166**
Army Report on Russian Trade Delegation, Constantinople 1922	**FO 371/8166**
Report from Paris on Eliza Arnold (probably from KL/1 a separate liaison section)	**KV 2/4030**
Dunderdale report on Soviet Foreign Policy 1920	**ADM 137/2280**
RSS on P5 Polish & Deuxième Bureau transmitter	**HW 34/8**
Bertrand's letters to Denniston (GC + CS)	**HW 65/1**
GC + CS dossier on French liaison	**HW 50/10**
Paris report on Bogovout-Kolomitzeff	**KV 2/4504**
Polish radio service	**FO 1093/317**
'C' ops in France post-WW2	**FO 1093/285**
June Dunderdale French Medal	**FO 372/6193**
Dunderdale's Rolls Royce	**FO 950/184**
Another GC + CS dossier on French liaison	**HW 25/15**
Dunderdale MBE	**FO 372/1782**
Dunderdale's reports from the Crimea	**ADM 137/2296**
Dunderdale's Bolshevik submarine	**FO 371/5433**
Information on Litauer to Dunderdale 1948	**KV 2/4217**
Dunderdale Crimea material sent in bulk:	**ADM 137/1735** **ADM 137/1743** **ADM 137/1752** **ADM 137/1753** **ADM 137/1758**

C Class submarines to Petrograd	**ADM 137/1247**
Bajanov India	**IOR 4/PJ/12/359**
SIS in France	**TNA 01-03-2014: 27/28**
P5 and Polish Radios	**TNA 31-07-2021**

SERVICE HISTORIQUE DE LA DEFENSE CHATEAU DE VINCENNES

Many hours were spent at Vincennes under the guidance of David Sbrava who could not have been more helpful and supportive, often suggesting additional files to those that I had requested. He was also helpful in guiding me through the process of requesting access to restricted files. The files listed below are the key ones consulted. Many 'dossiers' have more sub-files, too numerous to list here – for example the JADE FITZROY/AMICOL dossier has 184 sub-files, the Bertrand dossier more than 500.

Key files

- **DE 2016 ZB25/1-8**   Bertrand
- **GR 14YD 755**   Bertrand
- **GR 28 P4 363 à 366**   Réseau JADE FITZROY/AMICOL include individual files on Pierre Hentic, Claude Lamirault, Philip Keun, Paul Kilesso and Claude Arnould.
- **GR 16P 269357**   Sheelagh Greene
- **GR 16P 270357**   Charles Grey
- **GR 17P 129 1/2/3**   Réseau F2
- **GR 17P 124**   Réseau JOHNNY
- **GR 17P 131**   GROUPE 31/Madame Louis
- **GR 16P 461287**   Georges Paulin
- **GR 16P 551260**   Aileen Sleator/Schoofs
- **GR 16P 317903**   Jacques Kellner
- **GR 16P 541049**   Jean-Henri Schoofs
- **GR 16P 120255/56**   Georges Charadeau
- **GR 16P 120259**   Violette Charadeau
- **GR 17P 127**   Réseau FELIX 1+2
- **GR 72A 1/82/3/4**   Paul Paillole

FONDATION DE LA FRANCE LIBRE

An excellent source for early missions to France:
- Premières missions par Hubert Moreau
- A propos du Réseau JOHNNY par Jean Le Roux/André Malavoy

THE MAUTHAUSEN MEMORIAL PRISONER DATABASE

- **MM/Y50**
- **MM/Y43**
- **MM/Y/HPK**   Paul Kilesso
- **MM/Y36**

UNIVERSITY OF SOUTHAMPTON

- Mountbatten Diaries

YACHT MOTEUR CLUB DE FRANCE ARCHIVE

CHURCHILL COLLEGE CAMBRIDGE

- Papers of Admiral Godfrey

NATIONAL MARITIME MUSEUM

- Papers of Hugh Sinclair

REVUE DE LA FRANCE LIBRE

- *Revue De La France Libre*, vol 80, September 1954.
- *Revue De La France Libre*, vol 81, October 1954.
- *Revue De La France Libre*, vol 82, November 1954.

REVUE HISTORIQUE DE L'ARMÉE

- *Revue Historique De L'Armée*, vol 4, December 1952.

GUIDE ROSE PARIS

- 1926

GUIDE DES PLAISIRS À PARIS

NEWSPAPER ARCHIVES

- Gallica French Newspaper Archive (gallica.bnf.fr)
- The British Newspaper Archive

WEBSITES

- Conservatoire Collaboratif des message personnels (messages-personnels-bbc-39-45.fr)
- Levantine Heritage Foundation (levantineheritage.com)
- Libre Resistance (libreresistance.com)
- maho-hentic.com
- nilegioen.eu
- OSS Society (osssociety.org)
- Oxford Dictionary of National Biography (oxforddnb.com)
- Plan Sussex (plan-sussex-1944.net)
- Stew Ross Discovers (stewross.com)
- www.wikipedia.org

BOOKS

Aglan, Alya (1990). *Mémoires résistantes: Histoire du réseau Jade-Fitzroy, 1940–1944.* Cerf.

Aldrich, Richard J. (2003). *The Hidden Hand: Britain, America and Cold War Secret Intelligence.* Overlook Press.

Aldrich, Richard J. & Cormac, Rory (2016). *The Black Door: Spies, Secret Intelligence and British Prime Ministers.* William Collins.

Allfrey, Anthony (1989). *Man of Arms: The Life and Legend of Sir Basil Zaharoff.* Weidenfeld & Nicolson.

Alvarez, David (2016). *Spying Through a Glass Darkly: American Espionage Against the Soviet Union, 1945–1946.* University Press of Kansas.

Andrew, Christopher (1986). *Secret Service.* Hodder & Stoughton Ltd.

Andrew, Christopher (2019). *The Secret World: A History of Intelligence.* Penguin.

Atkin, Malcolm (2023). *Section D for Destruction: Forerunner of SOE and Auxiliary Units.* Pen & Sword Military.

Austin, Tim & Henry, Diana Mara (2021). *The Early Resistance in France.* Privately published.

Babington Smith, Constance (1958). *Evidence in Camera: The Story of Photographic Intelligence in the Second World War.* Chatto & Windus.

Baedeker, Karl (1911). *The Mediterranean, seaports and sea routes, including Madeira, the Canary Islands, the coast of Morocco, Algeria, and Tunisia: handbook for travellers.* Leipzig.

Baedeker, Karl (1931). *The Riviera. South-Eastern France and Corsica. the Italian Lakes and Lake of Geneva. Handbook for Travellers.* Leipzig.

Barker, Ralph (1969). *Aviator extraordinary: The Sidney Cotton story.* Chatto & Windus.

Bartz, Karl (1956). *The Downfall of the German Secret Service.* William Kimber.

Bazhanov, Boris (1990). *Bazhanov and the Damnation of Stalin.* Translated by D. Doyle. Ohio University Press.

Bazhanov, Boris (1979). *Bajanov révèle Staline. Souvenirs d'un ancien secrétaire de Staline.* Gallimard.

Beard, James & Watt, Alexander (1953). *Paris Cuisine.* Macgibbon & Kee.

Bennett, Gill (2007). *Churchill's Man of Mystery: Desmond Morton and the World of Intelligence.* Routledge.

Bertrand, Gustave (1973). *Enigma ou la plus grande énigme de la guerre 1939–1945.* Librairie Plon.

Bevan, John (2014). *Commander Crabb – What Really Happened?*. Submex.

Bower, Tom (1995). *The Perfect English Spy: Sir Dick White and the Secret War, 1935–90*. William Heinemann Ltd.

Bower, Tom (1989). *The Red Web: MI6 and the KGB Master Coup*. Aurum Press.

Brassai, Gyula Halasz (1977). *The Secret Paris of the 30's*. Pantheon.

Brissaud, André (1973). *Canaris*. Translated by I. Colvin. Weidenfeld & Nicolson.

Brook-Shepherd, Gordon (1998). *The Iron Maze*. Macmillan. William Heinemann Ltd.

Brook-Shepherd, Gordon (1988). *The Storm Birds*. Weidenfeld & Nicolson.

Brook-Shepherd, Gordon (1977). *The Storm Petrels: The First Soviet Defectors, 1928–38*. HarperCollins.

Budiansky, Stephen (2000). *Battle of Wits: The Complete Story of Codebreaking in World War II*. Simon & Schuster.

Bywater, H.C. & Ferraby, H.C. (1931). *Strange intelligence: memoirs of naval secret service*. Constable & Company.

Casey, William (1989). *The Secret War Against Hitler*. Simon & Schuster Ltd.

Cave Brown, Anthony (1975). *Bodyguard of Lies*. HarperCollins.

Cave Brown, Anthony (1988). *C: The Secret Life of Sir Stewart Graham Menzies, Spymaster to Winston Churchill*. Macmillan Pub Co.

Cave Brown, Anthony (1982). *The Last Hero: Wild Bill Donovan*. Times Books.

Cavendish, Anthony (1987). *Inside Intelligence*. HarperCollins.

Chatenay, Victor (1967). *Mon journal du temps du malheur*. Editions du Courrier de l'Ouest.

Clark, Freddie (1999). *Agents by Moonlight*. The History Press Ltd.

Collins, Larry & Lapierre, Dominique (1965). *Is Paris Burning?*. Simon & Schuster.

Cook, Andrew C. (2002). *On His Majesty's Secret Service: Sidney Reilly Codename ST1*. Tempus Publishing.

Couanault, Emmanuel (2016). *Agents Ordinaires, Le Réseau "Johnny" 1940–1943*. Locus Solus.

Cowles, Virginia (1941). *Looking for Trouble*. Harper & Brothers.

Cox, Geoffrey (1988). *Countdown to War: A Personal Memoir of Europe, 1938–1940*. Coronet Books.

Crowther Smith, H.F. (1919). *Night staff at the Bureau*. Privately published.

Dank, Milton (1978). *French Against the French*. Cassell.

Davies, Philip (2004). *MI6 and the Machinery of Spying*. Routledge.

Deacon, Richard (1985). *'C': Biography of Maurice Oldfield*. MacDonald.

Downing, Taylor (2011). *Spies in the Sky*. Abacus.

Dubicki, Tadeusz, Stirling, Tessa & Nalecz, Daria (eds) (2005). *Intelligence Cooperation between Poland and Britain during World War II. Vol 1*. Vallentine Mitchell & Co.

Dupouy, Alexandre (2019). *City of Pleasure*. Korero Press.

Elliott, Nicholas (1991). *Never Judge a Man by His Umbrella*. Michael Russell.

Elliott, Nicholas (1993). *With My Little Eye: Observations Along the Way*. Michael Russell.

Emerson, Maureen (2018). *Riviera Dreaming: Love and War on the Côte d'Azur*. Tauris Parke.

Erickson, Ben & Larsen, Peter (2018). *The Kellner Affair: Matters of Life and Death*. Dalton Watson Fine Books.

Faligot, Roger & Krop, Pascal (1989). *La Piscine: French Secret 1944: French Secret Service Since 1944*. Blackwell.

Furnham, Adrian & Taylor, John (2022). *The Psychology of Spies and Spying: Trust, Treason, Treachery*. Matador.

Fleming, Ian (1963). *From Russia with Love*. Jonathan Cape.

Fleming, Ian (1954). *Live and Let Die*. Jonathan Cape.

Forczyk, Robert (2017). *Case Red: The Collapse of France*. Osprey.

Fourcade, Marie-Madeleine (1974). *Noah's Ark*. E. P. Dutton & Co.

Fraser-Smith, Charles (1981). *Secret War of Charles Fraser-Smith: The Q Gadget Wizard of World War II*. Michael Joseph.

Garlinski, Józef (1980). *The Enigma War*. Scribner.

Gordon, Kevin (2017). *Secret Seaford*. Amberley.

Greene, Graham & Greene, Hugh (1957). *The Spy's Bedside Book*. Rupert Hart-Davis.

Guillaume, Paul (1948). *Au temps de l'héroïsme et de la trahison*. Librairie Loddé.

Hale, Don (2009). *The Final Dive: The Life and Death of 'Buster' Crabb*. The History Press.

Hampshire, Edward, Macklin, Graham & Twigge, Stephen (2008). *British Intelligence: Secrets, spies and sources*. Bloomsbury Academic.

Harris-Smith, Richard (1972). *OSS: The Secret History of America's First Central Intelligence Agency*. University of California Press.

Hayes, Paddy (2016). *Queen of Spies*. Duckworth.

Henry, Diana Mara (2024). *Agent André: The German Jew at the Heart of the SIS and French Resistance*. The History Press.

Hentic, Pierre (2009). *Agent de l'Ombre*. Editions Maho.

Herivel, John (2008). *Herivelismus and the German Military Enigma*. M.& M. Baldwin.

Herman, John (1998). *The Paris Embassy of Sir Eric Phipps*. Sussex Academic Press.

Hinsley, F.H. (1984). *British Intelligence in the Second World War*. H.M.S.O.

Humphrey, Dave (2014). *Legends and Heroes Behind the Lens*. Rosendale Books.

Hutton, Clayton (1960). *Officially Secret*. Max Parrish.

Hyde, H. Montgomery (1982). *Secret Intelligence Agent*. St. Martin's Press.

Jeffrey, Barbara (2019). *Chancers: Scandal, Blackmail, and the Enigma Code*. Amberley Publishing.

Judd, Alan (1999). *Mansfield Cumming and the Founding of the Secret Service*. HarperCollins.

Kazansky, Konstantin (1978). *Cabaret Russe*. Olivier Orban.

Kervella, André (2024). *Claude Arnould: industriel, résistant, homme d'influence, espion*. Nouveau Monde.

Kervella, André (2021). *Le Réseau Jade: L'intelligence Service britannique au cœur de la Résistance française*. Nouveau Monde.

King, Charles (2011). *Odessa – Genius and Death in a City of Dreams*. W. W. Norton & Company.

Kochanski, Halik (2022). *The Underground War in Europe, 1939–1945*. Penguin.

Kundahl, George G. (2017). *The Riviera at War: World War II on the Côte d'Azur*. I.B. Tauris.

Le Carré, John (1974). *Tinker Tailor Soldier Spy*. Pan Macmillan.

Le Roux, Jean (2010). *Le Réseau Johnny*. André H. Casalis (ed.). Lulu.

Lewis, Damien (2022). *The Flame of Resistance: American Beauty. French Hero. British Spy*. Quercus Books.

Lochery, Neill (2011). *War in the Shadows of the City of Light, 1939–1945*. PublicAffairs.

Lyman, Robert (2014). *The Jail Busters: The Secret Story of MI6, the French Resistance and Operation Jericho.* Quercus Publishing.

Madeira, Victor (2014). *Britannia and the Bear: The Anglo-Russian Intelligence Wars, 1917–1929.* Boydell & Brewer.

Mann, Carol (1996). *Paris Between the Wars.* Vendome Press.

Mansel, Philip (1995). *Constantinople: City of the World's Desire, 1453–1924.* John Murray.

Mansel, Philip (2010). *Levant: Splendour and Catastrophe on the Mediterranean.* John Murray.

McKeown, Michael (2020). *Matt. D'Arcy & Old Newry Whiskies.* Old Newry Publications.

Moats, Alice-Leone (2015). *No Passport for Paris.* Andesite Press.

Morris, Benny (2023). *Sidney Reilly.* Yale University Press.

O'Connor, Bernard (2010). *RAF Tempsford: Churchill's Most Secret Airfield.* Amberley.

Oliver, David (2005). *Airborne Espionage: International Special Duties Operations in the World Wars.* The History Press.

Olsen, Lynn (2019). *Madame Fourcade's Secret War: The Daring Young Woman Who Led France's Largest Spy Network Against Hitler.* Scribe UK.

Othen, Christopher (2020). *The King of Nazi Paris: Henri Lafont and the Gangsters of the French Gestapo.* Biteback Publishing.

Paillole, Paul (2004). *Fighting the Nazis: French Intelligence and Counter-intelligence, 1935–1945.* Enigma Books.

Paillole, Paul (1975). *Services Speciaux.* Robert Laffont.

Paillole, Paul (2016). *The Spy in Hitler's Inner Circle: Hans-Thilo Schmidt and the Intelligence Network that Decoded Enigma.* Translated by C. Key. Casemate.

Passy, Colonel (2000). *Mémoires du Chef des Services Secrets de la France Libre.* Odile Jacob.

Perrault, Giles (1990). *Paris Under the Occupation.* Vendome Press.

Phillips, Roland (2021). *Victoire: A Wartime Story of Resistance, Collaboration and Betrayal.* Bodley Head.

Picardie, Justine (2021). *Miss Dior: A Story of Courage and Couture.* Faber & Faber.

Pidgeon, Geoffrey (2003). *The Secret Wireless War.* Arundel Books.

Pollack, Guillaume (2022). *L'armée du silence: Histoire des réseaux de résistance en France 1940–1945.* Tallandier.

Pugh, Marshall (1956). *Commander Crabb.* Macmillan.

Read, Anthony & Fisher, David (1984). *Colonel Z: The Secret Life of a Master of Spies.* Hodder & Stoughton.

Richards, Brook (2013). *Secret Flotillas: Clandestine Sea Operations to Brittany 1940–44. Vol 1.* Pen & Sword Maritime.

Roosevelt, Kermit (1976). *The Overseas Target. Vol 2.* Walker & Co.

Ryan, Isadore (2017). *No Way Out: The Irish in Wartime France, 1939–1945.* Mercier Press.

Scott, J.D. (1962). *Vickers – A History.* Weidenfeld & Nicolson.

Sebag-Montefiore, Hugh (2000). *Enigma: The Battle for the Code.* Weidenfeld & Nicholson.

Slowikowski, Major General Rygor (1988). *In the Secret Service: Lighting the Torch.* Translated by G. Slowikowski. Windrush Press.

Smith, Michael (2010). *Six: A History of Britain's Secret Intelligence Service, Part 1: Murder and Mayhem 1909–1939.* Biteback.

Smith, Michael (2022). *The Real Special Relationship: The True Story of How* the British and US Secret Services Work Together. Simon & Schuster.

Smith, Simon C. (2008). *Reassessing Suez 1956: New Perspectives on the Crisis and Its Aftermath*. Routledge.

Soulier, Dominique (2013). *The Sussex Plan: Secret War in Occupied France 1943–1945*. Histoire et Collections.

Spicer, Tim (2021). *A Dangerous Enterprise: Secret War at Sea*. Barbreck Publishers.

Stead, Philip John (1959). *Second Bureau*. Evans Brothers.

Tanny, Jarrod (2011). *City of Rogues and Schnorrers: Russia's Jews and the Myth of Old Odessa*. Indiana University Press.

Thomas, Evan (1996). *The Very Best Men: Four Who Dared – Early Years of the CIA*. Simon & Schuster.

Tremain, David (2018). *Double Agent Victoire: Mathilde Carré and the Interallié Network*. The History Press.

Tsarev, Oleg & West, Nigel (2004). *Triplex: Secrets from the Cambridge Spies*. Yale University Press.

Turing, Dermot (2018). *X, Y and Z: The Real Story of How Enigma was Broken*. The History Press.

Tzu, Sun (2018 edition). *The Art of War*. Everyman's Library.

Vaughn, Hal (2006). *FDR'S 12 Apostles: The Spies Who Paved the Way for the Invasion of North Africa*. The Lyons Press.

Verity, Hugh (1978). *We Landed by Moonlight: Secret RAF Landings in France, 1940–1944*. Ian Allan Publishing.

Vogel, Steve (2019). *Betrayal in Berlin: The True Story of the Cold War's Most Audacious Espionage*. Custom House.

Wake-Walker, Edward (2011). *A House for Spies: SIS Operations into Occupied France from a Sussex Farmhouse*. Robert Hale.

Watson, Jeffrey (2002). *Sidney Cotton: The Last Plane Out of Berlin*. Hodder & Stoughton.

West, Nigel (2006). *At Her Majesty's Secret Service: The Chiefs of Britain's Intelligence Agency, MI6*. Naval Institute Press.

West, Nigel (1987). *GCHQ: The Secret Wireless War, 1900–1986*. Weidenfeld & Nicolson.

West, Nigel (2007). *Historical Dictionary of Cold War Counterintelligence – Historical Dictionaries of Intelligence and Counterintelligence*. Scarecrow Press.

West, Nigel (1983). *MI6: British Secret Intelligence Service Operations: 1909–45*. Weidenfeld & Nicolson.

West, Nigel (1988). *The Friends: Britain's Post-War Secret Intelligence Operations*. Weidenfeld & Nicolson.

West, Nigel (2005). *The Guy Liddell Diaries, Volume I: 1939–1942: 1939–1942: MI5's Director of Counter-Espionage in World War II*. Routledge.

Winterbotham, F. W. (1984). *From Victoria to Ultra: An Autobiography*. Equinox Press.

Winterbotham, F. W. (1969). *Secret and Personal*. William Kimber.

Winterbotham, F. W. (1978). *The Nazi Connection*. Weidenfeld & Nicolson.

Winterbotham, F. W. (1974). *The Ultra Secret*. Weidenfeld & Nicolson.

Wiser, William (2000). *The Twilight Years Paris in the 1930s*. Carroll & Graf.

Wrangel, Pyotr (1929). *Always with Honor: The Memoirs of General Wrangel*. Translated by S. Goulston.

Yardley, Herbert (1931). *The American Black Chamber*. The Bobbs-Merrill Company.

Young, Gordon (1957). *The Cat with Two Faces*. Putnam.

Yung-de Prévaux, Aude (2001). *Love in the Tempest of History: A French Resistance Story*. Free Press.